Revealing Britain's Systemic Racism

T0383621

Revealing Britain's Systemic Racism applies an existing scholarly paradigm (systemic racism and the white racial frame) to assess the implications of Markle's entry and place in the British royal family, including an analysis that bears on visual and material culture. The white racial frame, as it manifests in the UK, represents an important lens through which to map and examine contemporary racism and related inequities. By questioning the long-held, but largely anecdotal, beliefs about racial progressiveness in the UK, the authors provide an original counter-narrative about how Markle's experiences as a biracial member of the royal family can help illumine contemporary forms of racism in Britain. *Revealing Britain's Systemic Racism* identifies and documents the plethora of ways systemic racism continues to shape ecological spaces in the UK. Kimberley Ducey and Joe R. Feagin challenge romanticized notions of racial inclusivity by applying Feagin's long-established work, aiming to make a unique and significant contribution to literature in sociology and in various other disciplines.

Kimberley Ducey, PhD, is Associate Professor of Sociology at the University of Winnipeg in Manitoba, Canada. She is a public sociologist, whose work has appeared in such journals as *Canadian Ethnic Studies*, *Critical Criminology*, and *Genocide Studies and Prevention*. Her work also appears in *Animal Oppression*, the *Routledge Handbook of Public Criminologies*, *The Cambridge Handbook of Sociology*, the *Handbook of the Sociology of Racial and Ethnic Relations*, the *Routledge International Handbook of Public Sociology*, and *Educating for Critical Consciousness*. Her other books with Joe R. Feagin include *Racist America* (4th edn, Routledge, 2019), *Elite White Men Ruling* (Routledge, 2017), and *Liberation Sociology* (also with Hernán Vera; 3rd edn, 2014). Dr. Ducey has edited two books, *George Yancy: A Critical Reader* (2021, with Clevis Headley and Joe R. Feagin) and *Systemic Racism Theory: Making Liberty, Justice, and Democracy Real* (2017, with Ruth Thompson-Miller).

Joe R. Feagin, PhD, is Distinguished Professor and Ella C. McFadden Professor in Sociology at Texas A&M University. He has done much internationally recognized research on US racism, sexism, and political economy issues. He has written or co-written 74 scholarly books and 200-plus scholarly articles in his social science areas. His books include *Systemic Racism* (Routledge, 2006), *White Party, White Government* (Routledge, 2012), *Latinos Facing Racism* (Routledge, 2014, with José A. Cobas), *How Blacks Built America* (Routledge, 2015), *Elite White Men Ruling* (Routledge, 2017, with Kimberley Ducey), *Racist America* (4th edn, Routledge, 2019, with Kimberley Ducey), *Rethinking Diversity Frameworks in Higher Education* (Routledge, 2020, with Edna B. Chun), and *The White Racial Frame* (3rd edn, Routledge, 2020). He is the recipient of a 2012 Soka Gakkai International-USA Social Justice Award, the 2013 American Association for Affirmative Action's Arthur Fletcher Lifetime Achievement Award, and three major American Sociological Association awards: the W.E.B. Du Bois Career of Distinguished Scholarship Award, the Cox-Johnson-Frazier Award (for research in the African American scholarly tradition), and the Public Understanding of Sociology Award. He was the 1999–2000 president of the American Sociological Association.

Revealing Britain's Systemic Racism

The Case of Meghan Markle and the Royal Family

Kimberley Ducey and Joe R. Feagin

Routledge
Taylor & Francis Group

NEW YORK AND LONDON

First published 2021
by Routledge
52 Vanderbilt Avenue, New York, NY 10017

and by Routledge
2 Park Square, Milton Park, Abingdon, Oxon OX14 4RN

Routledge is an imprint of the Taylor & Francis Group, an informa business

© 2021 Taylor & Francis

Library of Congress Cataloging-in-Publication Data
A catalog record for this title has been requested

ISBN: 978-0-367-76545-3 (hbk)
ISBN: 978-0-367-76541-5 (pbk)
ISBN: 978-1-003-16743-3 (ebk)

Typeset in Garamond
by Newgen Publishing UK

For the global Black Lives Matter movement

Contents

Preface   ix
Chapter Overviews   xvi
A Note on Terminology for North American Readers   xviii
Acknowledgments   xx

1   Systemic Racism: Britain Now and Then   1

2   Straight Out of the White Racial Frame   57

3   Post-Racial Duchess or Trophy Wife of Diversity?   95

4   White Men Ruling and the Problem with Meghan Markle   122

5   Feminist Counter-Framer and Anti-Racist Counter-Framer: Disrupter of Elite White Dominance   153

6   "Where Is This Racism You Keep Talking About?": Sincere Fictions of the Virtuous White Self   183

7   Concluding Thoughts: The Royals, British Racism, and the Coronavirus Pandemic   218

Index   238

Preface

On January 8, 2020, the Duke and Duchess of Sussex—Prince Harry and Meghan Markle—announced on social media that they intended to step back as senior royals "and work to become financially independent, while continuing to fully support Her Majesty The Queen ... the Commonwealth, and [their] patronages." About an hour after their announcement, this statement from the queen followed: "Discussions with The Duke and Duchess of Sussex are at an early stage. ... We understand their desire to take a different approach, but these are complicated issues that will take time to work through."[1] The couple's aspiration to be part-time royals was something the House of Windsor—the reigning royal house of the UK and other Commonwealth realms—could not abide. In response to what has now been dubbed "Megxit" (a hybrid of "Meghan" and "exit," and playing on the word "Brexit"), the queen soon explained: "Although we would have preferred them to remain full-time working Members of the Royal Family, we respect and understand their wish to live a more independent life as a family while remaining a valued part of my family." At no time did the monarch make mention of the extensive, often gendered, racism that Markle had endured. She only said she was aware of the challenges the couple had "experienced as a result of intense scrutiny over the last two years and support their wish for a more independent life." She added, "I ... am particularly proud of how Meghan has so quickly become one of the family," an implicit allusion perhaps to her not being British or white.[2]

The House of Windsor forced a compromise of sorts on the Sussexes. The couple would divide their time between North America and the UK, retain their *private* patronages and associations, but would no longer be able to use their Royal Highness (HRH) titles or the phrase "Sussex Royal" in their public endeavors. The acclaimed royal expert Clive Irving has since called out the double standard, saying:

> [I]t's been an atrocious act of hypocrisy ... to [take the view] that it wasn't right for them to use a brand, Sussex Royal, to monetise the royal name, because [Prince] Charles was the first person ever to do that in a serious way, with the Duchy brand of grocery items. ... It never seemed to strike him or anybody else in the Royal Family that it

was hypocritical to attack Meghan and Harry for wanting to do their own brand, and in their case not to sell groceries but to do good work.[3]

Harry was stripped of honorary military appointments and his role as Commonwealth Youth Ambassador. Markle and Harry would no longer receive monies from the Sovereign Grant, which is funded by taxpayers and covers travel, employee's salaries, and palace maintenance and services. The couple ultimately moved near Los Angeles, Markle's hometown. They publicly stated they would continue to espouse the principles of the monarchy, even though as of March 21, 2020 they would no longer officially represent the queen.[4] Almost a year later, the couple decided to step back permanently from royal duties. "We can all live a life of service. Service is universal," they said at the time.[5]

In summer 2020, the much-anticipated book *Finding Freedom*, written by royal reporters Omid Scobie and Carolyn Durand, was published, purportedly chronicling key factors in the couple's decision to leave the royal fold and the UK. The authors spoke to friends, aides, other confidants of the Sussexes, and the couple themselves.[6] During press junkets coinciding with the book's release, author Scobie was questioned as to whether the pair's decision had anything to do with racial matters. "In terms of ticking those boxes that may ruffle feathers within an ancient institution" like the British monarchy, he explained, Markle "ticked all of them. Race did play a role." In his view, history will negatively judge the British monarchy for discarding a chance to actually diversify.[7] Elizabeth II, after all, is sovereign to 15 countries in addition to the UK, as well as head of the Commonwealth of Nations, which includes a third of the world's population. People of color are the majority there. India, for example, is the most populous member, with over 1 billion, while 19 Commonwealth countries are in Africa and another eight are in Asia.[8]

Much has been made of *Finding Freedom*'s supposed focus on racism as a divisive factor in the Sussexes's decision to step down as senior royals. The book upset Markle's most prominent white critics particularly for this reason (see Chapter 7). However, direct and indirect mentions of race, ethnicity, or racism appear only on 32 pages in this 347-page book. Even then, most such references fill a mere sentence or two. This rather brief attention to Britain's systemic racism has been enough to agitate much of the white establishment.

Similarly, but more broadly, conservatives in the ruling UK government began targeting critical race theory (CRT) in late 2020. The writer Daniel Trilling explains:

> [A]ccording to the parliamentary record … the term "critical race theory" had never once been uttered in the House of Commons chamber. By the end of the day on 20 October [2020], however, it was of such importance that the government declared itself "unequivocally against" the concept. "We do not want teachers to teach their white

pupils about white privilege and inherited racial guilt," warned the equalities minister, Kemi Badenoch [who is of Nigerian origin], at the end of a six-hour debate to mark Black History Month. "Any school which teaches these elements of critical race theory, or which promotes partisan political views such as defunding the police without offering a balanced treatment of opposing views, is breaking the law."[9]

A month earlier in the USA, President Donald Trump instructed federal agencies and contractors to halt subsidies to training programs based on "race-based ideologies." Theories that challenge subjective white-framed perspectives and practices, and the racially oppressive and exclusionary institutions and social systems created by whites over several centuries, were dubbed by Trump "a sickness that cannot be allowed to continue." He tweeted: "Please report any sightings so we can quickly extinguish!"[10]

CRT, like systemic racism theory, which is the focus of our book, casts doubts on the very foundation of liberalism. CRT emerged in the USA when legal scholars there grappled to understand racism as a permanent feature of society, and the law as a biased tool that could not effectively end racism. It has since become "shorthand" in the USA for an approach to race relations that asks whites to contemplate systemic advantages they possess within a foundationally racist system.

Trilling notes that in order to frighten white Britons, Johnson's Conservative government used CRT as part of its culture war on the left, after Trump began his attacks on critical race theorists. Moreover, like in the USA, conservatives in the UK have cast the Black Lives Matter movement as dangerously "extreme." Prime Minister Johnson even accused the Labour Party of being on the side of those who "want to pull statues down, to rewrite the history of our country … to make it look more politically correct." The definitive goal, of course, is to prevent conversations about systemic inequalities, including racism.[11] Our intent in this book is to give central and detailed attention to persisting and systemic racism.

In March 2020, immediately before social distancing measures for the coronavirus disease (COVID-19) took effect and the Black Lives Matter movement made global headlines, Markle and Harry returned to Britain for final appearances alongside the queen and other senior royals. Later the same month, after they returned to California, Harry's father and heir to the throne Prince Charles tested positive for the coronavirus but soon recovered.[12]

As people learned to adjust to the coronavirus pandemic, including to new ideas of what is work and what is home, systemic racial, class, and gender inequalities in the UK, as elsewhere, became all too visible. Rather quickly, claims of a post-racial UK society were again challenged and destroyed by obvious data—this time in the face of such revelations as black people in England and Wales being much more likely to die from the coronavirus than their white compatriots, and people of South Asian and other non-white backgrounds being at greater risk of dying from the disease than whites. Meanwhile, anti-Asian attacks caused numerous international students and tourists from Asia to flee the UK.[13]

As senior royals, such as the queen, Charles, William, and Kate, ignored the racial dimensions of the pandemic, white media commentators remained mostly silent too. Few, including among those engaging in the racist mobbing of Markle, saw the absurdity in their continuing rejection of the idea that UK racism thrives and is systemic. People of color felt differently, of course. Based on a June 2020 online survey of 1,535 British adults, which included at least 500 black and other "ethnic minority" respondents, CNN reported the following: "The outpouring of pent-up frustration about racism in the United Kingdom caught many White people by surprise. Who did not think the country had made big strides towards tolerance and equal opportunity over the past few decades? ... The answer: Many, many Black people, whose views of race and racism in the UK are profoundly different from those of most White people."[14]

Few white Britons recognize the systemic role that white racism has long played in their country. Powerful and ordinary whites continually demonstrate that they operate out of a white racial framing of their society, thereby preserving centuries-old systemic racism. Consider just a few examples of major politicians over the decades since the 1950s, as quoted by *The Guardian* columnist Gary Yonge. In the 1950s, the Labour Party's foreign secretary, Herbert Morrison, racially framed "independence for African colonies as comparable to giving a child of 10 'a latchkey, a bank account and a shotgun.'" Soon thereafter, Prime Minister Winston Churchill proclaimed that he would run in the national election against immigrants of color, with the mantra "Keep England White." Then, in the late 1960s, the Conservative Party's influential shadow secretary of state for defence, Enoch Powell, gave an infamous speech suggesting a "bloody" civil war might well result if significant non-white immigration from the Caribbean, India, and Africa to Britain continued. In the late 1970s, the future first female British prime minister, Conservative Margaret Thatcher, spoke out against the country being "swamped by people with a different culture," terminology used by numerous white conservative politicians ever since. In 2002, future Prime Minister Boris Johnson framed black people in very racist terms as "piccaninnies" with "watermelon smiles." More recently, in 2014, the influential leader of the far-right British UK Independence Party (UKIP), Nigel Farage, argued that "the basic principle" of Powell's earlier racist speech was "correct."[15]

Unsurprisingly, thus, Markle, with an African American mother and white American father, encountered an array of racist reactions and barriers in Britain, first when dating her future husband and then during her brief stint as a senior royal. What is actually at the heart of the racialized media coverage of Markle is that she is mixed-race, with a black mother. She is considered by many white Britons (and other whites) to be an interloper into important white spaces and a threat to centuries of powerful British whiteness.

We suggest that through her detailed story, one can visibly *see British racism for what it is*. Most white Britons cling to colorblind myths about their "democratic" country. The acclaimed black sociologist Stuart Hall once noted that the US mainstream media regularly mythologizes the country's democracy as genuine and asserts inaccurately but firmly that US society is "held together by common norms, including equal opportunity, respect for diversity, one person-one vote, individual rights and rule of law."[16] The same can be said of the mainstream media in Britain. Such a mythical façade involves widespread denial of the extensive white racism, including the gendered racism that Markle, and countless Britons of color, regularly face.

At this point, we should mention key differences in racism and migration in Britain and the USA. People of color in Britain are almost all voluntary immigrants—or their descendants—from the former British Empire or from the many former British colonies that joined the Commonwealth of Nations after independence. The USA is grounded in the violent land theft and other oppressions of Native Americans, the violent enslavement and forced migration of African workers, and then, later, in the capitalistic importation of racially subordinated Mexican and Asian laborers. The two nations have quite different histories of people of color over centuries. For many white Britons, Markle represents colonized peoples of color who are "taking over" the UK, while a key premise of ongoing white racist framing is the question of who is "authentically" British. Scobie and Durand argue that this is evident in "subtle acts of bias" and "micro-aggressions." For example, a palace staffer was surprised that Scobie, who is British with Iranian roots, spoke with a posh English accent. There was also the column titled, "Memo to Meghan: We Brits Prefer True Royalty to Fashion Royalty," which Scobie and Durand cite as an example of indirect micro-aggressions. The co-authors explain that while the journalist who penned this column appeared to be panning Markle's *Vogue* guest editorship, "there was another way to read it, and that was that to be British meant to be born and bred in the UK—and be white." "[T]he idea of a non-white person moving into the House of Windsor ruffled feathers," they write, and this is especially troubling to the so-called authentic Britons amid growing anti-immigration attitudes. "Some took to Meghan's Twitter and Instagram accounts to express racist feelings that were anything but subtle, including calling her the N-word or a 'mutt,'" write the authors.[17]

In this book we examine an array of white racist attacks on Markle, and on other people of color, that go well beyond subtle acts of bias and micro-aggressions. We assess the recurring denial of well-institutionalized racism by the mainly white members of the British commentariat and polity. One major goal is to *tell it like it is* about the centuries-old and systemic racism in Britain. We regularly highlight one key feature of this systemic racism, its dominant white racial frame: an old and regularized worldview operating over centuries of British history, to the present day (see Chapter 1). In our examination of the recurring white racial framing that has targeted

Markle, and of what it reveals about British systemic racism in general, we turn to critical social scientists and legal scholars who have developed conceptual tools that lead to sharper analyses than traditional racial relations and bias paradigms allow. As they have for the USA, these critical theories help advance an understanding of systemic racism in the UK by accentuating centuries-old and entrenched structures of racial oppression, and by calling out and assessing the reality, magnitude, and generative progression of that racial oppression today and, very likely, in the future.

An American divorcée and actress who usually identifies as biracial, Markle's admission into the senior ranks of the royal family has stirred much public discussion about racial issues. Perhaps only the election of Barack Obama to the US presidency has hitherto forced such an ongoing discussion of racial issues at this high level of a contemporary Western society. Her marital union with Harry provides an exceptional opportunity to interrogate systemic racism and its accompanying white racial frame.

Notes

1 Maria Puente, "Harry and Meghan 'Step Back' as Senior Royals; Queen Addresses 'Complicated Issues,'" *USA Today*, January 8, 2020, www.usatoday.com/story/entertainment/celebrities/2020/01/08/harry-meghan-were-stepping-back-senior-royals/2845950001/. Accessed May 3, 2020.
2 "Statement from Her Majesty The Queen," January 18, 2020, www.royal.uk/statement-her-majesty-queen-0. Accessed May 3, 2020.
3 "Prince Charles Slammed for Being 'Atrociously Hypocritical' of Meghan Markle," *The News International*, January 27, 2021, www.thenews.com.pk/latest/780758-prince-charles-slammed-for-being-atrociously-hypocritical-of-meghan-markle. Accessed January 28, 2021.
4 Omid Scobie and Carolyn Durand, *Finding Freedom: Harry and Meghan and the Making of a Modern Royal Family* (New York: HarperCollins), pp. 320, 329–330.
5 *Sky News* Staff, "Harry and Meghan: Duke and Duchess of Sussex tell the Queen they will not return as working members of Royal Family," *Sky News*, February 19, 2021 https://news.sky.com/story/duke-and-duchess-of-sussex-will-not-return-as-working-members-of-royal-family-12222693. Accessed March 1, 2021.
6 *Ibid.*, p. 349.
7 Brittany Vonow, "'SHE RUFFLED FEATHERS' Racism in the Monarchy 'Played a Role' in Meghan Markle and Prince Harry Quitting Royal Family, Author Claims," *The Sun*, August 10, 2020, www.thesun.co.uk/news/12363435/meghan-markle-prince-harry-racism-role-leaving-royals/. Accessed August 10, 2020.
8 Commonwealth Secretariat 2020, "Fast Facts on the Commonwealth," https://thecommonwealth.org/commonwealth-fast-facts. Accessed May 21, 2020.
9 Daniel Trilling, "Why is the UK Government Suddenly Targeting 'Critical Race Theory'?", *The Guardian*, October 23, 2020, www.theguardian.com/commentisfree/2020/oct/23/uk-critical-race-theory-trump-conservatives-structural-inequality. Accessed January 26, 2021.

10 Fabiola Cineas, "Critical Race Theory, and Trump's War On It, Explained," *Vox*, September 24, 2020, www.vox.com/2020/9/24/21451220/critical-race-theory-diversity-training-trump. Accessed January 26, 2021.

11 Trilling, "Why is the UK Government Suddenly."

12 Natalie Harmsen, "A Complete Timeline of Prince Harry and Meghan Markle's Relationship," *Elle*, April 1, 2020, www.ellecanada.com/culture/celebrity/a-complete-timeline-of-prince-harry-and-meghan-markles-relationship. Accessed May 13, 2020.

13 Haley Ott, "Black People in England and Wales are Four Times More Likely to Die from the Coronavirus, Data Shows," *CBS News*, May 7, 2020, www.cbsnews.com/news/coronavirus-britain-black-people-likely-die/. Accessed May 13, 2020; Sally Weale, "Chinese Students Flee UK after 'Maskaphobia' Triggered Racist Attacks," *The Guardian*, March 17, 2020, www.theguardian.com/education/2020/mar/17/chinese-students-flee-uk-after-maskaphobia-triggered-racist-attacks. Accessed May 10, 2020.

14 Richard Allen Greene, "Britain's Big Race Divide," *CNN*, June 22, 2020, https://edition.cnn.com/interactive/2020/06/europe/britain-racism-cnn-poll-gbr-intl/. Accessed August 12, 2020.

15 Gary Younge, "Given Britain's History it's No Surprise that Racism Still Infects Our Politics," *The Guardian*, November 29, 2019, www.theguardian.com/commentisfree/2019/nov/29/britain-history-racism-infects-politics-slavery-windrush. Accessed May 17, 2020.

16 Stuart Jeffries, "Stuart Hall's Cultural Legacy: Britain under the Microscope," *The Guardian*, February 10, 2014, www.theguardian.com/education/2014/feb/10/stuart-hall-cultural-legacy-britain-godfather-multiculturalism. Accessed May 17, 2020.

17 Scobie and Durand, *Finding Freedom*, p. 87.

Chapter Overviews

In Chapter 1, we detail the dominant *white racial frame*, which includes a beliefs aspect (racial biases, stereotypes, ideologies). It also includes integrating cognitive elements (racial interpretations and narratives), visual and auditory elements (racialized images and language use), a feelings aspect (racialized emotions), and an inclination to racialized actions (to discriminate). Since early in Britain's history, this predominant racist framing has incorporated a central subframe that forcefully emphasizes white virtuousness, racial superiority, morality, and motivation.

In Chapter 2, we consider major racialized events in Markle's life, mainly since her relationship with Harry became public in late 2016. These events illustrate key facets of systemic British racism, including the central white racial frame, its white virtuousness subframe, and its anti-black subframe. We reveal links between the white racial frame and the common male-sexist frame, and the resulting reality of gendered racism.

In Chapter 3, we explore the framing of Markle by many people as a "trophy" of diversity, someone to whom both elite and non-elite whites can point to as proof of an alleged "end of racism" within the UK. We show how this commonplace portrayal of her, and of the British context, obscures the white-racist policies and laws white Britons generally, even enthusiastically, support.

In Chapter 4, we examine how the British ruling elite operates within the white-racist, male-sexist, and capitalist-class subsystems of an all-encompassing *elite-white-male dominance system*. These specific concepts go beyond vague descriptions of this centuries-old inegalitarian society and call out more specific oppressive realities, their foundational depth, their specific operations and several inequalities, and their occasional structural changes. These systemic concepts offer numerous critical insights into why a great many white Britons, elite and non-elite, have often responded unfavorably to the duchess, and why she is seen as a serious threat to the overall British governing system, as well as to powerful white individuals.

In Chapter 5, we consider ways in which Britons who are subjugated by class, racial, and gender oppression regularly push back against those dominations and their legitimating frames. Specifically, we assess the degree to which Markle is a *feminist counter-framer* and *anti-racist counter-framer*. We also address her in-laws' front-stage acceptance of selected elements of her progressiveness, as well as their more subtle and covert attempts to rein in her more reformist social and political leanings.

In Chapter 6, we focus more centrally on illustrating collective myths wherein white Britons, like other white Westerners, see themselves as "not racist" and as "good people," even while they think and act in anti-black and other racist ways. We show how members of the British commentariat and polity, most especially white men, commonly view allegations of British racism as exaggerated or inaccurate. We demonstrate that they are ignoring much evidence to the contrary. Here, too, we assess the significant role of black Britons from Roman times onward and the racial oppression they have long endured. We also provide much detail on the many examples of senior royals' links to decades of white racism and fascism, with much lack of social virtue demonstrated there.

In Chapter 7, we conclude with a brief re-examination of earlier themes of systemic racism, this time as they were illustrated during the first six months or so of the coronavirus pandemic, including via the continued questioning and pillorying of Markle.

A Note on Terminology for
North American Readers

Referring to all Britons of color as "black" may seem strange to most North American readers, but this has been common terminology in the UK for decades. In addition, and more recently, most commentators and analysts in various British institutions customarily combine black people (those with African and Afro-Caribbean ancestry) and other racialized minority groups in the category "BAME," an acronym for black, Asian and minority ethnic people.

We should pause to note, however, that market researchers and other pollsters have found that responses from African- and Afro-Caribbean-descent Britons—black Britons in a narrow sense—tend to contrast considerably to those of other BAME groups. Media and other reports, thus, often give a mistaken impression of "one homogeneous opinion" for BAME respondents, explains Chris Hopkins, associate director of a market research group that collaborated with CNN on a major 2020 online survey. That survey asked 1,535 British adults how they viewed UK racial relations. It included a "nationally representative sample of 1,000 respondents, with a boost to guarantee at least 500 Black, Asian and minority ethnic respondents." As Hopkins explains, "[I]t is often the case that Black people are *considerably* more dissatisfied with race relations in Britain than other ethnic minorities and, while those views may be sharpened by the [Black Lives Matter movement], it does highlight the importance for statisticians and survey designers to try to avoid falling into the trap of assuming all BAME groups feel similarly when analyzing results."[1] Throughout this book we use available British survey data, including those which combine UK blacks and other racialized minority groups in the "BAME" category, although we would have preferred data broken down for specific groups.

Additionally, we should note that the older British use of "black" for all racialized minority groups has increasingly been criticized. In 2017, for example, the UK's Black Student Campaign—which represents students of African, Arab, Asian, and Caribbean descent—decided it was time to drop "black" as an umbrella term. Some have argued that this blanket designation diminishes British Asians' preferred Asian identities. Others argue that a too-broad black term does not distinguish the different varieties of white racism and other social prejudices that are faced by those of African/

Caribbean ancestry and those of Asian ancestry. As black journalist Charlie Brinkhurst-Cuff has underscored: "I didn't have the indignation of being compared to a terrorist and told I smelt of curry while growing up, as a few of my Asian classmates did, neither did they suffer from attitudes of anti-blackness imparted by other people of colour while they were a teenager, nor were they ever roughly called nigger by a group of sniggering adolescent boys at a party."[2]

Notes

1 Greene, "Britain's Big Race Divide." Italics added.
2 Aamna Mohdin, "'Political Blackness': A Very British Concept with a Complex History," *Quartz*, March 3, 2018, https://qz.com/1219398/political-blackness-a-very-british-concept-with-a-complex-history/. Accessed May 16, 2020.

Acknowledgments

We, the co-authors, include a Commonwealth citizen (Ducey) and an American (Feagin). Kimberley Ducey was born in Newfoundland, the native homeland of the Beothuk, Innu, and Mi'kmaq Indigenous peoples but established in 1610 as an English colony. In 1949, the colony joined Canada as the Province of Newfoundland. Joe R. Feagin, of Irish descent over numerous generations since the USA was founded in the late 1700s, is likely an American only because of a late-eighteenth-century ancestor being forced from Ireland by British monarchical control and oppression there.

In the preparation of this book, we have been indebted to many loved ones and supportive and helpful social science colleagues. Although regrettably we cannot name them all, we would particularly like to thank John Solomos, Sean Elias, Carly Jennings, and Melissa Ochoa for their help, comments, and suggestions on various drafts of this book. We are especially indebted to our savvy Routledge editor, Dean Birkenkamp, for his unceasing and enthusiastic support for this project and its underlying goals.

1 Systemic Racism
Britain Now and Then

Introduction

While many whites in Britain and elsewhere seemed shocked by the announcement that the Duke and Duchess of Sussex—Prince Harry and Meghan Markle—were stepping down as senior royals, black Britons seemed far less surprised. "Thank God they are free. ... All of this is about her race. I know it because as a Caribbean woman who did not grow up here, I have experienced it myself," said one Londoner. A *New York Times* headline read, "Black Britons Wonder What Took Harry and Meghan So Long," and quoted a former president of Cambridge University's Black and Minority Ethnic campaign.

> Most of the media is ignoring the whole racism factor that has clearly played a big role in the couple's decision. ... Racism issues are spoken about more in the popular discourse in the United States. ... People are more conscious of it, whereas here the black community is a lot smaller and it's not really raised as a significant issue regularly.[1]

A black student at the London School of Economics (LSE) said of the couple's decision: "The history of the royal family is built around the British Empire, so it was almost like it was coming full circle. ... [N]o matter how much we think we are accepted into society, we really aren't."[2] NBC reported on a group of black female teenagers in the UK who talked about the racist "angry black woman" image that they and Markle must endure. NBC noted that the group laughed at the notion that "Meghan's treatment was fair." "Of course, no one is going to call her an f----- N-word in a headline," the teenaged Peace Ogbuani said, censoring herself. "Maybe in America they would write that, but in Britain they are more subtly racist. Instead, you can see it in their mannerisms and the way they treat people."[3] These black teenagers, like the LSE student, plainly called out systemic racism in British institutions and the white Britons who implemented that racist action.

In the midst of the Black Lives Matter protests on both sides of the Atlantic in 2020, Labour Member of Parliament (MP) Dawn Butler remarked: "until we dismantle the systemic racism that exists in society, we are never going to make the progress that we need to see. ... [W]e have to have ... difficult and sometimes uncomfortable conversations to bring about the change we want to see." A daughter of Jamaican immigrant parents, this Member of Parliament was forced to close her office due to racist abuse she faced. "Ending this poisonous and dangerous political environment will help save our democracy, which is under threat from the politics of division and hate," she explained, "and with [Prime Minister Boris] Johnson and [his senior adviser Dominic] Cummings often implementing that exact strategy it is an uphill struggle." Butler called on policing agencies, the criminal justice system, social media companies, Parliament, and her own party to do much more to tackle systemic racism in Britain.[4]

In striking contrast to the LSE student, the black teens, and Butler, white members of the British commentariat and polity have long denied the existence of systemic racism, including claims that Markle was driven out of the UK by racist press coverage or racist Britons. They constantly insist on white virtuousness, a central feature of old white racial framing. "It's laughable," claimed an editor at *The Sun* tabloid. "The criticism of Meghan has got nothing to do with her race."[5] The celebrated author of books on royalty, Penny Junor appeared on *CBS This Morning* to counter claims that white racism had anything to do with the media treatment Markle received, telling hosts Gayle King and Tony Dokoupil: "The British were thrilled about her marrying into the Royal Family ... because she was mixed race." This comment prompted Dokoupil to ask: "Did you check in with any Black Brits before you made that determination?" and King added: "[T]o have your baby [Archie] portrayed as a chimp. ... That ... is, in fact, very racist." In response, Junor faltered: "I'm not denying that. ... What I'm saying is, that I think that the overweening sentiment of the British public was to be enthusiastic about Meghan. ... [I]t made a whole lot of coloured people in our country suddenly find that the Monarchy was relevant for them." King and Dokoupil did not respond to Junor's use of the epithet "coloured people"; however, in the UK the term is as offensive as it is in the USA.[6]

Further demonstrating that whites and blacks walk in different worlds were the numerous twitter responses to Junor's comments. Many people, who appear to be black, tweeted negatively in response to her use of the phrase "coloured people," similar to this example: "Penny girl, we do not believe you. The good folks from *Buzzfeed News* put together a comparison of media coverage of Kate and Meghan, which is striking. I think that some white people believe that if they do not use the N-word they're not racists, which is totally false."[7] These observers accented the recurring white racist framing in the mainstream media. Britain's systemic racism can be seen in all its major institutions, including in the mainstream media that we repeatedly analyze throughout this book.

Markle's experiences with white racially framed commentary and actions offer a clear lens through which to make sense of contemporary British racism. For centuries now, Britons of color have been racially framed and considered by whites as more tolerable if they deport themselves according to white norms and framing. If they do not, they are maligned or worse. Early on, the Kensington Palace staff, at the prominent residence of numerous white royals, branded Markle "Meghan the Menace" because of her "strong will"—code similar to "angry black woman." Markle's friends have since shed light on what is behind that supposedly "strong will"; she often "felt she had more to prove. Being biracial and not always knowing where she fit in, there was a part of her that just wanted people to see she was great at whatever she did."[8] Being a person of color in mostly white spaces usually creates unique and difficult pressures. What's more, hard work is not rewarded in a fair and colorblind manner in systematically racist societies like the UK and USA. During her lifetime, Markle has indeed had to work "twice as hard to get half as far," as her friends suggest.[9]

Entertainment reporter Britt Stephens wrote that "Meghan Markle is Being Called 'Difficult,' and Black Women Can Read Between the Lines" in an op-ed, thereby capturing well how white racist framing works. Responding to reports such as Markle's allegedly unreasonable demands for her wedding, her reprimand of a member of her sister-in-law's staff, and her personal assistant weepily quitting after a few months, Stephens notes the institutionalized character of the racist framing.

> It feels like every day there's a new story about Meghan not quite fitting in—and with each emerging rumor, it becomes easier for black women everywhere to read between the lines. … Meghan's blackness walked into the room before she did; that she was assumed to be "demanding" before she even made any demands, and she was considered to be "difficult" to work with even before anyone worked with her.[10]

In contradiction to Junor's aforementioned claim that Britons were delighted that Markle married into the royal family, the UK daily newspaper *The Guardian* examined articles published about the duchess between May 2018 (the month she wed Harry) and January 2020 (the month the couple announced their stepping down as senior royals), and found that she received *twice* as many unfavorable headlines as favorable ones. Of the 843 articles in 14 print newspapers, 43 percent were unfavorable, 20 percent were favorable, and 36 percent were neutral. The data suggest that assertions that Markle receives considerably more critical treatment than her sister-in-law Kate appear to be accurate. Of the 144 articles about Kate, 8 percent were unfavorable, 45 percent were favorable, and 47 percent were neutral. The statistical difference in how the press treats the women echoes an article revealing the strikingly different media coverage they regularly receive.[11] To take just one example, the *Daily Mail* ran a favorable story about Kate "cradling her baby bump," while condemning Markle for "vanity" for doing the same. *The Guardian* study also substantiates earlier research that found that of 29,000 tabloid and non-tabloid items published online about Markle in 2019, some 72 percent were unfavorable. In contrast, 31 percent of 14,000 tabloid and non-tabloid items published online about Kate were unfavorable.[12]

In the interview with commentators King and Dokoupil, Junor exclaimed that Markle and Harry "arrived like they were a golden couple. They were sprinkling fairy dust everywhere."[13] By mid-2018—a mere few months after their wedding—the percentage of articles that framed her unfavorably exceeded the percentage of favorable ones. Markle received a spike in negative coverage when she and Harry decided to keep specifics surrounding their son's birth and baptism private. Numerous articles quoted sources asserting that Markle was a "boastful" and "self-obsessed" celebrity who craved media attention, with this storyline strengthened when she guest-edited British *Vogue*. Another concentrated period of unfavorable press coverage ensued when the couple flew on private jets while sounding the alarm on climate change. Exposés concerning Markle's relationship with her father constituted nearly one third of unfavorable articles about her, and a number of articles connected Markle and the African American side of her family to drugs and violence.[14] Much of this negative media coverage barely conceals the commentators' white racist framing of Markle.

Some British politicians have spoken out about her racist treatment. A prominent member of the Labour Party described media reporting on Markle as "intrusive and racist."[15] In this book we examine closely the white racist attacks on Markle, the recurring denial of such racist attacks by mainly white members of the British commentariat and polity, and what that tells us about systemic racism and its central white racial frame in Britain today.

Systemic Racism and the White Racial Frame

Mainstream analysts researching contemporary UK racism make common use of attitudinal concepts like bigotry, bias, prejudice, and stereotyping. Examining white racism through such optics, though often valuable, tends to privilege individualistic analyses over systemic ones. It also focuses attention on certain elements of racial thought and framing that do not get enough into the foundational and systemic realities. For instance, the authors of *Finding Freedom* do not focus on these systemic realities. They frame the racism Markle encountered as a "more subtle problem with … attitudes," even as they note that she and Harry believe Britain has a broader problem with racism, and that her mixed-race heritage was an issue for some in the royal family and its network.[16] "When he first started seeing her, Harry, sensitive to even the slightest hint of *prejudice*, had fallouts within his own circle," the authors explain. "When some questioned his new relationship, and whether she was suitable, he would wonder, 'Is this about race? Is it snobbery?'"[17] Note here the proviso concerning his sensitivity to even the least "hint of *prejudice*." Contrasting the couple's different experiences with racism, the authors write: "While it might have been new territory for Harry, *bias—both unconscious and intentional*—had always been a part of Meghan's life."[18] Describing Markle's feelings, they write: "Meghan felt like some of the commentary and tabloid stories were more than a culture clash; they were sexist and *prejudiced*."[19]

Such attitudinal analyses do not provide the concepts necessary to make sense out of the highly racialized society that Britain is. Systemic racism theory, an early version of what is often called critical race theory (see Preface), fills this fissure by arguing that in the UK case, prevailing racist framing, practices, and institutions are collectively constructed and have been foundational to British society for centuries. Systemic racism theory suggests that in essential ways British society has progressed far less when it comes to racial matters than some more individualistic theoretical approaches suggest.

Here we give much credit to earlier British scholars, most with ancestry in British Caribbean and South Asian colonies, who pioneered a more critical and structural approach to British racism in their important book, *The Empire Strikes Back: Race and Racism in '70s Britain* (1982).[20] Its savvy contributors were among the first to place an analysis of whites' racist biases and ideology at the center of a critical understanding of British political (e.g., state, nationalism) and economic (e.g., capitalism, class struggle) matters. Still, for them "racism" often meant prejudice, bias, and ideology. They especially focused on white racist stereotyping and hostility directed at the many immigrants of color who arrived in Britain in the 1940s and 1970s.

Their approach was path-breaking for British racial studies. They accent white British racism and to some degree the anti-racist pushback, including from black workers and black feminists. In the preface to *Empire*, for example, the brilliant black historian Paul Gilroy—later, author of such influential books as *There Ain't No Black in the Union Jack* (1987), *The Black Atlantic: Modernity and Double Consciousness* (1993), *Against Race* (2000), and *Darker Than Blue* (2010)—describes the book's conceptual and activist foundation: "It is about racial divisions within the British class struggle. Our premise is therefore the problem of relating 'race' to class, not for sociological theory, but for socialist politics." Reviewing the 1950s and 1960s, the contributors to *Empire* reveal how British nationalism had changed to an even more openly white-supremacist form following the arrival of migrant laborers from the Caribbean and Indian subcontinent. Along with this influx of people of color came a perceived threat to the purported (white) British way of life. When the white-run state asserted its power during the 1973–1975 economic recession, a perfect racist storm took form. For Gilroy, what is of considerable importance is how overt white nationalism—especially via institutions of the white working class (e.g., trade unions)—encouraged racial divisions within the country's increasingly diverse working class. The nation's popular white discourse, he writes, "operates across the formal lines of class, and has been constructed against blacks."[21] In direct contrast, black Britons have been demanding genuine racial equality ever since large numbers of black workers emigrated from the Caribbean in the late 1940s and 1970s to help rebuild war-torn Britain.

These immigrants are often termed the "Windrush" generation after the ship *HMT Empire Windrush* that brought many to the UK. Sadly, in 2018 they were denied their legal rights and unlawfully harassed and deported in what became known as the Windrush scandal.[22]

A major influence on our thinking stems from the significant contributions of these anti-racist scholars to understanding British racism, as well as the limitations that come with their reliance on bias, prejudice, and ideology concepts when studying that racism. The concept *systemic racism* and its *white racial frame* suggest there are yet more specific dimensions to the reality and operation of that white racism than even the contributors to *Empire* suggest. As we show throughout this book, this dominant white frame has a strong white virtuousness center, one that is centuries old and hard for whites to see and understand. The dominant white frame is just one major part of the systemic racism common in the UK. That systemic racism also includes a strong racial hierarchy, great material inequalities along racial lines, and substantial patterns of *institutional* discrimination in politics, housing, employment, criminal justice, education, and culture.

While we deeply admire the early racism analyses of *Empire*, we seek here to take the next conceptual step to the "bigger picture" of an all-encompassing British elite-white-male dominance system, which has long operated mostly through its major white-racist, male-sexist, and capitalist-class subsystems. Most contemporary analysts of British racism have missed the opportunity to call out the top predatory capitalists explicitly by name and position; to emphasize that it matters that they are not just capitalistic but also mostly *white* and *male*; and to expose their actual capitalistic, racist, sexist, and other oppressive framings and actions. Rendering such realities constantly visible is, in our view, to greatly expand how well we understand contemporary oppressive societies like the UK, and how well we can do in crafting meaningful strategies for democratic societal change.

In numerous previous books we have detailed the limitations of individualistic conceptions when undertaking studies of systemic racism in the US case. We have demonstrated how concepts of systemic racism and its dominant white racial frame illuminate racial matters in the USA and other Western countries. These ideas are especially shaped by the long anti-racist tradition of analysis developed by African American scholars and activists. Here we apply this systemic racism theory, including its white frame concept, to the discourse and actions surrounding Markle and Harry, including their engagement, their wedding, the birth of their son, and their move away socially and geographically from the British royal family.

Throughout this book we argue that white-framed narratives about Markle persist because of strong racist views that have long been part of the UK's dominant white racial frame—an overarching white worldview that encompasses at least these important elements:

1) a beliefs aspect (racial stereotypes and ideologies)
2) integrating cognitive elements (racial interpretations and narratives)
3) visual and auditory elements (racialized images and language accents)
4) a feelings aspect (racialized emotions)
5) an inclination to negative action (discrimination)[23]

Since at least the seventeenth century this prevailing racial frame has provided the broad white-generated perspective from which whites and others in Western countries commonly view the social world. Such dominant frames are mostly created by the most powerful people at the top of a society. As Karl Marx and Friedrich Engels long ago underscored, "the ideas of the ruling class are in every epoch the ruling ideas: i.e., the class, which is the ruling material force of society, is at the same time its ruling intellectual force."[24] In the British case, white, mostly male, members of the ruling class have long dominated the creation, dissemination, and implementation of this system-generating and system-rationalizing racist frame in institutional arenas such as business, the media, politics and government, education, churches, and culture. They have routinely and invariably been assisted in this effort by the mass of ordinary white citizens.

Like a complex picture frame, with much detailed edging meant to enhance a print in it, the white racial frame includes numerous elements that operate to preserve and heighten myths and misconceptions of white superiority, virtuousness, civilization, and moral goodness. In this book we demonstrate that this centuries-old white frame plays a pivotal role in mythologizing "race" matters today in Britain, and in that process propagandizing for white nationalistic and nativistic nostalgia.

Since early in British history this overarching racist framing has included a *central subframe* that assertively accents a positive view of white virtue, moral goodness, and action. For centuries the white racial framing of this ingroup superiority, together with its framing of outgroup inferiority, has been *hegemonic*—that is, it has been part of a distinctive way of life and character structure that routinely governs much of contemporary society. For most white Britons, the white racial frame is more than one interpretive frame among many. Consistently centered as a way of everyday being, this broad perspective on life is fully internalized. It provides the language and interpretations that help structure, standardize, and rationalize white society's racialized actions, interactions, and institutions.

A key aspect of the white racial frame is its anti-others subframes. Psychological researchers who have probed the white racial mindset have shown that direct and indirect measures indicate that anti-black views and other negative racial subframes remain widespread.[25] Certainly, the anti-black subframe is evident in the mainstream media coverage of Markle. Not only racist bias but also racist imagery, narratives, and emotions regularly pervade this coverage. In 2016, when the *Daily Mail* titled an online story "Harry's Girl is (Almost) Straight Outta Compton," it duly provoked unprecedented critical remarks from Harry's office in Kensington Palace.

The prince condemned the "racial undertones of comment pieces" and "the outright sexism and racism of social-media trolls."[26]

Other royals and their advisors preferred that Harry remain silent, but his forceful remarks had precedent. One year prior, a strongly worded statement issued by William and Kate, and circulated worldwide to media outlets, reproached the British press for hounding their son, Prince George. And when in 2019 the media reported that Kate had had botox treatments following the birth of her third child, a palace spokesperson refuted the claim. Proxies for the royal family did more than remain silent in the face of press attacks against Markle, however; they sometimes concealed the nature of the racist attacks. For example, after the British Fashion Council (BFC) posted and then quickly removed a photo of Markle from its Instagram account, a palace source claimed it was because the image was meant to be a personal souvenir from the British Fashion Awards. However, the BFC reported it was removed because of a flood of racist comments posted beneath it.[27]

Racially *othering* Markle has since continued via pieces like *Tatler*'s "One Year of Meghanomania." This British magazine, targeted at the country's upper-middle and upper classes, is commonly referred to as "the bible of British aristocracy." Surveying Markle's first year as a royal, *Tatler* purported that Kensington Palace staff referred to her as "Me-Gain" because of the effort and attention she demanded. The story also mentioned the " 'Marie Antoinette' overtones of her [American] baby shower." While comparing the backlash Markle faces to that which Sarah Ferguson, Duchess of York, faced when marrying Prince Andrew in 1986, the white-run *Tatler* downplayed the *gendered racism* visited on the Duchess of Sussex, inaccurately writing that she "has seen nothing" on par with the negative attacks that the white Sarah had confronted.[28]

The British press regularly compares the treatment of these women. Sarah has even been dubbed "Meghan's predecessor," who "clearly knows what Meghan is experiencing."[29] Sarah, herself, has said "I know what Meghan is going through. ... I have been in Meghan's shoes, and I still am. ... I abhor bullying."[30] Lost on Sarah is the distinctive gendered-racist nature of the bullying and other attacks Markle has had to endure. As a highly privileged white woman, the Duchess of York has *never* been in Markle's shoes, and cannot possibility know what she has gone through as a biracial woman.

In early 2020, in the aftermath of Markle and Harry announcing they would be stepping down as senior royals, *Tatler* decided to reprint "One Year of Meghanomania," retitling it "Meghanomania Lives On." "As the country processes the Sussex Shock Statement, it occurs to *Tatler* that many of the 'Meghanomania' anecdotes from the May 2019 issue ring resoundingly true," the magazine stated with considerable white emotion.[31]

Prominent white Britons in and outside the press continue to stereotype and blame a supposedly dominant Markle for the couple's decision to leave the royal family. Stanley Johnson, father of Prime Minister Boris Johnson, referred to Markle as "the driving force behind" the decision.[32] The royal biographer Angela Levin, who said immediately following the couple's wedding that the African American preacher's sermon made her uncomfortable, has referred to Markle as a "mega-watt attention grabber" and a "fiercely ambitious woman who wants to be number one." While in his pre-Markle days Harry was "charismatic and accessible," according to Levin, he is now "a nervy, tense man who seems constantly on edge."[33] The socialite and author Lady Colin Campbell has compared Markle to Lady Macbeth, a leading character in the Shakespearean tragedy *Macbeth*, and wife of the play's ill-fated protagonist, who provokes her husband into committing regicide.[34] All these commentaries seem to have undertones of the old white-racist stereotype and image of assertive black women.

Markle has had much more to contend with than attacks by prominent white Britons. Very early on, she was inundated with violent threats and other hate mail arriving at various royal residences and via Kensington Palace's email and social media accounts. One white-racist note arrived in an envelope filled with innocuous white powder posing as anthrax. A security course, which she, like all royals—except the queen—was required to complete, occurred *before* her wedding because of the unprecedented number of alarming threats already against her person. The timing was highly unusual. Kate's security training, for example, took place *after* she had married William.[35] Routinely, Markle's black heritage has made her a target of white-racist abuse and threats.

Important in reproducing Britain's systemic racism is the regular assertion and transmission of the centuries-old pro-white and anti-others framing of people of color. A long-term historical creation, this white frame, as we have just demonstrated, is reproduced moment-to-moment within dense social networks that contextualize whites' lives, leaving them oblivious to the real costs of racism for racialized others or in denial of its existence. The scholar Maurice Halbwachs suggests that one should not seek where human understandings, images, and stereotypes are preserved just "in the brain or in some nook of my mind to which I alone have access." Instead, an individual's understandings, images, and knowledge bits hang together because they are "part of a totality of thoughts *common to a group*."[36] As in these examples and those that follow, we observe that whites gain most of their racialized understandings and framing from witnessing, imbibing, and testing the comments, reactions, and behavior of other whites, including parents, peers, and the media.

Systemic and Foundational Racism

White British Denials of the White Racial Framing of Meghan Markle

Unsurprisingly, many white Britons in and outside of the mainstream media regularly perpetuate a pervasive white-racist framing of Markle, yet often deny they do so. For instance, Camilla Tominey, editor of *The Telegraph*, is unwavering in her narrative that "race" is not an element in British press coverage of Markle. "When Meghan arrived here, she was really well received," she told the *New Yorker*, adding that Markle soon had detractors inside Kensington Palace, who were less besotted by the same attributes that made her alluring to the media, including her showbusiness background, self-confidence, and "feminist habits of assertion." Tominey went on to say, "This narrative of 'the press and the public have been attacking us,' and 'there's a racial undertone,' and Prince Harry talking about 'unconscious bias'—people are scratching their heads." In *her* narrative she meant *white* "people are scratching their heads," of course. Tominey even accused Markle of reverse-racism. In her white-framed column concerning Markle's *Vogue* editorialship, Tominey wrote: "I wonder whether Meghan was conscious of the bias she showed in choosing 15 'forces for change' for the *Vogue* cover, all of whom were women, of which only five were white? ... If I was pale, male and stale, I'd be feeling pretty discriminated against right now."[37]

One US entertainment writer astutely captures how the contemporary white-racist framing, within which Tominey operates here, actually works.

> Obviously, this is an inflammatory statement: Part of the "change" that Meghan (and so many others!) would like to see in the world is shifting attention away from white men, who have held the spotlight for far too long. It's no accident or even "bias" that Meghan selected "only" five white women—it was very specifically her goal to highlight women of color who know better than anyone the need for change, and have been denied a voice for generations. ... [T]o even use the word "discrimination" to describe their exclusion from a *Vogue* cover is a painful and insulting distraction from the true discrimination running rampant every day—in Britain, and across the world.[38]

Numerous ordinary folks on Twitter also called out Tominey, again capturing well how contemporary white-racist framing works. One example is this: "It's so telling that when a single edition of a single publication doesn't explicitly centre whiteness, Britain's right wing media goes into attack mode. This is how institutional racism works." Another person argued thus: "*The Telegraph* wants to lecture Meghan Markle about unconscious bias, as they continue their campaign against the first mixed race member of the royal family, who they've taken against for some mysterious reason they can't quite put their finger on."[39]

Australia's *60 Minutes* program came under criticism for a problematical segment titled "How Meghan Markle Lost Her Sparkle." The white-framed program failed to interview even one person of color, while giving the British white nationalist and media personality Katie Hopkins a platform to vilify the biracial duchess—again capturing well how contemporary white-racist framing works across many areas of the globe. Known for far-right views on immigration and racial matters, Hopkins was asked if the vitriol she holds for Markle is supported by a racist framing. She replied: "If I criticised Meghan, as we can hear I am, people say, 'Well, you're racist'. And, honestly, it's not even a second thought to me. ... So, this racist thing is really old and tired, but I think it's just people's way of sort of saying 'You must not criticise Meghan.'" Then, when asked "Why do you hate Meghan so much?" From her unreflective white-nationalist bubble, Hopkins responded, "Oh everything. ... It's my royal family. This is my country. Prince Harry is my Prince Harry."[40]

When Hopkins remarks, "It's my royal family. This is my country," what she means is that both the royal family and the UK should remain *white*. When she says "Prince Harry is my Prince Harry," what she means is that he should have married a *white* British woman. That a major newsmagazine such as *60 Minutes* would give a prominent white nationalist a platform to bash Markle—a white nationalist who has dubbed migrants "cockroaches" and "feral"; called for a "final solution" to terrorism; upheld "white genocide" conspiracy theories; referred to London as "Khan's Londonistan" (referencing London's mayor Sadiq Khan); and claimed there is "institutionalised discrimination against whites"—says much about how systemic racism and its legitimating racial frame operate in English-speaking countries.[41]

White denial of the white racism that Markle faces is not limited to overt white nationalists. Former press secretary to Diana, Princess of Wales, Patrick Jephson—who was also interviewed for this particular episode of Australia's *60 Minutes*—claimed that the issue of white racism was "entirely misleading. It's irrelevant and I would warn against anybody taking that line as any sort of explanation as to why Meghan sometimes doesn't get the press she necessarily wants." In response to Jephson's narrative, and referencing Harry's defense of Markle, the white *60 Minutes* reporter suggested that Harry had "played the racism card, to an extent." Diana's former press secretary disclosed that he "strongly advised [Harry] against doing that," adding "if you take that point of view then you're going to miss perhaps some more relevant reasons to why Meghan isn't as popular as she should be."[42] Note, too, that the phrase "played the racism card" is a relatively recent *white-created* term added to the dominant white-racist framing, in this case a phrase attempting to denigrate anyone who questions the centuries-old systemic racism of a country.

In response to claims that Markle and Harry believe Britain has a problem with white racism, Lady Colin Campbell remarked: "This is absolute poppycock. Britain is inclusive. It is outrageous to claim that."[43] In her recent book *Meghan and Harry: The Real Story*, this royal writer argues that Markle's biraciality was actuality a benefit for her in the eyes of white Britons, including royals. "Had Meghan not been a woman of colour," contends Campbell, "they would never have allowed the marriage. It was the only thing that was unreservedly in her favour.'" As for negative stories about the duchess, Campbell insists:

> most of the people who were spreading these stories were not racist or snobbish. Many ... were frankly concerned with the way Meghan and

Harry had been conducting themselves. They wanted them to behave in a less aggressive, assertive, and demanding manner. ... to conduct themselves the way ... William and Catherine did. ... [Racists in Britain are] so few and far between to be of no consequence ... though their existence would confuse the American press into thinking that Meghan was a victim of racism in Britain when nothing could have been further from the truth.[44]

This type of white denial of systemic racism, including the racist framing of black women, is by no means new. Today, white Britons commonly adopt a narrative that ignores or downplays the UK's extensive racist history or maintains that white racism has ceased to function as a major factor in contemporary society. The same narrative has been well-documented among whites in Markle's country of origin.

Defense of Empire and Other Contemporary British Denials of White Racism

The UK was indeed an important leader in the development of anti-racist legislation in 1960s and 1970s, soon after the postwar immigration of people of color from the Commonwealth. Yet, much of this legislation is, at best, weakly enforced. Moreover, the bulk of the country's long racial history is grounded in the extreme racial oppression that took the form of white slave-trading, slavery, colonialism, and imperialism. And though the UK saw a flowering of anti-racist movements and progressive legislation against discrimination sooner than other European countries, its extensive history of this slave-trading, slavery, colonialism, and imperialism has deeply shaped the legal, political, economic, educational, and other institutional systems of Britain. As one historian explained, the effects of the British Empire are tangible and enduring even if empire itself is "made silent, or invisible" in contemporary white memory, with the empire's white colonies still conjuring up a vanished era through the persisting narratives of "racial whiteness."[45] This global contemporary reality makes current claims of a *colorblind* or *post-racial* British society ill-informed and duplicitous.[46]

In recent years, nostalgia for the British Empire has been expressed by many whites, including members of the British commentariat and polity, leading scholars, and the public. The British historian Kim Wagner explains that this defense of empire commonly reveals "delusions of past grandeur" or a "persecution complex." Britain is regularly portrayed as both "a global power and a heroic underdog, single-handedly holding off the barbarians, whether Zulus, Nazis, immigrants or the EU." Wagner continues his overview:

to even suggest that the civilising mission might have been an essentially racialised project, or that the British could be quite as brutal as, say, the Belgians in Congo, is to challenge a particular *narrative* that so many people still hold dear. Ultimately, this is not about the past but the present, it is not about facts but feelings, and is not about history but identity.[47]

Wagner notes the work of prominent white historian Jeremy Black, who has written aggressively that "[b]laming imperial rule serves a variety of cultural, intellectual and political purposes, and at a number of levels. Domestically, aside from the 'culture wars' and identity struggles which ... appear to be becoming more active and potent, it is in part a strategy designed to create a new public identity."[48] While Wagner concludes there is a reasonable argument "against empire-bashing," he believes Black's work is highly problematic. He explains that the conservative historian "fails to acknowledge [that] while the brutality of the British empire may not have been historically unique, the way that it is still celebrated today as essentially a force for good perhaps is."[49] Wagner adds that recent opinion polls in Britain show that a significant majority of respondents view the British Empire as something of which to be proud, and that this is evidence that the views expressed by the historian Black are not uncommon.[50]

Oxford academic Nigel Biggar's article "Don't Feel Guilty About Our Colonial History" recently ignited controversy. Concerned that his work would be misread as demonstrative of the university's scholarship, other Oxford-based researchers wrote in protest of his cost-benefit analysis of British imperial history.[51] Backlash from right-wing newspapers soon followed that protest. The historian Jonathan Saha wrote the following in defense of Biggar's critics.

> To judge British colonial rule by its effects without taking into account its fundamentally racist legal and bureaucratic structures is to suggest that there are circumstances when white supremacy is acceptable. The argument that positive things were done through British imperialism that might excuse its inherent racism (let alone the numerous atrocities committed by British colonial regimes across the world) is ... a subtle defence of white supremacy. The claim that colonial rule did good because it "developed" colonized societies (with proponents of this position often citing improvements in medicine and infrastructure) rests on the implicit counter-factual view that without imperial intervention these societies would not have participated in modernity. ... It implies that only white rulers could have brought about these changes.[52]

Saha further reasons that Britons who glorify the Empire see any criticism of it as synonymous to impugning modern-day Britain or as a leftist guilt-inducing campaign. An example of this public "sensitivity," he explains, is the right-wing media's attack on Biggar's scholarly detractors. Another example is found in the actions of the former minister for universities and science, and brother of Boris Johnson, Jo Johnson. Jo Johnson criticized the necessary safe-space policies for students of color on historically white campuses, by suggesting that additional security for them to participate in higher-education settings is "an attack on (implicitly) white students' right to express themselves."[53]

To summarize, in defending the centuries-old British Empire, historians frequently proceed on three major assumptions, all out of a *white* racial framing of Western history. One, Western imperial rule is natural and inevitable, for it has been with us throughout the course of Western history. Accordingly, which nations realized imperial supremacy and how they have used it to prosper or fail should be our only empirical concerns. Two, British imperialists have been among the most benign colonizers in history, governing with more integrity, righteousness, and justice than not, and more fairly than their colonized nations' earlier or subsequent rulers. Three, the British Empire is unfairly condemned via modern-day historians' ideologies and political agendas, as opposed to objective assessments of the historical evidence.[54]

In *The Empire Project: The Rise and Fall of the British World System, 1830–1970*, John Darwin argues it is not helpful to keep fighting about whether the Empire was good or bad because there will never be agreement. He suggests an alternative way forward: understand how it worked and why it fell apart. Arguably, alas, we cannot move forward in such a way, given that when the former colonies achieved independence, agents of the withdrawing Empire expunged thousands of official records of transgressions committed against Indigenous peoples.[55] The concealment and destruction of such facts precludes important insights into how the British Empire actually operated and why it eventually failed.

Such cover-ups also conveniently circumvent needed reparations for past crimes. Take, for example, the story of the Koh-i-Noor diamond, which has been part of the British crown jewels for more than a century and a half. After imprisoning one heir to the Punjabi throne and forcing the other, a young boy, to sign a legal document relinquishing the gem and all claims to sovereignty, the diamond was given to Queen Victoria. Today, it is one of 2,868 diamonds that adorn Elizabeth II's Imperial State Crown. When she complained of the crown's weight, Twitter was abuzz with one suggestion on how to make it lighter: return the legendary Koh-i-Noor diamond to its rightful owners.[56]

The 2020 Black Lives Matter Movement and Racial Injustices in British Institutions

Building on systemic-racism theory and research, we show throughout this book how white-on-black and white-on-brown subjugation and oppression have underpinned British society since at least the seventeenth century. Reflecting on this centuries-old picture, one can ask the pivotal question of how the British system of racial oppression has been regularly *reproduced* over generations. As we demonstrate, a multi-generational approach to racial oppression is essential to a comprehensive understanding of its development and current institutions—i.e., the *social reproduction* of oppression. For Britain's systemic racism to persist across these many generations, it must routinely create and reproduce the necessary societal institutions and their internal normative structures. Today, as in the past, these include substantial control by elite and ordinary whites of British economic, political, legal, educational, and media institutions—all critical parts of the country's systemic racism. If you break a well-crafted, three-dimensional hologram into smaller parts and shine a laser through one part, you can project the whole holographic image again from that one part. Like such a hologram, each apparently separate British institution reflects in many ways the reality of centuries-old systemic racism. Unsurprisingly, each major institutional component of systemic racism is linked, directly or indirectly, to the other major institutional components.[57]

Each new generation of Britons inherits established social institutions that protect unjust enrichment, privileges, and power for whites and unjust impoverishment, disprivilege, and disempowerment for blacks and other Britons of color. Important too is reproduction over generations of the societal framing apparatus—that is, the white racial frame that aggressively rationalizes and legitimates long-lasting racial oppression in Britain.

Later in this book we provide many examples of the harms of systemic racism in Britain. Let us anticipate that discussion briefly by considering what impelled the 2020 British Black Lives Matter movement that developed in the midst of the coronavirus pandemic. Similarities in police mistreatment of black people in Britain and the USA were key to this movement. Recent statistics confirm that police in England and Wales are five times less likely to use force against whites, nine times less likely to stop and search them, and three times less likely to arrest whites than they are blacks. A black person in the UK is more than twice as likely to die in police custody, and with the police force more than twice as likely to be the cause of their death. In 2018–2019, a black person was ten times more likely to be stopped and searched in the UK than a white person, with 22 percent of searches resulting in a criminal justice outcome.[58] The lethal effects of police racism and the coronavirus pandemic, which protesters argued must be confronted simultaneously, also drove the Black Lives Matter demonstrations. Blacks in England and Wales were almost twice as likely to die from the coronavirus as whites, with poverty, congested housing, and employment in lower-paid and front-line jobs being contributing factors (see Chapter 7).

Moreover, a 2020 online survey of 1,535 British adults found that black and white respondents reported considerably different personal experiences with police officers. Forty-nine percent of black respondents said they "personally have not been treated with respect" by law enforcement versus 26 percent of white respondents who said the same. Fifty-nine percent of black respondents said a family member or friend had *not* been treated with respect by police versus 31 percent of white respondents who said the same. Surveyors also found that 54 percent of black respondents said British police are "institutionally racist," while just over a quarter of whites (27 percent) said the same.[59]

Beyond the survey data are stories like that of Cressida Dick, commissioner of the Metropolitan Police Service in London. In 2020, she told her officers not to take the knee in support of the Black Lives Matter movement. The pushback on her action was strong. "I think it is completely wrong to prevent officers—if they want to—from showing solidarity with Black communities, who are so often discriminated against and need support," responded Labour Member of Parliament Dawn Butler. Butler continued: "If our local police followed … Dick's diktats, she would take our policing backwards. … The [Black Lives Matter] movement has been so powerful and inspirational but now we must deliver on that call to action, and bring about true equity in society—where we remove *structural* and *systematic* barriers for all."[60]

In the interim, from his California home, Prince Harry spoke out publicly in support of Black Lives Matter, remarking that "institutional racism has no place in our societies, yet it is still endemic. Unconscious bias must be acknowledged without blame to create a better world for all of you."[61] And while several organizations associated with the monarchy, including the Queen's Commonwealth Trust, posted online support for the movement, Markle and Harry were the first British royals to publicly speak in support of the movement. When addressing graduating students at her former high school, Markle emphasized the US police killings of unarmed black Americans, including George Floyd and Breonna Taylor: "I wanted to say the right thing and I was really nervous that I wouldn't, or that it would get picked apart, and I realized the only wrong thing to say is to say nothing. Because George Floyd's life mattered and Breonna Taylor's life mattered and Philando Castile's life mattered and Tamir Rice's life mattered." "Black lives matter," she added.[62] Soon after, speaking to Rashad Robinson, the president of Color of Change—a US civil rights advocacy organization—Harry remarked, "we have to go to the *root of the problem*, to the *source of the problem*, and actually fix it there. … This is not down to the Black community, this is down to every single person who is on the planet right now." When Robinson himself remarked that we need to ensure that "we drive action towards structural and systemic change—changing the rules that have held people back," Harry said he could not agree more, adding, "You say it so beautifully."[63] Color of Change is just one group, among many, with whom Markle and Harry have engaged as they develop their awareness of systemic racism and publicly elevate the issue.

At the time of writing, Amelia Windsor, the queen's first cousin, is the only other British royal to publicly support Black Lives Matter. She backed the movement on a social media account and participated in at least one protest. A digital editor for *Town & Country* explained why few royals did the same: "A core tenant of the British monarchy is its apolitical nature. … Issues of racism and police brutality should not be considered political, but unfortunately they are politicized, which is just one of the possible reasons why, despite their significant platforms, the working royals are staying quiet at this moment."[64]

Speaking in defense of the royal family, a former press secretary to Elizabeth II responded to Markle's speech to the graduating students at her former Los Angeles high school as follows:

> What's happened in the states is an absolute tragedy and it should never have happened but unfortunately it did happen. Had Meghan and Harry still been in the U.K. and working members of the royal family that speech couldn't have happened. I'm talking about the whole speech . ... It's highly politicized because of the very nature of what it is.[65]

Note this ex-press secretary's qualification, "What's happened in the states," as if the killing of unarmed black men at the hands of white police is unique to the United States. Remember, too, that the duchess had said in the speech that "Black lives matter," a statement that should be moderate enough for other British royals also to utter.

The claim that the British royal family is apolitical is a myth. In 2001, Prince Charles—heir to the throne—complained about the European Convention on Human Rights, referring to it as "compensation culture" (see Chapter 6). Elizabeth II's well-known yearning for Scotland to remain in Britain and for Turkey to stay out of the European Union are two more recent examples that shatter the illusion of an apolitical royal family. In exchange for Adolf Hitler making no further demands for European lands, George VI publicly supported the 1938 Munich Pact—the international agreement that allowed Hitler to claim the Sudetenland in Czechoslovakia, which had a predominately German population (see Chapter 6). And there is, of course, the monstrous political legacy of monarchs like Queen Victoria during her long reign over violent British colonization across the globe, as documented in Mike Davis's *Late Victorian Holocausts*.[66] When a statue of Victoria was recently defaced in Manitoba (Canada), the scholar Jason Hannan explained why. Victoria "was in charge during the key period of relations between First Nations and a colonial occupying power, which kicked people off of their land, which forced Indigenous people onto reserves and, eventually, which led to policies like residential [Indian] schools."[67]

Admitting she was not surprised that the British royal family had mostly failed to publicly comment on the Black Lives Matter movement, writer Mikhaila Friel describes their most obvious link to institutionalized racism: the centuries of African slavery and the slave trade, for which the queen has failed to apologize, and from which she and her family have greatly benefitted. The failure to condemn this violent political legacy says much about the royal family's white privilege mentality, argues Friel. That the queen has not apologized is symptomatic of an absence of regret, of antipathy to addressing historic wrongs, and of a disingenuous commitment to multi-racial Britain.[68]

In summer 2020, this white-privilege mentality was on full display again, when a medal that the queen customarily awards to diplomats and senior Foreign Office officials who have served abroad was exposed as racist in its design. Created in 1818 under George III, this medal of the Order of St Michael portrays a white, blond, and blue-eyed Archangel trampling on a Satan figure who has dark skin and hair. The Scottish Nigerian musician Bumi Thomas offers a different interpretation of the medal, linking its imagery to centuries of British systemic racism and colonialism, and to the white American police officer who pressed his knee on George Floyd's neck long enough to kill him. She explains:

> It is not a demon; it is a black man in chains with a white, blue-eyed figure standing on his neck. It is literally what happened to George Floyd {whose death led to the global Black Lives Matter movement} and what has been happening to black people for centuries under the guise of diplomatic missions: active, subliminal messaging that reinforces the conquest, subjugation and dehumanisation of people of colour. It is a depiction on a supposed honour of the subjugation of the black and brown people of the world and the superiority of the white, a construct born in the 16th century. It is the definition of institutional racism that this image is not only permitted but celebrated on one of the country's highest honours. Whilst statues are being pulled down and relocated, emblems and symbols of this nature also need to be redesigned to reflect a more progressive, holistic relationship between Britain and the Commonwealth nations.[69]

Two other racialized events—the Grenfell Tower fire and the afore-mentioned Windrush scandal—serve as further links between the brutal police killing of Floyd in the USA and the British Black Lives Matter movement. The 2017 fire was the UK's deadliest domestic tragedy since World War II. It stemmed from what should have been a containable kitchen fire and caused the deaths of at least 71 people, mostly people of color. Anti-racism activists have argued that the fire was the direct result of systemic racism and systemic classism, including residents' unheeded pre-fire safety complaints. The engineer selected by Conservative Prime Minister Boris Johnson to lead an inquiry into the tragedy had previously headed an engineering industry group that had received a substantial grant from Arconic Corporation's charitable arm, the firm responsible for the tower's dangerous combustible casing.[70] As the scholar Maya Goodfellow explains, the "charred remains of Grenfell Tower stand in London's landscape as evidence of the deadly effects of austerity, deregulation, gentrification and legislated corporate greed."[71] We would add persisting systemic racism to this sad list.

The black anti-racist activist Doreen Lawrence has spoken out about the role institutionalized racism played in the 2017 fire. Since 1993, when her young son Stephen Lawrence was murdered by white youths, she has been fighting for racial justice. She was reminded of what an uphill battle that is when, in 2020, London's Metropolitan Police announced that its investigation into her son's murder would "move to an inactive phase." Over 20 years prior, an inquiry into his death concluded that "institutional racism" does affect British policing. That the police moved the investigation to inactive when the white conservative Boris Johnson was leading the country is significant. In articles Johnson penned in 1999–2000, he claimed that the inquiry into Lawrence's death had caused "the cowing of the police" and had trapped them in unjustified "racial awareness programs." When asked if he still holds these views 20 years later, the prime minister refused to answer.[72]

A year after the Grenfell Tower fire, thousands of blacks who had arrived in Britain in the decades between 1948 and 1971 from Commonwealth countries in the Caribbean and Africa (the "Windrush" generation) were erroneously told they were not lawfully in Britain (see Chapter 3). Political activist Patrick Vernon has suggested such discriminatory events highlight a number of questions for black Britons: "Are we really British? Are we valued? Is our contribution valued in this country? The whole Black Lives Matter thing crystallises that."[73]

According to a 2020 online survey of 1,535 British adults, some 55 percent of black respondents said they did not trust the government to prevent future Windrush-style racial discrimination; whereas, 55 percent of whites said they were confident that this would not happen again. This online survey also found that 33 percent of black respondents versus 11 percent of white respondents believe the UK has "not done anywhere near enough" to address historical racial injustices.[74] Today, a majority of white Britons, including the queen, prefer to ignore past centuries of racial oppression or to mentally separate that past oppression from the present.

Reproduction of systemic racism over long centuries has been considered more or less normal by most white Britons, and the ways and mechanisms by which this racist system has been reproduced and transmitted over generations have received too little attention in social science analyses. The large-scale racist institutions, such as the racialized economy and government, imbed white-controlled normative structures and social networks, and routinely perpetuate internal racial hierarchies and inequalities. These institutions are constantly created, recreated, and maintained by the processes of institutionalization, including legal processes, and by the racially conforming actions at the micro level of most whites. The so-called apolitical nature of the British monarchy is part of these processes. We pause now to consider some technicalities of the constitutional monarchy and further consider its allegedly apolitical nature.

A Powerful Constitutional Monarchy: A Brief History

Parliament is currently the legislative assembly of the UK. The political entity called the United Kingdom of Great Britain and Ireland (UK)—the sovereign state that existed between 1801 and 1922—was created by the

Acts of Union at the turn of the nineteenth century. (This state is now called the United Kingdom of Great Britain and Northern Ireland.) The UK has long had legislative assemblies called parliaments, early on with one branch of Lords (aristocrats and royals) and one of Commons (ordinary people). The parliaments have a long history of struggles to limit the power of British monarchs. The monarchy is centuries old, and for many of those centuries was absolutely powerful. By the late 1600s, the power of kings and queens had declined and the "relationship between the Lords and Commons had shifted in favour of the Commons." The 1832 Reform Act further modernized and democratized electoral procedures, as did other such Acts in the early and mid-1900s. Over time the House of Commons became by far the dominant branch of Parliament, as it is today.[75]

Nowadays, sessions of the British Parliament are opened with "a speech by the monarch from the throne in the House of Lords in the presence of members of the House of Commons. The speech, written by the government ... contains a list of proposals that the government intends to introduce in the upcoming parliamentary session."[76] Being told what to do by the leadership of the dominant political party suggests the British monarch is weak, irrelevant, and an anachronism. That is not true, for the monarch still has numerous political powers that are periodically utilized as "reserve weapons" of the British ruling elite, of which the monarch is a critical part.

At the end of Queen Victoria's long reign in 1901, that white-male elite spent much money building up the symbolic and ceremonial aspects of the British monarchy, and to protect certain reserve powers, even as voting rights of ordinary white men were expanded. In this way the refurbished monarchy has long been used via symbolic means to reinforce the country's traditional ruling class structure.[77] The monarchy and its accoutrements have remained a *critical symbolic backup* for the British elite-white-male dominance system, assisting in conning a majority of Britons to accept this hierarchical reality to the present day.

Moreover, the monarchy is still about more than just powerful symbolism. The reigning monarch is official head of the Privy Council, the oldest form of legislative assembly in Britain. Among other things, this powerful council plays a role in specific statutory regulatory bodies (e.g., healthcare, higher education). According to the royal website, "It is the court of final appeal for the UK overseas territories and Crown Dependencies, and for those Commonwealth countries that have retained the appeal to Her Majesty in Council, including Jamaica, Barbados, Antigua and Barbuda, Belize and Tuvalu." Approximately 700 elite political advisers serve on the Council, mostly major politicians and present or former members of the House of Commons and House of Lords. A handful of them attend monthly meetings where the Council secures the monarch's formal approval to a number of "Orders" previously discussed and approved by Cabinet ministers.[78]

The official royal website includes a superficial outline of what is discussed during the monthly meetings. Mainly, it includes who of the rotating roster of Cabinet ministers have been in attendance alongside the Lord President, who is always present. At the time of writing, Conservative Member of Parliament Jacob Rees-Mogg occupies this role. Council meetings are not open, leading *The Guardian* correspondent Jon Henley to describe how difficult reporting on the Council is: "Piercing the dense fog of obscurity that shrouds this most august of institutions" requires "exhaustive research undertaken in various dusty corners of the internet."[79] To imagine what goes on beyond the gilded gate, one might consider Rees-Mogg, who is typical of the top echelon of the elite: white, male, Christian, son of a Tory peer, and privately educated.

When asked to respond to a survey that found that 28 percent of then-Prime Minister David Cameron's wishlist of future Conservative Members of Parliament were schooled at Oxford or Cambridge, and that 52 percent were privately educated, Rees-Mogg replied: "Oxford and Cambridge are world-renowned universities that get the crème of British academic life. It would be absolutely perverse to be biased against some of the cleverest people in the country." Clearly, he is oblivious to how white male privilege and systemic racial, gender, and class oppressions work—a tendency among members of the white elite.[80]

Just *four* Cabinet ministers attend monthly Privy Council meetings with the queen, and Rees-Mogg is permanently in attendance, accenting the inner workings of the white British establishment. This reveals who closely advises the monarch, as does the fact that the overwhelming majority of the 700-member Council is white and male. Calculating from members listed on the Privy Council website as of mid-2020, we determined the gender and racial group of each via a search of news articles and biographies.[81] They are predominantly white men (541, or 77 percent), while another 105 (15 percent) are white women. Hence, whites make up 92 percent of the Council. Just 55 (about 8 percent) are people of color. Half of the people of color are from Commonwealth nations.

One of our goals is to move away from typical passive tenses and vague nouns in discussing those who have ruled Britain. To understand British society we must understand well its controlling private and public networks and organizations, such as the royal establishment manifested in the Privy Council. To understand what a society is, and to make solid predictions about its future, we must also study the dominant racial, class, and gender framing in the minds of elite white men who constitute, with a few others, the top decision-making class. Alas, few societal analysts have made systematic use of a specific analytical concept like *elite white men* for those who constitute the overwhelming majority of these most powerful decision-makers. Their everyday choices and actions regularly shape not only major British institutions but also some major institutions in Commonwealth countries across the globe.

This influential Privy Council advises the monarch on her/his required official duties, including enacting Acts of Parliament, issuing Royal Charters to various organizations, making treaties, awarding national honors, and making official appointments. The monarch's powers also include the ability to suspend parliament and even to "dismiss an elected government from office."[82]

Significantly, as James Kilby and Rob Sewell note, "We are led to believe that such powers ... are a relic of our feudal past." But these powers are far from hypothetical. For example, the significance of this power reserve was made clear during the 1975 Australian constitutional crisis when Elizabeth II—as Australian and British queen—dismissed Prime Minister Gough Whitlam of the Australian Labor Party. Besides the deposed prime minister and the queen, the crisis also involved Sir John Kerr (the governor general who formally dismissed Whitlam in his capacity as the queen's representative) and Malcolm Fraser (leader of the opposition and Liberal Party, appointed to replace Whitlam). This crisis was a type of coup against the Australian Labor government. Clearly, the British monarch can and does implement enduring stately power. "[T]hese powers ... are simply held back to be used as a last roll of the dice for the *ruling class*."[83]

Australian scholar Jenny Hocking writes that: "As an autonomous post-colonial nation, we assume that the Queen exercises no residual monarchical power over our system of governance. ... This assumption is misplaced." The queen was not politically impartial regarding Australia's political matters. Kerr's private papers disclose that Buckingham Palace was involved in the planning that led to Whitlam's dismissal. Hocking was forced to legally seek the release of secret letters between the queen and Kerr. "These historic letters, critical to our understanding of the dismissal, are held by our National Archives in Canberra [the capital of Australia] where they are kept hidden from us under the strict, and potentially indefinite, embargo of the Queen," explains Hocking.[84]

More recently, in 2019, the British Labour Party joined with the Liberal Democrats to call for the queen to intervene to stop the new Conservative Party leader, Boris Johnson, from suspending (proroguing) Parliament. Instead, the queen intervened to permit Johnson to take this action to continue with his aggressive plans to remove Britain from its long engagement with the European Union (Brexit). Her action created worry among the ruling elite because monarchical power works best when *hidden*. This use of the queen's prerogative to suspend Parliament, as one left-leaning commentator put it, "further revealed the rottenness of the British state. In normal times, the Monarchy's involvement in politics is kept to a minimum." Later, the British Supreme Court ruled Johnson's request to the queen for parliamentary suspension was illegal under the unwritten British constitution.[85]

In the future, moreover, this significant monarchical power can "be used against a left Labour government that attempts to challenge the power and privileges of the big banks and [corporate] monopolies. ... [T]his is the main role of the monarchy and the reason why it has been kept in being by the ruling class for so long."[86] One key aspect of this monarchical preservation is seen in vigorous efforts by the ruling white elite to keep the allegiance of the British population, which in the majority still supports the nationalistic symbolism and mystique of the white monarchy. Recent ratings of Elizabeth II by a nationally representative British sample found that 73 percent had a positive view of her, with just 10 percent stating a negative opinion. In addition, a 2020 survey of British adults found that a majority, 62 percent, thought that Britain should have a monarchy, versus 22 percent who were opposed.[87]

Who Owns Britain? Racial and Class Lessons from the Coronavirus Pandemic

The queen and her closest family members have colossal wealth in land and investments. This in itself is political, as is widening inequality. The coronavirus pandemic has further exposed these extreme societal inequalities. Take the Duchy of Cornwall, for example. Funding most of Prince Charles's yearly expenses, it includes 53,000 hectares spread across 23 UK counties. In 2016, the Duchy of Cornwall was valued at over £1 billion. In 2019, Charles received £21.6 million in proceeds from this country estate.[88] At Birkhall, his huge Scottish estate where he recovered from the coronavirus, he was isolated and waited on by servants. A royal reporter at *Vanity Fair* reported at the time: "There is a personal assistant on hand to assist and someone preparing his food and that is it. … The food is taken to the door, the staff member retreats, and the prince takes his meal."[89]

Weeks from her ninety-fourth birthday in 2020, the queen was chauffeured to Windsor Castle from Buckingham Palace during the pandemic for her own personal safety. Similarly, as a child she moved to Windsor Castle from Buckingham Palace during the German bombing against the UK. Spanning 13 acres and consisting of 1,000 rooms, Windsor is the largest occupied castle in the world. Buckingham Palace—with its 19 state rooms, 52 royal and guest bedrooms, 188 staff bedrooms, 92 offices, and 78 bathrooms—is located in the center of London and has 500 staff, making it less safe for the elderly monarch. Notably, 22 royal staff—including a chef, housemaid, personal butler, and the monarch's personal assistant and dressmaker—forfeited their home lives, perhaps even their health, to stay quarantined at Windsor Castle to serve the queen and her husband (Prince Philip) during the coronavirus pandemic.[90]

Prominent royal pundits, including Ingrid Seward, editor of the popular royal magazine *Majesty*, said little or nothing about the royal staff's potentially risky sacrifices or the queen's opulent surroundings. Rather, Seward equates the queen's life during the coronavirus pandemic to imprisonment, remarking: "The last time she was incarcerated in Windsor Castle was in 1940."[91] Of course, the queen's isolation was very different to that of actual British prison inmates—of which 12 percent are black, even though they account for 3 percent of the nation's population. During the pandemic, inmates generally had no more than 45 minutes a day outside their cells, resulting in growing rates of depression.[92]

Describing her very privileged existence under quarantine at Windsor Castle, a former spokesperson for the queen said she and Prince Philip "might well go outside for a walk as everybody else is doing. Windsor Home Park is [the private 655-acre estate of the castle] ... you could get lost in it without meeting anybody."[93] Note the assumption that *everybody* can similarly take a harmless walk. To the contrary, the coronavirus left many in Britain afraid of venturing outside, especially people of Asian origin, who feared the growth in anti-Asian hate crimes there before official quarantine even began (see Chapter 7).

A recent University of Exeter study found that access to a private garden translates into greater psychological well-being and that people with access to open-air spaces, such as a backyard, are more likely to stay physically fit. Here is an additional fact the former spokesperson and any well-off Briton hoarding many acres of green space for their private use seem willfully unaware of: low-paid working-class populations, in which people of color predominate, are nearly three times as likely not to have a private garden and to rely on local parks. Access to green space is therefore another example—along with the ability of more white Britons to work from home and the racialized death rates resulting from the coronavirus—of the racially coded nature of the pandemic.[94]

Not much was made about the choices senior British royals had when it came to where to live during the pandemic, despite the fact that at the opposite end of the spectrum were reportedly 4,266 "rough sleepers"—a British term for homeless people. Some researchers suggested the actual figure was much higher. Rough sleepers were particularly vulnerable to the coronavirus because they were much more likely to have pre-existing chronic health conditions and were unable to abide by necessary sanitation protocols.[95] Five years prior to the pandemic, the *Daily Mail* ran the headline "Homeless Migrants Sleep Huddled On Steps Just Metres From Queen's Residence," noting that many "men and women, believed to be mainly Romanian and Bulgarian nationals, can often be seen camped out on grass ... where homes can sell for tens of millions of pounds."[96]

In 2019, less than 1 percent of the population was exposed by Guy Shrubsole, an environmental activist, as owning *half* of England. Major landholders include the queen, numerous other aristocrats and gentry, Saudi princes, and wealthy business people. Not much in this severely skewed ownership pattern has changed for centuries, yet few Britons are cognizant of these facts. Shrubsole estimates that the land under the ownership of the royal family alone equals 1.4 percent of England. Additionally, the queen, by means of her Duchy of Lancaster, owns huge boggy areas for grouse hunting on her Whitewell Estate and in the North York Moors. Grouse moors are known to contribute to global warming, flooding, extinction of animals, fires, and other environmental destruction. An economist at the Institute for Public Policy Research, the UK's foremost progressive think tank, notes: "We have this idea that the class structures have changed so that the aristocracy is not as important as it used to be. What this demonstrates is the continuing importance of the aristocracy's wealth and power in our society."[97]

Unmistakably, highlighting these huge class inequalities provides an important take on the monarchy and its central role within the British ruling elite, including its colonial history and expansive expectations. But the research we draw on for this discussion badly needs to be broadened to explain how the contemporary ruling elite is not just a classed (i.e., capitalistic) elite but also a white-racist (and often male-sexist) elite, as we fully demonstrate throughout this book.

Systemic Racism: A Brief History of British Imperialism

The large-scale slaughter, colonization, and enslavement of Indigenous peoples is central to the emergence of Britain's systemic racism, in its onshore and offshore variations. Consider the famous admiral Sir John Hawkins (1532–1595). He appears to have been the first English colonizer to get rich off the backs of enslaved Africans. In 1562–1563, he enslaved at least 300 Guinea-coast Africans. Their destination was the Caribbean island of Hispaniola (currently Haiti and the Dominican Republic), where Hawkins sold them for a sizeable profit to Spaniards. At the time the powerful Queen Elizabeth I (1533–1603) sat on the English throne. She funded Hawkins's second slaving voyage in 1564–1565. Earlier, England's King Henry VII (1457–1509) commissioned the first explorers of the so-called new world. Led by John Cabot, a 1497 landfall on the coast of North America and the eventual settling of English, Irish, and Scottish people there caused, among other things, the extinction of the Beothuk—a group of Indigenous people living on the island of Newfoundland. Henry VII, like Elizabeth I after him, encouraged exploration and the conquering of lands and people, with the goal of procuring treasures.[98]

If we calculate the length of British involvement in the Atlantic slavery system from the date of Hawkins's first voyage to the African continent to the final abolition of slavery in the British colonies, the British transatlantic slave trade lasted for about 271 years. Additionally, the end of centuries of slavery was followed by extensive racial segregation and other discrimination targeting black Britons, to the present day. In contrast, the 1965 Race Relations Act—the first legislation in the UK to firmly address racial discrimination—was a mere 53 years old when Markle married Harry, and it has not been aggressively enforced. These numbers reveal in glaring terms the length of time that British society's foundational social structure has encompassed extensive racial oppression and white racial tyranny.[99]

In addition to central participation in the slave trade, the English elite launched major overseas colonies starting in the sixteenth century. Many involved substantial slavery systems. Eventually, English (later British) control was so global that at any one time there was daylight in one of the territories, leading to the maxim, "the Empire on which the sun never sets." Put another way, at its pinnacle in 1920, the British Empire ruled

over approximately 412 million people, or 23 percent of the global population. At its height, this highly racialized empire included 57 colonies,
dominions, territories, and protectorates from Australia, Canada, and India
to Fiji, Western Samoa, and Tonga. From London, the mostly white male
elite governed and ruled virtually a quarter of the world's landmass.[100]

The British Empire lasted half a millennium, if one marks its beginning from Cabot's voyage in 1497 to the transfer of Hong Kong to China
in 1997. Others mark the end of the Empire officially in 1947, when the
British cabled Washington, DC that they no longer had the wherewithal
to defend Greece or Turkey as the USSR loomed large.[101] Most of those
colonized, exploited, or killed off in this imperialism were, to use contemporary terminology, people of color. Globalized English (later British)
oppression conspicuously reveals the length of time that eurocentric (later
white racial) supremacy has been a standard part of the UK's foundational
political and social structure.

Since the eighteenth century, the explicitly racial hierarchy at the
heart of systemic racism has been a dominant and powerful force within
the UK, as in North America. "The Secret Teacher," an anonymous blog
by experienced teachers, captures well how the historically oppressive
treatment of people of color by white Britons, including the elite, awk-
wardly coincides with the British rhetorical values of freedom, justice, and
the rule of law.

> Race issues are increasingly being discussed ... thanks in part to social
> media and movements such as #BlackLivesMatter. ... But the UK edu-
> cation system does not prepare children to have these conversations. ...
> Amid the units about the slave trade, abolition and the Civil Rights
> movement in the US, we forget the Civil Rights movement in the UK,
> unless teachers choose to include specific case studies. The brutalities
> and crimes of the British empire are ignored. Even Winston Churchill,
> who ... believed in racial hierarchies and eugenics, escapes scrutiny
> beyond his war hero reputation. Students are led to believe racism and
> discrimination came out of the ether in this country. That adds to the
> marginalisation many feel, and has a profound impact on students'
> understanding of racism. ... In whitewashing the discrimination and
> bloodshed ... is it any such a wonder that parts of society are racist,
> misogynistic and prejudiced?[102]

Notice the continuing significance of the British Empire, as its brutal
and criminal realities are frequently ignored inside and outside the class-
room. The white elite that shapes the culture of learning in British schools
is central to this whitewashing. In 2013, the education secretary—a white
male member of the Conservative Party—claimed that the teaching of
British history was too often about "post-colonial guilt." However, he
was forced to redraft plans to modify the more honest history curriculum
after widespread condemnation by teachers at all levels. Critics were justly

concerned that his proposals were saturated by white nationalism. Even though the curriculum was rewritten, calls for more "British history"— code for white history—have not disappeared. Such white nationalistic claims were bolstered by the Brexit debates, especially on immigration, and the election of white nationalists Boris Johnson in the UK and Donald Trump in the USA. The USA has seen similar calls for sanitizing and ignoring its white-racist history coming out of white supremacists in the Trump White House.[103]

Legacies of a Racialized Empire: Contemporary Racial Discrimination

Efforts in the UK to remedy systemic racial discrimination and inequality in education, employment, housing, politics, and other legacies of British imperialism and slavery are regularly met with contradictory and incongruous claims of "reverse-racism," as in the USA. Assertions that officially ending legal discrimination was sufficient and that further attempts generate unjust impediments for whites, especially white men, are popular among white Britons. Such assertions discount the continuing consequences of British imperialism, as centuries of systemic racial oppression continue to influence racial discrimination and disparities in the present day. These contradictory and incongruous claims help to legitimate persisting and huge racial inequality, as is evidenced in the average black college graduate earning approximately a quarter less than the average white graduate; in the black unemployment rate being roughly twice as high as the white rate; and in black Britons being considerably less likely than white Britons to attend a leading university or attain a managerial position.[104]

We should note the demography of British racial groups (also called ethnic minorities) at this point. In the most current population estimates for England (2016), whites make up 84.9 percent of the population, a slight decline since the 2011 census, with the remaining 15.1 percent being people of color. The latter are listed as 3.5 percent black (mostly African British, African Caribbean British), 8 percent South and East Asian, and 3.7 percent mixed-race or other (mostly black white, Asian white, Arab British).[105]

These Britons of color remain vastly under-represented in positions of influence, including in politics, academia, and the judiciary. Consider the British Parliament. Before the 2015 general election, in which Boris Johnson (then London mayor, soon after prime minister) was running for a House of Commons seat, a broadcaster suggested that voters had a choice between him and another white man who had attended primary school with Johnson, or a white man who had been at secondary school with Johnson. The broadcaster's observations capture the reality of the old white boys' network, which remains at the heart of the British elite. In that election, Members of Parliament—hailed as the most diverse group ever—included a mere 29 percent that were women, even though women comprise half the UK population. Racial minority Members of Parliament totaled 6 percent of the newly elected Parliament, in spite of representing more than double that percentage in the overall population that year. To put the numbers here in proportion, consider that voters would have needed to elect 130 additional women and more than twice the number of racial minority Members of Parliament to be representative of the UK population. Clearly, UK political parties and norms are not dedicated to that democratic principle.[106]

Racial discrimination and inequality remain well-institutionalized and thus systemic. White Britons, on average, have more wealth, more education, and higher incomes than Britons of color, and many whites rationalize this unjust reality by drawing on the timeworn white framing of Britons of color as lazy, uncivilized, or inferior to whites. Many whites continue to ardently support and actively maintain racial inequalities in various societal settings, including engaging in everyday discrimination that has a weighty impact on Britain's social structure. A recent survey of 1,000 Britons of color found they were consistently more likely to encounter negative everyday experiences (usually related to racial discrimination) than whites in a comparison poll. Some 43 percent reported having been discriminated against in regard to job promotions in recent years, as compared to 18 percent of whites. Britons of color were "three times as likely to have been thrown out of or denied entrance to a restaurant, bar or club in the last five years" as whites. Britons of color were much more likely than whites to report having been "wrongly suspected of shoplifting in the last five years." They were more than twice as likely as whites to have faced abuse from strangers during the last week. Just over half said they had suffered discrimination because of their physical appearance, as compared with less than a third of whites. They also reported they had to work harder to succeed than whites and were paid less than whites for comparable work.[107]

These findings came a year after Prime Minister Theresa May (2016–2019) published a "race disparity" audit. This audit combined government statistics and covered racial breakdowns in 130 areas across health, education, housing, employment, and criminal justice. Among the audit's findings were: "Bangladeshi and Pakistani households had an average income of nearly £9,000 a year less than white British households between 2014 and 2016, and the gap between white and black Caribbean and black British families was £5,500." Some 41 percent of Britons of color reported having been treated as *not* British in the last year. When dining out or shopping, they were twice as likely as whites to have been mistaken for staff in restaurants and stores. Half of black Britons reported job discrimination, as did 41 percent of Asian Britons. Britons of Middle Eastern descent (typically Muslim) were more likely to face discrimination than people of other religious backgrounds; this included being unfairly stopped by police and whites not sitting next to them on buses and trains. The government report also found that "black Caribbean pupils are permanently excluded from school at three times the rate of white British pupils" and that "black men are more likely to be found guilty at crown court" than whites with comparable cases. The "race disparity" audit also reported that unemployment rates for Britons of color were significantly higher than for whites across the country.[108]

A recent investigation by the BBC's *Inside Out London* program uncovered anti-black racism in UK rental housing. Posing as a white landlord, an investigative reporter asked ten real estate agents not to rent his property to African Caribbean people. All ten agents agreed. "We cannot be shown discriminating against a community. But obviously we've got our ways around that. Ninety-nine per cent of my landlords don't want Afro-Caribbeans, or any troublesome people," explained one white agent. "Afro-Caribbeans" and "troublesome people" are often synonyms in white racial framing. Words matched deeds; a white investigator who asked to view the rental property was granted access; whereas, a black investigator, with the exact same credentials, was told the property was already rented. Contemporary discrimination often involves this sort of racialized lying and opportunity hoarding by whites.[109]

Contemporary social scientists and other social researchers detail the pervasiveness and centrality of this racial oppression and inequality. Their research makes clear that whites as individuals and collectively are adept in safeguarding the country's systemic racism and its white power and privileges. Rather than inactive bystanders or insurgent allies working to dismantle systemic racism, most whites in the UK, as in other white-dominant nations like the USA and Canada, work to protect unjust racial opportunities and benefits within the economic, social, political, and legal institutions that were originally constructed to create, champion, and protect white power and privilege. As African American philosopher George Yancy maintains, white privilege cannot be separated from "the oppressive consequences and implications tied to it in relationship to Black [and we would add brown] bodies."[110] In our view, to have any real chance at challenging systemic racism in the UK, white Britons must first accept the harsh truths about what being white really means in a Western society that was created, and has been maintained to systemically empower, enrich, and privilege whites.

The Enduring Significance of the First Lords of Modern Predatory Capitalism

The Legacies of British Slavery and Colonialism

In the immediate run-up to the 2018 wedding of Markle and Harry, much was made of an enslaved African American woman, Nancy Bowers. She was Markle's great-great-great-great maternal grandmother and was born into slavery in 1820s Georgia, a new US slave state at the time.[111] In mainstream media discussions of Bowers, much less was said about the centuries of *British* slavery and their extensive consequences for Britain, to the present day. This capitalistic slavery became foundational for modern British economic development.

White English colonists established a modern slave society in Barbados in the early seventeenth century, basing the territory's economy on enslaved labor. Plantation slavery developed over centuries throughout the Caribbean, South America, and the southern USA, where Bowers was born. Markle's four-times great-grandmother was thus born into a reality of horror and anguish, perfected by white English colonists, among whom were the forbearers of the family that Markle married into—a royal family who, like others in the British elite, benefitted immensely from the profitable triangle of trade between the west coast of Africa, the Americas, and England (soon Britain). Britain could not have become the dominant economic force on the planet by the turn of the nineteenth century without controlling many of the world's major slave plantations, enslaving in excess of 800,000 people by that time.[112]

The extensiveness of this enslavement history is glaringly obvious, given its many graphic legacies. There is the fact that approximately 33 percent of the properties under the care of the National Trust for Places of Historic Interest or Natural Beauty are linked to slavery and colonialism. Remarkably, the director of culture and engagement for the National Trust said the release of this data is not meant to be a judgment on history. "We're presenting information based on research, allowing people to explore and draw conclusions for themselves. No one alive today can ever be held responsible for the wrongs of the period when slavery took place, but we can seek to understand this better."[113] His words suggest a *white fragility* or a misdirected sensitivity to issues surrounding this history. It is likely that the director is afraid of offending white Britons and hence his understated prose. His comments are also problematic given the massive wealth transfers that even the National Trust references. Writing on behalf of the Trust, Lucy Porten explains the following about the East India Company, whose "conquest of India," she argues, "almost certainly remains the supreme act of corporate violence in world history."

> For over 250 years, [the company] led a complex global trading network. ... At least 229 landed estates were purchased in Britain by those who had made their fortune either as employees of the company or as independent merchants in India between 1700 and 1850. Among the properties now cared for by the National Trust, at least 50 have a connection to the company, be it through past owners or their family members, those who worked for, supplied, supported or opposed it, or through the items in our collections, their commission, acquisition or subject matter. Often, such a connection can be found across several generations, even if the property in question changed hands.[114]

The historical vestiges of slavery and colonialism also include buildings named in honor of slaveowners and statues as memorials to them. Seventeenth-century slave trader Edward Colston, who gave huge sums of money to the city of Bristol in southwest England, is but one example. He made his fortune on the blood, sweat, and tears of the 85,000 Africans he helped enslave while managing the Royal African Company (RAC). Significantly, following the 2020 killing of yet another unarmed black man by a white police officer in the USA, protesters in Bristol tore down a Colston statue and dumped it into the harbor.[115] The actual significance of this protest act—acknowledging the foundational nature of British racism—was lost on Conservative Prime Minister Boris Johnson, who insisted that such anti-racist demonstrations had been "subverted by thuggery."[116]

The actual violent *thugs* were men like Colston, who should have been knocked off their prestigious pedestals long ago. Johnson's reaction to the statue's destruction is no surprise. In 2016, he questioned why US President Barack Obama had removed a bust of the openly racist Winston Churchill from his presidential office, writing, "Some said it was a snub to Britain. Some said it was a symbol of the part-Kenyan President's *ancestral dislike* of the British empire—of which Churchill had been such a fervent defender. ... [I]f that's why Churchill was banished from the Oval Office, they could not have been more wrong."[117]

On several occasions during the 2020 Black Lives Matter protests, Johnson admitted that UK racism exists, although minimizing the issue. An ardent white-racist framer, he re-victimized people of color, laying the blame in part at their feet, saying: "What I really want to do as Prime Minister is change the narrative so we *stop the sense of victimization* and discrimination, we stamp out racism and *we start to have a real sense of expectation of success*." While he announced a new cross-governmental commission to investigate racism and discrimination, he had previously failed to implement findings arising from earlier government inquiries and reports on racist practices. What's more, he appointed his political advisor Munira Mirza to head the new commission. She is an elite acolyte of his, one with a conservative colorblind ideology even though a woman of color. She has openly referred to institutional racism as a myth.[118] People of color often operate, because of societal pressure or personal choice, out of some version of the dominant white racial frame. White racial framing has never been limited to just whites.

During this same period, Home Secretary Priti Patel—also a woman of color and elite acolyte with a conservative colorblind ideology (see Chapter 5)—labeled the political acts of Black Lives Matter protesters "sheer vandalism" and vowed to bring them to justice.[119] No mention was made by Johnson or Patel of the fact that almost a third of all UK police custody deaths in the past two years (2019–2020) were of black people.[120]

On June 7, 2020, anti-racist protesters in central London added the accurate words "was a racist" to Winston Churchill's statue in Parliament Square. While video footage showed a small group trying to protect the statue, a larger group of protesters chanted "Churchill was a racist" and "Boris [Johnson] is a racist." Signs containing the words "British Colonialism is to blame" and "What if it was your son?" were left at the base of the statue.[121]

Nearly two decades before these anti-racism protests, Johnson had referred to the continent of Africa as a "mess." Writing, as usual, from his strong white-racist framing, he explained his imperialistic view.

> [W]e must … not blame Britain, or colonialism, or the white man. The continent may be a blot, but it is not a blot upon our conscience. The problem is not that we were once in charge, but that we are not in charge any more. … The best fate for Africa would be if the old colonial powers, or their citizens, scrambled once again in her direction; on the understanding that this time they will not be asked to feel guilty.[122]

Johnson, unsurprisingly, leaves out of his calculus the huge white-enriching exploitation and impoverishment of Africa over several centuries, to the present day—exploitation that helped greatly in making Britain a wealthy Western country. Contrast Johnson's reaction to the Black Lives Matter protests to that of historian David Olusoga, who duly explains: "Statues are about saying 'This was a great man who did great things.' That is not true, [Colston] was a slave trader and a murderer." The mayor of Bristol, Marvin Rees—who like Markle is mixed-race—also argues in defense of those who consider Colston's statue "an affront to humanity," saying their views should be taken seriously.[123]

Significantly, a 2020 online survey of 1,535 British adults found that black respondents were more than twice as likely as white respondents to say they are "offended by statues of people who were involved in the slave trade or colonization." Two-thirds of black adults agreed, but just under a third of whites did. Additionally, blacks were roughly twice as likely as whites to support the removal of such statues. Moreover, 81 percent of black respondents and 64 percent of white respondents said they understood why people would want the offensive monuments removed.[124]

To comprehend the continuing oppression that takes form in police misconduct against black and brown bodies, one must do at least two things. One, expose who actually runs the country, as well as their racial, class, and gender framing. Two, recognize that the white-racist oppression of people of color is not new but has been foundational to and systemic in UK society since at least the seventeenth century. Both actions are at the heart of the 2020 Black Lives Matter protests. The anti-racism activist who said, "You can't enslave people, have the largest colonial empire in history and be like 'Yeah let's be peaceful—let's talk.' It don't work like that," understands the necessity of doing both, as do scholars like Olusoga.[125] Nearly 300 years after the death of Colston, elite white men and their acolytes mostly still do not recognize the necessity of doing either, which is key to the furtherance of systemic racism.

Another instance of whites' downplaying the historical suffering of enslaved human beings is the fact that the Royal African Company (RAC), which Colston managed, had earlier been named the Company of Royal Adventurers Trading to Africa. Such linguistic denial is important to the dominant white frame, now over several centuries. "Adventurers Trading to Africa" sounds more like a bunch of innocuous globetrotters than predatory capitalists, mass murderers, and enslaving captors. Such white misrepresentations of slavery's brutality and wealth-generating profitability have long been intentional.

The powerful and wealthy RAC was established by City of London merchants and the Stuart royal family. The Stuart King Charles II (1660–1685) granted the RAC a royal monopoly on the expanding slave trade. RAC vessels brought more enslaved African workers to the Americas than any other such capitalistic enterprise. Charles II is actually an ancestor of Camilla, Duchess of Cornwall, Prince Harry's step-mother. Family trees of the British elite conspicuously reveal the intergenerational connections between them and their enslaving ancestors. Note that in the run-up to the 2018 royal wedding, the enslaved great-great-great-great grandmother of Markle made headlines, yet far less was made of the fact that huge British fortunes, including current country homes, are directly linked to white slaveowning and slave-trading ancestors. To this day, slavery's cultural bequest also permeates the palates of elite and non-elite whites alike, from sweetened tea to silver service to cotton clothwork, and, of course, in the pervasive racial and class inequalities that typify daily life in the contemporary UK. Despite these critical historical facts, many Britons have a clearer understanding of US slavery than of British slave-trading in Africa or British-owned slave plantations in the Caribbean. This, too, is intentional, part of a grander white racial framing—indeed, whitewashing—of British history.[126]

Slavery: Foundations of Modern British Capitalism

Note, too, how the heavy British involvement in the Atlantic slavery system was closely linked to the emergence of modern capitalism and the modern state in Britain. Centuries of unpaid black labor had a significant role in both creating the massive surplus capital that was the basis of much of the country's capitalistic economic development and expansion, and in creating much material prosperity and wealth for numerous generations of white individuals and families, especially many in the white British elite, including the royal family.

Many powerful white men in Britain—including leading political, business, and intellectual figures inside and outside the royal family—were substantially involved in slavery's investments and profits. Stockholders of the famous British South Sea Company, established to transport enslaved workers from Africa to overseas colonies, included the leading scientist Isaac Newton, influential authors like Jonathan Swift and Daniel Defoe, and the founder of the Bank of England, the Earl of Halifax. They also included numerous members of the House of Lords and House of Commons. These influential white men, and others like them, viewed slavery as an acceptable wealth-generating investment, one they often passed along to later generations of whites.[127]

Over time, capitalized slavery profits became central to building up the great wealth and power of Britain as the first modern industrialized nation. As Britain's Industrial Revolution was expanding, in the 1740s, one business pamphleteer wrote about the source of much British wealth in this era.

> The most approved Judges of the Commercial Interests of these Kingdoms have ever been of the opinion that our West-India and African Trades are the most nationally beneficial of any we carry on. It is also allowed on all Hands, that the trade to Africa is the Branch which renders our American Colonies and Plantations so advantageous to Great Britain. ... The Negroe-Trade therefore, and the natural consequences resulting from it, may be justly esteemed an *inexhaustible* Fund of Wealth and Naval Power to this Nation.[128]

This pamphlet accents the central and continuing role of the African-origin labor in British shipping and manufacturing, and in creating an "inexhaustible Fund of Wealth and Naval Power" for the country, but especially for British capitalists. One historian, Robin Blackburn, has estimated that by the 1770s the British trade profits connected to this Atlantic slavery system were huge, making up "between 20.9% and 55% of Britain's gross fixed capital formation."[129]

Cities like London, Liverpool, Manchester, Birmingham, and Bristol developed major slave-shipping ports and thriving factories off this ever-expanding fund of slavery-based capital. Textile manufacturing in northern England and New England in North America was the core industry of the Industrial Revolution, and most of the cotton used in these factories was grown by enslaved black laborers. The profits resulting from this slavery–manufacturing nexus, together with the British and related international trade in other slave-produced products, often became capital circulating through many banking enterprises. These profits provided a substantial part of the large-scale investments in yet other emerging British and American industries. The enslaved labor of millions of Africans over several centuries was the ultimate foundation of modern capitalism, and thus of our modern industrial and technological age.[130]

White Mythical Tales of the Abolition of Slavery and Persisting Systemic Racism

A common British version of the white racial frame would have us believe that British slavery ceased to exist because of the moral transformation of slavery-involved whites. In contrast, historian of slavery and Prime Minister of Trinidad and Tobago Eric Williams (1962–1981) long ago argued effectively that slavery in the British Empire was abolished because this form of predatory capitalism stopped being economically advantageous for many white slaveholders. This interpretation is in keeping with African American scholar Derrick Bell's description of the *interest convergence* that sometimes takes place between part of the white elite and dissenting people of color, as it did in the era of racial change that led to British slavery's abolition.[131] That is, at about the same time that Markle's ancestor Nancy Bowers was born into slavery in 1820s Georgia, slavery was starting to conflict with a new economic approach that many British capitalists were increasingly excited about—free trade across the Empire. For instance, British merchants exporting East Indian, Brazilian, and Cuban sugar to Britain were not benefitting from the export protections that maintained the sugar monopoly of the West Indian slave plantations, and so wanted them ended. Meanwhile, with the onset of new transport and military technologies (e.g., railways, steamships, gunboats), British predatory capitalists recognized they could amass profits in previously difficult-to-reach places, including distant Australia and South America. By 1833, when British slavery was abolished, the economic system of slavery was already substantially declining due to other globalizing investments of elite whites and their acolytes.[132]

Most white Britons did not care that the opulence of post-abolition Britain, and the continuing poverty and suffering of post-abolition Caribbean areas, were still intimately joined. Many decades later, the prime minister of Antigua and Barbuda, Baldwin Spencer, reasoned that black Caribbeans' ongoing travails were unequivocally the consequences of such earlier economic exploitation. Speaking at a meeting of the heads of government of the Caribbean Community, he linked past colonialism to the present.

> We know that our constant search and struggle for development resources is linked directly to the historical inability of our nations to accumulate wealth from the efforts of our peoples during slavery and colonialism. ... These nations that have been the major producers of wealth for the European slave owning economies during the enslavement and colonial periods entered independence with dependency straddling their economic, cultural, social and even political lives.[133]

Currently, the economic systems of Antigua, Barbados, and Jamaica continue to suffer as a result of the black loss of inherited family wealth over those many colonial generations, and because of their historically imposed reliance on foreign capital and other financial arrangements.[134]

Recently, a research team that examined the records of the 1830s Slave Compensation Commission found that they contain a census of British slavery as of August 1834, just after the slavery system was terminated.

The census includes a complete record of slaveowners, where the enslaved lived, and how much revenue the enslavers collected. Given this comprehensive data, the many decades of white success in downplaying Britain's slavery history is all the more remarkable—making the white racial frame's concealing power today even more striking. After all, British ships carried at least 3.4 million enslaved Africans to the Americas.[135]

The Slavery Abolition Act of 1833 officially emancipated about 800,000 enslaved African-descended people in the Caribbean and South Africa, as well as a smaller number in Canada, who were legal property of British slaveowners. The Act included a provision for financial damages to be paid to slaveowners by British taxpayers for loss of enslaved human property. The Commission oversaw the British government allotment of £20 million (about 40 percent of all government expenditures for 1834) as compensation. Today, that sum is estimated at £17 billion. Until the bailout of British banks during the 2009 Great Recession, reparations to Britain's 46,000 slaveowners represented the largest monetary bailout in British history. Yet those who had been enslaved received no compensation. In fact, for four years after their liberation, they were bound under the Act to work 45 hours a week (unpaid labor, misleadingly known as *apprenticeship*) for those who had hitherto enslaved them.[136]

Placing the arrogance and duplicity of this white racial framing on full display, historian Kris Manjapra hauntingly explains: "During this period of apprenticeship, Britain declared it would teach blacks how to use their freedom responsibly, and would train them out of their natural state of savagery. But this training involved continued unpaid labour for the same masters on the same plantations on which they had worked the day before."[137] The cruel hypocrisy of the pro-white subframe (e.g., whites are virtuous and superior) is blatantly evident here. Who in this scenario is the real savage—the oppressor or the oppressed? Even for adamant supporters of the dominant white frame, this enforced apprenticeship should be hard to defend. Consider the label *apprentice*, with its synonyms, including amateur, beginner, and newcomer. These words suggest a lack of prior knowledge, despite their years of enslavement and work experience. And if formerly enslaved workers are *apprentices*, are former slavemasters *mentors*? According to the mythical thinking of the pro-white subframe, the absurd answer has to be "yes."

Hired in Britain, government magistrates were sent to plantation colonies to ensure that apprentices followed the strict dictates of former slavemasters. They could have them reprimanded, even tortured, for any number of things, including racially stereotyped laziness. The treadmill, a torture device intended to instill fear in black apprentices, was a rotating wheel with wood planks, from where they hung by their hands from a plank, typically for hours, as they "danced" unshod. They were also often tortured with a whip.[138] Yet again, whites were extraordinarily hypocritical in framing black workers who did most plantation work as lazy. Reflecting on centuries of enslavement, the contemporary

African American entrepreneur Claud Anderson memorably said that if non-blacks had been the better workers, "why would supposedly bright [white] businessmen spend 250 years traveling half way around the world to kidnap [millions of] innocent, but lazy blacks, then knowingly bring them to America to do work that other ethnic groups could do better?"[139]

These harsh ironies were created and sanctioned by major figures of the time, including John Gladstone (1764–1851), father of Victorian prime minister William Gladstone (1809–1898). As a politician, William Gladstone espoused reimbursement for enslavers and supported the so-called system of apprenticeship. He defended West Indian slaveholders' interests. John Gladstone was paid a huge compensation (£80 million in current pounds) for the 2,508 people he enslaved on nine plantations. Unsurprisingly, in his inaugural speech in Parliament, Prime Minister Gladstone defended slavery.[140]

Researchers recently examining Slave Compensation Commission data have confirmed that Charles Blair (1776–1854), the great-grandfather of famous author George Orwell (1903–1950), was at that time paid £4,442 for the 218 men and women he enslaved. Ancestors of the novelist Graham Greene (1904–1991), the poet Elizabeth Barrett Browning (1806–1861), and the architect Sir George Gilbert Scott (1811–1878) all received significant monetary reparations after slavery's abolition. An ancestor of David Cameron, the UK prime minister from 2010 to 2016, also received such compensation.[141]

Arguably more noteworthy is the finding that British slavery was much more commonplace than earlier recognized. While a majority of whites who enslaved their fellow human beings were men, scaled-down slavery involvement among the middle class included some widows and single women, who owned no land in the Caribbean but rented out their "human property" to white landowners. Approximately 40 percent of white enslavers in the British colonies were women, and they often had inherited human property through their husbands. Still, most of the government's compensatory money went to the "richest citizens, who owned the greatest number of slaves."[142]

And while British slavery is often assumed to be a pursuit restricted to whites in slave-trading ports like London and Bristol, records show that slaveowners lived throughout Britain. The general conclusion of the contemporary researchers examining the Slave Compensation Commission data is that British colonial slaveownership was of far more importance for Britain than has hitherto been acknowledged. As the historian David Olusoga has agonizingly explained, millions of black people know that as descendants of the enslaved they "carry the same English surnames that appear in the ledgers of the Slave Compensation Commission—Gladstone, Beckford, Hibbert, Blair, etc.—names that were imposed on their ancestors, initials that were sometimes branded on their skin, in order to mark them as items of property."[143]

Early on, racial oppression and consequent inequality were embedded deeply in major UK institutions. But the white racial frame's mythologies and misrepresentations often prevail over historical truth. The scholar Catherine Hall, who helped spearhead the Slave Compensation Commission research, explains that "Britons were the first in the world to abolish slavery. ... That's the way in which the history's been written. ... [F]or example, in Macaulay's great *{The} History of England*, he scarcely mentions slavery— scarcely mentions the Caribbean—but he celebrates the fact of abolition. And that's a very common pattern." Hall recognizes the true cost of this dominant racial framing: "Slavery has left the most terrible marks and legacies on not just people's material lives. ... [T]he levels of inequality, the levels of under-development of the Caribbean in terms of health and education are deeply shocking ... [and] there's also the psychic histories connected with that. ... *They aren't just over. They carry on.*"[144]

In 2018, Prince Charles belatedly described Britain's part in the slave trade as an "atrocity." He included the oft-cited line, "Britain can be proud that it later led the way in the abolition of this shameful trade" in the same sentence in which he condemned "the abject horror of slavery," saying it should "never be forgotten."[145] Despite his words, from 1807 to the present day, no money has been paid by the government to the African workers that white Britons enslaved or to their descendants over many later generations. Additionally, not a single word of official *apology* has ever been uttered to them. In 1993, Bernie Grant, a reparations activist and one of the first black British Members of Parliament, demanded an apology from the British state for the legacies of slavery. "I am going to write to the Queen. I know she is a very reasonable woman," he announced in a speech in Birmingham. He died in 2000 without an apology. In 2015, during an official visit to Jamaica, then-Prime Minister David Cameron announced it was time to "move on from this painful [slavery] legacy and continue to build for the future."[146]

As for Charles's 2018 critique of British slavery, it does not come close to making amends for the unfathomable misery British royals and other whites have long inflicted on black people, in the past or present. "It's not enough for the son of the monarch to apologize," observed the pop-culture pundit Kristen Meinzer, "The monarch should."[147] To which we would add: concrete reparations and a genuine commitment to dismantling contemporary systemic racial oppression must also be made. Charles's good-bad rhetoric, the British state's reticence, the queen's silence, and Cameron's whitewashing sentiments are typical of the white elite, both those inside and outside the royal family. That is part of the contemporary reality of elite whites' racial framing. Acknowledging white Britain's crimes against humanity over centuries, and providing substantial restitution to black Britain, is something the elite has *never* been willing to do.

Elite white insensitivity and tactlessness knows no bounds. In 2018, in a tweet complete with an image of Africans being marched in yokes and ropes into slavery, the Treasury Department wrote: "Here's today's surprising #FridayFact. Millions of you have helped end the slave trade through your taxes. ... In 1833, Britain used £20 million, 40% of its national budget, to buy freedom for all slaves in the Empire. The amount of money borrowed for the Slavery Abolition Act was so large that it wasn't paid off until 2015. Which means that living British citizens helped pay to end the slave trade."[148]

The white-run Treasury Department got the facts *wrong*. The British slave trade was not abolished in 1833, but in 1807. And slavery was not abolished in all parts of the British Empire in 1833, for that law applied to the British Caribbean, Mauritius, and the Cape Colony, and in the area of today's South Africa, but not to Ceylon (now Sri Lanka) or British India. In addition, no freedom was purchased for plantation slaves in 1833 because the enslaved were forced to work without pay and under the persistent threat of penalty until 1838. Nor did the Treasury Department's tweet reference the fact that generations of British taxpayers had been paying off a government loan that reimbursed well-off white enslavers, not enslaved black workers and their families. The tweet reeked of white framing. As historian Olusoga flawlessly responded, "[This] is what happens when those communities for whom this history can never be reduced to a Friday factoid remain poorly represented within national institutions."[149]

Postcards from a Mythologized British Past: White Saviors

Drawing on recent Oscar-nominated British films *Victoria & Abdul*, *Darkest Hour*, and *Dunkirk*, the writer Amrou Al-Kadhi aptly describes the conveniences and impacts of whites racially framing, or whitewashing, this racist history of Britain. Such films are "postcards from a mythologized Great Britain," functioning to expunge or distort British history in order to advance white-nationalist nostalgia. Considering the lore surrounding Harry's four-times great-grandmother Queen Victoria, Al-Kadhi explains that the recent biographical drama *Victoria & Abdul*, about the relationship between the queen and her Indian Muslim servant Abdul Karim, is "absurdly rose-tinted," with Victoria portrayed as anti-racist, even though "she was a notorious racist."[150] Revealing the film's visibility outside of Britain, a *Washington Post* critic noted that, while there had been friendship between Victoria and Abdul, "by keeping the focus on court gossip it misses the political structure that allowed Victoria to control Abdul at her whims. ... This kind of shallow Raj [Empire] revisionism is possible because of how little we've confronted the enduring and painful legacy of the British Empire."[151]

In *Victoria & Abdul*, civilized Indian development is depicted as beholden to the British. In reality, Britain's Industrial Revolution was buttressed by predatory capitalist endeavors in this South Asian nation. Britain's extensive exploitation of India, including its agriculture for export, reduced the country's share of the world economy from 23 percent to 4 percent, and in the process triggered major famines, killing about 20 million South Asians.[152]

While stories of Markle's enslaved great-great-great-great-grandmother were featured in news reports in the run-up to the 2018 royal wedding, little or no mention was made of Harry's great-great-great-great-grandmother's racist reign as Queen of the United Kingdom of Great Britain and Ireland

and Empress of India. Queen Victoria reigned over a white-racist, ruthless, and predatory empire from 1837 to 1901. Under her rule, for example, the 1857–1858 "Indian Uprising" was suppressed. In defiance of punitive land taxes and hostile British-style reforms, the Indians had bravely rebelled against one of the most influential and brutal companies ever to exist, the British East India Company. Following the failed uprising, the British government transferred power from deviation from conventional white India's Mughal monarch, who had ruled Delhi for centuries, to the British Crown. The British Raj—the term for British rule of the Indian subcontinent—was erected on the blood and bones of people of color. The subcontinent's societies, politics, and territorial lines were forever changed.[153] Notably, Victoria is widely known to be much admired by her great-great-granddaughter, Elizabeth II.

If we reconsider how the British elite has hidden its slaveowning and slave-trading history, we often observe white racial framing in full operation. For example, in the seventeenth and eighteenth centuries, thousands of white families made their riches by means of the slave trade or from the sale of slave-produced products. Nowadays, slave traders are frequently whitewashed and vaguely referred to as "West Indian merchants," while slaveowners are referred to as "West Indian planters." Alongside such euphemistic terms are thousands of positive family profiles written in commemoration of prominent seventeenth- and eighteenth-century Britons, profiles relegating their proprietorship of human beings to mere footnotes or otherwise purging the bloody specifics from the historical record. While the geography of British slavery has helped to make this *white amnesia* possible (i.e., unlike in the USA, British slavery was mostly overseas), certain elements of the dominant white racial frame, especially its *white savior* myth, have played an important role in the cover-up.[154]

The much-celebrated abolitionist William Wilberforce (1759–1833) has long served as a diversion from the factual and complete picture of British slavery. The pomp and circumstance surrounding him and other white abolitionists has functioned to protect the sanitized white framing of British racial history in several ways. In Holy Trinity Church in Clapham, a well-off London suburb, a stained-glass window above the altar depicts Wilberforce breaking the news of the 1807 British government's abolition of the slave trade to a black woman. She is shown kneeling before him in a prayer-like stance. A second male white savior figure appears in the artwork alongside a black male standing and rubbing his wrists, having been newly freed of golden-colored chains the second white man is now holding. In another patent example of the frame's white savior myth, there are no less than 32 images of Wilberforce in London's National Portrait Gallery. This famous gallery houses numerous portraits of illustrious Britons but contains a mere four images of black abolitionists and other anti-slavery activists from the same era. Through the lens of the pro-white subframe of the dominant white frame, we again see how white virtuousness is foregrounded, including in words and visual images. Reducing chronicles of the abolition of slavery to tales of white saviors, who nobly bestowed freedom on black people, fits well into the dominant racial framing of British society.[155]

The anti-others subframe of the dominant white frame is in operation here too. That view would have us believe that enslaved people were convinced of their personhood and desire for freedom mainly because of beneficent whites. This is false. Black uprisings for freedom were common across the slavery era. By the 1810s and 1820s, when Nancy Bowers, Markle's ancestor, was born, slave societies in the British Caribbean were experiencing serious black revolts. In 1816 in Barbados, the enslaved population revolted for their freedom. In 1823, those enslaved in Demerara (modern-day Guyana) rose up. Shortly after Christmas in 1831 in Jamaica, around 60,000 enslaved people went on strike for their liberty, burning sugar cane fields, and destroying sugar mills. These courageous souls exhibited incredible discipline, jailing slaveowners on estates but never harming them. Conversely, when the tide turned against the rebellion, the white British Jamaican government reacted quite brutally, slaughtering hundreds in the ensuing conflict, on scaffolds or by firing squad.[156]

As white-framed institutions like the National Portrait Gallery remind us, heroic stories about enslaved souls resisting white oppression are deliberately overshadowed by whites' need to frame themselves as saviors, rescuers, or protectors. This may explain why the bicentenary of the abolition of the transatlantic slave trade produced only one serious film. The British-American biographical drama, *Amazing Grace*, focused on the campaign against the slave trade in the British Empire led by Wilberforce. This is white racial framing personified. As Aidan McQuade, the Director of Anti-Slavery International, put it:

> [Wilberforce's] portrayal as [the] "one voice [that] changed the lives of millions" does not fully take into account the fact that abolition of the trade was not the result of the efforts of any one individual. Africans resisted their enslavement from the moment of capture. The revolts on the ships and uprisings in the Americas and Caribbean were pivotal in causing plantation owners to question whether the slave trade was still economically viable.[157]

What's more, Wilberforce did not even "believe in racial equality," even though he thought that, with training, Africans had the potential to become "a grateful peasantry."[158]

The tremendous strength of the white racial frame is seen in the fact that not until 2010 did researchers launch an examination of the records of the nineteenth-century Slave Compensation Commission, mentioned previously. The 1830s Commission was directed to administer the compensation to slaveowners for loss of *their* human property following the abolition of slavery. And it was authorized to provide a roughly complete census of slaveownership in the Empire at the time.[159] That Western academics did not dive into this treasure trove of data long before 2010 is testament to the persistence of the dominant white frame, and the continuing influence of the white elite that benefits most from its perpetuation and from white amnesia and denial of racial oppression.

The British had been engaged in the transatlantic slave trade for more than 200 years by the time it was officially abolished in 1807 (see Chapter 2). The complete abolition of slavery did not follow for another generation, as the actual census of slaveownership in the British Empire in the 1830s illustrates.[160]

The contemporary research team that launched an examination of the detailed records of the 1830s Commission determined how payouts from the end of British slavery greatly stimulated capitalism. Like earlier capital made off the backs of those enslaved, this new infusion of capital stemmed from those enslaved. Again, this unjustly gained capital funded manufacturing, subsidized railways, sponsored mining firms, bankrolled merchants and banks, financed insurance companies, supported museums, and helped elite whites to build country estates and amass major art collections. The Bank of England, UK's central bank, and other major banks across England and Wales benefitted hugely from these compensatory payments to former white slaveholders. Unfortunately, the *slavery origins* of modern capitalism are rarely recognized, even today.[161]

Slavery researchers have also exposed the extraordinarily vicious and violently oppressive nature of numerous white slaveowners and their overseers. Consider the wealthy white slaveholder Thomas Thistlewood (1721–1786). Operating from Jamaica in the mid-1700s, his own diaries record *3,852 acts of rape* that he committed with *136 enslaved women* in almost four decades, including his long-term coercive relationship with Phibbah, his enslaved "wife." In an entry from 1756, Thistlewood writes about the cruel punishment he inflicted on an enslaved black man. "Gave him a moderate whipping, pickled him well," he wrote, "made Hector shit in his mouth, immediately put a gag in it whilst his mouth was full and made him wear it 4 or 5 hours."[162] The ongoing white savior myths about British slavery certainly have no room for such harsh realities imposed by elite British men. Once again, we see how old and strong the dominant white racial frame has been, from centuries ago to the present day.

A Comparative Note on Slavery in the UK and the USA

Comparisons of the UK and the USA are significantly improved by understanding how the two societies began and developed historically. The historical origins are different, including the timing and entry of contemporary groups of color. The American colonies (later the USA) developed by the 1700s into a slavery-centered society in which much of the economy, especially that beyond the subsistence farms of whites, was controlled by white slaveholders and merchants, shipbuilders, insurers, and bankers linked, directly or indirectly, to slave plantations and the Atlantic slave trade. Much of the international economic system for centuries was centered in slavery, slave-produced products, trade with plantations, and the economic recirculation of capital from the profitable slave economy. Various British cities were central to this international slave trade. In the USA, millions of Africans and their descendants became central to the manual labor force, and thus to building up great wealth for some whites and to create economic success for many others.[163]

No one group of color in the UK has been so central to the creation of the internal wealth and political constitution of the nation as African Americans have been to the USA. Unlike in the UK, the USA (as of 1787–1790) began as a slavery-centered political economy and nation. Coupled with whites' violent seizure of Indigenous American lands, African American enslavement was essential to much economic development and wealth creation. The US Constitution (1787) was written by powerful slaveholders and the merchants, bankers, lawyers, and other white men economically associated with them. That Constitution has at least a dozen provisions designed to uphold the US slavery system.[164]

Without the millions of enslaved African Americans, there likely would not have been the economic development that led to the political-economic creation of the US nation at that time—and its economic and territorial expansion thereafter. Ironically, substantial capital used to fight the revolutionary "freedom" struggle against imperial Britain came off the backs of enslaved African Americans. By the 1700s, the development of this slavery-centered system led to the production by leading whites of sermons, newspaper articles, and books that were central to the creation of a broad white racial frame designed to justify and maintain the unjust enrichment of whites from slavery and related commercial efforts. This 246-year history of enslavement was followed by nearly a century of Jim Crow segregation for African Americans (altogether 82 percent of US history). This explains why, for four centuries now, African Americans have been central to the development of racial inequality, racial hierarchy, and racial framing. Over this long period, together with Native Americans, African Americans have been central in the development and persistence of many racial aspects of US society, including its foundational institutions—more so than later immigrant groups of color, such as Asian and Latino/a Americans, who have also been racially oppressed since the mid-nineteenth century. This white-racist system, and its racist framing of African Americans and other Americans of color, has endured in many ways to the present.[165]

In contrast, the UK was not founded as a nation on enslaving millions of non-European people who were fully racialized within its territorial borders. The UK did not develop early on the kind of slavery system, with its racial hierarchy and constitutional buttressing, that made up the political-economic core of the new United States of America. In contrast, by the early 1700s, Britain was directly and increasingly involved in the Atlantic slave trade that transported many enslaved Africans to North America and the Caribbean. Britain itself never had a large enslaved population within its territory, and its fully developed white racial frame thus evolved gradually over time. The historian Olusoga has explained: "Whereas the cotton plantations of the American south were established on the soil of the continental United States, British slavery took place 3,000 miles away in the Caribbean. That geographic distance made it possible for slavery to be largely airbrushed out of British history, following the Slavery Abolition Act in 1833."[166]

Mythical English National Culture: The Politics of Race and Nation

Let us return to film critic Al-Kadhi's apt analysis of the Oscar-nominated British films from 2017, *Darkest Hour* and *Dunkirk*. He comments sharply on *Dunkirk*'s white racial framing: "I'm not sure if Christopher Nolan [who wrote and produced the film] has an aversion to people of colour, because there is not a single one in his movie. Its dystopian quality is only accurate in how it relays what the world would be like if solely inhabited by white men. The film … literally erases the fact that almost 5 million Commonwealth soldiers … fought in the war, and that British Indians had a prominent role at Dunkirk." Of *Darkest Hour*, Al-Kadhi writes that it is "one in a long line of British period dramas that view [Sir Winston] Churchill as a national hero, conveniently muting the reality of his racist tyranny (it's telling that many of Churchill's imperialist exploits abroad are not widely known)."[167] These and other recent films regularly perpetuate white-virtuousness mythologies that remain central to the UK's dominant white racial frame.

A major challenge to the UK's enduring white racial frame is found in social historian Paul Gilroy's brilliant examination of anti-black racism and contemporary culture in his book *There Ain't No Black in the Union Jack*. Gilroy's study of major black contributions to British culture, typically framed as standing on a purely white Christian history, provides a conceptual model that allows one to make sense out of a highly racialized UK society.[168] As one reviewer wrote, Gilroy "shrewdly refrains from the usual explanations of racism as a peculiar evil on the margins of British society and shows how the history of British racism is bound up with an imaginary English 'national culture' which is supposedly homogenous in its whiteness and Christianity."[169] For example, Gilroy demonstrates that black music is a major illustration of a counter-culture in Britain. His work comes to mind when reflecting on the meaning of Markle in the era of Brexit and the related debates over non-white and other immigration to Britain. Take, for example, the black gospel choir performing *Stand by Me* at her racially diverse wedding, a song influenced by an early black American gospel composer (Charles Tindley), and composed by a black songwriter (Ben E. King) and his white associates. Markle's deviation from conventional white royal norms attests to the importance of Gilroy's message, which critically questions white notions that black culture has meaning in Africa only and that European culture is purely white.[170]

Conclusion

In the UK, the oppressive treatment of people of color coexists uneasily with professed ideals of freedom, justice, and equality before the law. Social scientists have developed various perspectives to explain racial inequalities and the enduring UK racial hierarchy. We argue that *systemic racism* and the attendant concept of the *white racial frame* offer a valuable analytical framework from which to understand British systemic racism, including the pervasive racial dynamics surrounding the entry of Meghan Markle into the royal family. Certainly, a significant aspect of systemic racism theory, which originated in the black American race-critical tradition (see Chapter 2), is that it sets racial subjugation and discrimination in a rich historical context, and accentuates the many ways in which racial oppression is systemic in white-dominated societies.

We trace the ways in which the racial pecking order, racial inequalities, and racial discrimination have long been reproduced at the core of British society. In opposition to claims that white-imposed racism is gradually declining, even becoming a negligible part of UK society, data on and analyses of UK racism help in making sense of the hyper-racialization of Markle, and show that the character and markers of racial oppression begun centuries ago persist in copious ways in the present era.

White racial framing is important to legitimating and rationalizing the continuation of systemic racial discrimination and inequalities throughout all UK areas and institutions, including in governmental, legal, educational, and economic bodies. In modern-day Britain, one moderate version of white framing characteristically translates into rather timid or sanitized discussions of racial inequality and discrimination. Markle's biracialism, for example, is something many in the white-dominated press are fixated on, while at the same time they seem resistant to address more openly its many ties to systemic racism. This is characteristic of moderate versions of the dominant racial frame. Certainly, part of how the white racial frame functions is by weakening attention to and the discourse surrounding the still-pervasive systemic racial disparities in British society.

Notes

1 Ceylan Yeginsu, "Black Britons Wonder what Took Harry and Meghan So Long," *The New York Times*, January 16, 2020. www.nytimes.com/2020/01/10/world/europe/harry-meghan-markle-racism.html. Accessed May 3, 2020.

2 Alexander Smith, "Meghan Markle and British Racism: What her Saga Says to Black Britons," *NBC*, February 10, 2020, www.nbcnews.com/news/world/meghan-markle-british-racism-what-her-saga-says-black-britons-n1132181. Accessed February 16, 2020.

3 *Ibid.*

4 Dawn Butler, "Dawn Butler: 'To Dismantle Systemic Racism, We Need Uncomfortable Conversations,'" *Tribune*, August 1, 2020, https://tribunemag.co.uk/2020/08/dawn-butler-to-dismantle-systemic-racism-we-need-uncomfortable-conversations. Accessed August 7, 2020.

5 Smith, "Meghan Markle and British Racism."
6 Blue Telusma, "Gayle King Checks Royal Family Biographer over Meghan Markle Racial Remark on 'CBS This Morning,'" *The Grio*, January 13, 2020, https://thegrio.com/2020/01/13/gayle-king-checks-royal-family-biographer-over-megan-markle-racial-remark-on-cbs-this-morning/. Accessed April 29, 2020.
7 @Kikoqua1990, Twitter, https://twitter.com/Kikoqua1990/status/1216772 702742159361. Accessed February 16, 2020.
8 Omid Scobie and Carolyn Durand, *Finding Freedom: Harry and Meghan and the Making of a Modern Royal Family* (New York: HarperCollins), p. 16.
9 Christopher D. DeSante, "Working Twice as Hard to Get Half as Far: Race, Work Ethic, and America's Deserving Poor," *American Journal of Political Science*, 57 (2) (April 2013), p. 342.
10 Britt Stephens, "Meghan Markle is being Called "Difficult," and Black Women can Read between the Lines," *Pop Sugar*, December 17, 2018, www.popsugar.com/news/Meghan-Markle-Racism-Op-Ed-45574616. Accessed June 19, 2019.
11 Pamela Duncan and Polly Bindman, "Meghan Gets Twice as Many Negative Headlines as Positive, Analysis Finds," *The Guardian*, January 18, 2020, www.theguardian.com/global/2020/jan/18/meghan-gets-more-than-twice-as-many-negative-headlines-as-positive. Accessed April 29, 2020.
12 Duncan and Bindman, "Meghan Gets Twice as Many Negative Headlines."
13 Telusma, "Gayle King Checks Royal Family Biographer."
14 Duncan and Bindman, "Meghan Gets Twice as Many Negative Headlines."
15 James Rodgers, "Meghan Markle and Prince Harry's Lawsuit over Letter to her Father Lets the Tabloids Win," *NBC*, April 25, 2020, www.nbcnews.com/think/opinion/meghan-markle-prince-harry-s-lawsuit-over-letter-her-father-ncna1191776. Accessed April 29, 2020.
16 Rebecca English, "New Biography Author Drops a Hint that Royal 'Racism' was Directed at Meghan Markle, by Suggesting Some Individuals 'May Like to Take a Look at how they View the World,'" *Daily Mail*, July 24, 2020, www.dailymail.co.uk/news/article-8558725/Kate-snubbed-Meghan-final-royal-engagement.html. Accessed August 7, 2020.
17 Mehera Bonner, "10 Bombshell Reveals from Meghan Markle and Prince Harry's New Biography *'Finding Freedom,'*" *Cosmopolitan*, July 29, 2020, www.cosmopolitan.com/entertainment/celebs/a33456758/finding-freedom-meghan-markle-prince-harry-biggest-revelations/. Accessed August 7, 2020. Italics added.
18 Scobie and Durand, *Finding Freedom*, p. 87. Italics added.
19 *Ibid.*, p. 250.
20 Centre for Contemporary Cultural Studies (ed.), *The Empire Strikes Back: Race and Racism in 70s Britain* (Abingdon: Routledge, 1982).
21 Paul Gilroy, "Steppin' Out of Babylon—Race, Class, and Automony," in *The Empire Strikes Back: Race and Racism in 70s Britain*, ed. Centre for Contemporary Cultural Studies (Abingdon: Routledge, 1982), pp. 275, 278.
22 Nosheen Iqbal, "Has Meghan Markle Changed Britain's Attitude to Race and Royalty?" *The Observer*, May 13, 2018, www.theguardian.com/uk-news/2018/may/13/has-meghan-markle-changed-britains-attitude-race-and-royalty. Accessed June 12, 2019.

23 Joe R. Feagin, *The White Racial Frame: Centuries of Racial Framing and Counter-Framing*, 3rd edn (New York: Routledge, 2020), et passim.

24 Karl Marx and Friedrich Engels, *The German Ideology*, ed. R. Pascal (New York: International Publishers, 1947), p. 39.

25 Andrew Scott Baron and Mahzarin R. Banaji, "The Development of Implicit Attitudes: Evidence of Race Evaluations from Ages 6 and 10 and Adulthood," *Psychological Science*, 17 (2006), pp. 52–53; John F. Dovidio, John C. Brigham, Blair T. Johnson, and Samuel L. Gaertner, "Stereotyping, Prejudice, and Discrimination: Another Look," in *Stereotypes and Stereotyping*, eds C. Neil Macrae, Miles Hewstone, and Charles Stangor (New York: Guilford, 1995), pp. 276–319; Sonja M.B. Givens and Jennifer L. Monahan, "Priming Mammies, Jezebels, and Other Controlling Images: An Examination of the Influence of Mediated Stereotypes on Perceptions of an African American Woman," *Media Psychology*, 7 (2005), pp. 102–103.

26 "A Statement by the Communications Secretary to Prince Harry," www.royal.uk/statement-communications-secretary-prince-harry. Accessed June 19, 2019.

27 Scobie and Durand, *Finding Freedom*, pp. 95, 246, 249.

28 *Tatler* Staff, "One Year Of Meghanomania," *Tatler*, March 25, 2019, www.tatler.com/article/meghan-markle-mania. Accessed June 19, 2019.

29 Perry Carpenter, "Sarah Ferguson Feels Sorry for Meghan Markle and Prince Harry but Refuses to Offer Advice for this Reason," *ShowBiz Cheatsheet*, December 14, 2019, www.cheatsheet.com/entertainment/sarah-ferguson-feels-sorry-for-meghan-markle-and-prince-harry-but-refuses-to-offer-advice-for-this-reason.html/. Accessed May 3, 2020.

30 Alexandria Gouveia, "Exclusive: Sarah, Duchess of York Talks Meghan Markle, Princess Diana, and those Jeffrey Epstein Claims," *Vogue Arabia*, December 11, 2010, https://en.vogue.me/culture/vogue-arabia-may-issue-do-it-yourself/ Accessed May 3, 2020.

31 David Jenkins, "Meghanomania Lives On," *Tatler*, January 9, 2002, www.tatler.com/article/meghan-markle-mania. Accessed April 29, 2020.

32 Abe Hawken, "DRIVE OF HIS WIFE Meghan Markle was behind Megxit as She's in 'Driving Seat' of her and Prince Harry's Marriage, Stanley Johnson Thinks," *The Sun*, May 1, 2020, www.thesun.co.uk/news/11525365/meghan-markle-behind-megxit-driving-seat/. Accessed May 2, 2020.

33 Angela Levin, "Harry and Meghan Seem to Bring out the Worst in Each Other," *The Telegraph*, July 26, 2020, www.telegraph.co.uk/men/relationships/harry-meghan-seem-bring-worst/. Accessed August 7, 2020.

34 Ben Griffiths, "LADY MEGBETH Royal Biographer Lady C Says 'Weak' Harry was Taken Away from his Family by 'Shakespeare Villain' Meghan," *The Sun*, August 1, 2020, www.thesun.co.uk/news/12289741/lady-c-harry-shakespeare-villain-meghan/. Accessed August 7, 2020.

35 Scobie and Durand, *Finding Freedom*, pp. 161, 182.

36 Maurice Halbwachs, *On Collective Memory*, ed. and trans. Lewis Coser (Chicago, IL: University of Chicago Press, 1992), pp. 38, 52. Italics added.

37 Rebecca Mead, "Prince Harry and Meghan Markle's Fractured Fairy Tale," the *New Yorker*, April 20, 2020, www.newyorker.com/magazine/2020/04/20/prince-harry-and-meghan-markles-fractured-fairy-tale. Accessed April 29, 2020.

38 Louisa Ballhaus, "Meghan Markle's *Vogue* was Deemed 'Not White Enough' by British Press & Twitter is Fuming," *She Knows*, August 6, 2019, www.sheknows.com/entertainment/articles/2077790/meghan-markle-vogue-not-white-enough-criticism/. Accessed April 29, 2020.

39 As quoted in Ballhaus, "Meghan Markle's *Vogue*."

40 News.com.au Staff, "'Bottom of the Barrel': 60 Minutes Blasted over Damning Meghan Markle Segment," *news.com.au*, September 9, 2019. www.news.com.au/entertainment/tv/bottom-of-the-barrel-60-minutes-blasted-over-damning-meghan-markle-segment/news-story/ef4d6ecb1673a42da68a375adedfd127. Accessed August 25, 2020.

41 Jon Sharman, "TV Station Condemned for Featuring Racist Katie Hopkins in Megan Markle Documentary," *The Independent*, September 6, 2019, www.independent.co.uk/news/world/australasia/katie-hopkins-meghan-markle-documentary-60-minutes-australia-a9093816.html. Accessed November 5, 2019.

42 News.com.au Staff, "'Bottom of the Barrel.'"

43 Griffiths, "LADY MEGBETH."

44 Julie Miller, "Lady Colin Campbell, Author of the *Other* Harry and Meghan Book, Swears it's not a Takedown," *Vanity Fair*, July 30, 2020, www.vanityfair.com/style/2020/07/lady-colin-campbell-swears-its-not-a-takedown?itm_content=footer-recirc. Accessed August 14, 2020.

45 Bill Schwarz, *The White Man's World (Memories of Empire)* (Oxford: Oxford University Press, 2011), pp. 14, 164.

46 Stefano Fella and Emanuela Bozzini, "Fighting Racism in the United Kingdom: A Multicultural Legacy and a Multi-Faceted Movement," in *Anti-Racist Movements in the EU*, eds Carlo Ruzza and Stefano Fella (London: Palgrave Macmillan, 2013).

47 Kim Wagner, "Imperial Legacies by Jeremy Black Review—Whitewash for Britain's Atrocities," *The Guardian*, August 10, 2019, www.theguardian.com/books/2019/aug/10/imperial-legacies-jeremy-black-review-empire-multiculturalism. Accessed May 16, 2020. Italics added.

48 Jeremy Black, "Identity Politics and the Empire Debate," *Quadrant*, June 27, 2018, https://quadrant.org.au/magazine/2018/06/identity-politics-empire-debate/. Accessed August 20, 2020.

49 Wagner, "Imperial Legacies."

50 *Ibid.*

51 "Ethics And Empire: An Open Letter from Oxford Scholars," *The Conversation*, December 19, 2017, https://theconversation.com/ethics-and-empire-an-open-letter-from-oxford-scholars-89333. Accessed August 7, 2020.

52 Jonathan Saha, "Safe Spaces for Colonial Apologists," *Critical Legal Thinking*, January 8, 2018, https://criticallegalthinking.com/2018/01/08/safe-spaces-colonial-apologists/. Accessed August 7, 2020.

53 Saha, "Safe Spaces."

54 Jeremy Black, *Imperial Legacies: The British Empire Around the World* (New York: Encounter Books, 2019).

55 John Darwin, *The Empire Project: The Rise and Fall of the British World System, 1830–1970* (Cambridge: Cambridge University Press, 2009); Erica Gerald Mason, "How Prince Harry and Meghan Markle could Actually Combat Colonialism's Destructive Legacy," *Vanity Fair*, August 14, 2020, www.vanityfair.com/style/2020/08/how-prince-harry-and-meghan-markle-could-actually-combat-colonialisms-destructive-legacy. Accessed August 14, 2002.

56 Lorraine Boissoneault, "The True Story of the Koh-i-Noor Diamond—and Why the British Won't Give it Back," *Smithsonian Magazine*, August 30, 2017, www.smithsonianmag.com/history/true-story-koh-i-noor-diamondand-why-british-wont-give-it-back-180964660/. Accessed August 14, 2020; Anurag Verma, "'Return Koh-i-Noor': Internet has Solution to Queen Complaining about Crown being Heavy," *News18 Buzz*, March 4, 2020, www.news18.com/news/buzz/return-koh-i-noor-internet-has-solution-to-queen-complaining-about-crown-being-heavy-2524591.html. Accessed August 23, 2020.

57 For more details on social reproduction of racism, see Joe R. Feagin, *Systemic Racism: A Theory of Oppression* (New York: Routledge, 2006).

58 Joseph Lee, "George Floyd: Five Factors behind the UK Black Lives Matter Protests," *BBC*, June 13, 2020, www.bbc.com/news/uk-52997848. Accessed June 20, 2020; Butler, "Dawn Butler."

59 Richard Allen Greene, "Britain's Big Race Divide," *CNN*, June 22, 2020, https://edition.cnn.com/interactive/2020/06/europe/britain-racism-cnn-poll-gbr-intl/. Accessed August 12, 2020.

60 Butler, "Dawn Butler." Italics added.

61 Meaghan Wray, "Prince Harry Breaks Silence on Black Lives Matter Movement during Speech at Diana Awards," *Global News*, July 2, 2020, https://globalnews.ca/news/7131211/prince-harry-black-lives-matter-diana-awards-speech/. Accessed August 7, 2020.

62 Caroline Hallemann, "How Prince Harry and Meghan Markle are Getting Involved in the Black Lives Matter Movement," *Town & Country*, June 21, 2020, www.townandcountrymag.com/society/tradition/a32884318/prince-harry-meghan-markle-black-lives-matter-movement/. Accessed August 7, 2020.

63 Simon Perry, "Prince Harry Says it is 'Down to Every Single Person' to Act against Racial Injustice," *People*, August 10, 2020, https://people.com/royals/prince-harry-everyone-must-act-against-racial-injustice/. Accessed August 10, 2020. Italics added.

64 Hallemann, "How Prince Harry and Meghan Markle are Getting Involved."

65 *Ibid.*

66 Maya Oppenheim, "Queen's Birthday: Five Times Elizabeth II Dropped the Veil of Neutrality and Revealed her Political Opinions," *The Independent*, April 20, 2016, www.independent.co.uk/news/people/queens-birthday-five-times-elizabeth-ii-dropped-her-veil-of-neutrality-and-revealed-her-political-a6992781.html. Accessed August 7, 2020; London Staff, "Chamberlain's Return From Munich," *The Guardian*, October 1, 1938, www.theguardian.com/news/1938/oct/01/leadersandreply.mainsection. Accessed June 15, 2020; Robert Rhodes James, *A Spirit Undaunted: The Political Role of George VI* (London: Abacus, 2004); Mike Davis, *Late Victorian Holocausts: El Niño Famines and the Making of the Third World* (Brooklyn, NY: Verso, 2017).

67 Caitlyn Gowriluk, "Quietly Removing Paint on Queen Victoria Statue a 'Missed Opportunity' for Conversation, Expert Says," *CBC News*, June 25, 2020, www.cbc.ca/news/canada/manitoba/queen-victoria-statue-winnipeg-paint-missed-opportunity-1.5626816. Accessed August 7, 2020.

68 Mikhaila Friel, "The British Royal Family has Turned a Blind Eye to its Racist Past," *Insider*, August 7, 2020, www.insider.com/british-royal-family-racist-history-black-lives-matter-2020-8. Accessed August 9, 2020.

69 Simon de Bruxelles, "Calls for Redesign of Royal Honour over 'Offensive' Image," *The Guardian*, June 22, 2020, www.theguardian.com/uk-news/2020/jun/22/calls-for-redesign-of-royal-honour-over-offensive-image. Accessed September 7, 2020.

70 Lee, "George Floyd"; Robert Booth, "Grenfell Survivors Consider Boycotting Inquiry over Conflict of Interest," *The Guardian*, January 24, 2020, www.theguardian.com/uk-news/2020/jan/24/grenfell-survivors-consider-boycotting-inquiry-over-conflict-of-interest. Accessed June 21, 2020.

71 Maya Goodfellow, "The Connection between Grenfell and Finsbury Park," *Al Jazeera Media Network*, June 21, 2017, www.aljazeera.com/indepth/opinion/2017/06/connection-grenfell-finsbury-park-170621075822519.html. Accessed June 21, 2020.

72 Robert Hutton, "Police End Stephen Lawrence Murder Probe that Showed U.K. Racism," *Bloomberg News*, August 11, 2020, www.bnnbloomberg.ca/police-end-stephen-lawrence-murder-probe-that-showed-u-k-racism-1.1478760. Accessed August 14, 2020.

73 Lee, "George Floyd."

74 Greene, "Britain's Big Race Divide."

75 "Parliament," *Britannica Academic Online*, https://academic-eb-com.srv-proxy2.library.tamu.edu/levels/collegiate/article/Parliament/58522#215007.toc. Accessed February 13, 2021.

76 *Ibid.*

77 Alan Woods, "The Crisis of Capitalism and the Role of the Monarchy," *Socialist. Net*, www.socialist.net/royal-powers-revealed-abolish-this-rotten-relic.htm. Accessed March 19, 2020.

78 *The Royal Household*, "The Queen and Privy Council," www.royal.uk/queen-and-government?ch=7#bio-section-6. Accessed May 24, 2020.

79 Jon Henley, "The Privy Council Meeting: What May Have Happened. Possibly," *The Guardian*, October 30, 2013, www.theguardian.com/uk-news/2013/oct/30/privy-council-press-rubber-stamps-charter. Accessed May 24, 2020. Italics in original.

80 Andy McSmith, "State School Pupils are 'Potted Plants', Says Tory," *The Independent*, October 5, 2006, www.independent.co.uk/news/uk/politics/state-school-pupils-are-potted-plants-says-tory-418767.html. Accessed May 24, 2020.

81 The Privacy Council Office, "Privy Council Members," https://privycouncil.independent.gov.uk/privy-council/privy-council-members/. Accessed May 24, 2020. All numbers are approximates. We entered their names and/or titles exactly as listed by the Privy Council Office and located photographs and other biographical information where available.

82 James Kilby and Rob Sewell, "Royal Powers Revealed: Abolish this Rotten Relic," *Socialist.Net*, www.socialist.net/royal-powers-revealed-abolish-this-rotten-relic.htm. Accessed March 19, 2020.

83 *Ibid.* Italics added.

84 Jenny Hocking, "Unmasking History: The Queen, the Governor General and the Whitlam Dismissal," *The Guardian*, December 5, 2018, www.theguardian.com/australia-news/2018/dec/06/unmasking-history-the-queen-the-governor-general-and-the-whitlam-dismissal. Accessed April 29, 2020.

85 *Ibid.*

86 Woods, "The Crisis of Capitalism."

87 "Survey on Monarchy," *YouGov*, https://yougov.co.uk/topics/travel/survey-results/daily/2020/02/18/8b405/1. Accessed March 20, 2020.

88 Robert Stevens, "The Berries of Wrath: Prince Charles Demands 'Hard Graft' from Furloughed Workers," *World Socialist Website*, May 21, 2020, www.wsws.org/en/articles/2020/05/21/frui-m21.html. Accessed May 21, 2020.

89 Katie Nicholl, "'He Might Be in Isolation, But He is Not Isolated': How Prince Charles is Spending his Coronavirus Quarantine," *Vanity Fair*, March 27, 2020. www.vanityfair.com/style/2020/03/prince-charles-coronavirus-quarantine. Accessed April 29, 2020.

90 Leah Silverman, "These are All of Queen Elizabeth's Homes," *Town & Country*, December 12, 2017, www.townandcountrymag.com/leisure/real-estate/g14106752/queen-elizabeth-homes/. Accessed April 29, 2020; Milly Vincent and Claire Toureille, "Inside 'HMS Bubble': Memo from Queen's Master of the Household Reveals how Her Majesty and Prince Philip are Relying on 22 Staff who have Said Goodbye to their Families for the Duration of Coronavirus Lockdown to Protect the Royals at Windsor," *Daily Mail*, April 26, 2020, www.dailymail.co.uk/femail/article-8258257/Queen-94-Duke-Edinburgh-98-isolating-22-members-staff.html. Accessed May 22, 2020.

91 Jack Royston, "Wartime Theme in Queen's Speech Came after Coronavirus Lockdown Triggered Memories of Evacuation, Royal Author Says," *Newsweek*, April 6, 2020, www.newsweek.com/wartime-theme-queens-speech-came-after-coronavirus-lockdown-triggered-memories-evacuation-royal-1496388. Accessed August 9, 2020.

92 Alasdair Lane, "British Prisoners and their Families—The Forgotten Victims of COVID-19," *Forbes*, July 23, 2020. www.forbes.com/sites/alasdairlane/2020/07/23/british-prisoners-and-their-families-the-forgotten-victims-of-covid-19/. Accessed August 9, 2020; Benjamin Kentish, "Revealed: How 'Racial Bias' at the Heart of Criminal Justice System Means Black People in UK More Likely to be in Prison than those in US," *The Independent*, September 8, 2017, www.independent.co.uk/news/uk/home-news/black-people-prison-uk-more-likely-us-lammy-review-a7935061.html. Accessed August 20, 2020.

93 Jack Royston, "Queen Elizabeth II will have Stopped Horse Riding during Coronavirus Lockdown, Says Former Press Secretary," *Newsweek*, April 2, 2020, www.newsweek.com/queen-elizabeth-ii-will-have-stopped-horse-riding-during-coronavirus-lockdown-says-former-press-1495683. Accessed August 9, 2020.

94 Various authors, "Instant Opinion: Coronavirus has Left Brits Scared to Go Outside," *The Week*, May 5, 2020, www.theweek.co.uk/instant-opinion/106914/instant-opinion-coronavirus-has-left-brits-scared-to-go-outside. Accessed August 20, 2020; Michael Goodier and Josh Rayman, "COVIDd-19 is Highlighting Cities' Unequal Access to Green Space," *CityMetric*, June 3, 2020, www.citymetric.com/fabric/covid-19-highlighting-cities-unequal-access-green-space-5168. Accessed August 20, 2020.

95 Winnie Agbonlahor, "Coronavirus: 'Too Many Homeless Still Sleeping Rough,'" *BBC*, April 15, 2020, www.bbc.com/news/uk-england-52299498. Accessed April 29, 2020.

96 Stephanie Linning, "Down and Out at Buckingham Palace: Homeless Migrants Sleep Huddled on Steps Just Metres from Queen's Residence,"

Daily Mail, June 25, 2015, www.dailymail.co.uk/news/article-3138713/Homeless-migrants-sleep-huddled-steps-one-London-s-prestigious-address-just-metres-grounds-Buckingham-Palace.html. Accessed April 29, 2020.

97 Rob Evans, "Half of England is Owned by Less than 1% of the Population," *The Guardian*, April 17, 2019, www.theguardian.com/money/2019/apr/17/who-owns-england-thousand-secret-landowners-author. Accessed April 29, 2020; Guy Shrubsole, "Revealed: The Aristocrats and City Bankers Who Own England's Grouse Moors," *Who Owns England?* August 12, 2018, https://whoownsengland.org/2018/08/12/revealed-the-aristocrats-and-city-bankers-who-own-englands-grouse-moors/. Accessed April 29, 2020.

98 Peter Fryer, *Staying Power: The History of Black People in Britain* (London: Pluto Press, Kindle Edition), pp. 7–8; Richard Halloran, "The Sad, Dark End of the British Empire," *Politico*, August 26, 2014, www.politico.com/magazine/story/2014/08/the-sad-end-of-the-british-empire-110362_Page2.html. Accessed June 10, 2019.

99 East of England Broadband Network, "British Involvement in the Transatlantic Slave Trade," *The Abolition Project*, http://abolition.e2bn.org/slavery_45.html. Accessed June 10, 2019.

100 Mason, "How Prince Harry"; Halloran, "The Sad, Dark End."

101 Halloran, "The Sad, Dark End."

102 Secret Teacher, "Secret Teacher: The UK has a Complex Racial History. Why Aren't We Teaching It?," *The Guardian*, January 20, 2018, www.theguardian.com/teacher-network/2018/jan/20/secret-teacher-uk-history-of-race-bloody-racism. Accessed June 9, 2019.

103 Warwick Mansell, "Michael Gove Redrafts New History Curriculum after Outcry," *The Guardian*, June 21, 2013, www.theguardian.com/education/2013/jun/21/michael-gove-history-curriculum. Accessed June 9, 2019; Secret Teacher, "Secret Teacher."

104 Equality and Human Rights Commission, "Race Report Statistics," December 27, 2018, www.equalityhumanrights.com/en/race-report-statistics. Accessed April 29, 2019; UK government, "Lammy Review," September 8, 2018, www.gov.uk/government/publications/lammy-review-final-report. Accessed April 29, 2019; Kimiko de Freytas-Tamura, "U.K. Reports Big Rise in Hate Crime, Citing Brexit and Terrorist Attacks," *The New York Times*, October 17, 2017, www.nytimes.com/2017/10/17/world/europe/uk-hate-crime-brexit-attacks.html. April 29, 2019; Kris Manjapra, "When Will Britain Face Up to its Crimes against Humanity?," *The Guardian*, March 28, 2018, www.theguardian.com/news/2018/mar/29/slavery-abolition-compensation-when-will-britain-face-up-to-its-crimes-against-humanity. Accessed June 18, 2019.

105 UK Office For National Statistics, "Research Report on Population Estimates by Ethnic Group and Religion," December 2019, www.ons.gov.uk/peoplepopulationandcommunity/populationandmigration/populationestimates/articles/researchreportonpopulationestimatesbyethnicgroupandreligion/2019–12–04/. Accessed December 18, 2019.

106 Jennifer Hudson and Rosie Campbell, "UK Elects Most Diverse Parliament Ever but it's Still Not Representative," *The Conversation*, May 13, 2016, https://theconversation.com/uk-elects-most-diverse-parliament-ever-but-its-still-not-representative-41626. Accessed June 10, 2019.

107 Robert Booth and Aamna Mohdin, "Revealed: The Stark Evidence of Everyday Racial Bias in Britain," *The Guardian*, December 2, 2018, www.theguardian. com/uk-news/2018/dec/02/revealed-the-stark-evidence-of-everyday-racial-bias-in-britain. Accessed June 10, 2019.

108 Anushka Asthana and Helena Bengtsson, "Audit Lays Bare Racial Disparities in UK Schools, Courts and Workplaces," *The Guardian*, October 9, 2017, www.theguardian.com/uk-news/2017/oct/09/audit-lays-bare-racial-disparities-in-uk-schools-courts-and-workplaces. Accessed June 10, 2019.

109 Hugh Muir, "'Post-Racial' Britain And What Lies Beneath The Surface," *The Guardian*, October 13, 2013, www.theguardian.com/uk-news/2013/oct/13/post-racial-britain-beneath-the-surface-bbc-inside-out. Accessed June 12, 2019.

110 George Yancy, *Backlash: What Happens When We Talk Honestly about Racism in America* (Lanham, MD: Rowman & Littlefield, 2018), p. 75.

111 Christopher Wilson, "Now That's Upwardly Mobile! How in 150 Years, Meghan Markle's Family Went from Cotton Slaves to Royalty via Freedom in the U.S. Civil War...While Her Dad's Ancestors Included a Maid at Windsor Castle," *Daily Mail*, November 29, 2017, www.dailymail.co.uk/femail/article-5130473/Meghan-Markles-upwardly-mobile-family.html. Accessed December 9, 2019; Rachel West, "Meghan Markle's Family Tree Includes Royal Roots and Ties to Slavery," *ET Canada*, May 18, 2018, https://etcanada.com/news/328734/meghan-markles-family-tree-includes-royal-roots-and-ties-to-slavery/. Accessed June 10, 2019.

112 Manjapra, "When Will Britain Face Up."

113 John Orna-Ornstein, "Beautiful Places, Challenging Histories," *National Trust Blog Post*, September 21, 2020, www.nationaltrust.org.uk/blogs/directors-blog/beautiful-places-challenging-histories. Accessed October 17, 2020.

114 Lucy Porten, "The East India Company" in *Interim Report on the Connections between Colonialism and Properties Now in the Care of the National Trust, Including Links with Historic Slavery*, eds Sally-Anne Huxtable et al. (Swindon: National Trust, Heelis, 2020), pp. 45, 47.

115 BBC Staff, "George Floyd Death: Protesters Tear Down Slave Trader Statue," *BBC*, June 7, 2020, www.bbc.com/news/uk-52954305. Accessed June 7, 2020.

116 Manjapra, "When Will Britain Face Up"; Emine Saner, "Renamed and Shamed: Taking on Britain's Slave-Trade Past, from Colston Hall to Penny Lane," *The Guardian*, April 29, 2017, www.theguardian.com/world/2017/apr/29/renamed-and-shamed-taking-on-britains-slave-trade-past-from-colston-hall-to-penny-lane. Accessed June 18, 2019.

117 Boris Johnson, "Boris Johnson: UK and America Can Be Better Friends than Ever Mr Obama... If We LEAVE the EU," *The Sun*, April 22, 2016, www.thesun.co.uk/archives/politics/1139354/boris-johnson-uk-and-america-can-be-better-friends-than-ever-mr-obama-if-we-leave-the-eu/. Accessed June 7, 2020. Italics added.

118 Greene, "Britain's Big Race Divide." Italics added.

119 Claire Schofield, "Why Was a Winston Churchill Statue Defaced? The Life and Views of the Wartime PM as Graffiti Brands Him 'Racist,'" *Edinburg Evening News*, June 8, 2020, www.edinburghnews.scotsman.com/news/people/why-was-winston-churchill-statue-defaced-life-and-views-wartime-pm-graffiti-brands-him-racist-2878135. Accessed June 8, 2020.

120 Stephen Colegrave, "12 Facts That Prove Black Lives Don't Matter in Britain," *Byline Times*, June 8, 2020. https://bylinetimes.com/2020/06/08/black-lives-dont-matter-in-britain/. Accessed June 9, 2020.

121 Schofield, "Why Was a Winston Churchill Statue Defaced?"

122 Boris Johnson, "The Boris Archive: Africa is a Mess, But We Can't Blame Colonialism," *The Spectator*, July 13, 2016, www.spectator.co.uk/article/the-boris-archive-africa-is-a-mess-but-we-can-t-blame-colonialism. Accessed June 7, 2020.

123 BBC Staff, "George Floyd Death."

124 Greene, "Britain's Big Race Divide."

125 Martin Robinson and Mark Duell, " 'I Tagged the Statue of Churchill Because he's a Confirmed Racist': Defiant Black Lives Matter Protester Says he Desecrated the Wartime PM's Plinth Because he Fought the Nazis to Protect Colonialism—NOT for 'People of Colour,' " *Daily Mail*, June 8, 2020, www.dailymail.co.uk/news/article-8398909/Defiant-Black-Lives-Matter-protestor-says-desecrated-Churchills-statue.html. Accessed June 8, 2020.

126 Manjapra, "When Will Britain Face Up"; Saner, "Renamed and Shamed"; David Olusoga, "The History of British Slave Ownership Has Been Buried: Now its Scale can be Revealed," *The Guardian*, July 12, 2015, www.theguardian.com/world/2015/jul/12/british-history-slavery-buried-scale-revealed. Accessed June 10, 2019.

127 Rafael Tammariello, "The Slave Trade," *Las Vegas Review-Journal* (February 8, 1998), p-1E.

128 J.H. Parry and P.M. Sherlock, *A Short History of the West Indies*, 3rd edn (New York: St. Martin's Press, 1971), pp. 110–111. See also William M. Wiecek, *The Sources of Antislavery Constitutionalism in America, 1760–1848* (Ithaca, NY: Cornell University Press, 1977), pp. 15–16. Italics added.

129 As summarized by Matt Wrack, "Book Review of *The Making of New World Slavery: From the Baroque to the Modern, 1492–1800*", *Socialism Today*, 13 (November 1998), http://socialismtoday.org/archive/33/slavery33.html. Accessed December 16, 2019. See also Robin Blackburn, *The Making of New World Slavery: From The Baroque To The Modern, 1492–1800* (London: Verso, 1997).

130 See Eric Williams, *Capitalism And Slavery* (Chapel Hill, NC: University of North Carolina Press, 1994 [1944]), pp. 98–107; Douglass C. North, *The Economic Growth of the United States, 1790–1860* (Englewood Cliffs, NJ: Prentice Hall, 1961), pp. 38–45; Barbara L. Solow and Stanley L. Engerman, "British Capitalism and Caribbean Slavery: The Legacy of Eric Williams: An Introduction," in *British Capitalism And Caribbean Slavery: The Legacy Of Eric Williams* (Cambridge: Cambridge University Press, 1987), pp. 8–9.

131 Manjapra, "When Will Britain Face Up"; Derrick Bell, "Brown v. Board Of Education and the Interest Convergence Dilemma," *Harvard Law Review* 93(3) (1980), p. 518.

132 Manjapra, "When Will Britain Face Up."

133 Sam Jones, "Follow the Money: Investigators Trace Forgotten Story of Britain's Slave Trade," *The Guardian*, August 27, 2013, www.theguardian.com/world/2013/aug/27/britain-slave-trade. Accessed June 18, 2019.

134 *Ibid.*

135 Olusoga, "The History of British Slave Ownership Has Been Buried"; East of England Broadband Network, "British Involvement in the Transatlantic Slave Trade."

136 Historica Canada, "Slavery Abolition Act, 1833," *The Canadian Encyclopedia*, 2019, www.thecanadianencyclopedia.ca/en/article/slavery-abolition-act-1833. Accessed June 10, 2019; Olusoga, "The History of British Slave Ownership Has Been Buried."

137 Manjapra, "When Will Britain Face Up."

138 *Ibid.*

139 Claud Anderson, *Black Labor, White Wealth* (Edgewood, MD: Duncan & Duncan, 1994), p. 97. See also Joe R. Feagin, *How Blacks Built America: Labor, Culture, Freedom, and Democracy* (New York: Routledge, 2015), pp. 15–48.

140 Catherine Hall and Nick Draper, "William Ewart Gladstone Profile & Legacies Summary," Legacies of British Slave-Ownership Project, University College London, www.ucl.ac.uk/lbs/person/view/2146630326. Accessed June 18, 2019. For a more detailed examination of William Gladstone's views on slavery, see Roland Quinault, "Gladstone And Slavery," *The Historical Journal*, 52 (2) (2009), pp. 363–383.

141 Catherine Hall and Nick Draper, "Jamaica St Thomas-in-the-East, Surrey 291 (East Prospect Estate)," Legacies Of British Slave-Ownership Project, University College London, www.ucl.ac.uk/lbs/estate/view/2830. Accessed June 18, 2019; Manjapra, "When Will Britain Face Up."

142 Manjapra, "When Will Britain Face Up."

143 Olusoga, "The History of British Slave Ownership Has Been Buried."

144 As quoted in Jones, "Follow The Money." Italics added.

145 Kevin Rawlinson and Agency, "Prince Charles says Britain's Role in Slave Trade Was an Atrocity," *The Guardian*, November 5, 2018, www.theguardian.com/uk-news/2018/nov/05/prince-charles-says-britains-part-in-transatlantic-slave-trade-was-atrocity. Accessed June 18, 2019.

146 Manjapra, "When Will Britain Face Up."

147 Friel, "The British Royal Family."

148 David Olusoga, "The Treasury's Tweet Shows Slavery is Still Misunderstood," *The Guardian*, February 12, 2018, www.theguardian.com/commentisfree/2018/feb/12/treasury-tweet-slavery-compensate-slave-owners. Accessed June 18, 2019.

149 Manjapra, "When Will Britain Face Up"; Olusoga, "The Treasury's Tweet."

150 Amrou Al-Kadhi, "Great Britain Was Never a White Utopia. It's Time to Confront Our Real Past," *The Independent*, April 15, 2018, www.independent.co.uk/voices/great-britain-racism-winston-churchhill-imperial-colonial-history-dunkirk-queen-victoria-a8304826.html. Accessed June 10, 2019.

151 Bilal Qureshi, "Why Does Hollywood Keep Churning Out Racist Fantasies Like 'Victoria & Abdul'?," *The Washington Post*, October 9, 2017, www.washingtonpost.com/news/posteverything/wp/2017/10/09/why-does-hollywood-keep-churning-out-racist-fantasies-like-victoria-abdul/. Accessed June 19, 2019.

152 Al-Kadhi, "Great Britain Was Never a White Utopia."

153 Manjapra, "When Will Britain Face Up"; Saner, "Renamed and Shamed"; Qureshi, "Why Does Hollywood." For more on the East India Company, see Lucy Porten, "The East India Company" in Huxtable et al. (eds), *Interim Report*, pp. 45–48.

154 Olusoga, "The History of British Slave Ownership Has Been Buried."

155 Age Fotostock, "Stock Photo—Clapham London England Holy Trinity Church Slavery Window Stained Glass Window William Wilberforce

and Slaves," 2019, www.agefotostock.com/age/en/Stock-Images/Rights-Managed/TRI-10602790. Accessed June 18, 2019; Manjapra, "When Will Britain Face Up."

156 Age Fotostock, "Stock Photo"; Manjapra, "When Will Britain Face Up."

157 GO LONDON, "Amazing Grace or Disgrace?," *GO LONDON Newsletter*, March 22, 2017, www.standard.co.uk/go/london/film/amazing-grace-or-disgrace-7169498.html. Accessed June 19, 2019.

158 *Ibid.*

159 Catherine Hall and Nick Draper, "The Database," Legacies of British Slave-Ownership Project, University College London, www.ucl.ac.uk/lbs/. Accessed June 18, 2019.

160 Sam Jones, "Follow the Money."

161 *Ibid.*

162 Manjapra, "When Will Britain Face Up."

163 Joe R. Feagin and Kimberley Ducey, *Racist America: Roots, Current Realities, And Future Reparations*, 4th edn (New York: Routledge, 2018), et passim.

164 *Ibid.*

165 *Ibid.*

166 Olusoga, "The History Of British Slave Ownership Has Been Buried."

167 Al-Kadhi, "Great Britain Was Never A White Utopia."

168 Paul Gilroy, *There Ain't No Black In The Union Jack: The Cultural Politics of Race and Nation*, 2nd edn (New York: Routledge, 2002), et passim.

169 Bryan Cheyette, "BOOK REVIEW/Still Ain't No Black In The Union Jack: 'The Black Atlantic' – Paul Gilroy: Verso, 11.95," *The Independent*, December 11, 1993, www.independent.co.uk/arts-entertainment/books/book-review-still-aint-no-black-in-the-union-jack-the-black-atlantic-paul-gilroy-verso-1195–1466777.html. Accessed June 9, 2019.

170 Gilroy, *There Ain't No Black In The Union Jack*, et passim.

2 Straight Out of the White Racial Frame

Introduction

In 2016, Prince Harry publicly condemned the British media for their "wave of abuse and harassment" of then-girlfriend Meghan Markle, citing a smear campaign on the front page of a national newspaper, racial undertones of newspaper opinion pieces, and "outright sexism and racism of social media trolls and web article comments."[1] Three years later, 72 female Members of Parliament from across party lines spoke out against the "distasteful and misleading nature" of newspaper stories about Markle, now the Duchess of Sussex. The Members of Parliament noted old colonial undertones in the white-framed reporting.[2]

In 2019, the couple publicly discussed their ongoing struggles with the British press. Media pressure was aggravated, the duchess explained, given that between 2018 and 2019, they faced the combined pressures of being newly married and expecting their first child. Around the time of this admission, the Sussexes brought legal action against conservative British newspapers. Markle sued the tabloid *The Mail on Sunday* (owned by the media baron Jonathan Harold Esmond Vere Harmsworth, 4th Viscount Rothermere), charging the paper with unlawfully publishing a private letter she wrote to her father. Harry sued *The Sun* (part of arch-conservative Rupert Murdoch's News Corporation) and the *Daily Mirror* (operated by white-male-run Reach PLC) for purported illegal interception of personal voicemail messages.[3]

The duchess's legal team was prohibited by a judge from arguing in court that *The Mail on Sunday* was "dishonest, stirred up trouble and had an anti-Meghan agenda" because those claims "were irrelevant in law, presented to the court inadequately, or disproportionate to investigate." In response, Markle's lawyers stated: "Whilst the judge recognizes that there is a claim for breach of privacy and copyright, we are surprised to see that his ruling suggests that dishonest behaviour is not relevant."[4] Significantly, the duchess is biracial and we should not therefore discount the history of racism that unquestionably shapes an underhanded anti-Markle agenda or creates distress for the Sussexes.[5] Following a two-year legal battle, Markle ultimately won the high court privacy case, referring to it as a "comprehensive win" over the tabloid's "illegal and dehumanising practices."[6]

The seemingly unending racist and sexist headlines have included, "How in 150 Years, Meghan Markle's Family Went from Cotton Slaves to Royalty," which charted Markle's so-called "Dirt Poor in the Deep South" family branch.[7] Markle was dubbed the "Duchess Difficult" by tabloids and other media outlets, some reporting she snubbed British designers in favor of foreign ones. Countless "Meghan Markle bridezilla reports" appeared. Some media outlets claimed Markle demanded to wear a specific tiara from the monarch's collection on her wedding day, with her insistence exasperating the queen. Endless reporting claimed the bride-to-be complained about everything from the temperature in Windsor Castle to the medieval chapel's proximity to Heathrow Airport. Allegedly, she made her soon-to-be sister-in-law Kate Middleton cry over her demands for Middleton's daughter's bridesmaid's dress. News reports also appeared about the newly married duchess's overburdened staff, with her demands on them allegedly causing many to quit.[8]

The mainstream media is not above racially framing Markle either. The BBC repeated the outwardly flattering phrase "modern couple" so often that it led one Twitter user to ask: "[W]hat other kind of couple would they be? Medieval?" The Twitter user suggested that "modern couple" was code for Markle's mixed-race background.[9] Then there was the CNN story about the impending birth of the couple's child that was titled, "How Black Will the Royal Baby Be?" The headline led a US human rights author and politician to tweet: "My God @CNN just legitimately asked 'How black will the royal baby be?' and 100% un-ironically warned [that] 'commentators who reinforce dangerous racist stereotypes are totally unaware of the damage.'"[10]

Untold negative comments were left on the couple's Instagram page targeting Markle, her values, and her family after she and Harry announced their plans to step down as senior royals. "Some people naturally destroy families. Harry, you need to wake up before your son will grow up in a broken family like Markle's," posted one commenter accenting racist stereotypes about black families. Another remarked: "Spoiled little brats. Probably [M]eghan pretending to be the innocent victim again." Other commentators saw the gendered-racist comments for what they were, with one Instagram user writing, "I thought the reports of how poorly she's been treated were exaggerated but, after reading these comments, I see she was spot on. I would say the press and the people are the ones who have driven H&M out and it looks like a smart move on their part."[11]

Though Markle's purported liberal views are frequently used as cover for gendered-racist attacks on her, she and Harry arguably appear to be moderately progressive (see Chapter 3). They have publicly discussed the contemporary mental health crisis "but not its causes ... environmental catastrophe but not its causes ... the Grenfell Tower fire but not its causes ... nothing on austerity, inequality or poverty."[12] At the time of writing, however, there have been modest signs of change. Recall from Chapter 1, for example, that Markle admitted to being "really nervous" about getting "picked apart" if she said *black lives matter*. But she said it anyway, even if her remarks did not address systemic racism in the UK or the USA.[13] In the run-up to the 2020 US presidential election, the Sussexes urged Americans to reject "misinformation" and "hate speech" in what the duchess called "the most important election of our lifetime."[14]

In our examination of the white racial framing of the Duchess of Sussex, and what it reveals about systemic racism in Britain today, in this chapter we turn to critical social scientists and critical legal scholars who have developed conceptual and interpretive tools that lead to sharper analyses than older and traditional "racial relations" paradigms allow.[15] These critical and probing theories help advance an understanding of the UK's systemic racism by accentuating entrenched structures and assessing the magnitude and generative progressions of racial oppression over time.

In North America, from where this book's authors originate, such methodical and explanatory theories have typically derived from the counter-mainstream historical tradition of scholars and activists of color. These include African American abolitionists David Walker (1796–1830) and Frederick Douglass (1818–1895), and African American sociologists W.E.B. Du Bois (1868–1963), Anna Julia Cooper (1858–1964), Ida B. Wells-Barnett (1862–1931), and Oliver C. Cox (1901–1974). Strikingly, too, in more recent decades, typically those working within the counter-mainstream historical tradition have been scholars and activists of color and Indigenous scholars and activists. Such pioneering voices have, to name but a few, included Kwame Ture (1941–1998), Rodolfo Acuña (1932–), Richard Delgado (1939–), Derrick Bell (1930–2011), Mari Matsuda (1956–), Angela Y. Davis (1944–), Adrian Piper (1948–), Audra Simpson (Mohawk) (1969–), Haunani Kay-Trask (Hawaiian) (1949–), and Linda Tuhiwai Te Rina Smith (Ngāti Awa and Ngāti Porou iwi) (1950–).

In the UK, a counter-mainstream historical tradition of scholars and activists of color is also thriving. Using an extensive range of methodologies—including storytelling via critical race theory, autobiography, geographically rooted longitudinal ethnographies, and in-depth interviewing—black and post-colonial feminist scholars have pioneered new approaches to studying multiple identity, diaspora, religion, culture, sexuality, and other important areas. Researching the social and moral control of black women, and black women's resulting resistance in our neo-colonial times, including in education, work, family, and the media, these UK scholars and activists have contributed enormously to critical race and post-colonial feminist thinking there and elsewhere.[16]

Sociologist Stuart Hall is central as a theorist of race in Britain and globally. Venerated US philosopher Cornel West said of this preeminent Jamaican-born sociologist: "[W]e all grew up reading Stuart. We wouldn't be here without him. We all stand on his shoulders." Early on, one of Hall's most substantial arguments was to perceive the "internality of race" in all societal processes, and to use race as a lens through which larger societal structures can be studied. As Hall reportedly described his work, "I have never worked on race and ethnicity as a kind of subcategory. I have always worked on the whole social formation which is racialized." The following sentiments illustrate his powerful work.

> What is the relationship between the mobilisation or performance of racialised and other forms of ethnicity and identity at the local, micro, more ethnographic level and the large thing that brought us into the field at the beginning, namely a racialised world ... a world in which material and symbolic resources continue to be deeply unequally distributed. Why are you in this field if you are not concerned about that?[17]

We focus in this chapter on that racialized world and are very cognizant of this centuries-long counter-system tradition. In examining the meaning of Markle in Britain, we demonstrate how the dominant white racial frame has always routinely intersected with other major societal frames. Frequently, once a racial frame is in play, concomitant frames and subframes also come into play (e.g., Islamophobia-oriented, colonial-oriented, class-oriented, and gender-oriented framing). To fully understand the societal worlds inhabited by Markle as a member of the royal family, we must recognize that from the first century of British colonialism, such orientations have been faithfully linked to the white racial frame. In Markle's case, we must also name the gendered viciousness directed at her, which is part of a larger male-sexist frame and closely connected to the overriding white racial frame. (See especially Chapter 4.)

In the decades before and after 1900, US scholar-activists Ida B. Wells-Barnett (1862–1931) and Anna Julia Cooper (1858–1964) emphasized the gendering of the racial hierarchy. They considered the extensive empirical data on the despotic segregation faced by black women and black men, in addition to gendered discrimination faced by women. They wrote about their own experiences with gendered racism, and they made constant use of counter-framed ideas, such as subjugation, domination, and subservience, in their sociological analyses.[18] Together with more recent scholars of gendered racism like Angela Y. Davis, Philomena Essed, and Patricia Hill Collins (see below), their insightful ideas shed much light on the meaning of Markle in twenty-first-century Britain.

As explained in Chapter 1, the white racial frame is far-reaching and multifaceted, and includes not only a beliefs aspect (racial stereotypes, prejudices, ideologies) but also integrating cognitive elements (racial interpretations and narratives), visual and auditory elements (racialized images and language use), a feelings aspect (racialized emotions), and an inclination to action (to discriminate). Since early in Britain's colonial history, this predominant racist framing has incorporated a central subframe that forcefully emphasizes white righteousness, superiority, honor, morality, and ethical conduct (*a white virtuousness subframe*). It also features a robust negative placement of racialized "others" who are subjugated and oppressed by whites (*unvirtuousness subframes*). For centuries the white racial framing of ingroup supremacy and outgroup subordination has been, to borrow

Antonio Gramsci's term, *hegemonic* (i.e., part of a distinct way of life that routinely governs society). For a vast majority of white Britons and some Britons of color, this white racial frame is consistently internalized and embodies an all-encompassing worldview. From cradle to grave, it affords white Britons a language and narratives that allow them to rationalize and legitimate racist structures, actions, and events.

Now we can consider numerous racialized events in the life of Markle since she met and married Prince Harry. These events illustrate and reproduce key facets of the white racial frame, the anti-black subframe, and gendered racism—both contemporarily and historically.

British Nationalist Consciousness: White Fetishization, White Amnesia, and White Denial

Just as in the past when a white-male elite created a legitimating white racial frame that was highly gendered, today the still mostly white-male elite perpetuates gendered racism in the UK. Unsurprisingly, Markle is a casualty of the current version of this still-dominant frame. For example, the elite whites who control British tabloid papers have regularly conducted gendered-racist campaigns against her. In 2019, in an emotional letter to announce the legal action the Sussexes were launching against the publishers of such tabloids, Harry referred to such press intrusion as "ruthless," with no thought to their harmful personal impacts.[19]

Prior to her life as a royal, as an actress in North America, Markle was open with her feelings about how her racial identity impacted her career—her "ethnically ambiguous" skin color, as she put it. "I wasn't black enough for the black roles and I wasn't white enough for the white ones," she explained, "leaving me somewhere in the middle as the ethnic chameleon who couldn't book a job."[20] When she married Harry it was expected that the airing of such public sentiments would end. Historically, or so it is claimed, royals are apolitical. In an apparent departure from royal convention, in 2019, after the couple had filed lawsuits against British tabloids, Harry released a statement concerning the couple's relationship to the problematical media. Describing the "intrusive" and "unlawful" media reporting that has tenaciously targeted the duchess with the intent to disparage her, the prince remarked: "There is a human cost to this relentless propaganda." Most memorably, the prince hauntingly compared the irresponsible media coverage of his wife to that of his late mother Diana, Princess of Wales: "I've seen what happens when someone I love is commoditized to the point that they are no longer treated or seen as a real person. I lost my mother and now I watch my wife falling victim to the same powerful forces."[21] Harry's general point is well-taken; however, the mainstream media treatment of the white aristocrat Diana has been vastly different to the gendered-racist coverage of Markle.

Jordanian-Palestinian counter-framer Rami Yasir has eloquently described white fetishization, amnesia, and denial as part of a white-nationalist consciousness in Britain. He brings attention, for example, to white racially framed representations seen in recent television dramas like *The Crown*, *Downton Abbey*, and *Peaky Blinders*. These series wax nostalgic for a lost Britain, while mostly erasing the colonial roots of white prosperity.[22] Black British author Candice Carty-Williams has similarly remarked that *"The Crown* or *Downton Abbey* ... never [have] any black people. There is a history of them not having any interest in us."[23] To be sure, *Downtown Abbey* did finally feature one black actor as a Jazz singer in its fourth season, who was widely described as a "royal gigolo." The show's only other character of color was named Kemal Panuk, a Turkish diplomat actually played by a white actor.[24]

The black Jazz singer in *Downton Abbey* was said to be a version of Grenada-born cabaret star Leslie Hutchinson. In real life the latter was, for a brief moment, on friendly terms with the British elite, including Edward, Prince of Wales, and Lord Louis Mountbatten's wife Edwina, with whom he had an affair. To combat budding gossip of the white aristocrat sleeping with a black man, George V demanded that Edwina sue a newspaper that had hinted at such an affair. She did, and she won. When the white royals thereafter closed ranks on Hutchinson many career opportunities dried up for him.[25]

White fetishization, amnesia, and denial are critical to the overriding *white frame of reference* and *frame of mind* at the heart of British reactions to Markle, including the smear campaigns on the front pages of several national newspapers; the archaic, racial, and colonial undercurrents of newspaper opinion pieces; and the consummate "sexism and racism of social media trolls and web article comments."[26] Additionally, white selective memory about racial matters covers all of British popular culture (indeed, all of British life), including the aforementioned television series and books on British royalty. Compare acclaimed biographer Robert Hardman's criticisms of the Netflix series *The Crown* in his book about Elizabeth II, titled *Queen of the World*, to that of Yasir's or Carty-Williams's evaluations of the show. Hardman's critical assessment is limited to inaccurate storylines about the queen and her husband. He takes issue with the show's suggestion that the main incentive behind an official royal tour of Ghana in 1961 was personal inadequacies the monarch felt in comparison to the dazzling US first lady Jackie Kennedy.[27] Hardman appears oblivious to the more substantial racial issues that whitewashed shows like *The Crown* omit. For example, a former British colony, Ghana had gained independence just four years earlier in 1957.

A white racial framing of royal tours can be seen in a 1955 *Life* magazine article describing the queen's sister, Princess Margaret, who was visiting the British West Indies. She is depicted as "a gay and pretty 24-year-old girl who might have liked the glamor of a movie actress or the fun of ordinary life [moving] radiantly through the wearisome tasks of a working princess. She puts in 17-hour days. ... with every graceful gesture [she] was strengthening all the *warm, heartening little sentimentalities on which the empire rests*."[28] Of course, there is no space in this *Life* magazine story, with its sentimental musings on empire, for the brutal history of slavery in the still racially impoverished British West Indies. Ugly racist remnants of the British Empire are obscured in favor of a description of a self-sacrificing white princess who might rather be doing something glamorous or fun.

Also in 1955, the British Council of Churches and the Consultative Committee on Overseas Coloured Workers published a guide for white Britons in dealing with new Caribbean migrants to Britain. Numerous Anglican churches had closed their doors to these newcomers. The guide stresses the importance of "generosity" and "good will," but is paternalistic and white-framed. With its missionary slant, the black newcomers are rendered amiable but "childlike and naïve," while cultural differences between them and the "British people" (that is, whites) are underscored as related to skin color. On the issue of marriage, the white reader is asked to ponder how a "mixed race child" will be met by (white) society.[29]

Sociologist Jennifer Sims has more recently studied the perception of mixed-race people in the UK and the USA. Her analysis indicates that while there is some variation in how people of color, including mixed-raced individuals, experience racism in the two countries, the UK is certainly *not* a refuge from recurring white racism. UK mixed-race participants who identify as black-and-white describe treatment akin to that which Markle has faced as a result of her black ancestry. Whites everywhere mostly frame mixed-race people like Markle *as black*. And powerful whites have the ability to craft and impose racial identities, now for centuries, in both countries. The UK and the USA are both still strongly marked by many types of anti-blackness.[30]

Recall that fewer than 100 years ago, the British Crown ruled over a fifth of the earth's inhabitants. The white elite then emphasized racist notions of white British superiority and the inferiority of racialized others—as they often do now—and committed a myriad of violent atrocities against their colonial subjects. Such large-scale atrocities include those committed under the reign of Elizabeth II, who became queen in 1952. For example, there was the "Mau Uprising" (1952–1960) in Kenya against British rule, when colonial forces murdered many Indigenous Kenyans seeking freedom.

In *Imperial Reckoning: The Untold Story of Britain's Gulag in Kenya*, historian Caroline Elkins captures the inhumaneness, including torture and rape, and deception involved in British colonial rule in this East African nation. Her research demonstrates the power of the white-racist framing of British officials during the uprising. She underscores contradictions between mythical British notions of exporting democracy and the actual reality of anti-democratic British regimes in African countries that were undergirded by racially framed clichés of white civility, racial superiority, and ultranationalism. Notably, this gulag-type oppression took place a few years after thousands of Kenyans had fought alongside British soldiers in World War II. The inhumanity and oppression of an implemented white racial frame is seen in the fact that a mere seven years after the defeat of

Adolf Hitler and the horrors of the Holocaust were fully revealed, the British colonial government detained a half-million Kikuyu—that is, almost the entire population of Kenya's largest ethnic minority. Elkins's data, exposing this hidden history of empire, are disturbing, including her descriptions of brutal prisons and oppressive work camps where thousands of Kikuyu perished. This was a single-minded attempt by the white British elite to extinguish their quest for freedom and independence. Kenya finally gained independence in 1963. But it was not until 2013 that many of the colonial victims entered talks with the British government over a legal settlement, and 5,228 of them were set to receive payments totaling £19.9 million in British reparations.[31]

Significantly, historian Stephen Howe is among several white British historians who have criticized Elkins's account as "too inclined to place all blame for violence on the British, the settlers, and their [local] allies."[32] The language here suggests an unreflective white British framing of these horrific events. The British were *not* "the settlers," but colonizing white invaders—of course, as viewed by the Indigenous Africans who were invaded. The British inaugurated this colonial oppression and violence.

If ostensibly democratic countries like Britain are serious about ending systemic racism, whites the world over, including television show runners, filmmakers, royal biographers, historians, and even royals, must discontinue these roles as perpetrators or bystanders in the whitewashing of colonial and imperial histories. Bemoaning Elizabeth II's erroneous depiction regarding Jackie Kennedy, while ignoring the erasure of massive racist and colonial injustice, is a dramatic example of *collective forgetting*. Important for white Britons' perpetuation of systemic racism today is this sustained forgetting of harsh historical realities. Perpetuating racial oppression over the long term requires much collective disremembering and selective remembering, most of which abandons white responsibilities for past oppression and glorifies white achievements in line with whites' racial-group interests.[33] This is not a minor matter. The refusal of most white Britons, including many historians, to remember clearly and accept responsibility for a long and bloody past of racial oppression is harmful, including morally, to them as individuals and to society as a whole.

Early White Racial Framing: Rationalizing Slavery and Empire

Eighteenth-Century Racial Framing

Even a quick review of the centuries of British history reveals the racially oppressive actions that the dominant white racial frame rationalizes to the present day, including by means of white racial fetishization, amnesia, or denial. As we discuss in Chapter 1, this includes much historical mythmaking about British history. Let us consider a bit more of that history and its enduring white rationalizations and myths.

By the seventeenth and eighteenth centuries, the growing English slave trade and the barbaric exploitation of human beings on Caribbean sugar plantations were rationalized by early versions of the white racial frame. African-origin people were framed as innately inferior to white Europeans in most respects, including culturally, psychologically, ethically, and spiritually. And since they were commonly framed as uncivilized, un-Christian, and "subhuman savages," there could be no indignity or immorality in the barbarous slave trade. In other words, white racial framing did not steer English traders and merchants into the African slave trade, but their predatory capitalistic framing did so. Profits came first; legitimating white-racist framing came very soon after.

White Europeans' political and economic goals have been at the heart of systemic racism and this white-racist framing from the beginning. Take, for example, Barbados. First occupied by the British in 1627 and continuing as a British colony until full independence was granted in 1966, the small island on the eastern end of the Caribbean became one of the most vicious and lucrative slave systems in history. In effect, it was a Caribbean concentration camp where hundreds of thousands of enslaved Africans labored to make huge profits for British slaveowners, traders, and investors. About 5 percent of all victims of the Atlantic slave trade (approximately 600,000 Africans) arrived on the island in chains. As early as 1661, before slavery had taken full root in the USA, the colonial government there passed a law that described all "negroes" as treacherous thugs, who could be branded, whipped, and gelded like livestock. The law was later embraced by the British colonies in Jamaica and South Carolina.[34] As the scholar Paul Fryer explains, aggressive white-racist framing "emerged in the oral tradition in Barbados in the seventeenth century, and crystallized in print in Britain in the eighteenth, as the ideology of the plantocracy, the class of sugar-planters and slave-merchants that dominated England's Caribbean colonies."[35]

In the eighteenth century, one infamous British racist writer was Edward Long (1734–1813), a colonial administrator and historian born in the British Jamaican colony. In *The History of Jamaica* (1774), he more brashly and "scientifically" than anyone before him combined claims of black inferiority to the justification of slavery. For example, he vindicated enslavement with denigrating claims that "negroes" in the Americas possessed the same "bestial manners, stupidity and vices which debase their brethren" in Africa.[36] His brashness and so-called "scientific" claims came at an opportune time, giving a reputable white-framed shield and specious legitimacy to the growing slave trade and established slave plantations, which were starting to provoke significant disapproval and resistance at home.

As Fryer writes, Long's *History of Jamaica* influenced the way English whites understood black Africans, predisposing the former to see a parallel between the "human-like beasts of the 'dark' continent" and the region's purportedly "beast-like human beings." Similar to Long, other leading whites of the time, such as the celebrated Irish novelist and playwright Oliver Goldsmith (1728–1774), deemed the "black race" as unintelligent, lazy, and otherwise ill-behaved.[37] By the late eighteenth century, defending slavery from a white-racist framing had gained much traction in Britain.

Commencing in the 1770s, three key incidents—the British abolition movement and the French and the Haitian Revolutions—collectively transformed the British Atlantic Empire and slavery in the Caribbean. The abolition movement was early on spurred by a specific decision by an eminent British judge. In 1772, during the reign of George III, the British Lord Chief Justice William M. Mansfield ruled that enslavement of persons in England could not be upheld by British law, in a particular case involving an enslaved black man, James Somerset. Somerset had been purchased in the USA by the British customs officer Charles Stewart. When taken to England some years later, he managed to escape his slaveowner. Yet, he was apprehended and put on a ship headed to an overseas slave plantation. His family, working with abolitionists, applied for a writ of *habeas corpus*, which brought the matter to the highest British court. Lord Chief Justice Mansfield then set Somerset free.[38]

In spite of Mansfield's major decision in this particular case, for decades many black people continued to be enslaved in England and overseas. Still, the significance of the ruling cannot be overstated. Many other enslaved people were inspired by Somerset and demanded freedom. Some were successful; others were not. Not until 1833 were all freed from enslavement in Britain.[39]

The Mansfield ruling alarmed elite whites throughout the Empire, especially slaveholders and those in business with them. They feared a British legal or parliamentary decision that would interfere with or prohibit slavery, including in continental North America and the British West Indies. One important white elite was that in the American colonies, which included a large contingent of white slaveholders and other white men involved in the profitable slavery system (e.g., merchants and bankers). There, the substantial pro-slavery press published many commentaries seething against Mansfield's ruling. Articles and editorials cautioned American whites of the possibility that the British Parliament might ban slavery or otherwise interfere with it. Especially in the southern American colonies, those with huge slave populations, the ruling against enslavement was viewed as an escalation of British despotism.[40] Many in that white American elite soon sought their independence from Britain, a break motivated to some degree by their fear that slavery might be abolished there. In the case of Britain, that feared abolition decision did not come until 1833, during the reign of William IV (1830–1837), the king who had been an outspoken advocate for slavery earlier in his life.

In private papers and public proclamations the young Prince William (third son of George III, who would succeed his elder brother George IV as king) offered insight into the monarchy's position on slavery during this eighteenth-century age of revolutionary turmoil. In 1787, remarking on a visit to the Caribbean island of Dominica, the young prince observed in a letter to his father: "The trade in slaves at this island is very great owing to our supplying the French with that valuable commodity."[41] His positive view of colonial slavery would not change in the years ahead, despite gossip that he had been involved in sexual relationships with black women while on Navy duty in the Caribbean. He became an object of satirical cartoons, such as James Gillray's *Wouski* (1788). That image depicts the prince, then 22 and fully dressed, holding the hand of a black woman, with his other hand on her shoulder, as she lies between his legs.[42]

Regardless of the truth behind the caricature, when debates about the African slave trade intensified in the 1790s and early nineteenth century, Prince William—by then the Duke of Clarence—was an outspoken champion of colonial slavery. In 1799, in a widely reprinted pro-slavery speech in the House of Lords, he cited the enduring history of profitable European involvement in the African slave trade. Noting his firsthand observations of enslavement conditions in the Caribbean, he argued that abolitionists were miscalculating the consequences of the slave trade on Africa and Africans and distorting the handling of those enslaved in the British sugar colonies. Abolition, he reasoned, was radical and misguided and acutely destructive to Britain's continuing economic welfare. The duke's ardent defense of colonial slavery helped to postpone its abolition.[43]

Twelve years before William delivered this speech, Ottobah Cugoano, who was born in what is modern-day Ghana, became the first African British man to publicly demand the full abolition of slavery. Employed as a free black man in England, in 1787 he published a powerful contribution to the abolition campaign, titled *Thoughts and Sentiments on the Evil and Wicked Traffic of the Slavery and Commerce of the Human Species*. He was the earliest African British opponent of slavery to publish on abolition and the first to freely demand complete abolition—a stance that hardly any white opponent of slavery had taken by this time. He sent a copy to King George III and to the conservative philosopher-politician Edmund Burke. There is no confirmation that either man read Cugoano's words. If anything, it would appear that the top royals were generally against abolition of the slave trade, given William's broadly dispersed pro-slavery speech. And Edmund Burke, a prominent conservative Whig in Parliament, abandoned his previous effort to quash the slave trade for fear of Whig electoral losses in Parliament.[44]

Despite the royals' unequivocal or implied defenses of British colonial slavery over the course of George III's long reign (1760–1820), much racial change transpired across the Empire. The realm gained new territories and acquired a racial diversity of subjects as part of the 1763 Treaty of Paris, which marked the end of the Seven Years' War (1756–1763). King George III also lost his American colonies in 1783, following the American War of Independence. It was during his reign that the British slave trade was finally abolished in 1807.

Nineteenth-Century Racial Framing

Today, as in the past, white Britons often seem ignorant of the fact that Britain's communities of color have substantial internal distinctions of nationality, culture, religion, and language.[45] This has long been apparent, including when one considers the swift expansion of the British Empire in the nineteenth century. During this period, white academic publications claiming scientific variations among the "races" mushroomed, while elite whites fervently accepted the racial pecking order, with themselves at the white top.

The historian Bill Schwarz captures the enduring quality and impact of this literature, which was as concerned with race as it was with sovereignty. To coalesce the Anglo-British spirit through domestic and foreign policies, these scientific works included a populist impulse founded on a belief in the superiority of the white "race" (then known as English, British, Anglo-Irish, Caucasian, Teuton, or Anglo-Saxon). According to Schwarz, this racial-ethnic populism is well-represented in Charles Dilke's *Greater Britain* (1868), John Robert Seeley's *Expansion of England* (1883), and James Anthony Froude's *Oceana, or England and Her Colonies* (1886). All three major authors aimed to reimagine the character of the "English" or "British." Even though the elite had long expressed hope that English civilization could be established in foreign parts, it was not until the nineteenth century that "race" became a familiar and specific "arbiter of civilization." As Schwarz explains, the shared goal of scholars Dilke, Seeley, and Froude was to establish through their writings that their fellow subjects living at home in Britain could take part in the construction of a Greater Britain. This large "imagined community of the white empire" was, according to Schwarz, "more an ideological force-field, traversed by many contrary political currents, than a single political reality."[46]

In the twentieth century (especially the 1950s–1970s), decolonization had just as much an effect in the homeland as abroad. The immediacy of numerous new black migrants entering Britain triggered recollections of the former imperial era, especially memories of comprehensive white authority. "For the white man could only be a white man in relation to his others," wrote Schwarz, "his whiteness and his masculinity acquired meaning only in relation to those who had no claims, or lesser claims, to whiteness or to masculinity."[47] Note, again, how systemic racism is intertwined with the male dominance of systemic sexism.

In *Empire* a ground-breaking book in its critical and structural approach to British racism—women of color wrote scholarly essays on institutional sexism in this same era, including early black feminist resistance to it. Decades later, feminist scholar Gargi Bhattacharyya wrote that these women scholars had already positioned black feminism centrally.

> [T]his was an approach where analysis of the experiences of racism and sexism was essential to any understanding of workplace struggles, where feminism was central to the struggle but white feminism was critiqued for an ignorance and sometimes an antipathy to the concerns of black women, and where ideologies of idealised families and parallel

imaginings of gender and sexuality were identified as part of the repertoire of racist logic that informed state racisms.[48]

As we see it, sexism, like racism, is too frequently viewed by analysts as mainly involving a prejudiced perpetrator and a target. However, in the tradition of *Empire*, we believe sexism like racism cannot be reasonably understood in just an individualistic and interpersonal framework. These asymmetrical relationships are part of larger societal systems within which more powerful people repeatedly impose their interests and goals on those less powerful. At the heart of an analysis of institutional sexism, and thus of gendered racism, is also the *material* reality of highly gendered economic, political, and social exploitation.

Considering non-elite and less educated whites in Britain, note too the effects of the social psychological processes Schwarz describes above. For them, the dominant frame was transmitted via popular culture, including mainstream media, comic books, children's magazines, and advertisements. Through racist narratives there, protagonists of the British Empire regularly engaged in pro-white and anti-others framing.

The anti-black subframe was common in children's comics and magazines, serving to legitimize British colonialism on the African continent and white supremacy in Britain among schoolchildren. This framing included both verbal elements (terms) and visual images to communicate the anti-black subframe to white children and their parents. The transmission of the white racial frame is also distinctly seen in popular music of the time. That is, the anti-black framing includes racialized sounds. Scholar John Mullen has written about the popular minstrel shows and "coon" songs, similar to those in the USA. He illustrates that the parodied "black other" was intended as the "mirror image of the Victorian and Edwardian respectable gentleman and lady"—hence illustrating how black people could be depreciated and desired by whites simultaneously.[49]

Also in the nineteenth century, the famous author Charles Dickens (1812–1870), commonly applauded for his sympathies to disadvantaged social classes, perpetuated and popularized the dominant white-racist frame widely in his journalism and fiction. While he did not stand in the way of people of color or advocate for legal segregation or employment discrimination, he was enthusiastic in his belief in European male supremacy. He was contemptuous toward what he deemed "primitive" cultures. His notion of British virtue epitomized the historical pro-white center of the white frame. He prized white British nationalism and pilloried non-European cultures. In step with various racist views of his day, Dickens had the utmost hostility toward Indigenous peoples in the British colonies, including black Africans. The latter needed prompt civilization by white Europeans, he reasoned.[50]

In assessments of peoples of color almost all white British scientists and other intellectuals agreed with Dickens's white-supremacist views. By the mid-nineteenth century, the squashing of non-whites' freedom on various continents had been justified by widespread white framing of white superiority and virtuousness. The accent of white virtuousness is seen, for example, in the travel book of the relatively liberal Member of Parliament Charles Wentworth Dilke (1843–1911). In *Greater Britain: A Record of Travel in English-Speaking Countries* (1868), Dilke considers Britain superior despite what he deems archaic institutions like the monarchy and an oligarchic Parliament. As the scholar Peter Fryer explains, white men like Dilke portrayed the English future in the most glowing terms—Englishmen parading west towards "universal rule" and the "setting sun," with unparalleled "intelligence," and as the "only extirpating race on earth."[51]

Sir Edward Bulwer Lytton (1803–1873), an English writer and politician who served as secretary of state for the colonies, told British Members of Parliament in 1858 that their common interest was "to fulfill the mission of the Anglo-Saxon race, in spreading intelligence, freedom, and Christian faith wherever Providence gives us the dominion of the soil." Scottish essayist Thomas Carlyle (1795–1881) believed that the English had a duty to master half the globe or more. Influential capitalist Cecil Rhodes (1853–1902) thought similarly. He served as prime minister of the British Cape Colony, and famously remarked on his trek across South Africa: "I looked up at the sky and down at the earth and I said to myself this should be British." He further declared, "We are the first race in the world, and … the more of the world we inhabit the better it is for the human race."[52]

Later Prophets of British Imperialism: Race and Empire

No historical discussion of the British white racial frame and accompanying subframes would be complete without mention of famous diplomat and poet Rudyard Kipling's (1865–1936) racist and imperialist belief in the God-given right of white men to rule the world. His ill-reputed 1899 poem titled "The White Man's Burden: The United States and the Philippine Islands" illustrates well the dominant racial frame and its subframes. Written after the US victory in the Spanish–American War (1898), Kipling's dehumanizing and brutalizing sentiments about people of color there and elsewhere (whom he termed "sullen peoples, half devil and half child") were meant to relay to white America its duty to civilize non-white colonial subjects. "Burden" in the poem's title signifies Kipling's belief that white men everywhere are responsible for this task of cultural dominance and conversion.[53] An 1890s soap advertisement even used "White Man's Burden" to encourage white Britons to teach hygiene to colonial peoples in order to mimic purported white purity. The ad read: "The first step towards lightening 'The White Man's Burden' is through teaching the virtues of cleanliness. Pears' Soap is a potent factor in brightening the dark corners of the earth as civilization advances while amongst the cultured of all nations it holds the highest place."[54]

Kipling's style of white racial framing is still with us. A 2008 television commercial—a joint effort by the United Nations Children's Fund and Procter & Gamble, makers of Pampers—features a white woman being persuaded by women of color and their children to buy pampers in return for the company providing vaccines to non-Western children. The commercial was dubbed "white woman's burden" by the sociologist Lisa Wade, who noted this is a "fascinating example of the way in which white Westerners are seen as rescuing the rest of the world."[55]

According to George Orwell, Kipling was an early "prophet of British imperialism."[56] In *Burmese Days*, Orwell wrote of the relationship between the colonizer and the colonized, and the devastating effects of British colonialism on both. He challenged and problematized the dominant white frame of his day, including white men's imperial expansion, economic exploitation, and extraction of resources of non-white colonial subjects.[57]

How fitting then that Stuart Hall, a prominent black UK scholar known as the "godfather of multiculturalism," would much later remark: "I'm expected to speak for the entire black race on all questions theoretical, critical, etc. and sometimes for British politics, as well as for cultural studies. This is what is known as the *black person's burden*."[58] Hall further remarked on this black person's burden in an interview with a white journalist, telling him: "I am not a liberal Englishman like you. In the back of my head are things that can't be in the back of your head. That part of me comes from a plantation, when you owned me. I was brought up to understand you, I read your literature, I knew [your poem] 'Daffodils' [inspired by flowers in the English Lake District] by heart before I knew the name of a Jamaican flower. You don't lose that, it becomes stronger."[59] Notably, too, the "Daffodils" author was the conservative poet William Wordsworth, who himself insisted that "slavery is not in itself at all times and under all circumstances to be deplored."[60]

John MacKenzie's analysis of the effects of the British Empire's propaganda, including symbols of royalty, on various aspects of white popular culture helps us better understand this black man's burden. During the long imperial period, non-elite white Britons' lives, including their everyday consumption, were closely tied to the international trade and commercialization stemming from imperial Britain's many exploitive colonies. MacKenzie explains:

> The most aggressive and innovative advertisers of the day were companies dependent on the imperial economic nexus, in tea, chocolate, soaps, and oils, tobaccos, meat extracts, shipping and later rubber. They set out to illustrate not only a romantic view of imperial origins, a pride in national possession of what [leading imperialist British politician] Joseph Chamberlain called the imperial "estates," but also to identify themselves with *royal* and military events, to score from the contemporary cult of the personality.[61]

As sociologist Stuart Hall makes quite clear, white zeal for anti-black and anti-other framing did not die with the likes of Charles Dickens and

Rudyard Kipling. It still flourishes today. Despite lighter skin and what some have described as an ability to "pass as white," Markle regularly encounters similar anti-black perspectives. If Dickens and Kipling were to miraculously return to modern-day Britain, they would recognize much of the contemporary pro-white and anti-black framing Markle has faced, including the racist emotions lying behind it (e.g., white anger, hostility). In assessing the *white-virtuousness* material that is central to the contemporary racial framing of Markle, one finds much that has persisted over centuries. Whites as a group remain at the top of the racial hierarchy, while white racist views, values, and framing remain fully and centrally normative in the UK.

Evidence of this persistence was unmistakable in 2012 when, upon arriving on the Pacific island of Tuvalu—an independent nation within the Commonwealth—William and Kate were carried by local men of color from their plane on a double-throne. Writing uncritically, a reporter for *The Telegraph* describes the dramatic scene as such:

> The couple looked delighted when 25 men in traditional Polynesian dress emerged with the home-made double throne, on which they were carried to a tribal hall on the main island of the group for a raucous welcoming ceremony. ... Garlands of flowers were placed on the heads of the Duke and Duchess, like crowns, before the couple began a tour of the main island.[62]

Significantly, the white racial framing and complicity of royals in such racially symbolic acts usually does not register in the white-dominated press. Reporters are more likely to write about other *so-called* controversies, such as when Kate "wore wedges" or "bought the same dress twice."[63] Such British mainstream press coverage often averts attention away from the clear evidence of systemic racism and the remnants of racialized empire.

The only critical reaction we could find to such photos was an online contest launched by *OkayAfrica*, spotlighting a different royal tour, when the couple were also carried on thrones by people of color. The critical competition was actually titled "Prince William & 'The Savages' Photo Caption Contest." This digital media platform, dedicated to African culture, music, and politics, asked its readers to "caption this racist photo of Prince William being carried on a throne by Africans." Next to the picture of William, *OkayAfrica* placed a cartoon of the titular protagonist of *The Adventures of Tintin* also being carried on a throne by Africans. The white Belgian cartoonist Georges Remi created this well-known, racially stereotyped comic series in 1929. It is still published today and has spawned an animated television series and several films. These productions have been broadly denounced in recent years, including by Britain's Commission for Racial Equality, for their racially stereotyped simianization of Africans and other white-racist framing.[64] That *OkayAfrica* could so compellingly link the two images speaks volumes about the royal family's white-privilege mindset and its insincere commitment to a multiracial Commonwealth of Nations. That in 2019 the *Tintin* comic was still being called "one of Belgium's great gifts to the children of the world" says much about how globally dominant the white racial frame and its anti-black subframe still are.[65]

Anti-Black Framing

We next detail a large array of mainstream media and social media accounts that demonstrate the nature of the aggressive anti-black framing directed at Markle. We need to emphasize the point, documented here and throughout this book, that many whites relish such racist commentaries and performances. Disturbingly, they obtain pleasure from gendered-racist jokes and other anti-black humor. That is, the racial targeting of the Duchess of Sussex and her son are unmistakably a source of racialized "fun" for many whites.

Animalistic and Related Imagery

During her first post-engagement interview alongside Harry, which was streamed on a live video app, the words "Jungle fever," "gold digger," "biracial commoner," "whitest black girl," and "unsuitable" flashed on the screen—all comments from viewers.[66] On the same day, a hostile Twitter user tweeted: "The tribe [referencing a British writer with African heritage] is already trying to use Prince Harry's engagement to erase British identity."[67] These views are in keeping with the strong emotions (e.g., anger, resentment) that have since accompanied the dominant racial framing of Markle.

Racially framed views of black Britons are regularly used, refurbished, and passed along in white social networks, often from one generation to the next. These networks are fundamental to the operation of systemic racism, today as in the past. A great many whites still view black people in terms of old racist stereotypes (e.g., unintelligent, lazy, criminal). Among the outrageous stereotypes and images found within the anti-black subframe of the white racial frame are simian slurs and other negative animalistic imagery. As for why the white frame has long associated animals, especially simians, with people of African descent, we should consider the elite English scientist Charles Darwin (1809–1882).

In his influential writings, Darwin applies the evolutionary idea of natural selection to human "races." In spite of his path-breaking ideas about evolution, he did not escape the crude racist framing common then among influential white scientists. In the 1874 edition of his book *The Descent of Man*, he insists that Africans' and Australian Aborigines' consanguinity is much closer to apes than are the other "races of man." He asserts that "at some future period, not very distant as measured by centuries, the civilized races of man will almost certainly exterminate and replace throughout the world the savage races."[68] Darwin is describing a hierarchy from the so-called civilized (white) races to what he deems the "savage races" (black and brown peoples).

By the late 1800s, white pseudoscientists, promoting *social Darwinism*, were arguing that racially inferior races were less evolved and more ape-like than superior white races. Elite social scientists like the Briton Herbert Spencer and the American William Graham Sumner were aggressive white-racist framers, arguing broadly that social life is a life-and-death struggle in which the best individuals will win out over their inferiors. Spencer (1820–1903), an influential classical liberal of the Victorian era, coined the term "survival of the fittest." He argued that to fathom the minds of primitive races, the civilized races needed to look at the minds of their own children. He claimed the primitive races had permanently infantile intellects, unlike those of children in the civilized races.[69] For Spencer and other social Darwinists, wealthy whites were the virtuous products of natural selection and essential to the advancement of civilization.

By the late nineteenth century, an influential, racialized, and politicized *eugenics* movement was spreading among elite white scientists and other intellectuals in Britain. These eugenicists, almost all white men, accented the importance of breeding the right (that is, white) types of human groups. Francis Galton, a leading British physical scientist and cousin of Darwin, argued for improving the so-called superior white race by vigorous human intervention. Galton invented the term eugenics, and he and others of this racist bent argued that allowing the unfit races to survive would destroy the superior race and civilization so grandly cultivated by northern Europeans. In Britain, the USA, Canada, and other white-dominant countries, many elite whites concluded that those from the so-called lesser non-white races should be sterilized or excluded from immigration. These and similar versions of the dominant racial frame were regularly supported by influential white scientists, politicians, and business leaders. This racist eugenics framing has persisted to the present day.[70]

Perhaps most important about this old white racial framing is what it tells us about the minds of powerful white decision-makers across several eras, those whose racial (and class and gender) framing of society has greatly shaped their important societal decisions—and thus the minds and lives of white and non-white Britons. The present and future shape of British society is still substantially in the hands of people (mostly men) like these. The eugenics perspective remains a central part of this common white framing, such as in whites' political views of non-white immigrants to the UK as somehow inferior, contaminating, or unfit.

Consider too that the average British citizen would not have read the elite scientific journals or had access to this racialized scholarship in the nineteenth century, yet popular culture was playing a decisive role in propagating Darwinist and Galtonian ideas, including strong anti-black framing. There were the books *King Solomon's Mines* and *She* by English author H. Rider Haggard (1856–1925). This adventure fiction was set in so-called exotic locales, mainly in Africa. In the nineteenth and twentieth centuries, white English schoolboys were often trained to think of black people by means of popular books, such as the adventure stories of George Alfred Henty (1832–1902). Henty, the most widely read author of boys' adventures in Britain prior to World War I, sold more than 25 million copies of his books in the postwar era. His books were still selling 50 years after his death. Still later, Art Robinson (1942–), a conservative Republican nominee for the US House of Representatives, marketed Henty's virulently racist 1884 novel *By Sheer Pluck: A Tale of the Ashanti War* through his Christian home-schooling curriculum in the USA. As late as 2010, Robinson's Home Schooling Curriculum website made this claim about Henty's books: "American young people should read not a few Henty books, but all 99 of them." Operating out of an extreme white-supremacist version of the white racial frame, in *By Sheer Pluck* Henty wrote that:

> the intelligence of an average negro is about equal to that of a European child of ten years old. A few, a very few, go beyond this, but these are exceptions. … Living among white men, their imitative faculties enable them to acquire a considerable amount of civilization. Left alone to their own devices they retrograde into a state little above their native savagery.[71]

Sociologists Les Back and John Solomos have explained what is going on in such influential examples of popular literature.

> We need to remember that most Victorians had no personal contact with the "exotic" peoples and places that they were assuming responsibility for. Their opinions were formed according to the sources of their information, and these sources were for the most part the popular press and literature. The linkages between colonialism and racism became evident throughout the late nineteenth and early twentieth centuries in the form of the articulation between nationalism and patriotism in the construction of the very definition of "Englishness" and "Britishness."[72]

This popular racist framing has persisted, for children and adults. Later influential English writers, such as children's author Enid Blyton (1897–1968), continued to spread the white racial frame, with its positive framing of whites as virtuous and negative framing of black people as unvirtuous, to yet more generations of children. Her books are unmistakably racist and xenophobic, as well as sexist and otherwise elitist. With more than 600 million copies sold and translated into at least 90 languages today, her white-racist and imperialistic thinking has been passed to innumerable children across the globe. In her 1965 book *The Little Black Doll*, a doll named "Sambo" (a derogatory term for a person with African or Indigenous heritage) is despised by the child who owns him and by other toys due to his purported "ugly black face." Shockingly illustrating the anti-black subframe, Sambo runs away, only to return (to a now welcoming) home after the rain changes his face from black to white.[73]

Over 25 years earlier, in 1939, Agatha Christie's mystery novel *Ten Little Niggers*, named after the very racist US minstrel song, had been published. On the eve of war with the Nazis, this still-esteemed white author and her white publisher thought it acceptable to use the racist N-word as a literary device. This says much about how white Britons positively viewed their racist empire, as opposed to how they negatively saw German imperialism. An understanding of these influential white writers' enduring legacies, together with the legacies of other racist books for children and adults, is central to understanding systemic racism in Britain today.

Significantly, it was not until 2020 that the title of the French version of Christie's mystery novel was changed from *Dix Petits Negres* to *Ils Etaient Dix (They Were Ten)*. The French word "negre," the rough equivalent of the English N-word, appeared 74 times in the book. In 2020, it was replaced with the word "soldat" or "soldier"; additionally, "Ile du Negre" where the murder mystery occurs is now titled "Ile du Soldat" ("Soldier Island"). The change has not been met with universal support in France. The white journalist François Busnel called the alteration "absurd," and the daily morning newspaper *Le Figaro* called it "another triumph for political correctness."[74] Powerful and ordinary whites in France, too, often operate out of an obvious or inconspicuous white racial framing.

This white racial framing, whose escalation such prominent examples sketch, has been fundamental to the lived realities of ordinary white and black people in Britain and beyond for centuries. Some might consider these racist books irrelevant and from a bygone era, but they are still read and, more importantly, the white-racist framing these influential white writers helped to spread throughout the world has persisted in contemporary books and other media presentations. The global impact is quite important. Blyton's story of black Sambo brings to mind a recent advertisement by a Chinese cosmetics company (Leishang), one illustrating the worldwide reach of the white racial frame. The ad includes a black man who is forced to eat a pouch of Qiaobi cleaning liquid. He is then shoved into a washing machine by a smiling Chinese woman. At the end of the spin cycle, the woman opens the machine to find a light-skinned Chinese man. As the man emerges, he flashes a smile to the viewer before the company's motto appears: "Change begins with Qiaobi." People of color can also operate out of elements of the white racial frame, and those that do often maintain their performances are not racist. In this case, a Leishang representative, speaking for top corporate management, asserted that the foreign media was "too sensitive" in negatively reacting to the ad and that the company had "never thought about the issue of racism." This naïve remark suggests how deeply imbedded white-created, anti-black framing now is, even in Asia.[75]

In the same year that Markle started dating Harry, the sentiment behind the story of black Sambo had taken this new form in the Qiaobi advertisement. And roughly a decade before she, a mixed-race woman with African heritage, married into the British royal family and before her son was born, the hyper-racist Enid Blyton had been voted Britain's best-loved author. One commentator has raised perhaps the most important question about the influential Blyton—i.e., who is still buying her millions of racist books? An equally significant point was raised by Amnesty International, reporting that only 7 percent of children's books published in the UK in one recent year featured positive characters of color.[76] Given the global reach and enduring dominance of the white racial frame, is it any wonder that Markle and her son Archie have been targets of abhorrent animalistic and other racist imagery from both elite white and ordinary white sources?

Characteristically, animalistic imagery is accompanied by joking. Clearly, this is an attempt on the part of whites to veil their racist framing. An example relating to Archie involves the prominent BBC radio broad-caster Danny Baker. He was fired after tweeting a photo of a human couple, each holding the hand of a chimpanzee, with the heading, "Royal baby leaves hospital." The chimpanzee was of course meant to represent then-newly born Archie. Baker had brought the harsh simian framing of black-descended people, customarily reserved for whites-only backstage "joking," to the public multiracial frontstage. Following significant pushback, he deleted the tweet, initially referring to it as a "gag." He said he had not considered the racist undertones of the "joke" because his mind is "not diseased." His purported ignorance is impossible to believe. After all, to understand the "joke," one must understand the long-standing white simianization of black people.[77] In contrast, he had not said the same thing about Prince George, Princess Charlotte, or Prince Louis, the children of William and Kate, all of whom were born before Archie and all of whom are white. Baker had not said the same thing about the queen's other *white* great-grandchildren—all born prior to the arrival of Archie.

Given that the British royal family is an historically all-white insti-tution, and that Markle has received scrutiny because she has African heritage, Baker's white-virtue defenses are quite unacceptable.[78] As one Twitter user put it: "Sadly there are so many posts that equate ... Markle with a 'Monkey' or an 'Ape' that it's inconceivable how ... Baker thought portraying a mixed race baby as a chimpanzee was fine! ... [W]e can't pre-tend this vile racism doesn't exist." This particular Twitter user pointed to other posts, such as those titled "Prince Harry Marries Half Ape Meghan Markle" and "Planet of the Apes: Meghan Markle Births First African Royal."[79] Significantly, too, this Twitter user was met with such distain for calling out Baker that he felt compelled to issue follow-up tweets. The first addition read in part: "I really am at a loss [as to] why so many people are supporting Danny Baker."[80] A second read: "I've taught kids who've been called 'Monkeys' or had 'ohh' noises made at them & the fact someone with 500,000 followers [Baker] thinks that's cool hit a nerve with me. Given his interest in football surely he was aware of racist chants?"[81] This critical Twitter commentator is correct. To throw bananas in front of black sportspeople is a frequent racist provocation in the UK and across Europe today. The practice is so rampant that Harry's brother, William, who is president of the Football Association, has condemned it. William has cited recent abuse endured by footballers like a black Belgian player who had monkey chants directed at him.[82]

Consider another example of simian-related racial slurs, this one involving the Duchess of Sussex's actions when she visited a charity that helps street sex workers. She wrote messages such as "you are strong" and "you are special" on bananas that were part of packed lunches for the women. Her act of kindness drew vile racist backlash. She was, for example, dubbed the "banana baroness," photoshopped eating a banana with the words "you're a sucksess" written on the image, and compared to a monkey.[83] White-racist commentaries stereotyping and imaging Markle and her son as simian-like are easy to locate, including on all major social media sites. For instance, a photo of the duchess with black South African children during an official royal tour in 2019, posted to the couple's official Instagram page, included a one-word reply, "Monkey," followed by two smiling emojis.[84] Then there are a few of the numerous racist lines that the celebrity Jo Marney texted to a male friend some weeks before beginning a dating relationship with the leader of the UK Independence Party (UKIP), an arch-conservative political party: "[Markle is] obsessed with race. And her seed [will] taint our royal family. Just a dumb little commoner. Tiny brain. She's black. This is Britain, not Africa."[85] Expectedly, in a systemically racist UK, a mixed-race duchess and her son have become targets of the dominant white racial frame. Repeated negative characterizations of Markle and Archie activate and reinforce many whites' broad negative framing of black people and other people of color.

We would be remiss not to point out that such racist characterizations are reminiscent of the still-common stereotyping and imaging of US President Barack Obama (2009–2017) and his family. As a case in point, a major white female county development official in the USA slammed Michelle Obama as "an ape in heels" in a Facebook comment. This statement was also praised by the white mayor of a local city and other white commentators online.[86]

The Duchess of Sussex has been targeted by white racial framing in the USA as well. Twitter permanently suspended US Republican congressional candidate Paul Nehlen for a racist post about Markle. The self-avowed "pro-white" politician took the couple's official engagement photo and an image of Cheddar Man, a dark-skinned, blue-eyed Mesolithic man thought to be one of the first modern people to inhabit Britain, and superimposed the man's face on Markle's face. Nehlen captioned his tweet, "Honey does this tie make my face look pale?"[87] As documented throughout this book, many whites seek significant gratification, amusement, and pleasure from engaging in white-framed, anti-other racist performances.

When called out for their racist performances, most whites fervently maintain they are not racist. Danny Baker is a case in point. Jo Marney is too. When her male friend called her out for being racist during their texting, Marney replied: "Not wanting other races and cultures to invade your own culture doesn't mean I hate their race. Just means I don't want their cultures invading mine."[88] The frequency of such racist performances directed at Markle and her son; the emotional amusement, entertainment, and enjoyment whites get from it; and the vehemently self-justifying and self-protective reactions by whites when they are called out for such acts exposes the mental, emotional, and social depth of Britain's systemic racism in what is frequently purported to be a colorblind society.

Criminality

Simianizing stereotypes merge with other emotionally loaded stereotypes and images, including those alleging black criminality, in whites' racial framing. Animalistic imagery has long justified whites' targeting of blacks for discrimination, including when they come into contact with the police. Researchers have concluded that whites' visual and verbal dehumanization of blacks as ape-like assists the process by which the latter become targets of "cruelty, social degradation, and state-sanctioned violence."[89]

Allegations of black criminality are also part of the white racial framing that Markle has had to endure. In 2016, following the disclosure that she was dating Harry, the conservative *Daily Mail* ran a story titled, "Harry's Girl is (Almost) Straight Outta Compton: Gang-Scarred Home of her Mother Revealed—So Will He be Dropping By for Tea?" The subsequent text included the following:

> Prince Harry's new girl *Suits* star Meghan Markle is from Crenshaw, LA.
>   Crenshaw has endured 47 crimes in the past week—including murder.
>   Gangs, including the Bloods, count the neighborhood as their territory.
>   Markle' social worker mom, Doria Ragland, lives in the run-down area.
>   And the actress's aunt, Ava Burrow, is in nearby gang-afflicted Inglewood.[90]

Notably, what the ignorant white reporter falsely refers to as "Crenshaw" is the View Park-Windsor Hills neighborhood. It is an affluent and pre-dominantly African American community. The home of Doria Ragland— Markle's mother—is located in the hills above the Crenshaw area.[91] The *Daily Mail* also mentions the supposedly "gang-scarred" neighborhood where Ragland lives, but not her master's degree in social work or that she is a clinical therapist. Such thorough white-racist framing was common-place in this early period of Markle's relationship with Harry.[92]

Gendered Racism

The white racial frame's negative portrayals of women of color and men of color share many parallels but are not transposable. We see this when considering gendered-racist depictions of Markle. The white-male-controlled media remains central to the dissemination of this negative framing. In 2019, for instance, the BBC network aired a comedy segment titled *Meghan Markle's Royal Sparkle*, written and performed by a black woman, who later defended it. The segment presented a 3D digital animation of the duchess that critics panned as racist and otherwise disrespectful. In the segment, the animated version of the duchess attempts to resume her television career. She begins by taking questions from fans. When asked what makes her angry, she mentions the time her sister-in-law Kate Middleton borrowed her hairbrush. "I say no because that's gross, and then I leave my room and come back ... and I can tell she's used my hairbrush anyway because it's covered in skanky hair that's going grey and I say, 'Stay the f*** out of my trailer or I'll cut you, Kate.'" The animated duchess also lambastes a fan by accusing her of "trying to lay claim to my man."[93] As one commentator put it, the "caricature of Meghan not only darkened her skin tone dramatically, but also spoke incredibly crudely, which has some people accusing the show of trying to perpetuate negative stereotypes about black women."[94]

Recall Chapter 1's discussion of how the pro-white and anti-black subframes often work in unison to problematize women of color, including by promoting the angry-black-woman stereotype. Here again, we witness this form of *jungle book theme*: a cartoon Duchess of Sussex with darker skin and with a caricatured urban accent threatens to knife the Duchess of Cambridge (white Kate). In this latter imagery we again observe the criminality stereotype that is important in common versions of whites' anti-black framing. The mock black-language accent is also a major way to mark people of color as "other" (i.e., not like white Britons).[95]

From their lived experience, black women have advanced well-defined systems of knowledge that are key to understanding gendered racism. One early and famous analyst of the intersections of racism, classism, and sexism is Angela Y. Davis, a US scholar-activist. In her work she assesses how enslaved black women are exploited for their productive labor as workers and their reproductive labor in creating enslaved children. These black women endure gendered racial oppression. Philomena Essed, a scholar of color renowned for introducing the concepts of *everyday racism* and *gendered racism* in Europe, brilliantly documents how in modern societies black women's encounters with discrimination are routinely gendered. Essed's work has been applied in a series of countries, including the UK. Yet another trailblazing social scientist, US sociologist Patricia Hill Collins, demonstrates how a formidable black feminist counter-frame rejects and analyzes numerous detrimental stereotypes of black women. White-generated stereotypes include the docile mammy, domineering matriarch, promiscuous prostitute, and negligent welfare mother. Such gendered-racist framings of black women, some of which are applied to yet other women of color, endure because they are promoted by white-dominated mainstream media and thereby generate more white discrimination. In their research on black women, researchers like Davis, Essed, and Collins—as well as Elizabeth Higginbotham, Yanick

St. Jean, and Adia Harvey Wingfield—regularly emphasize the importance of emancipating women of color from racial, gender, and gendered-racist stereotypes and discrimination.[96]

An early British analyst of the intersections of racism, classism, and sexism is Claudia Jones, who was persecuted for communist activities in the USA and deported to the UK in 1955. Her 1949 article in *Political Affairs* titled "An End to the Neglect of the Problems of the Negro Woman!" showcases what would later be known as intersectionality (see Chapter 5). From her Marxist perspective, she observes:

> The capitalists know, far better than many progressives ... that once Negro women begin to take action, the militancy of the whole Negro people, and thus of the anti-imperialist coalition, is greatly enhanced. ... As mother, as Negro, and as worker, the Negro woman fights against the wiping out of the Negro family, against the Jim Crow ghetto existence which destroys the health, morale, and very life of millions of her sisters, brothers, and children. Viewed in this light, it is not accidental that the American bourgeoisie has intensified its oppression, not only of the Negro people in general, but of Negro women in particular.[97]

Turning to current British women scholars who have pioneered in the area of gendered racism, we should note Heidi Mizra, one of the UK's first black female professors. Through the post-colonial feminist approaches that Mirza adopts, one comes to more fully understand the continuing power of British colonialism as it appears in the production and reproduction of contemporary marginalized, racialized, and gendered British social worlds. As with the aforementioned US scholars, using an intersectional approach, Mirza studies the intricacies of black female marginality, wherein race, class, and gender are theorized as lived and interlinking realities. Recently tweeting that "Black on black is the only way to build our capacity in academia as white establishment has wantonly not [delivered] with equality and diversity," she continues the fight for parity and freedom for Britons of color.[98]

Black women authors seeking popular audiences have also contributed to an increase in writings dealing with racist and gendered-racist realities in Britain. For example, Reni Eddo-Lodge's *Why I'm No Longer Talking to White People About Race* (2017) was the first book by a black British author to take the top spot on Nielsen Book's weekly bestseller chart. She has recently underscored that her "work stands on the shoulders of so many black British literary giants—Bernadine Evaristo, Benjamin Zephaniah, Zadie Smith, Andrea Levy, Stella Dadzie, Stuart Hall, Linton K Johnson, Jackie Kay, Gary Younge."[99]

Cultural Decline

For many in the large anti-Markle camp, she symbolizes cultural decline. Akin to large-scale immigration to Britain, she threatens the British people and their culture—i.e., whites and white culture. A recurring theme in the tabloids, and among hordes of critics on social media, is the corrupting effect she purportedly has had on the entire royal family, especially on Harry. In keeping with framing Markle as a symbol of cultural decline, there is the prevalent hashtag #Megxit. It was used by her detractors on social media before she and Harry stepped down as senior royals and the tabloids adopted this portmanteau to denote the couple's move to North America. A cruel take on Brexit, it conveyed a strong desire for Markle to leave the UK, which she soon did. Within the first six weeks of 2019—a year before the couple announced they were stepping down as senior royals—approximately 3.5 million online users were exposed to #Megxit. The #Megxit conversation was primarily motivated by women, with about 75 percent of gender-categorized authors using the negative hashtag actually registering as female. Its strongest use originated from users based in the USA, followed by Canada, and then the UK. While some who tweeted #Megxit did so to convey displeasure with its message, accompanying hashtags suggested that a majority tweeting it were not fans of the duchess.[100]

In 2019, CNN examined 5,000 tweets incorporating anti-Markle hashtags. They found that just 20 Twitter accounts were driving 70 percent of the negative coverage. While the media giant could not determine how many people were behind the accounts, they concluded it was not just automated bots because the tweets appeared to be mostly personalized.[101]

A senior researcher at Hope Not Hate, a UK advocacy group that campaigns against racism and fascism, has explained how the duchess "fits into this bigger idea of the West and the UK in decline."

> She does that by not fitting in, by being who she is, which is mixed race. [White] People tie these things ... to what they think it means to be British, which is white. ... [I]t has a racial element to it. But there's also this idea of cultural decline—what we were before, a strong palace, a monarchy, an empire ... is falling apart, and that of course is brought on by these other far-right conspiratorial ideas, like what mass immigration is doing with our society, the replacement of British people of British culture.[102]

In keeping with the idea of cultural decline, in 2019 an individual calling herself "Gifted Welsh" (based in Wales) started a change.org petition titled, "Stop UK Funding for Meghan Markle & Prince Harry's Lifestyle." Gifted Welsh alleged that Markle "has shown little or no understanding of British culture, traditions or history. ... [S]he recently accused British universities of racism by not hiring enough black people and even called eminent professors 'Male Pale and Stale.'"[103]

The reference to "Male Pale and Stale" concerns Markle's response to UK professors being predominantly white men (68 percent). About 23 percent are white women; approximately 6.5 percent are black and minority ethnic

(BME) men; and roughly 2 percent are BME women.[104] Upon seeing these figures, when visiting the Association of Commonwealth Universities, of which she was patron, Markle had actually said: "Oh my god. ... This is quite a shock to see and clearly we have some way to go."[105] She never uttered the words *male, pale, and stale*, at least not publicly. Rather, the white-controlled mainstream media have linked this phrase to the progressive "Decolonising the Curriculum" campaign currently active in Britain.[106] The *Daily Mail*, for example, actually had a writer describe the campaign as challenging "the legacies of the empire and racism on campuses" and promoting "black and female thinkers instead of 'male, pale and stale' ones."[107] Generally, the mainstream media, like many UK university administrations, have failed to understand the importance of this democratizing campaign. In addition to advocating for "more black and non-Western scholars" on student reading lists, it also contends that reforms must deal with diversifying the current pedagogy that is often "rooted in imperial and colonial ideas about knowledge and learning, at an institutional level." Predictably, this progressive campaign is contentious, indeed with only a fifth of British universities currently committed to restructuring their academic curriculums with attention to these important diversifying and democratizing matters.[108]

Here, again, we observe a strong white racial framing of Markle. Her racial perceptiveness and black heritage make her doubly foreign and threatening. As Yomi Adegoke, author of *Slay in Your Lane: The Black Girl Bible*, has said, the Duchess of Sussex is an alien deviation from what most whites think of when they think of the British royal family today. The aforementioned change.org petition, likely started by a conservative white person, illustrates once more how the dominant racial frame gives rise to related frames or subframes, including in this case those that are gender-oriented.[109]

White Spaces and Double-Standards

Markle courts controversy and scorn simply by occupying what the dominant racial frame considers privileged *white spaces*, including when she served as guest editor for a 2019 issue of British *Vogue*. In contrast, Harry guest-edited *The Today Programme*, an early-morning BBC news programme, on several occasions without drawing ire. He was even applauded for his interview with Barack Obama. Notably, three of *The Today Programme*'s four regular hosts are white like Harry. In contrast, the editor of *Vogue*, responsible for Markle's gig there, is Edward Enninful, who is black. Prince Charles's two-time guest editorship of *Country Life*, the "quintessential English magazine" with its wealthy white readership, was also commended. Kate Middleton's one-day stint as guest editor of the UK's *Huffington Post* came with plenty of praise for her dedication to children's health issues, and rightly so. But when assuming the guest editorship of *Vogue*, Markle was admonished for the edition's (modest) focus on racial diversity and labeled anti-white. Recall, from Chapter 1, that Camilla Tominey, editor of *The Telegraph*, accused Markle of reverse-racism and sexism for selecting only five white women to feature among a total of 15 female "forces for change." For the cover, Markle selected the women, mostly models and actors, but also the Nigerian writer Chimamanda Ngozi Adichie and New Zealand Prime Minister Jacinda Ardern, the latter having received international praise for her response to violent white-supremacist attacks on mosques in her country.[110]

The type of criticism Markle faced afterwards involved time-honored tropes aimed at people of color who enter important white spaces without seeking the approval of whites, or who revel in their own non-white heritage. *Vogue* editor Enninful and the duchess have much in common. He is a gay Ghanaian immigrant to the UK and the first non-white (and male) editor in the magazine's 103-year history; she is American-born and the first mixed-race senior member of the British royal family. Markle and Enninful court controversy by just ontologically *being*, and especially by occupying what the dominant racial frame considers privileged white spaces. Even the announcement that Markle would guest-edit the *Vogue* issue incited backlash, including some maliciously racist media op-eds.[111]

To be sure, there are valid reasons to criticize the collaboration between the Duchess of Sussex and *Vogue*. While noting that Markle displayed "moments of genuine radicalism" in her work as guest editor, the journalist Helen Lewis captured her personal discomfort with the collaboration, writing that it "reveals not only the limits [Markle] must grapple with—all British royals are expected to remain studiously apolitical—but also the contradictions of today's social-justice movements, which often preach radical change while being embraced by corporations. It is inevitably jarring to nestle feminist advocacy among ads for $2,800 dresses." Lewis clarifies she is not trivializing Markle's progressive intent or the significance of diversity issues considered in the magazine. Rather, she explains: "Increasing the visibility of women of color is a social good by itself, and under Enninful, *Vogue* has consistently challenged the racism of the fashion industry. But there are sharp limits on the activism of royals."[112]

The duchess herself somewhat recognized the paradox of which Lewis wrote. "There is one caveat for you to remember: this is a magazine," Markle noted. "It's still a business, after all. I share that to manage expectations for you: there will be advertising sections that are requisite for every issue, so while I feel confident that you'll feel my thumbprint on most pages, please know that there are elements that just come with the territory." Still, argues Lewis, because of the expectation that royals remain apolitical, "Markle can talk about marginalized women who struggle to find clothes for job interviews [in her royal patronage with a British organization offering unemployed women job interviews and wardrobe assistance] … but she cannot address the causes of poverty."[113]

Whether Markle and Harry will fully address the systemic nature of racial, gender, and class injustices now that the shackles of the royal family's allegedly apolitical stance are removed remains to be seen. But there is some reason to hope. There were the duchess's recent comments on the Black Lives Matter movement. In Harry's interview with anthropologist Jane Goodall for the *Vogue* issue that the duchess edited, he included a discussion of unconscious bias leading to racist actions, though not of blatant or systemic racism. However, more recently he has uttered the phrases *systemic racism* and *institutional racism*.

Conclusion

The overall white racial frame and its subframes are ubiquitous in all Western and many other societies across the globe. They operate in expected and unexpected ways, while significantly shaping UK and global society, now over centuries of time. In the numerous examples of racist and gendered-racist framing of the Duchess of Sussex, we witness verbal elements of the prevailing racial frame, constantly connected to graphic visual imagery and impassioned verbal sentiments. Some of the imagery and sentiments are easily recognizable, while others become more noticeable if we first consider the racialized actions of white people over the long course of British history. Throughout this history there is a distinctive predacious longing for material wealth, which is a main stimulus for whites' racist actions and framing.

Intensely anti-black actions have also often involved a visceral animosity, what US social scientist Joel Kovel calls the everyday "madness" of white racism. In his sociopsychological examination of *fear*, also a dominant white sentiment, Kovel argues that many whites reject black bodies because they project their own racial fears, typically rooted in childhood, into the murky abnormality of a black individual reified as a threat to whites. In one's youth, argues Kovel, most whites are socialized to see blacks as unclean, treacherous, unknowing, and/or strange.[114] This anti-black framing is generated and supported by more than childhood socialization. That framing has a lifetime of reinforcements in a long series of interactions in white networks. Family and friendship networks pressure members to think and act in line with their collective racial framing. Within these networks, frequent repetition of racist understandings of many kinds, together with related racist emotions and inclinations, keeps them strong and circulating over long periods of time.

As an object of white animosity, blacks and other people of color are routinely "othered." As racialized others, they become for most whites the common "they" or "you people"—as opposed to "us" or "us people"—and are thus relegated to inferior status and otherwise negatively differentiated. In everyday practice, white-racist framing and its resulting nefarious deeds require a major interruption of affirmative human sentiments, such as empathy, compassion, sympathy, mercy, and commiseration. Destroying positive feelings and reactions, especially empathy, appears to be essential to forming a broad and durable system of white racial oppression.

Even white Britons with access to much contrary socio-racial information frequently appear to act, knowingly or involuntarily, out of an unsophisticated version of the white racial frame and its corresponding subframes, including by accenting white virtuousness and the glories of empire. It is usually Britons of color—and not whites—who recognzie that the royal family would not exist today (at least in its current form), or have vast wealth, if not for centuries of bloody colonialist and imperialist actions across the globe. For example, Elizabeth II's great-great-grandmother Queen Victoria was made Empress of India by an Act of Parliament in Britain, justifying bloody British government control over what had been the Mughal Empire, which had governed most of India and Pakistan previously. Even when India and Pakistan gained full independence in 1947, the title of Emperor of India was not relinquished by George VI, Elizabeth II's father, until a year later.[115]

Britain has long embodied and implemented the white racial frame, with the royal family benefitting immensely from it. While Markle's entry into the royal family and the birth of her son are undeniably salient for their impact on British society and the Commonwealth of Nations, the romanticized view of a post-racial Britain, as we show throughout this book, is very much out of touch with the everyday realities of continuing and systemic racial hostility and discrimination in the UK.

Notes

1 Communications Secretary, "Statement by the Communications Secretary to Prince Harry," *The Royal Household*, November 6, 2016, www.royal.uk/statement-communications-secretary-prince-harry. Accessed April 29, 2019.
2 Tim Teeman, "British Women in Parliament Send Letter of 'Solidarity' to Meghan Markle in her Fight against U.K. Media," the *Daily Beast*, October 29, 2019, www.thedailybeast.com/british-women-in-parliament-stand-in-solidarity-with-meghan-markle-in-her-fight-against-uk-media. Accessed November 8, 2019.
3 Danica Kirka, "Duchess of Sussex Calls 1ˢᵗ Year of Marriage Difficult," *Associated Press*, October 21, 2019, https://apnews.com/da2af3150df044799b b592fd756025f8. Accessed November 9, 2019.
4 Hannah Furness, "Meghan Markle Privacy Claim: *Mail On Sunday* Publisher Wins First High Court Skirmish," *The Telegraph*, May 1, 2020, www.telegraph.co.uk/royal-family/2020/05/01/meghan-markle-vs-mos-duchess-sussex-high-court-case-suing-mail/. Accessed May 21, 2020.
5 Tim Rhydderch, "'British Tabloids Will Ruin Your Life': Confronting Racism in the Portrayal of Meghan Markle," *The McGill International Review*, September 26, 2020, www.mironline.ca/british-tabloids-will-ruin-your-life-confronting-racism-in-the-portrayal-of-meghan-markle/. Accessed October 12, 2020.
6 Caroline Davies, "Meghan Wins Privacy Case against *Mail on Sunday*," *The Guardian*, February 11, 2021. https://www.theguardian.com/uk-news/2021/feb/11/meghan-markle-father-duchess-sussex-mail-on-sunday-wins. Accessed February 14, 2021.
7 Stephanie Eckardt, "Meghan Markle's Mom and Oprah Hung Out for Six Hours, Reportedly Planning a Tell-All Interview on Racism," *W Magazine*,

May 7, 2018, www.wmagazine.com/story/meghan-markle-mom-doria-ragland-oprah-winfrey-racism-interview. Accessed on November 9, 2019.

8 Martha Ross, "The Meghan Markle Bridezilla Report: Tiara Demand Annoyed Queen Elizabeth," *The Mercury News*, November 9, 2018, www.mercurynews.com/2018/11/09/the-meghan-markle-bridezilla-report-tiara-demand-annoys-queen-elizabeth/. Accessed November 16, 2019; Jack Royston, "Meghan Made Kate Cry," *The Sun*, November 28, 2018, www.thesun.co.uk/fabulous/7839296/meghan-markle-kate-middleton-cry-princess-charlotte-royal-wedding-dress/. Accessed November 16, 2019; Yomi Adegoke, "What the Meghan Markle Rumors Say about Britain and the World," *The Washington Post*, February 8, 2019, www.washingtonpost.com/opinions/2019/02/08/what-meghan-catherine-feud-narrative-says-about-britain-world/?utm_term=.723d0a42a7b0. Accessed June 9, 2019.

9 Meg Hanson, "Meghan Markle Targeted in Racist, Sexist, Classist Reporting," *Pop Dust*, n.d., www.popdust.com/meghan-markle-press-2640834758.html. Accessed November 11, 2019.

10 Sarah Taylor, "CNN Gets Taken to the Woodshed after Asking 'How Black Will the Royal Baby Be?' *The Blaze*, May 7, 2019, www.theblaze.com/news/cnn-gets-taken-to-the-woodshed-after-asking-how-black-will-the-royal-baby-be. Accessed November 9, 2019.

11 Laura Hanrahan, "People are Blaming Meghan Markle for Her and Prince Harry's Decisions to Step Back from Royal Duties," *Woman's Day*, January 9, 2020, www.womansday.com/life/entertainment/a30456972/prince-harry-meghan-markle-leaving-royal-family-reaction/. Accessed May 3, 2020.

12 Tanya Gold, "Meghan Markle is the Duchess the Royal Family Needs," *The New York Times*, May 6, 2019, www.nytimes.com/2019/05/06/opinion/royal-baby-meghan-markle.html. Accessed June 12, 2019.

13 Jack Royston, "Meghan Markle Black Lives Matter Speech Supported by Majority of U.K.—Poll," *Newsweek*, July 26, 2020, www.newsweek.com/meghan-markle-black-lives-matter-support-british-poll-1513532. Accessed August 8, 2020.

14 Catriona Harvey-Jenner, "Donald Trump Just Responded to Meghan and Harry's Voting Plea with a Harsh Swipe," *Cosmopolitan*, September 24, 2020, www.cosmopolitan.com/uk/reports/a34138875/donald-trump-meghan-markle-insult/. Accessed October 12, 2020.

15 See Patricia Hill Collins, *Black Feminist Thought: Knowledge, Consciousness, and the Politics of Empowerment* (Boston, MA: Unwin Hyman, 1990); Joe R. Feagin and Hernán Vera, *White Racism: The Basics* (New York: Routledge, 1995); Eduardo Bonilla-Silva, "Rethinking Racism: Toward a Structural Interpretation," *American Sociological Review*, 62 (June 1997), pp. 465–480; the scholars in Richard Delgado and Jean Stefancic (eds), *White Studies: Looking Behind The Mirror* (Philadelphia, PA: Temple University Press, 1997); Joe R. Feagin, *Systemic Racism: A Theory of Oppression* (New York: Routledge, 2006).

16 For a discussion of this work, see Heidi Safia Mirza, "Plotting a History: Black and Postcolonial Feminisms in 'New Times,'" *Race Ethnicity and Education*, 12 (1) (February 2009). DOI: 10.1080/13613320802650899.

17 Claire Alexander, "STUART HALL AND 'RACE,'" *Cultural Studies*, 23(4) (2009), p. 469.

18 Anna Julia Cooper, *The Voice of Anna Julia Cooper*, eds Charles Lemert and Esme Bhan (Lanham, MD: Rowman & Littlefield, 1998); Ida B. Wells-Barnett, *A Red Record* (Chicago, IL: Donohue and Henneberry, 1895).

19 HRH Prince Harry, Duke of Sussex, "Statement by His Royal Highness Prince Harry, Duke of Sussex," *Sussex Official*, October 1, 2019, https://sussexofficial. uk/. Accessed November 10, 2019.
20 Hanson, "Meghan Markle Targeted."
21 HRH Prince Harry, Duke of Sussex, "Statement by His Royal Highness."
22 Rami Yasir, "The Depraved Violence of Britain's 'Subtle' Racism," *Intersectional Feminist Media*, August 9, 2019, https://wearyourvoicemag.com/race/britain-violence-of-british-racism. Accessed November 10, 2019.
23 Afua Hirsch, "Why a Royal Meghan Markle Matters," *Time*, May 17, 2018, http://time.com/5281096/meghan-markle-multicultural-britain/.   Accessed June 6, 2019.
24 Christopher Wilson, "The Scandalous Truth about *Downton Abbey*'s Royal Gigolo 'Jack Ross,'" *The Telegraph*, October 14, 2013, www.telegraph.co.uk/culture/tvandradio/downton-abbey/10377794/The-scandalous-truth-about-Downton-Abbeys-royal-gigolo-Jack-Ross.html. Accessed May 21, 2020.
25 *Ibid.*; Angela Cobbinah, "Leslie 'Hutch' Hutchinson: Scandal in the Wind," *Camden New Journal*, October 25, 2018, http://camdennewjournal.com/article/leslie-hutch-hutchinson-scandal-in-the-wind. Accessed May 18, 2020; Michael Thornton, "The Royal Gigolo: Edwina Mountbatten Sued over Claims of an Affair with Black Singer Paul Robeson. But the Truth was Even More Outrageous," *Daily Mail*, November 14, 2008, www.dailymail.co.uk/femail/article-1085883/The-royal-gigolo-Edwina-Mountbatten-sued-claims-affair-black-singer-Paul-Robeson-But-truth-outrageous-.html. Accessed May 18, 2020.
26 Communications Secretary, "Statement by the Communications Secretary."
27 Robert Hardman, *Queen of the World* (London: Century, 2018), p. 137.
28 "A Working Princess on the Road," *Life Magazine*, 38(8) (February 1955). Italics added.
29 Wilfred Easton, *Your Neighbour From The West Indies* (London: British Council of Churches: Churches Together in Britain and Ireland, 1955).
30 Rachel Hatzipanagos, "Royalty, Social Class Could Not Shield Meghan from Racism in Britain," *The Washington Post*, January 16, 2020, www.washingtonpost.com/nation/2020/01/16/meghan-obama-class-race/. Accessed February 16, 2020.
31 Caroline Elkins, *Imperial Reckoning: The Untold Story of Britain's Gulag in Kenya* (New York: Holt Paperbacks, 2005); Ian Cobain and Jessica Hatcher, "Kenyan Mau Mau Victims in Talks with UK Government over Legal Settlement," *The Guardian*, May 5, 2013, www.theguardian.com/world/2013/may/05/mau-mau-victims-kenya-settlement. Accessed November 12, 2019; BBC News Staff, "Mau Mau Torture Victims to Receive Compensation—Hague," *BBC News*, June 6, 2013, www.bbc.co.uk/news/uk-22790037. Accessed November 12, 2019.
32 Stephen Howe, "Colonising and Exterminating? Memories of Imperial Violence in Britain and France," *Histoire@Politique*, 11(2) (2010), p. 12.
33 For more on collective forgetting, see Feagin, *Systemic Racism*.
34 J.M. Opal, "The Resilience of Barbados Counters Trump's 'Sh-thole' Remarks," *The Conversation*, November 13, 2018, https://theconversation.com/the-resilience-of-barbados-counters-trumps-sh-thole-remarks-106902. Accessed December 9, 2019.
35 Peter Fryer, *Staying Power: The History of Black People in Britain* (London: Pluto Press, Kindle Edition), pp. 136–137.
36 As cited by Wilson Armistead, *A Tribute for the Negro: Being a Vindication of the Moral, Intellectual, and Religious…1848* (London: William Irwin, 1848), p. 35.

37 Fryer, *Staying Power*, p. 164.
38 Joey La Neve DeFrancesco, "The American Counterrevolution," *Commune*, July 4, 2019, https://communemag.com/the-american-counterrevolution/. Accessed December 10, 2019.
39 *Ibid.*
40 *Ibid.*
41 GEO/MAIN/44732–44735, "Prince William to His Majesty King George III," written aboard *HMS Pegasus* in the English Harbour, January 7, 1787, https://georgianpapers.com/2019/01/21/uncovering-royal-perspectives-on-slavery-empire-and-the-rights-of-colonial-subjects/. Accessed August 19, 2020.
42 Jim Sherry, "Wouski," www.james-gillray.org/pop/wouski.html. Accessed December 9, 2019.
43 Thomas Clarkson, *The History of the Rise, Progress, and Accomplishment of the Abolition of the African Slave-Trade by the British Parliament*, vol. 2 (London: L. Taylor, 1808), https://oll.libertyfund.org/titles/clarkson-the-history-of-the-abolition-of-the-african-slave-trade-vol-2. Accessed December 9, 2019.
44 Fryer, *Staying Power*, pp. 102–105.
45 Paul Gilroy, *Small Acts: Thoughts on the Politics of Black Cultures* (London: Serpents Tail, 1993), p. 54.
46 Bill Schwarz, *Memories of Empire, Volume I: The White Man's World* (Oxford: Oxford University Press, 2011), pp. 71, 397–398.
47 *Ibid.*, pp. 11, 20–21.
48 Gargi Bhattacharyya, "Rereading *The Empire Strikes Back*," *Ethnic and Racial Studies*, 37 (10) (2014), p. 1805.
49 John Mullen, "Antiblack Racism in British Popular Music (1880–1920)," *Revue Française De Civilisation Britannique*, XVII-2 (2012), pp. 61–80.
50 David Scott Kastan, *Oxford Encyclopedia of English Literature*, vol. 1 (Oxford: Oxford University Press, 2006), p. 157; Sally Ledger and Holly Ferneaux, *Dickens in Context* (Cambridge: Cambridge University Press, 2011), pp. 297–299.
51 Peter Fryer, *Staying Power*, pp. 184–185.
52 *Ibid.*, pp. 184–187.
53 Rudyard Kipling, "The White Man's Burden" (1899), www.shmoop.com/white-mans-burden/poem-text.html. Accessed November 10, 2019.
54 Lisa Wade, "Colonialism, Soap, and the Cleansing Metaphor," *Sociological Images*, August 10, 2010, https://thesocietypages.org/socimages/2010/08/10/colonialism-soap-and-the-cleansing-metaphor/. Accessed May 21, 2020.
55 Lisa Wade, "The White Woman's Burden," *Sociological Images*, June 13, 2014, https://thesocietypages.org/socimages/2014/06/13/the-white-womans-burden/. Accessed August 21, 2020.
56 Camilla Turner, "Rudyard Kipling's 'If' Poem Scrubbed off Wall by Students Who Claim He was a 'Racist,'" *The Telegraph*, July 18, 2018, www.telegraph.co.uk/education/2018/07/18/rudyard-kiplings-poem-scrubbed-wall-students-claim-hewas-racist/. Accessed November 11, 2019.
57 Isam M. Shihada, "Racism in George Orwell's *Burmese Days*," *The IUP Journal of English Studies*, 9(3) (September 2014), pp. 80–99.
58 Stuart Jeffries, "Stuart Hall's Cultural Legacy: Britain under the Microscope," *The Guardian*, February 10, 2014, www.theguardian.com/education/2014/feb/10/stuart-hall-cultural-legacy-britain-godfather-multiculturalism. Accessed May 17, 2020. Italics added.

59 Tim Adams, "Cultural Hallmark," *The Guardian*, September 23, 2007, www.theguardian.com/society/2007/sep/23/communities.politicsphilosophy andsociety. Accessed May 17, 2020.

60 *The Letters of William and Dorothy Wordsworth: The Later Years*, Vol. 2., ed. Ernest De Selincourt (London: Clarendon Press, 1939), p. 648.

61 John MacKenzie, *Propaganda and Empire: The Manipulation of British Public Opinion, 1880–1960* (Manchester: Manchester University Press, 1988), p. 16. Italics added.

62 Gordon Rayner, "Duke and Duchess Carried on Thrones in Tuvalu," *The Telegraph*, September 18, 2012, www.telegraph.co.uk/news/worldnews/ australiaandthepacific/tuvalu/9549814/Duke-and-Duchess-carried-on-thrones-in-Tuvalu.html. Accessed August 9, 2020.

63 Alex Warner and Bianca Rodriguez, "Kate Middleton's Most Controversial Moments," *Marie Claire*, July 30, 2020, www.marieclaire.com/culture/ g19599018/kate-middleton-most-controversial-moments/?slide=1. Accessed August 9, 2020.

64 Vanessa Wruble, "FOH: Prince William & "The Savages" Photo Caption Contest," *OkayAfrica*, September 20, 2012, www.okayafrica.com/prince-william-racist-photo-africans-tintin/. Accessed August 20, 2020; Bruno Waterfield, "Racism Row Overshadows 90th Birthday Edition of Tintin's Congo Adventure," *The Times*, January 11, 2019, www.thetimes.co.uk/art-icle/racism-row-overshadow-s-90th-birthday-edition-of-tintin-s-congo-adventure-2j2jbqplv. Accessed August 20, 2020.

65 Paul Aleixo, "Tintin: As the Eternal Youth Turns 90, He's Still Teaching Children about the World," *The Conversation*, January 9, 2019, https:// theconversation.com/tintin-as-the-eternal-youth-turns-90-hes-still-teaching-children-about-the-world-109533. Accessed August 30, 2020.

66 Hanson, "Meghan Markle Targeted."

67 @westland_will, Twitter, November 27, 2017, https://twitter.com/ westland_will/status/935233411903471616?ref_src=twsrc%5Etfw% 7Ctwcamp%5Etweetembed%7Ctwterm%5E935233411903471616 &ref_url=https%3A%2F%2Fgraziadaily.co.uk%2Fcelebrity%2Fnew s%2Fmeghan-markle-racism-twitter%2F. Accessed November 11, 2019.

68 Charles Darwin, *The Descent of Man, and Selection in Relation to Sex*, 2nd edn (London: John Murray, 1874), p. 154.

69 Peter Fryer, *Staying Power*, pp. 182–183.

70 John Higham, *Strangers In The Land* (New York: Atheneum, 1963), pp. 96–152; William H. Tucker, *The Science and Politics of Racial Research* (Urbana, IL: University of Illinois Press, 1994), p. 35ff.

71 Troutfishing, "Viciously Racist Book Sold by GOP Candidate for the 4th Congressional District," *Daily Kos*, June 29, 2010, www.dailykos.com/stories/ 2010/6/29/880205/-. Accessed December 9, 2019.

72 Les Back and John Solomos (eds), *Theories of Race and Racism: A Reader*, 1st edn (New York: Routledge, 2000), p. 14.

73 Robert Druce, *This Day Our Daily Fictions: An Enquiry into the Multi-Million Bestseller Status of Enid Blyton and Ian Fleming* (Amsterdam: Editions Rodopi, 1992).

74 Agence France-Presse (AFP) Staff, "N-Word Dropped from French Edition of Agatha Christie Novel," *France24*, August 26, 2020, www.france24.com/ en/20200826-n-word-dropped-from-french-edition-of-agatha-christie-novel. Accessed August 30, 2020.

75 Emma Graham-Harrison, "Black Man is Washed Whiter in China's Racist Detergent Advert," *The Guardian*, May 28, 2016, www.theguardian. com/world/2016/may/28/china-racist-detergent-advert-outrage.   Accessed November 17, 2019.

76 Ceri Radford, "Enid Blyton 50 Years On: Let's Be More Critical about Books Venerated in the Past," *The Independent*, November 27, 2018, www.independent. co.uk/arts-entertainment/books/features/enid-blyton-50-years-anniversary-death-legacy-childrens-books-author-a8648281.html.   Accessed November 11, 2019; @AmnestyUK, Twitter, October 30, 2019, https://twitter.com/ AmnestyUK/status/1189571160394096642. Accessed November 17, 2019.

77 Kara Fox, "BBC Radio Presenter Fired over Racist Royal Baby Tweet," *CNN*, May 9, 2019, www.msn.com/en-ca/lifestyle/lifestyleroyals/bbc-radio-presenter-fired-over-racist-royal-baby-tweet/ar-AAB8gML.   Accessed   June 8, 2019.

78 Micha Frazer-Carroll, "Baby Archie's First Race Row May Be a Taste of Things to Come," *The Guardian*, May 9, 2019, www.theguardian.com/commentisfree/ 2019/may/09/royal-baby-archie-british-racism. Accessed June 9, 2018.

79 @Jim_Sheridan, Twitter, May 9, 2019, https://twitter.com/Jim_Sheridan/ status/1126471807714897920. Accessed November 9, 2019.

80 @Jim_Sheridan, Twitter, May 9, 2019, https://twitter.com/Jim_Sheridan/ status/1126474665474625360. Accessed November 9, 2019.

81 @Jim_Sheridan, Twitter, May 9, 2019, https://twitter.com/Jim_Sheridan/ status/1126477501579038720. Accessed November 9, 2019.

82 Hannah Furness, "Duke Of Cambridge 'Fed Up' with 'Outrageous' Racism in Football as he Vows to 'Do Something About It,'" *The Telegraph*, September 6, 2019, www.telegraph.co.uk/royal-family/2019/09/06/prince-william-fed-outrageous-racism-football-vows-do-something/.   Accessed   November   10, 2019; Tom Jacobs, "Studies Expose 'Apelike' Stereotype among Whites," *Pacific Standard*, June 1, 2018, https://psmag.com/social-justice/studies-expose-apelike-stereotype-among-whites-20708. Accessed November 11, 2019.

83 Emily Mee, "The Trolling of Meghan," *Sky News*, n.d., https://news.sky.com/ story/trolling-of-meghan-how-duchess-is-abused-over-race-and-pregnancy-11696606. Accessed June 9, 2019.

84 @SierraBo22, Twitter, October 18, 2019, https://twitter.com/SierraBo22/ status/1185199851430121472. Accessed November 9, 2019.

85 Glen Owen, "'Meghan's Seed Will Taint Our Royal Family': UKIP Chief's Glamour Model Lover, 25, is Suspended From the Party over Racist Texts about Prince Harry's Wife-To-Be," *Daily Mail*, January 13, 2018, www.dailymail. co.uk/news/article-5266657/Ukip-leaders-girlfriends-racist-Meghan-Markle-messages.html. Accessed November 11, 2019.

86 Clarence Page, "Michelle Obama's Burden—And Ours," *Chicago Tribune*, July 26, 2016, www.chicagotribune.com/news/opinion/page/ct-michelle-obama-racism-perspec-0727–20170726-story.html. Accessed November 11, 2019; see also Mia Moody, "New Media-Same Stereotypes: An Analysis of Social Media Depictions of President Barack Obama and Michelle Obama," *The Journal of New Media & Culture*, 8 (Summer 2012), www.ibiblio.org/nmediac/ summer2012/Articles/obama_facebook.html. Accessed November 11, 2019.

87 Emily Sullivan, "Twitter Bans GOP Contender for Racist Tweet Targeting Meghan Markle," *NPR*, February 13, 2018, www.npr.org/sections/thetwo-way/2018/02/13/585339969/twitter-bans-gop-contender-for-racist-tweet-targeting-meghan-markle. Accessed November 11, 2019.

88 Owen, "Meghan's Seed."

89 Kayla Hounsell, "'There's No Shortage of Negative Things': Pregnant Meghan Faces Online Bullying," *CBC News*, March 1, 2019, www.cbc. ca/news/world/meghan-markle-duchess-of-sussex-faces-online-bullying-1.5037143. Accessed June 17, 2019.

90 Ruth Styles, "EXCLUSIVE: Harry's Girl is (Almost) Straight Outta Compton: Gang-Scarred Home of Her Mother Revealed—So Will He be Dropping by for Tea?," *Daily Mail*, November 2, 2016, www.dailymail.co.uk/news/article-3896180/Prince-Harry-s-girlfriend-actress-Meghan-Markles.html. Accessed April 29, 2019.

91 Sandi Rankaduwa, "Meghan Markle is the Future of a Monarchy with Racist Baggage," *BuzzFeed*, November 30, 2017, www.buzzfeednews.com/article/sandirankaduwa/itsamodernmarkle. Accessed November 11, 2019; Regan Morris, "'Meghan Who?' LA Shrugs over Harry's Hometown Girlfriend," *BBC News*, www.bbc.com/news/world-us-canada-41391607. Accessed November 11, 2019.

92 Saada Branker, "We Get it British Press—Meghan Markle is Biracial," *CBC*, November 20, 2016, www.cbc.ca/news/opinion/meghan-and-harry-1.3857742. Accessed April 30, 2019.

93 Blue Telusma, "BBC Slammed for 'Racist' & 'Disrespectful' Cartoon of Meghan Markle," *The Grio*, June 25, 2019, https://thegrio.com/2019/06/25/bbc-racist-cartoon-of-meghan-markle. Accessed November 10, 2019.

94 Rae Batchelor, "BBC's 'Racist' and 'Disrespectful; Cartoon of Meghan Markle Faces Heavy Backlash," *Diply*, June 26, 2019, https://crafty.diply.com/61196/bbcs-racist-and-disrespectful-cartoon-of-meghan-markle-faces-hea. Accessed November 10, 2019.

95 Anne-Marie O'Connor, "Opinion: Meghan Markle vs. the Tabloid Mob," *Los Angeles Times*, October 4, 2019, www.latimes.com/opinion/story/2019–10–04/meghan-markle-prince-harry-royals-tabloid-racism. Accessed November 11, 2019.

96 Angela Davis, "Reflections on the Black Woman's Role in the Community of Slaves," *Black Scholar*, 3 (December 1971), pp. 2–15; Philomena Essed, *Understanding Everyday Racism* (Newbury Park, CA: Sage, 1991); Patricia Hill Collins, *Black Feminist Thought: Knowledge, Consciousness, and the Politics of Empowerment* (Boston, MA: Unwin Hyman, 1990); Elizabeth Higginbotham, *Too Much To Ask: Black Women in the Era of Integration* (Chapel Hill, NC: University of North Carolina Press, 2001); and Yanick St. Jean and Joe R. Feagin, *Double Burden: Black Women and Everyday Racism* (New York: M.E. Sharpe, 1998).

97 Claudia Jones, "An End to the Neglect of the Problems of the Negro Woman!" Reprinted from *Political Affairs*, June 1949, pp. 3–4.

98 @HeidiMirza, Twitter, November 14, 2019, https://twitter.com/heidimirza?lang=en. Accessed November 17, 2019.

99 @renireni, Twitter, June 16, 2019, https://twitter.com/renireni/status/12729 14087949844480. Accessed August 9, 2020.

100 CNN Staff, "Racist Online Abuse of Meghan Markle Puts Royal Staff on High Alert," *CNN*, March 7, 2019, https://wtop.com/europe/2019/03/racist-online-abuse-of-meghan-markle-puts-royal-staff-on-high-alert/. Accessed June 20, 2019; Hounsell, "'There's No Shortage of Negative Things.'"

101 NPR Staff, "Inside The Racist Online Attacks on Meghan Markle," *NPR*, March 10, 2019, www.npr.org/2019/03/10/701987112/inside-the-racist-online-attacks-on-meghan-markle. Accessed November 11, 2019.

102 Max Foster and Hilary McGann, "The Racist Online Abuse of Meghan has Put Royal Staff on High Alert," *CNN*, March 8, 2019, https://edition.cnn.com/2019/03/07/uk/meghan-kate-social-media-gbr-intl/index.html. Accessed June 8, 2019.

103 Gifted Welsh, "Stop UK Funding for Meghan Markle & Prince Harry's Lifestyle," *change.org*, www.change.org/p/uk-parliament-stop-uk-funding-for-meghan-markle-prince-harry-s-lifestyle. Accessed November 16, 2019.

104 Leigh Mcmanus, "Meghan Markle Backs Campaign to 'Decolonise the Curriculum' by Adding More Black Women to University Staff Instead of 'Male, Pale, and Stale' Professors in her First Political Intervention since Joining the Royal Family," *Daily Mail*, February 17, 2012, www.dailymail.co.uk/news/article-6713833/Meghan-Markle-backs-campaign-decolonise-curriculum-UK-universities.html. Accessed August 21, 2020; Tobi Oredein, "Meghan Markle is Right, British Universities are Pale, Male and Stale," *Grazia*, February 20, 2019, https://graziadaily.co.uk/life/in-the-news/meghan-markle-british-education/. Accessed August 21, 2020.

105 Scobie and Durand, *Finding Freedom*, p. 264.

106 Oredein, "Meghan Markle is Right."

107 Mcmanus, "Meghan Markle Backs Campaign."

108 David Batty, "Only a Fifth of UK Universities Say they are 'Decolonising' Curriculum," *The Guardian*, June 11, 2020, www.theguardian.com/us-news/2020/jun/11/only-fifth-of-uk-universities-have-said-they-will-decolonise-curriculum. Accessed August 21, 2020.

109 CNN Newsource Staff, "Online Abuse of Meghan Markle"; @YankeeWally, Twitter, https://twitter.com/YankeeWally. Accessed November 16, 2019.

110 BBC News Staff, "Prince Harry Edits Radio 4's *Today*: Obama And Charles Interviewed," *BBC News*, December 27, 2017, www.bbc.com/news/uk-42488837. Accessed November 11, 2019; Emine Saner, "Country Life's Editor: 'We'll Be the Last Magazine on the Last News-Stand,'" *The Guardian*, November 17, 2013, www.theguardian.com/media/2013/nov/17/country-life-editor-prince-charles. Accessed November 11, 2019; *Country Life* Staff, "A Look Inside HRH The Prince of Wales' Guest-Edited Issue of *Country Life*," *Country Life*, November 14, 2018, www.countrylife.co.uk/country-life/prince-wales-guest-edit-188725. Accessed November 11, 2019; *Hello!* Staff, "Kate Middleton Turns Editor for a Day for the Huffington Post," *Hello!*, February 17, 2016, https://ca.hellomagazine.com/royalty/2016021768956/kate-middleton-guest-editor-huffington-post-uk/. Accessed November 11, 2019; Rebecca Mead, "Prince Harry and Meghan Markle's Fractured Fairy Tale," the *New Yorker*, April 20, 2020, www.newyorker.com/magazine/2020/04/20/prince-harry-and-meghan-markles-fractured-fairy-tale. Accessed April 29, 2020; Helen Lewis, "The Issue with Meghan Markle's *Vogue* Issue," *The Atlantic*, August 2, 2019, www.theatlantic.com/international/archive/2019/08/meghan-markle-vogue-radical-royalty/595288/. Accessed November 11, 2019.

111 Afua Hirsch, "Vogue's Edward Enninful: 'Was the Criticism of Meghan Markle Racist? Some of It, Yes,'" *The Guardian*, September 21, 2019,

www.theguardian.com/fashion/2019/sep/21/edward-enninful-vogue-meghan-markle-criticism-racist?utm_term=Autofeed&CMP=twt_gu&utm_medium=&utm_source=Twitter&CMP=aff_1432&utm_content=The+Independent&awc=5795_1570047331_ea0b85ac96958a191489674b5ab361d0#Echobox=1569054598. Accessed November 11, 2019.
112 Lewis, "The Issue with Meghan Markle's *Vogue* Issue."
113 *Ibid.*
114 Joel Kovel, *White Racism: A Psychohistory* (New York: Columbia University Press, 1984), pp. xl; xli–xlvii. See also Joe R. Feagin, Hernán Vera, and Pinar Batur, *White Racism, The Basics*, 2nd edn (New York: Routledge), pp. 1–33.
115 *The Royal Household* © Crown, "Victoria (r. 1837–1901)," www.royal.uk/queen-victoria. Accessed November 10, 2019; *The London Gazette*, 1948, Issue 38330, p. 3647 www.thegazette.co.uk/London/issue/38330/page/3647. Accessed November 10, 2019.

3 Post-Racial Duchess or Trophy Wife of Diversity?

Introduction

Despite customary declarations to the contrary by elite whites such as former UK Prime Minister John Major, various British ambassadors, and members of the royal household, the British queen and her family do *not* currently possess a universal appeal. People of color throughout the former Empire and the Commonwealth of Nations, and some whites too, have long questioned and laid bare the systemically racist foundations on which the monarchy rests.[1] As we show throughout this book, many critics also argue that the monarchy is anti-democratic and a feudal vestige that embodies and underpins modern-day class inequality, while promoting "phonily apolitical" conservatism. The British journalist and Labour Party political aide Seumas Milne explains.

> As things now stand, Britain (along with 15 other former island colonies and white settler states) has now chosen its next three heads of state—or rather, they have been selected by accident of aristocratic birth. The descendants of warlords, robber barons, invaders and German princelings—so long as they aren't Catholics—have automatic pride of place at the pinnacle of Britain's constitution.[2]

In spite of this reality, a recent survey found that 70 percent of the British public, which is majority-white, is in favor of the current monarchy, while two-thirds regard the former British Empire positively.[3] Celebrated British author Candice Carty-Williams, who is of Jamaican and Indian descent, has remarked that the "royal family don't stand for us." Growing up in the UK in the 1980s, the monarchy made the author Afua Hirsch, who like Meghan Markle is mixed-race with a black mother, feel excluded and painfully aware of her "visible otherness."[4] The scholar Kehindre Andrews refers to the royal family as an enduring symbol of whiteness, empire, pure bloodlines, and colonialism.[5] For these women, as for countless other people of color, an almost exclusively white royal family has served to reinforce the view that Britishness and whiteness are one and the same.

All of this serves as a harrowing reminder of how deeply entrenched the royal family is in the white racial frame and its subframes, and begs the question of whether celebrating Markle is akin to idealizing the long overdue and superficial embrace of people of color into institutions that have historically harmed, subjugated, and exploited them racially and in other terms. Sri Lankan Canadian writer Sandi Rankaduwa has captured well the strains people of color experience when it comes to simultaneously praising royals, including Markle's entry into the royal family, and reconciling the role monarchy plays in perpetuating systemic racism historically and contemporarily. Some of Rankaduwa's ancestors were colonial subjects in the British Colony of Ceylon (now the Commonwealth nation Sri Lanka) and died at the hands of the British during uprisings against colonialism. Still, a close family member adored Elizabeth II and Diana, Princess of Wales.[6]

In this chapter, we explore the framing of Markle as a trophy of diversity, someone to whom both elite and non-elite whites can point as proof of the alleged end of racism within the UK. We show how this portrayal of her and of the British context obscures the white-racist policies and laws white Britons generally, even enthusiastically, support.

A Post-Racial Duchess?

As Britons readied for the May 2018 wedding of Markle and Harry, many white commentators, including royal historian Ted Powell, believed it hard to exaggerate the implications of a biracial woman, and one reveling in her diverse heritage, joining the royal family. Powell was encouraged by the wedding. After all, it occurred in the face of Brexit, controversies over immigration by people of color, and the infamous 2018 Windrush scandal, in which many (mostly Caribbean) immigrants of color who had come to Britain decades before were denied their current legal rights, unlawfully harassed, and deported.[7] In stark contrast to Powell, commentators of color largely argued that Markle could not possibly have the kind of major positive influence on the UK that some white folks were forecasting.[8] Two years later, after the couple stepped down as senior royals, headlines again suggested they could work miracles—this time, successfully combatting the legacy of colonialism, including through their Archewell charity.[9]

Personification of a Post-Racial Duchess via Her Family Tree

Markle's great-great-great-great grandmother was born into slavery in the USA and worked as a laborer following emancipation from slavery. According to genealogists, who tend to exaggerate, the Duchess of Sussex's ancestors also include immigrants from 1860s England who became coal miners in Pennsylvania. Her great-great-great grandmother on her father's side, Mary Smith, was born in Ireland and moved to London in the 1800s. Smith married a British soldier and may have worked as a servant in Windsor

Castle for Queen Victoria in the 1850s. Her father, Thomas Markle, shares distant ancestors with US presidents George W. Bush, George H.W. Bush, Gerald Ford, Richard Nixon, Herbert Hoover, Calvin Coolidge, Chester Arthur, and James Garfield.[10]

Markle's family tree purportedly includes royalty. According to the New England Historic Genealogical Society, she and Harry are "distant cousins in more than 200 ways."[11] Other genealogical experts trace her royal roots all·the way back to the first Norman King of England, who reigned from 1066–1087.[12] The New England Historic Genealogical Society claims that Markle's heritage mirrors contemporary USA, UK, and European history. "Related to millions of Americans and many Britons, including notables in both countries," the Society observes, "Markle is perhaps the newest solidifying figure in Anglo-American kinship and American-British relations."[13]

Certainly prior to her return to California, such talk elevated false claims that the UK had entered a post-racial era by using Markle as a solidifying post-racial figure. For many whites her racial and ethnic background, real and imagined, remains key in her personification as a post-racial Duchess.

From Trophy Wife of Diversity to Harry's Misfortune

Markle is a trophy of diversity, someone to whom elite and non-elite whites point to as proof of the alleged end of racism in the UK, while obscuring the white-racist policies, laws, and other aspects of systemic racism they enthusiastically support.[14] Her supposed wholehearted embrace of diversity and progressive activism helps to drive this persisting white narrative. When she and Harry stepped down as senior royals, it should have become patently clear that much work was needed to combat Britain's systemic racism. Instead, many white pundits attacked suggestions that white racism played any role in the couple's decision, leading the Scottish Pakistani writer Amna Saleem to remark: "It seems that much of Britain desperately wants to be absolved [of] its racist history without doing any work to combat racism—treating marginalisation and discrimination like imagined annoyances not worth confronting. But looking at the fate of a royal couple that was supposed to symbolise progression and a supposedly post-racial British society, it seems clear that there is still much work to be done."[15]

The Myth of a Post-Racial Society

When Markle married Harry, she wore a veil embroidered with the national flowers of 19 African countries, seven Asian nations, 13 countries in the Caribbean and the Americas, three European nations, and 11 countries in the Pacific region. Her incorporation of the Commonwealth of Nations led some to suggest she had symbolically carried billions of people of color with her up the aisle of St George's Chapel at Windsor Castle.[16] The dress designer has since explained that the national flowers were meant "to bring the world into the journey of the ceremony. ... [I]t would be a very personal ceremony with so many choices that would reflect [the couple's] heritage and their unique way of being incredibly inclusive, genuine and generous."[17] Britons with Caribbean roots, such as those living in Brixton—a multicultural district of south London—rejoiced on Markle's wedding day. Prior to the wedding, the future duchess had visited Brixton's mostly Afro-Caribbean community, "one not previously on the royal family's radar."[18]

Early on, liberal commentators applauded Markle for her philanthropy, but warned that it was unlikely she would use her royal status to bring awareness to British racial issues or their root causes in systemic racism. The historian Valerie Wade suggested that we would be sadly disappointed if we were to expect Markle to speak out against police brutality affecting men and women of color, or on other matters especially affecting black women. Wade also warned people to be cognizant of the meaning of the duchess's main self-identification as biracial, and usually not as black. We should judiciously scrutinize the meaning of Markle, she argued, a mixed-race woman of African descent marrying into the royal family: "It's possible to be happy for her and still desire royalty that is more than decorative."[19]

In the same month that the couple wed, a UN special rapporteur on racism criticized Britain's escalating racial, ethnic, and religious "intolerance" following the referendum on Brexit. The rapporteur emphasized systemic racism—the surges in hate crimes following that referendum; the disproportionate criminalization of UK blacks; the human rights violations and indignities black Britons have long faced; and the persistent vilification of British Muslims, who are in effect racialized via the government's so-called counter-radicalization scheme.[20] This indictment was a far cry from claims of a post-racial era that many whites suggested had dawned in the wake of the royal wedding.

In this white version of a mythical colorblind society, all people of color can transcend their racial categorization. If they do not, the fault lies within the individual. In the interim, Markle and Harry themselves continued to mostly speak about transforming individuals as opposed to transforming the UK, a white-dominated and still systemically racist society.

Roughly 19 months after the wedding, Harry told Russian pranksters—who had deceived him into thinking they were the environmental activist Greta Thunberg and her father—that Donald Trump "has blood on his hands" for "pushing the coal industry." Of Boris Johnson the prince spoke more positively, but again with no attention to systemic racial issues: "I think he is a good man, so you are one of [the] few people who can reach into his soul and get him to feel and believe in you."[21] In contrast to Harry's favorable impression of Johnson, 58 percent of blacks in the UK considered the governing Conservative Party institutionally racist, while 31 percent of blacks considered the opposition Labour Party institutionally racist, according to a 2020 online poll. The same poll found that 39 percent of whites believed the governing Conservative Party to be institutionally racist and 34 percent of them believed the opposition Labour Party to be institutionally racist.[22]

Significantly, at no time during his telephone conversations with the Russian pranksters did Harry mention British racism. He and Markle had stepped down as senior royals to protect Archie, he explained, but did not say from whom. Stepping down had given them the potential "to say things and do things" they might have been unable to do otherwise, he indicated. But of their struggle with the media, he spoke in broad terms of bullying.

> From the moment that I found a wife that was strong enough to … stand up for what we believe in together, has basically scared [the tabloid papers] so much that they've now come out incredibly angry, they've come out fighting, and … they will try [to] … destroy our reputation. … But what they don't understand is the battle we are fighting against them is far more than just us. … Even though they want to make it personal they are scared because we are some of the first two people willing to stand up to their bullying.[23]

Claims of Racial Transcension

Markle's links to several racial and ethnic groups seem to authenticate her supposedly post-racial identity. This is a crucial factor in convincingly presenting her as a trophy wife of diversity. To emphasize this, in a 2016 essay for *Elle* magazine, she reflects on her identity as a biracial woman. "Biracial" here is the word she prefers. She ponders the possibility of dwelling as an actress in a racial chasm of internal confusion or of discovering an identity outside that chasm. "You push for color-blind casting," Markle writes; "you draw your own box" when filling out a form. The overall message of her essay led many black women to conclude that she should not be spontaneously willed the title "black princess," a designation she likely does not covet.[24]

Markle also writes about the discrimination that her black mother, Doria Ragland, faces when reflecting on an episode in which a seventh-grade teacher told the future duchess to check the box for "Caucasian" on a form because that is "how you look." Hence, we see the reason for Markle's reference to drawing "your own box." The future duchess recalls not following her teacher's advice because she feared the "pit-in-her-belly sadness" her mother would experience if she were to discover that checked box: "I left my identity blank—a question mark, an absolute incomplete—much like how I felt." In the essay, Markle also shares that people often enquire about her racial background, asking from where her parents originate. She writes: "While I could say Pennsylvania and Ohio, and continue this proverbial two-step, I instead give them what they're after: 'My dad is Caucasian and my mom is African American. I'm half black and half white.' "[25]

While Markle's life before and after she became a duchess has been anything but colorblind, a false narrative is perpetuated by many commentators that she and all people of color are today free from discriminatory treatment based on racial grouping. In *White Privilege: The Myth of a Post-Racial Society*, Kalwant Bhopal explains how whites have crafted this post-racial myth, including the commonplace assertion that most whites "do not see color" in this contemporary era. The use of such self-justifying repartee, when unjustly gained white privilege and resources are still linked to persisting racial inequality, is fundamental to contemporary racial framing. White denial of historical discrimination and unjust and systemic disadvantages long faced by people of color is persisting and tenacious. The root of the problem is unjust white privilege and resources. The white racial frame flourishes by *othering*—i.e., oppressing and victimizing—people of color, while often accenting supposed virtuous white colorblindness to deflect attention.[26]

Markle herself, perhaps inadvertently, fed this portrayal with her comment that a person just needs to draw their "own box" (i.e., make an individual choice). Yet, racial identities in Western societies involve much more than such individual choices. Because of systemic racism, identities are routinely forced on people, especially people of color, from the outside. This is true for Markle in the UK and the USA. Strikingly, she has spoken of a "gray" area surrounding her self-identification. Achromatic gray, as Markle used it, is much in keeping with the racialized views of whites who construct the mythical colorblind perspective.

This colorblind viewpoint has major consequences, including rationalizing racial inequality. The sociologist Eduardo Bonilla-Silva has researched it, chronicling how it supports practices that reproduce US racial discrimination, such as voter disenfranchisement, housing discrimination, and police brutality. Similarly, Bhopal charts the ways in which this colorblind perspective legitimizes specific white-racist practices that maintain racial discrimination and inequalities in the UK.[27] In both countries, white claims of colorblindness are a dangerous part of the dominant racial framing precisely because they can prevent genuine discussions of the extreme racial inequality they maintain.

In both countries, there is also substantial emphasis on individualism. The sociologist Adia Harvey Wingfield describes the paradoxical nature of emphasizing individualism. In regard to racial matters, whites generally benefit from such an emphasis because they as individuals commonly profit from existing racial stratification, while the positive evaluation of their group's "whiteness is normalized." From an early age, individuals of color, on the other hand, must be vigilant of the fact that they will be negatively appraised on the basis of their racial group membership, with harmful racist stereotypes routinely conferred upon them by whites.[28] As we show throughout this book, Markle is constantly judged on the basis of her racial group membership, with long-established negative racial framing conferred upon her by elite and non-elite whites alike.

2016 and 2020 US Presidential Elections

In the oft-cited comments Markle made about Donald Trump before she married Harry, there is little attention to white racism. Prior to his election in 2016, Markle vowed to vote for his opponent Hillary Clinton. Appearing on a Comedy Central program, the then-actress remarked: "Of course Trump is divisive—think about female voters alone. I think it was in 2012, the Republican Party lost the female vote by 12 points. That's a huge number and as misogynistic as Trump is, and so vocal about it, that's a huge chunk of it."[29]

She makes no mention of *gendered racism* and demonstrates no cognizance of that important intersectionality, despite Trump's decades-long history of racism and his tendency to negatively target black people, and especially black women. For some years Trump had played a prominent role in what is termed the *birther movement*, which falsely claims that Barack Obama is not US-born. By the time Markle made her comments on Comedy Central, Trump's numerous racist remarks had spanned more than 40 years, including when announcing his bid for the presidency, when he infamously vilified ordinary Mexican immigrants as rapists and gang members. Despite Markle's attention to Trump's misogyny, she did not take the opportunity to call out the clearly intertwined realities of systemic sexism and systemic racism—experiences she herself has long faced.[30]

In the lead-up to the 2020 presidential election, the duchess joined 99 other prominent American women, including Michelle Obama, Hillary Clinton, Oprah Winfrey, and Alexandria Ocasio-Cortez, to share why she would be voting that November. Likely in a nod to being silenced by the royal establishment, she explained: "I know what it's like to have a voice, and also what it's like to feel voiceless. ... I also know that so many men and women have put their lives on the line for us to be heard. And that opportunity, that fundamental right, is in our ability to exercise our right to vote and to make all of our voices heard. ... That is why I vote."[31]

Roughly 11 weeks before that election, Markle had participated in a virtual "voter registration couch party," co-hosted by the non-profit group When We All Vote, which was co-chaired by Michelle Obama and aimed to increase voter turnout and "close the race and age voting gap by changing the culture around voting." At the time, Markle said: "We all know what's at stake this year. I know it. I think all of you certainly know it. You're just as mobilized and energized to the change that we all need and deserve." She added: "We vote to honor those who came before us and to protect those who will come after us—because that's what community is all about and that's specifically what this election is all about." The duchess also spoke in basic terms about the problem of voter suppression and the significance of women's rights, highlighting the 19th Amendment to the US Constitution, which granted *white* women the right to vote but not women of colour. "If you're not going out there and voting, then you're complicit," she said, "We can make the difference in this election and we *will* make the difference in this election."[32]

Several prominent white men, well-known critics of Markle, weighed in. Dan Wootton—executive editor of *The Sun* tabloid, owned by arch-conservative Rupert Murdoch—accused her of "actively campaigning against Donald Trump." Piers Morgan said the Sussexes' royal titles should be removed because Markle "spout[ed] off about foreign elections in such a brazenly partisan way." Social conservative and former member of the UK Independence Party (UKIP) David Kurten, who is of British and Jamaican descent, agreed. He tweeted that Markle is "obviously no longer politically neutral" and that she and Harry "should be stripped of their Sussex titles."[33]

Markle soon after joined Gloria Steinem for a pre-recorded discussion of political representation and why every vote matters. Steinem began by saying: "we've been rescued by women of color in all of our recent elections because of a vote of conscience and compassion. The heart of the Democratic Party has been Black women, actually, and now there is a potential Vice President who is Black and that's exciting." The duchess replied optimistically, and said she was excited about biracial Senator Kamala Harris's nomination for vice-president, addressing her own experiences being biracial: "growing up, whether it was a doll or a person in office, you need to see someone who looks like you in some capacity. As many of us believe, you can only be what you can see."[34]

When Steinem said she, too, felt hopeful, Markle referenced *Algorithms of Oppression: How Search Engines Reinforce Racism*, a 2018 book by the scholar Safiya Umoja. Markle explained:

> [I]t talks about how the digital space really shapes our thinking about race. For example, it wasn't that long ago that when you'd start to type in a search engine 'why are white women…' it would start to autofill with words like 'so pretty' or 'so beautiful.' And then when you would type 'why are black women…' it would autofill with words like 'so angry' or 'so loud.' You get to see how our minds are being shaped by something so much bigger than what we're actually feeling or putting out there.[35]

The duchess also shared with Steinem her concern for voter suppression via intimidation tactics, and described the opportunity she had to speak about it to Stacey Abrams—the first black woman in the USA to be a major party's nominee for state (Georgia) governor.[36]

During their discussion of the coronavirus pandemic, Markle and Steinem seemed at least partially to miss the boat on how even it is not colorblind. "I wonder if the COVID-19 disaster—which is an unmitigated suffering and a very unequal suffering … —is teaching us something," pondered Steinem, "because it doesn't recognize race, gender or nationality. It sees human beings as human beings. And perhaps we're beginning to see that too." Markle added: "On top of that, it's just giving everyone this moment of reset; to reevaluate what actually matters. I think it's often forgotten how women like you and so many others before you fought for us to just be where we are right now."[37] Even as Steinem spoke of *unequal suffering* and Markle gave a nod to her feminist forebearers, both failed to address the fact that even if the virus may not *recognize race, gender or nationality*, the people with the power to stop it certainly do, including powerful white men like Boris Johnson and Donald Trump (see Chapter 7). And, of course, contrary to Markle's sentiments here, not everyone has the privilege to reset or reevaluate during the health crisis, whether it concerns one's priorities or anything else. Many people were trying to just survive somehow in systemically racist, sexist, and classist societies.

Again, stressing the grave importance of casting a ballot that year, six weeks before the November 2020 US presidential election, Markle and Harry appeared on the American Broadcasting Company's (ABC) and *Time* magazine's televised celebration of the world's 100 most influential people. "We're six weeks out from the election, and today is voter registration day. Every four years, we're told the same thing, 'This is the most important election of our lifetime.' But this one is," the duchess said. "When we vote, our values are put into action, and our voices are heard." Harry implored viewers to "reject hate speech, misinformation, and online negativity." Though the couple did not endorse a candidate, they were accused of doing so by media pundits and social media users. In response, and targeting Markle only, President Donald Trump said at the time: "I'm not a fan of hers. ... And I would say this—and she probably has heard that—but I wish a lot of luck to Harry, because he's gonna need it."[38] Among social media users who condemned the couple's statements was Piers Morgan, who tweeted: "Prince Harry poking his woke nose into the US election and effectively telling Americans to vote against President Trump is completely unacceptable behaviour for a member of the Royal Family."[39]

Individualistic Understandings of Racism versus Awareness of Systemic Racism

In examining centuries of racial oppression in Britain, throughout this book we have extended the conceptions of societal framing and emphasized the central importance of a broad, long-dominant white racial frame, one that Markle is victim of and of which she often seems unsophisticatedly informed. This elite-created racial frame provides an overarching and generally destructive white worldview, one now extending and intersecting across white divisions of class, gender, sexuality, age, nationality, and religion. Since its inception, this powerful frame has provided the vantage point from which white Britons have constantly viewed society. Its centrality in elite and ordinary white minds is what makes it a dominant frame throughout the UK and much of the Western world, as well as numerous other places (e.g., recall the discussion of China in Chapter 2). Over time, this powerful frame has also been accepted by or imposed on the minds of many people of color, because it is the dominant *frame of mind* and *frame of reference* in regard to racial matters in every white-dominated society.

We see evidence of Markle internalizing the dominant racial frame, at least to some degree, in an interview with British *Pride* magazine and in the aforementioned *Elle* essay. In *Pride*, she claims that she doesn't "care if I'm fair-skinned and I don't care what it is, that's who I am and that's my family. … My hope is for the world to get to a place where it's colour blind."[40] Clearly, she did not call out white racism for its central role in shaping the racial identities, and the skin-color preferences, for people of color.

Astutely, some then questioned whether Markle realizes how her physical appearance may have influenced the supposedly race-neutral casting that landed her a starring role on the US *Suits* television series from 2011 to 2017.[41] Others have speculated that if Markle had had a darker complexion, it is doubtful she would have dated, let alone married, Harry. Still others suggest that if Harry had been direct heir to the British throne, not sixth in line at the time, she would have been out of the running for the role of bride-to-be. As one BBC commentator explained, "mixed race is the acceptable face of blackness already … fetishized by the elite."[42] Many white Americans have a similar view. A black writer at *Vogue* magazine describes Markle as the kind of black person that the "majority of right-leaning white America wishes we all could be, if there were to be blackness at all."[43]

Markle's self-identification as biracial, and what some see as a lack of understanding on her part of the disadvantages that dark-skinned people of color face as compared to those with lighter skin (*colorism*), have generated critical discussions among black women. For some, her timid or uncritical comments on race and racism issues render her unfamiliar or even offensive. In the 2015 *Elle* essay, the future duchess arguably illustrates an unawareness of colorism and how it benefits *her* as an actress. For example, she writes:

> Being "ethnically ambiguous", as I was pegged in the industry, meant I could audition for virtually any role. Morphing from Latina … to African American … [as] varied as an Eighties Benetton poster. Sadly, it didn't matter: I wasn't black enough for the black roles and I wasn't white enough for the white ones, leaving me somewhere in the middle as the ethnic chameleon who couldn't book a job.[44]

Markle continues:

> This is precisely why *Suits* stole my heart. … a dramedy about a NY law firm. … Enter Rachel Zane, one of the female leads and the dream girl—beautiful and confident with an encyclopedic knowledge of the law. "Dream girl" in Hollywood terms had always been that quintessential blonde-haired, blue-eyed beauty. … But the show's producers … were simply looking for Rachel. In making a choice like that, the producers helped shift the way pop culture defines beauty.[45]

In response, the historian Valerie Wade explains what should be obvious, that such casting decisions do not alter societal beauty standards. Many fans of the show, adds Wade, did not even know that the Rachel Zane character was black until an African American actor appeared as her father.[46]

Wade contrasts Markle's self-proclaimed "ethnically ambiguous appearance" to that of an earlier mixed-race Hollywood actress, Lena Horne (1917–2010). While Horne was aware that her light skin was exploited by the white-dominated film industry, Markle seems far less mindful of her own exploitation. We can see the stark difference between the actresses' consciousness regarding colorism if we compare Markle's words in the *Elle* essay to the words of Horne. While Markle commends *Suits*'s producers on race-neutral casting and transforming definitions of beauty by casting her instead of a "quintessential blonde-haired, blue-eyed" thespian, Horne recognizes that she "was unique in that [she] was a kind of black that white people could accept." Horne remarked: "I was their daydream. I had the worst kind of acceptance because it was never for how great I was or what I contributed. It was because of the way I looked." And while that of which Horne so genuinely speaks—the malleability of light-complexioned black women—is still with us, this fact seems mostly lost on Markle, at least according to the 2015 *Elle* essay and her comments to *Pride* magazine that same year.[47]

In 2012, when Markle participated in the *Erase the Hate* campaign, which strives to strengthen and fast-track front-line anti-hate and pro-inclusivity efforts in the USA, she said: "I'm biracial, most people can't tell what I'm mixed with, and so, much of my life has felt like being a fly on the wall. ... [S]ome of the slurs I've heard or the really offensive jokes, or the names, it's just hit me in a really strong way, and then ... a couple of years ago, I heard someone call my mom the N-word." Of people's perceptions of her, Markle explained: "Certain people don't look at me and see ... a black woman or a biracial woman. ... They treat me differently I think than they would if they knew what I was mixed with, and I think ... it can be a struggle as much as ... a good thing depending on the people that you're dealing with." She also shares painful memories of her first encounters with close-mindedness when she moved away from her hometown, Los Angeles; her eyes were "really opened ... to a mentality that still exists that [she] thought was backdated" and isolated to her black grandfather's generation. She also speaks of her pride in her "heritage on both sides" and of her hopes "that by the time I have children that people are even more open-minded to how things are changing and that having a mixed world is what it's all about."[48]

There is certainly a lot to unpack here in Markle's words. She speaks of "slurs," "offensive jokes," and (racist) "names," and refers to racial discrimination as closed-mindedness. Examining white racism through these optics, though beneficial, privileges individualistic analyses over systemic ones. She thus fails to address the foundational and systemic realities of US racism. She also discloses that she had recently believed racism to be isolated to her grandfather's era—which raises many questions about what others have named Markle's ability to "pass as white." This might explain her gradual racial awakening in the very systemically racist US society in which she grew up. She also seems to refer to *passing as white* as simultaneously "a good thing" and "a struggle." And although she was 31 years old when she spoke these words, she hoped her children would be born when "having a mixed world is what it's all about." This suggests that she does not fully understand how foundational and systemic white racism is. In her hopes for her future children, she appears to suggest that being mixed-race—as, say, opposed to being black—is the preferred norm. Still, when it comes to biracial people, Markle appears to recognize that being part-black is possibly less desirable in the estimation of many white Americans, as is indicated by her words "treat me differently … if they knew what I was mixed with."

Significantly, the same year that she contributed to the *Erase the Hate* campaign, there were synchronized attempts across the USA to suppress the votes of people of color. Then-President Barack Obama was being variously described as an African tribal chief, a foreign Muslim, Indonesian, and Kenyan—in other words, as *The New York Times* put it, "as a man fundamentally ineligible to be our president."[49] Fifty-one percent of Americans conveyed overt anti-black attitudes in 2012, compared to 48 percent in 2008.[50] The year 2012 was also when Trayvon Martin, an African American teen, was fatally shot by a neighborhood watch volunteer. The same year, the *Ella Baker Center for Human Rights*—named in honor of the black civil rights and human rights activist—noted: "racism is alive and well in America. It manifests itself differently from what most Americans believe racism to be. … The school to prison pipeline that criminalizes rather than educates our children, particularly Black boys, is an example. … Mass incarceration is another manifestation … which has allowed America to become the world's largest incarcerator, especially of Black and Brown males."[51]

In the wake of the Black Lives Matter protests in 2020, some of the same tabloids that published racist and gendered-racist stories about Markle reproduced her 2012 *Erase the Hate* message, leading one royal expert to comment: "I think it is a bit much for the tabloids … to highlight her messages about racism as the papers have no interest in acknowledging their roles [in] the unfavorable, sometimes racist coverage" of the duchess.[52] Piers Morgan displayed the same hypocrisy. This white supporter of the British Conservative Party and long-time detractor of Markle, actually commended her on her 2020 address to students at her former Los Angeles high school in which she mentioned Black Lives Matter. After President Donald Trump set police forces and National Guard troops loose on peaceful protesters with tear gas, flash grenades, and rubber bullets, a headline in Morgan's *Daily Mail* column read: "Mr. President … listen to Meghan Markle and stop dividing and start uniting a country crying out in pain."[53] Morgan's duplicity was on display earlier the same year when he said he had probably taken things too far with prior negative comments about Markle and Harry, adding that he would soften how he talks in the future. Still, he did not acknowledge the extensive white racism Markle had faced, something he has long denied. What's more, he would return to his gendered-racist commentary of her soon after.[54]

In the interim, the couple's increasing—albeit still narrow—understanding of systemic racism was visible in their public commitment to the progressive campaign *Stop Hate for Profit*. Launched in mid-2020, it calls on Facebook to "stop valuing profits over hate, bigotry, racism, antisemitism, and disinformation," including permitting posts inciting violence against anti-racism protesters.[55] Jim Steyer, the head of Common Sense Media—an important resource on entertainment and technology recommendations for families—said the couple contacted him, asking: "'Which companies can we help target?" "They jumped on board," he said.[56] Apparently, the couple are eager to address online hate speech and to work alongside anti-racist and civil rights groups on the issue. They have worked to persuade "global CEOs to stand in solidarity with a coalition of civil and racial justice groups," such as the National Association for the Advancement of Colored People (NAACP), the Anti-Defamation League, and Color of Change—all of whom are working to enact "structural changes" to the online world.[57] In appreciation for their work, the NAACP tweeted: "We are grateful for the leadership of the Duke and Duchess of Sussex in recognizing the importance of solidarity in this moment. Your commitment to truth, justice, and equality are appreciated."[58]

Disapproving of Markle

Markle and Harry began their public life together by playing it relatively safe—mindful perhaps of the importance of mass appeal—and appearing to have little genuine understanding of systemic racial discrimination. Also, of course, the apolitical nature of their roles as senior royals loomed large.[59]

Back then, Harry openly expressed his passionate support for the monarchical institution in which he was born and what it represents. He also asserted that he wanted to help ensure the monarchy's survival.[60] Even after he and Markle made the decision to step down as senior royals, he said: "Our hope was to continue serving the Queen, the Commonwealth and my military associations without public funding. Sadly that wasn't possible. … It brings me great sadness that it has come to this."[61]

The many forms of racial and other inequalities that the monarchy's survival ensures seemed lost on Harry, leading the political commentator Bill Maher to memorably say:

> I give Harry and Meghan some credit, but not a lot. … If they want to be seen as a modern couple way hipper than the other stuffy ones in the family, okay, then go all the way and say it. Say, We're not just taking a step back from royalty, we're renouncing the whole outdated, racist, anachronistic lot of it. We're saying loud and proud, what is this

bullshit that some people are royal? ... Say it's 2020 [and] I hereby
decree this birthright nonsense from the Middle Ages is stupid.[62]

Mass appeal is strategic and arguably the most important reason why the
British royal family has outlasted or overshadowed other European royal
houses. Acceptance among the masses has been acknowledged as crucial to
the survival of the British royal family since at least 1917, when George
V ordered all British royals to dispense with the use of German surnames
and titles because of anti-German sentiment during World War I. This
included changing his surname from the Germanic Saxe-Coburg-Gotha to
the very English-sounding Windsor. Also during World War I, George V
failed to save the Russian imperial family, his kin, from being executed
by Communist revolutionaries. He offered the deposed tsar and his family
asylum in Britain, only to retract the proposal and later conceal the about-
turn. The British elite, including the king and his private secretary, feared
that the presence of the autocratic tsar in England could fuel the mounting
republican movement in Britain at the time, and topple the monarchy.[63]

Nowadays, the British royals' popularity among Britons is regularly
measured by opinion polls. YouGov poll ratings, for example, gauge the
popularity and prominence of the most senior royals on a positivity scale. In
2017, Elizabeth II was ranked most popular (72-percent positivity rating).
In 2018, Harry jumped to first place ahead of his grandmother, with a 77-
percent positivity rating. He was described as fun-loving, admirable, and
affable. Markle was less popular among Britons than her husband, landing
in sixth place and scoring a 55-percent positivity rating. This ranking put
her behind Harry, the queen, William, Kate, and Prince Phillip (the queen's
husband). A year later, a survey found that only Prince Andrew, the queen's
disgraced son (see Chapter 4), was less popular than Markle. Significantly,
this later poll established that the Duchess of Sussex was well-liked among
left-leaning individuals and younger Britons (66 percent for 18- to 24-
year-olds versus 28 percent for those aged 55 to 64).[64]

The 2018 royal wedding, according to another survey, failed to rouse
excitement among most Britons. The pre-wedding poll commissioned
by the anti-monarchist group Republic found that two out of three
respondents were "not very interested" or "not interested at all" in the
nuptials of Markle and Harry. Sixty percent reported that they planned to
spend the wedding weekend in pursuit of regular activities.[65] The poll's
results seem to contradict claims such as those made by Penny Junor (see
Chapter 1) that Markle and Harry "arrived like they were a golden couple"
and were celebrated by most Britons.[66]

The results of a 2019 poll conducted by Opinium Monarchy Tracker
found that, among those surveyed, Elizabeth II was still the most popular
female royal with a 70-percent approval rating. Despite Markle's novelty,
and the anticipation of the birth of her first child, she ranked just ahead
of Camilla (wife of Charles), with a 39-percent approval rating. Among
male royals, William outranked Harry (74 percent versus 70 percent).

Respondents were asked whether they agreed with Markle's and Harry's decision to not disclose particulars about the upcoming birth of their first child. The majority of respondents viewed the decision as positive. When queried whether they believe the couple have a significant role to play in society, specifically in regard to charitable activities, most respondents agreed. General support for the royal family then stood at 63 percent, higher than for the leading political parties. An analyst with the Opinium pollster concluded that given that UK politics was then tumultuous and the country's place in Europe unclear, "it's good to see support for a longstanding British institution."[67]

When it comes to public funding of royals by taxpayers, a recent poll found that Markle and Harry did not fare as well as other royal couples. This was a key issue when they stepped down as senior royals. They did not want to be beholden to public funding and would soon be paying their own way. Thirty-eight percent of the public said the new royal couple should receive money from the public purse, compared to 60 percent who said William and Kate should.[68]

Royal author Phil Dampier offers the following explanation for Markle and Harry not being as popular among Britons as other royal couples: "The public don't like being lectured on climate change by a couple who take private jets or being told they can't see Archie's christening when they've paid for Frogmore Cottage [the couple's Windsor home] to be renovated."[69] Dampier, like so many other white commentators, makes no mention of the potential impact of gendered racism on the polling results. Although lagging in the polls as a couple, the Sussexes gained 9.9 million Instagram followers in less than one year of joining the social media platform.[70]

Of 1,000 adult Britons surveyed online for a UK tabloid the day after the couple announced they were stepping down as senior royals, a majority agreed they should be evicted from Frogmore Cottage and reimburse taxpayers for the £2.4 million of public money spent on its refurbishing. Markle was held responsible by a majority of respondents for the decision to leave the royal fold, with a mere 4 percent holding Harry accountable. The couple's popularity took a nosedive in the wake of the announcement, with Markle ranked "a lowly tenth place among the royals" and Harry—the perennial favorite—ranked fifth. Notably, too, 60 percent of respondents agreed that the couple had treated the queen "shoddily," while 76 percent said they should receive no financial support from Buckingham Palace or the British government, and no protection from the Metropolitan Police Service, if they left the UK.[71]

Of 1,500 adult Britons surveyed online for the US magazine *Newsweek* four months after the couple stepped down, 54 percent of respondents said they should not return to royal duties. *Newsweek* asked respondents how the royal family's response to the coronavirus pandemic had impacted their opinion of various royals. The following data were compiled:

Asked about Meghan, 36 percent said they had a more negative view of the duchess following the outbreak with 20 percent saying their view became more positive. For Harry, 33 percent said they had a worse view of him compared to 19 percent whose opinion improved. ... Elizabeth II saw 35 percent of [respondents] say their impression of her had improved compared to 14 percent who said it worsened. ... William was viewed more positively by 33 percent and less positive by 11 percent, while Kate Middleton was seen more favorably by 29 percent and less by 14 percent.[72]

It would appear that the important work Markle and Harry engaged in at this point during the coronavirus pandemic was undervalued by or unknown to many Britons. This included Harry's video call to British parents trying to get their critically ill kids on a coronavirus vulnerability list, and the couple's $112,000 donation to Feeding Britain, an independent charity that aims to end hunger and its root causes, and helped families with children left hungry due to the cessation of free school meals during the pandemic.[73] Even if those surveyed viewed the couple less positively following the outbreak of the coronavirus, Feeding Britain's national director certainly did not. He called their donation a "godsend," explaining it would "keep breakfast, lunch and dinner, so three square meals, on the table of many tens of thousands of children across our network."[74]

During the pandemic, a 2020 *Tatler* magazine survey of 4,174 British adults found that two-thirds of respondents believe the Sussexes should have their royal titles removed, while a majority (63 percent) said Markle should not publicly comment on US politics. Thirty-five percent of those surveyed said that they believe Markle "wants to be president of the United States one day."[75] Another survey by *YouGov* during the same period asked 3,250 British adults if the couple should "be stripped of their royal titles." This survey broke down responses by political persuasion, with 70 percent of Conservative supporters, 31 percent of Labour supporters, and 39 percent Liberal Democrat supporters answering in the affirmative.[76]

Royal Protocol: Expedient Paths to Dominant Racial Framing

Royal protocol signals that senior royals should not share publicly their political opinions. The Royal UK site reads: "As Head of State The Queen has to remain strictly neutral with respect to political matters, unable to vote or stand for election."[77] The BBC put it this way: "The Queen can vote, as can members of her family, but they do not do so because in practice it would be considered unconstitutional."[78] Hence, we understand Harry's aforementioned comment to the Russian pranksters that stepping down had given the couple the potential "to say things and do things" they might have been unable to do otherwise.[79]

All technicalities aside, even Elizabeth II has been reproached for breaching this protocol after saying Scots should "think very carefully about the future" before the 2014 Scottish independence referendum. And while her online royal biography stated that Markle is proud to be a feminist, and she early on appeared to be primed to advocate for gender equality in her work as a senior royal, she was expected to remain apolitical when she married into the royal family.[80] But during her brief stint as a senior royal, Markle breached this royal protocol. A few months before her wedding, she enthusiastically spoke in support of the Time's Up and #MeToo feminist movements. She was criticized for being politically progressive. The criticism was based on Markle's public remarks:

> I hear a lot of people speaking about girls' empowerment and women's empowerment—you will hear people saying they are helping women find their voices. I fundamentally disagree with that because women don't need to find their voices, they need to be empowered to use it and people need to be urged to listen. Right now with so many campaigns like MeToo and Time's Up there's no better time to continue to shine a light on women feeling empowered and people supporting them.[81]

Royal historian Anna Whitelock explained the conservative backlash to this viewpoint: "The monarchy cannot stop being based on hierarchy and has to be founded on privilege and birth rather than merit. It is founded on deference and the sense that some people are better than others."[82]

Markle's pre-royal social media accounts grant unique access to her political and social views at that time. Those archived online or detailed in secondary sources suggest that even if she could have spoken openly during her brief stint as a senior royal she would have likely capitalized on moderate racial framing, including remaining silent on police brutality and other issues greatly affecting black people, and advocating for a type of commercialized feminism (see Chapter 4). In so doing, Markle may have been attempting to position herself as a biracial actress, and later a biracial duchess, acceptable to most whites.

Indeed, Markle and Harry appear to draw on a form of race-neutrality during their first official joint interview in 2017 after their engagement was announced. When asked about scrutiny concerning her "ethnicity," Markle makes no explicit reference to racism. She frames the scrutiny as social noise that can be effortlessly drowned out by the kind of love she has with Harry. She comments that it is a shame that there is "the climate in this world to focus that much on that." Ultimately, she adds, "I'm really just proud of who I am and where I come from, and [Harry and I] have never put any focus on that." She clarifies that she and Harry concentrate on who they are as a *couple*—presumably, as opposed to individuals, with one mixed-race female American divorcée and the other a white elite male born into the British royal family. "And so when you take all those extra layers away and all of that noise," she explains, "I think it makes it really easy to just enjoy being together and tune all the rest of that out."[83] Sadly, within less than 24 months, Markle would come to see that true love cannot conquer all, telling a British television documentarian that she was adversely affected by the ever-present media intrusion and criticism. Soon thereafter, she and Harry left the royal family and the UK altogether.

In a follow-up question during the engagement interview, Harry is asked if the couple's different backgrounds mean they "represent something new for the royal family."[84] He replies that his soon-to-be wife would simply become "another team player as part of the bigger team." He clarifies that they want to "be able to carry out the right engagements, carry out our work and try and encourage others in the younger generation to be able to see the world in the correct sense rather than perhaps ... just having a distorted view."[85] What he means by "right engagements," "correct sense," and "distorted view" remains a mystery because he immediately starts to describe his love for Markle. He also says that she will "be really unbelievably good at the job" and that that is a huge relief for him "because she'll be able to deal with everything else that comes with it." Harry also refers to himself and Markle as "a fantastic team": "We hope to over time try and have as much impact for all the things that we care about as much as possible."[86] The couple did not know it then, but within a mere 764 days they would publicly announce they wished to no longer play for Team Senior Royals.

The assumption that Markle would be "really unbelievably good" in the role of royal wife (apparently because she was an actress), and "be able to deal with everything else that comes with it," seemed naïve at the time, as it does now. The larger significance of marrying a mixed-race American divorcée seemed lost on Harry. Still, by the time this interview took place, he had already taken the unprecedented step of publicly condemning specific racial and gender "abuse and harassment" that Markle had previously faced (see Chapter 2).[87] Now as his fiancée, she would miraculously "be able to deal with everything." Perhaps it was the security protection that she would now have that made Harry more hopeful. Yet, his interview comments reveal the prince's ignorance about the systemic character of the gendered racism that women of color face.[88]

The couple successfully avoided acknowledging the historic nature of their engagement, especially the significance of her status as a mixed-race fiancée of the grandson of the current British monarch. Even when asked directly by the interviewer about scrutiny over her "ethnicity," Markle herself makes no mention of the social or political implications of a mixed-race American divorcée marrying into the white British royal family. The significance is either lost on Harry, too, or purposely ignored. Markle would soon come to privately agonize over the questioning of her appropriateness as a royal bride, and the unfavorable contrasts made between her and Harry's aristocratic (white) ex-girlfriends by the British media and public.[89]

In her first official interview with Harry in 2017, as well as in the previously mentioned 2015 *Elle* magazine essay and the interview with *Pride* magazine the same year, Markle appears to be operating from a perspective of what might be termed *race transcension*. She presents herself as above race. In her apparent attempt to transcend race, she faces the paradoxical dilemma of positioning herself racially as someone who is black enough to be a symbol of a colorblind Britain, but not too black for most whites, including her royal in-laws and perhaps even her husband.

As we show throughout this book, when Markle has addressed racism, she has mostly avoided its systemic nature. Consider the often-cited story of the Barbie doll family that she coveted when young. The set included two children and their parents. A "perfect nuclear family ... sold in sets of white dolls or black dolls," Markle recalls in the *Elle* magazine essay. "I don't remember coveting one over the other, I just wanted one," she writes. Then on Christmas morning in 1988 she found her Barbie family under the tree: "a black mom doll, a white dad doll, and a child in each colour." Her father had tailored the families, buying two sets and combining them, to reflect their family. Here, Markle gives the impression that she and her father do not seem to comprehend that neither of the dolls is mixed-race.[90]

Markle's partial white ancestry and assumed benign racial status are subtly communicated to whites via such childhood narratives. Identifying and being identified as mixed-race arguably have the same effect. What's more, claims that anyone can select their own racial identity irrespective of physical appearance is uncorroborated in extensive research. Social identities are regularly *imposed* by outsiders, whatever one's personal choice may be. Researchers have shown that whites, especially those with significant social power, have been the primary generators of racial identities in both Britain and the USA, now for centuries.[91]

Pushing Meghan Markle: Internal and External Racist Forces

The contemporaneous *lived experiences* of people self-identifying as biracial, multiracial, or mixed-race accentuate the fact that in both the UK and the USA racial identities are socially, not biologically, constructed. In their study of the meaning of racial identity for multiracial people in contemporary society, Kerry Ann Rockquemore and David Brunsma document the extensive assortment of racial identities utilized and encountered by individuals with one black and one white parent. The young people interviewed, most of whom have a black and a white parent, usually do not choose one racial identity. Rather, like Markle, they accentuate a gray or biracial (black-and-white) identity, irrespective of how other people label them. Significantly, however, the identity *imposed* on them by white outsiders—especially those with power—was *black*. The researchers also found that even being classified as in-between black and white on the US racial continuum does not translate into equality of rights and privileges.[92]

In research on white racial framing during the 2008 US presidential election, Adia Harvey Wingfield and Joe R. Feagin remarked on how biracial Americans inevitably face racial discrimination. Studying the white framing of Barack Obama, who like the Duchess of Sussex dabbled in colorblind-speak and has a white mother and black father, they write:

> As young biracial Americans grow older and move beyond their more supportive friendship groups and home environments into the larger society, especially white-dominated employment, political, and housing settings, most learn hard societal lessons, including that many whites impose a racial identity and target them for discrimination no matter how assimilated to whiteness they may be. Discrimination often prevents them from achieving their life goals and pushes them and their identities ever more in the direction of personally and fully identifying as black American.[93]

As Markle has moved from television actress to senior royal, from mixed-race bride of a prince to mixed-race wife and mother of a son in line to the British throne, and now to a non-working member of the royal family, she has learned hard societal lessons, including that whites impose a racial identity and target her for discrimination no matter what she prefers or how assimilated to whiteness she may appear to be. The white framing and discrimination she has faced—including the racist tone of British newspaper pieces and the "outright sexism and racism of social media trolls and web article comments"—always had the potential to prevent her from achieving her goals as a senior royal.[94] That chronic discrimination stood in the way of her family's happiness, so much so that she, Harry, and Archie soon moved to the United States of America.

Whether Markle would have found supportive friendship groups and a supportive home environment in the royal spaces she seemed destined to occupy is now a moot point. Her tearful comments captured in the 2019 television documentary *Harry & Meghan: An African Journey*, in which she admitted that few people ask if she is alright in light of the media scrutiny she receives, were a harbinger of things to come. She admitted she felt especially vulnerable while pregnant and that the external criticism made her feel even more stressed.[95] "It's not enough just to survive something, right? That's not the point of life," she told the documentarian, revealing that she even tried to "adopt the British stiff upper lip." "[W]hat that does internally is probably really damaging," she added.[96]

On this tour, when the couple visited *The Justice Desk* initiative in South Africa, Markle gave a memorable speech to a women's group, assertively relating to them across both gender and racial lines. She remarked: "On one personal note, may I just say that while I am here with my husband as a member of the Royal Family, I want you to know that for me, I am here with you as a mother, as a wife, as a woman, as a woman of color, and as your sister. I am here with you, and I am here for you."[97] At an earlier event celebrating a cookbook by women affected by the 2017 Grenfell Tower fire (see Chapter 2), for which she wrote the foreword, Markle similarly related to the women, most of whom were women of color. Assembled at a communal cooking space at the Al Manaar Muslim Cultural Heritage Centre in West London, she told the women she "felt so immediately embraced" by them when she moved to London. "[T]o see in this one small room how multi-cultural it was," she explained, "I feel so proud to live in a city that can have so much diversity." Referring to the "twelve countries represented in this one group of women," she added it is "pretty outstanding."[98] Her comments suggest that Markle may think and behave differently in mostly non-white settings. Through her gendered-racist experiences in the white spaces that British royals generally occupy, she may have been pushed beyond the racial and ethnic ambiguousness that a smaller film stage or television studio had earlier allowed her to secure.

Conclusion

The Duchess of Sussex could do nothing to end British racism, nor did her rank as a senior royal expunge the royal family's continuing role in global white supremacy and other aspects of systemic racism. Dominant social frames, including the white racial frame, are powerfully shaped and sustained by the highest echelons of society, even though this creation and dissemination takes place in routine interaction with the views and practices of acolytes and other non-elites. Those with greater power typically have a larger capacity to enforce their racial frames on others. The duchess does not possess that power.

The white, mostly male, members of the UK ruling class have long controlled the design, dialogue, and distribution of a system-rationalizing racist frame, including by means of the constitutional monarchy, the well-established aristocracy, the corporate elite, and the top leadership in Parliament. While there is much non-elite-generated racial stereotyping, imagery, and interpretation, even popular white racial framing is typically vetted, codified, and embellished by the white elite. Leading British aristocrats, including royals, have long been part of the creation and dissemination of the dominant white frame and other elements of systemic racism. They are central actors in the intergenerational transmission of all of Britain's systemically racist institutions, as well as of the centuries-old racist framing that still reinforces them.

With very few exceptions, immediate royal family members who support the reigning monarch have all been white. Markle, an exemption to the rule, appears at best to have been—at least for a time—a trophy wife of diversity. In accentuating her mixed-race status and her speaking out mostly about sexism—but not about gendered racism—first as an actress and later as a senior royal, Markle helped reinforce the commonplace view that racial characteristics are somewhat inconsequential in contemporary UK and US societies. She bolstered, perhaps unintentionally, the white-framed idea that racial characteristics are no longer as meaningful as they truly are in determining the life chances of people of color or their presentation of self in everyday life.

Notes

1 Robert Hardman, *Queen of the World* (London: Century, 2018), pp. 4–6.
2 Seumas Milne, "Britain's Royal Family: Cut this Anti-Democratic Dynasty out of Politics," *The Guardian*, July 23, 2013, www.theguardian.com/commentisfree/2013/jul/23/cut-anti-democratic-dynasty-out-of-politics. Accessed November 24, 2019.
3 James Bickerton, "Meghan Markle and Prince Harry Snubbed as Majority Say they Shouldn't Get Public Funding," *Daily Express*, November 24, 2019, www.express.co.uk/news/royal/1208522/Meghan-Markle-news-Duchess-of-Sussex-Prince-Harry-funding-William-Kate-Middleton. Accessed November 24, 2019; Valerie Wade, "What Meghan Markle's Engagement to Prince Harry Says about How We Think of Black Royalty," *Allure*, November 29, 2017, www.allure.com/story/meghan-markle-engagement-black-royalty Accessed April 30, 2019.
4 Afua Hirsch, "Why a Royal Meghan Markle Matters," *Time*, May 17, 2018, http://time.com/5281096/meghan-markle-multicultural-britain/. Accessed June 6, 2019.
5 Nosheen Iqbal, "Has Meghan Markle Changed Britain's Attitude to Race and Royalty?," *The Observer*, May 13, 2018, www.theguardian.com/uk-news/2018/may/13/has-meghan-markle-changed-britains-attitude-race-and-royalty. Accessed June 12, 2019.
6 Sandi Rankaduwa, "Meghan Markle is the Future of a Monarchy with Racist Baggage," *BuzzFeed*, November 30, 2017, www.buzzfeednews.com/article/sandirankaduwa/itsamodernmarkle. Accessed November 11, 2019.
7 Iqbal, "Has Meghan Markle Changed Britain's Attitude?"
8 Caitlin Logan, "'Ignorant and Insulting': Anti-Racist Activists Push Back on Image of the Royal Wedding as a Beacon of Progress," *Common Space*, May 18, 2018, www.commonspace.scot/articles/12781/ignorant-and-insulting-anti-racist-activists-push-back-image-royal-wedding-beacon. Accessed June 12, 2019.
9 See, for example, Erica Gerald Mason, "How Prince Harry and Meghan Markle Could Actually Combat Colonialism's Destructive Legacy," *Vanity Fair*, August 14, 2020, www.vanityfair.com/style/2020/08/how-prince-harry-and-meghan-markle-could-actually-combat-colonialisms-destructive-legacy. Accessed August 14, 2002.
10 Gary Boyd Roberts, "The Royal Ancestry of Meghan Markle," *American Ancestors*, www.americanancestors.org/Royal-Ancestry-of-Meghan-Markle.aspx. Accessed June 12, 2019; *Irish Central* Staff, "Meghan Markle Has a Surprising Irish Connection," *Irish Central*, May 7, 2019, www.irishcentral.com/roots/ancestry/meghan-markle-irish-roots. Accessed June 12, 2019.
11 Roberts, "The Royal Ancestry of Meghan Markle."
12 Rachel West, "Meghan Markle's Family Tree Includes Royal Roots and Ties to Slavery," *ET Canada*, May 18, 2018, https://etcanada.com/news/328734/meghan-markles-family-tree-includes-royal-roots-and-ties-to-slavery/. Accessed June 10, 2019; *Irish Central* Staff, "Meghan Markle Has a Surprising Irish Connection."
13 Roberts, "The Royal Ancestry of Meghan Markle."
14 Logan, "'Ignorant and Insulting.'"
15 Amna Saleem, "Harry and Meghan were Meant to Embody Post-Racial Britain. So Much for That," *The Guardian*, January 11, 2020, www.theguardian.com/commentisfree/2020/jan/11/post-racial-britain-harry-meghan-tabloids. Accessed August 9, 2020.

16 Amy Mackelden, "Meghan Markle's Wedding Veil Had the Sweetest Surprise for Prince Harry," *Harper's Bazaar*, September 22, 2018, www.harpersbazaar.com/celebrity/latest/a23376285/meghan-markle-wedding-veil-commonwealth-flowers-prince-harry-surprise. Accessed November 29, 2019.

17 Chloe Foussianes, "Clare Waight Keller Talks Designing Meghan Markle's Royal Wedding Dress in Touching Instagram Post," *Town & Country*, April 23, 2020, www.townandcountrymag.com/society/tradition/a32253302/clare-waight-keller-meghan-markle-wedding-dress-anniversary-instagram/. Accessed May 21, 2020.

18 Omid Scobie and Carolyn Durand, *Finding Freedom: Harry and Meghan and the Making of a Modern Royal Family* (New York: HarperCollins), p. 205.

19 Wade, "What Meghan Markle's Engagement."

20 Damien Gayle, "UK Has Seen 'Brexit-Related' Growth in Racism, Says UN Representative," *The Guardian*, May 11, 2018, www.theguardian.com/politics/2018/may/11/uk-has-seen-brexit-related-growth-in-racism-says-un-representative. Accessed June 12, 2019.

21 Chris Kitching, "Prince Harry Hoax Call in Full from Megxit Agony to Thoughts on Trump and Boris Johnson," *Mirror*, March 11, 2020, www.mirror.co.uk/news/uk-news/prince-harry-hoax-call-full-21671641. Accessed May 21, 2020.

22 Richard Allen Greene, "Britain's Big Race Divide," *CNN*, June 22, 2020, https://edition.cnn.com/interactive/2020/06/europe/britain-racism-cnn-poll-gbr-intl/. Accessed August 12, 2020.

23 Kitching, "Prince Harry Hoax."

24 Meghan Markle, "Meghan Markle: I'm More Than an 'Other,'" *Elle*, December 22, 2016, www.elle.com/uk/life-and-culture/news/a26855/more-than-an-other/. Accessed November 21, 2019.

25 *Ibid.*

26 Kalwant Bhopal, *White Privilege: The Myth of a Post-Racial Society* (Bristol: Polity Press, 2018), pp. 23, 101, 74–76.

27 Eduardo Bonilla-Silva, *Racism Without Racists: Color-Blind Racism and the Persistence of Racial Inequality in America* (Lanham, MD: Rowman & Littlefield, 2003); Bhopal, *White Privilege*, pp. 23, 101, 74–76.

28 Adia Harvey Wingfield, "Color-Blindness is Counterproductive," *The Atlantic*, September 13, 2015, www.theatlantic.com/politics/archive/2015/09/color-blindness-is-counterproductive/405037/. Accessed November 24, 2019.

29 Amanda Harding, "This is What Meghan Markle Said about Donald Trump before She Was a Royal," *Showbiz CheatSheet*, June 3, 2019, www.cheatsheet.com/entertainment/this-is-what-meghan-markle-said-about-donald-trump-before-she-was-a-royal.html/. Accessed June 21, 2019.

30 David A. Graham, Adrienne Green, Cullen Murphy, and Parker Richards, "An Oral History of Trump's Bigotry," *The Atlantic*, June 2019 Issue, www.theatlantic.com/magazine/archive/2019/06/trump-racism-comments/588067/. Accessed June 22, 2019; Harding, "This is What Meghan Markle Said."

31 Emily Dixon, "Meghan Markle Opens Up to *Marie Claire* about Why She's Voting in November," *Marie Claire*, August 11, 2020, www.marieclaire.com/celebrity/a33572727/meghan-markle-why-im-voting-marie-claire/. Accessed August 14, 2020.

32 Maija Kappler, "People are Furious Because Meghan Markle Encouraged Americans to Vote," *Huffington Post*, August 23, 2020, www.huffingtonpost.ca/entry/meghan-markle-royals-voting_ca. Accessed August 26, 2020.

33 *Ibid.*

34 Caroline Hallemann, "Meghan Markle Opens Up about Prince Harry's Feminism with Gloria Steinem," *Town & Country*, August 26, 2020, www.townandcountrymag.com/society/tradition/a33807343/meghan-markle-prince-harry-feminism-gloria-steinem-quote/. Accessed August 30, 2020.

35 Meghan Markle, "My Conversation With Gloria Steinem," *MAKERS*, August 26, 2020, https://ca.style.yahoo.com/meghan-the-duchess-of-sussex-my-conversation-with-gloria-steinem-151902708.html. Accessed August 26, 2020.

36 Hallemann, "Meghan Markle Opens Up."

37 Markle, "My Conversation."

38 Caroline Hallemann, "President Trump Reacts to Prince Harry and Meghan Markle's Voting Video," September 24, 2020, *Town & Country*, www.townandcountrymag.com/society/tradition/a34133544/president-trump-response-prince-harry-meghan-markle-voting-video/. Accessed October 12, 2020.

39 Emily Ferguson, "Royal Poll: Should Meghan Markle and Prince Harry Campaign in US Politics? VOTE HERE," *Daily Express*, September 23, 2020, www.express.co.uk/news/royal/1338958/meghan-markle-prince-harry-us-election-2020-royal-family-politics-poll-time100.   Accessed   October 12, 2020.

40 Nicole Stinson, "Meghan Markle Speaks Candidly about Racism Growing-Up—Before Romantic Holiday with Harry," *Daily Express*, August 7, 2017, www.express.co.uk/news/royal/837778/meghan-markle-harry-proposal-rumours-romantic-holiday-prince-speaks-about-racism. Accessed November 17, 2019.

41 Wade, "What Meghan Markle's Engagement."

42 Nicole Stinson, "'If Meghan Markle Had Darker Skin there Would NOT Be a Wedding'—BBC Guest Blasts Royals," *Daily Express*, November 28, 2017, www.express.co.uk/news/royal/885132/Meghan-Markle-Prince-Harry-engagement-racism-debate-BBC-Newsnight-wedding. Accessed June 20, 2019.

43 Elaine Musiwa, "The Problem with Calling Meghan Markle the "First Black Princess"," *Vogue*, November 28, 2017, www.vogue.com/article/meghan-markle-biracial-identity-politics-personal-essay. Accessed June 20, 2019. Italics in original.

44 Markle, "Meghan Markle."

45 *Ibid.*

46 Wade, "What Meghan Markle's Engagement."

47 *Ibid.*

48 Antoinette Bueno, "Meghan Markle Powerfully Stands Up against Racism in 2012 Video," *ET*, June 2, 2020, www.etonline.com/meghan-markle-powerfully-stands-up-against-racism-in-2012-video-147529. Accessed August 10, 2020.

49 Steven Hahn, "Political Racism in the Age of Obama," *The New York Times*, November 10, 2012, www.nytimes.com/2012/11/11/opinion/sunday/political-racism-in-the-age-of-obama.html. Accessed August 22, 2020.

50 Associated Press, "AP Poll: Majority Harbor Prejudice against Blacks," *NBC News*, October 27, 2012, http://usnews.nbcnews.com/_news/2012/10/27/14740413-ap-poll-majority-harbor-prejudice-against-blacks?lite. Accessed August 22, 2020.

51 *Ella Baker Center for Human Rights* Staff, "Racism in America in 2012," April 2, 2012, *Ella Baker Center For Human Rights*, https://ellabakercenter.org/blog/2012/04/racism-in-america-in-2012. Accessed August 22, 2020.

52 Mikhaila Friel, "The British Tabloids Have Finally Acknowledged Meghan Markle's Struggle with Racism—But they're 6 Months Too Late," *Insider*, June 9, 2020, www.insider.com/british-tabloids-finally-acknowledged-meghan-markles-racism-struggle-2020-6. Accessed August 10, 2020.

53 *Ibid.*

54 Brent Furdyk, "Piers Morgan Admits He Took His Criticism of Meghan Markle 'Too Far,'" *ET Canada*, May 10, 2020, https://etcanada.com/news/641360/piers-morgan-admits-he-took-his-criticism-of-meghan-markle-too-far/. Accessed May 17, 2020.

55 Stop Hate For Profit, www.stophateforprofit.org/, Accessed August 10, 2020.

56 Simon Perry, "How Meghan Markle and Prince Harry are Making Their Mark in the Facebook Boycott Campaign," People, July 1, 2020, https://people.com/royals/how-prince-harry-and-meghan-markle-are-making-their-mark-in-facebook-boycott-campaign/. Accessed August 10, 2020.

57 Victoria Murphy, "Prince Harry and Meghan Markle Support the Facebook Advertising Boycott," *Town & Country*, June 27, 2020, www.townandcountrymag.com/society/tradition/a32987335/meghan-markle-prince-harry-facebook-advertising-boycott/. Accessed August 10, 2020.

58 @NAACP, Twitter, June 26, 2020, https://twitter.com/NAACP/status/1276715688837689344. Accessed August 10, 2020.

59 Scobie and Durand, *Finding Freedom*, et passim.

60 Katie Nicholl, *Harry: Life, Loss, and Love* (New York: Hachette Books, 2018), p. 238.

61 Thomson Reuters, "Prince Harry Says He's Saddened by Move to Step Back, But Wants 'More Peaceful Life.'" *CBC*, January 19, 2020, www.cbc.ca/news/world/queen-all-smiles-after-harry-meghan-announcement-1.5432694. Accessed August 9, 2020.

62 Devon Ivie, "Bill Maher Hopes Meghan and Harry Screw the Royals Even Further," *Vulture*, January 18, 2020, www.vulture.com/2020/01/bill-maher-on-meghan-markle-and-prince-harry-leaving-royals.html. Accessed August 9, 2020.

63 Helen Rappaport, *The Race to Save the Romanovs: The Truth Behind the Secret Plans to Rescue Russia's Imperial Family* (New York: St Martin's Press, 2018). Rappaport explains, for example, that Russian geography played a role in the inability to save the Tsar and his family. The fault does not lie solely with George V, as has been accepted wisdom for the last century.

64 Becky Pemberton, "FIRM CHOICE The UK's Favourite Royal Has Been Named…And It's Not the Queen," *The Sun*, November 13, 2018, www.thesun.co.uk/fabulous/7726409/uks-favourite-royal-not-queen/. Accessed June 21, 2019; Latifa Yedroudj, "Meghan Markle in Popularity Shock as Poll Says Duchess Liked by Just Over HALF of Britons," *Daily Express*, November 13, 2018, www.express.co.uk/news/royal/1044790/meghan-markle-news-prince-harry-the-queen-kate-middleton-popularity-poll. Accessed June 21, 2019; Rebecca Sullivan, "Meghan Markle's Downfall: Why the World Has Turned Against the Duchess," *now TO LOVE*, May 1, 2019, www.nowtolove.com.au/royals/british-royal-family/meghan-markle-feud-53096. Accessed June 21, 2019; Joel Day, "Meghan Markle and Prince Andrew Dubbed 'Most Unpopular' in Royal Family in New Poll," *Daily Express*, November 5, 2019,

www.express.co.uk/news/royal/1199665/royal-family-latest-prince-andrew-public-popularity-polls-meghan-markle. Accessed October 13, 2020.

65 Denis Staunton, "Monarchy in the UK: The Royal Family's Uncertain Future," *Irish Times*, May 19, 2018, www.irishtimes.com/news/world/uk/monarchy-in-the-uk-the-royal-family-s-uncertain-future-1.3500174. Accessed June 21, 2019.

66 Blue Telusma, "Gayle King Checks Royal Family Biographer over Megan Markle Racial Remark on 'CBS This Morning,'" *The Grio*, January 13, 2020, https://thegrio.com/2020/01/13/gayle-king-checks-royal-family-biographer-over-megan-markle-racial-remark-on-cbs-this-morning/. Accessed April 29, 2020.

67 *now TO LOVE* Staff, "A New Poll Has Revealed Who the Most Popular Members of the Royal Family Are in the UK," *now TO LOVE*, May 13, 2019, www.nowtolove.com.au/royals/british-royal-family/kate-meghan-popularity-poll-55677. Accessed June 22, 2019.

68 James Bickerton, "Meghan Markle and Prince Harry Snubbed as Majority Say they Shouldn't Get Public Funding," *Daily Express*, November 24, 2019, www.express.co.uk/news/royal/1208522/Meghan-Markle-news-Duchess-of-Sussex-Prince-Harry-funding-William-Kate-Middleton. Accessed November 24, 2019.

69 *Ibid.*

70 *Ibid.*

71 Simon Walters, "Fury Over Meghan and Harry's 'Shoddy' Treatment of the Queen: Poll Shows Britons Want Royal Pair Stripped of Titles and Public Money as their Popularity Plunges," *Daily Mail*, January 10, 2020, www.dailymail.co.uk/news/article-7874669/Majority-Britons-say-Harry-Meghan-treated-Queen-shoddily.html. Accessed August 9, 2020.

72 Jack Royston, "Exclusive Poll: Majority of British People Say Prince Harry and Meghan Markle Should Not Return to Royal Duties," *Newsweek*, April 17, 2020, www.newsweek.com/britons-oppose-prince-harry-meghan-markle-coronavirus-response-1498454. Accessed August 9, 2020.

73 Royston, "Exclusive Poll"; Jack Royston, "Prince Harry and Meghan Markle Donate $112,000 Royal Wedding Footage Earnings to Hungry Coronavirus Families," *Newsweek*, April 16, 2020, www.newsweek.com/prince-harry-meghan-markle-donate-112000-royal-wedding-footage-earnings-hungry-coronavirus-1498251. Accessed August 9, 2020.

74 Royston, "Prince Harry and Meghan Markle Donate $112,000."

75 Hannah Furness, "Harry and Meghan Should be Stripped of Royal Titles and Stay Out of Politics, Two Thirds Say in British Poll," *National Post*, September 26, 2020, https://nationalpost.com/news/world/harry-and-meghan-should-be-stripped-of-royal-titles-and-stay-out-of-politics-two-thirds-say-in-british-poll. Accessed October 13, 2020.

76 Frederica Miller, "Meghan Markle and Harry 'Should Lose Royal Titles' Say 40% of Britons in New Poll," *Daily Express*, September 29, 2020, www.express.co.uk/news/royal/1341476/meghan-markle-prince-harry-lose-royal-titles-poll-results-uk. Accessed October 13, 2020.

77 "The Queen's Role in Government," www.royal.uk/queen-and-government. Accessed November 24, 2019.

78 As quoted in Francesca Specter, "Can the Royal Family Vote? Does Queen Elizabeth II Vote in the General Election?," *Daily Express*, February 2, 2018,

www.express.co.uk/life-style/life/913564/queen-elizabeth-royal-family-vote-kate-middleton-prince-william. Accessed November 24, 2019.

79 Kitching, "Prince Harry Hoax."

80 *The Royal Household*, "The Duchess of Sussex," www.royal.uk/duchess-sussex, Accessed August 22, 2020.

81 Maya Oppenheim, "Meghan Markle: How the Chomsky-Reading Trump Critic Will Have to Bite Her Tongue When She Enters the Palace," *The Independent*, May 17, 2018, www.independent.co.uk/news/uk/home-news/meghan-markle-trump-royal-wedding-politics-feminism-prince-harry-a8356001.html. Accessed June 22, 2019.

82 *Ibid.*

83 Lesley Messer and Michael Rothman, "Full Transcript of Prince Harry and Meghan Markle's Engagement Interview," *ABC News*, November 27, 2017, https://abcnews.go.com/Entertainment/full-transcript-prince-harry-meghan-markles-engagement-interview/story?id=51415779. Accessed June 20, 2019.

84 *Ibid.*

85 *Ibid.*

86 *Ibid.*

87 Communications Secretary, "Statement by the Communications Secretary."

88 Messer and Rothman, "Full Transcript."

89 Scobie and Durand, *Finding Freedom*, p. 104.

90 Markle, "Meghan Markle."

91 See John Solomos, *Race and Racism in Britain*, 3rd edn (New York: Palgrave Macmillan, 2003), passim; and Joe R. Feagin and Kimberley Ducey, *Racist America: Roots, Current Realities, and Future Reparations*, 4th edn (New York: Routledge, 2019), et passim.

92 Kerry Ann Rockquemore and David L. Brunsman, *Beyond Black: Biracial Identity In America*, 2nd edn (Lanham, MD: Rowman & Littlefield Publishers, 2007). We draw here on the foreword by Joe R. Feagin.

93 Adia Harvey Wingfield and Joe R. Feagin, *YES We Can! White Racial Framing and the 2008 Presidential Campaign* (New York: Routledge, 2010), p. 19.

94 Communications Secretary, "Statement by the Communications Secretary."

95 Danica Kirka, "Duchess Of Sussex Calls 1st Year of Marriage Difficult," *Associated Press*, October 21, 2019, https://apnews.com/da2af3150df044799b b592fd756025f8. Accessed November 9, 2019.

96 Aramide Tinubu, "A Royal Expert Pinpointed the Moment Megxit Became Inevitable for Prince Harry and Meghan Markle," *ShowBiz Cheatsheet*, April 13, 2020, www.cheatsheet.com/entertainment/prince-harry-meghan-markle-megxit-inevitable-moment.html/. Accessed May 3, 2020.

97 *OK United!* Staff, "Meghan Markle to South African Crowd: I Am Here 'As a Woman of Color & as Your Sister,'" *OK United!*, September 24, 2019, https://okmagazine.com/photos/meghan-markle-powerful-speech-south-africa-royal-tour/. Accessed December 9, 2019.

98 Omid Scobie and Carolyn Durand, *Finding Freedom: Harry and Meghan and the Making of a Modern Royal Family* (New York: HarperCollins), p. 280.

4   White Men Ruling and the Problem with Meghan Markle

Introduction

In Britain, elite white men hold almost otherworldly societal rank and privilege. The top-ranked among them, a small minority, were long ago positioned at the apex of the political-economic governing system. Among them are oligarchs, who can be described as "immoral business leaders who, as Russia's Vladimir Putin defined them in the *Financial Times*, use their 'proximity to the authorities to receive super profits.'"[1]

The white-racist, male-sexist, and capitalist-class structures and framing of which the oligarchs and other members of the elite benefit are interlocking, codetermining, and coreproducing, as if forming an integrated triple social helix.[2] In this chapter, we examine how this elite operates within the white-racist, male-sexist, and capitalist-class subsystems of an all-encompassing *elite-white-male dominance system* in Britain. We continue to move beyond vague descriptions of this centuries-old inegalitarian society to call out more specific oppressive realities, their foundational depth, their particular operations and several inequalities, and their occasional structural changes. These systemic concepts offer numerous critical insights into why many elite and non-elite white Britons have responded unfavorably to the Duchess of Sussex, and why she is seen as a *threat* to the overall governing system, as well as to powerful white individuals.

Meghan Markle's global popularity and status as an international icon, especially among people of color, is also seen as a *threat* to white hegemony. To hear many white Britons tell it, by moving to the USA and making clear why she did so, she has deliberately made a supposedly post-racial Britain look racist. The gendered-racist narrative thus continues in an attempt to demean and diminish her credibility as a primary witness to Britain's very systemic racism.

As for the monarchy's failure to understand the need to shield Markle from gendered-racist attacks by the mainly white members of the British commentariat and polity, the Sri Lankan Canadian writer Sandi Rankaduwa explains.

> [G]iven the overwhelming whiteness of the monarchy, it's not surprising they aren't cognizant of a crucial factor in being an active ally:

stepping up and speaking out (much like Harry has done through his warnings to the press, frank interviews, and … lawsuits). … You can't expect to benefit from the perks, PR, and fanfare of having a "biracial princess" if she isn't given the space to feel empowered, heard, and accepted. … The racism Meghan has experienced is treated as benign, when in reality it chips away and infects. … And when royals lead pampered, sheltered lives … it's not surprising they don't (at least yet) understand this. The same seems true of many others, in the media and beyond.[3]

To this, we would add that the royal family's very survival is tied to the white-racist, male-sexist, and capitalist-class subsystems of the all-encompassing elite-white-male dominance system. The monarchy thus invests heavily in this system's survival, as opposed to investing in anti-racist and related social justice movements for genuine and radical change to British society's persisting oppressions.

Racialized and Gendered Reactions to Meghan Markle

The many negative reactions to the duchess noted throughout this book can generally be understood through two or more of the three major subsystems of the elite-white-male dominance system, most especially at the intersection of systemic racism and systemic sexism. Through this intersectional lens (i.e., *gendered racism*), the rawness and authenticity of her experiences as a woman of color inhabiting historically white spaces are made excruciatingly visible (see also Chapter 6). Through this lens, we can most effectively understand why many white Britons (especially older and more conservative ones) tend to fear Markle and see her as sullying *their* royal family.

Of course, white Britons are not alone in these gendered-racist sentiments. Recall from Chapter 3, for example, that six weeks before the November 2020 US presidential election, Markle and Harry urged American voters to "reject hate speech, misinformation, and online negativity" and to vote. Notably, the couple did not endorse President Donald Trump's political rival, Joe Biden, who would go on to win the election. They did not even mention the candidates. Nevertheless, a US political reporter for the British tabloid the *Daily Mail* told the president that the couple had "essentially encouraged people to vote for … Biden." Trump responded: "I'm not a fan of [Markle]. … She probably has heard that. But I wish a lot of luck to Harry because he's going to need it." Note that even though both Markle and Harry urged Americans to vote, and the reporter claimed *the couple* had basically endorsed Biden, Trump censured only the duchess.[4]

Prominent conservative white Britons and the white-male-controlled tabloids in the UK similarly blame Markle for the ruination of Harry, including getting him to quit smoking, consume less alcohol, engage in yoga and other physical exercise, adopt more healthy eating habits, and leave his family, country, and royal duties behind and move to the USA. They disseminate the belief that an easily manipulated Harry has adopted his wife's purported "prima donna Hollywood ways," having grown "grumpy and aloof" under her influence. The white press accuse the duchess of cunningly airbrushing her husband's lifelong friends out of his life. They report that the "old Harry" happily mingled with them during foreign tours, while "married Harry" did not. When the couple failed to socialize with the mostly white press corps during a visit to Australia, a paparazzo described the good old days: "We'd get together [with Harry] in a pub and we'd talk about everything, get it off our plate. It would be frank and open, and you never reported it. Now, it's not even 'Good morning.'"[5]

The public picked up on these misogynistic themes. The following are typical of the countless anti-Markle online comments, which journalist Deepansh Duggal calls "some good ol' misogyny and 'blame it on the woman' attitude."[6]

> I think she love bombed [Harry], projected her political agenda onto him, turned him against his family, shut the public out apart from when it suited her and has created this "us against them" mentality that controlling people in relationships do. Harry looks so miserable with her.[7]
>
> Harry is no longer the happy type of individual he was prior to this thing with this woman.[8]

When Markle and Harry announced they were stepping down as senior royals, the prominent media commentator Piers Morgan similarly tweeted: "People say I'm too critical of Meghan Markle. But she ditched her family, ditched her Dad, ditched most of her old friends, split Harry from William (and) has now split him from the Royal Family."[9] Similarly, a former girl-friend of the queen's youngest son, the notorious Prince Andrew, remarked: "What really stings is that it does not feel like it was a long-term plan, but it simply came about when Meghan re-read the membership rules, months after signing on the dotted line, and decided it cramped her style. ... [H]er new life became burdensome and an inconvenience when she discovered she could not run her own show."[10]

Never mind that Markle converted to the Church of England, changed countries of residence, abandoned a flourishing acting career, and left her beloved mom and friends back on the North American continent. Never mind that Markle gave up her right to vote, abandoned her political activism, disregarded her public voice, and closed down her social media accounts, leading the scholars Laura Clancy and Hannah Yelin to argue her "activist voice has been either silenced or appropriated by the monarchy."[11] In the prevailing public chronicles, Harry was said to have been adversely transformed by a controlling wife. Yet, behind closed doors, Markle was often left in tears, so controlled by the royal establishment that she could not even defend her mother against white-racist media attacks. Markle told a friend: "I gave up my entire life for this family. I was willing to do whatever it takes."[12]

In direct contrast, when the queen quashed the couple's aspirations to take a *hybrid* role as royals—i.e., pursuing personal goals and representing her—there was much fuss made regarding what Harry was giving up for Markle, including military appointments. But it was the queen and her advisors, not Markle, who imposed this on Harry, even though he had served on active duty for a decade and held the rank of captain.[13] Of the decision, Markle privately said: "It was so unnecessary. ... And it's not just taking something away from him; it's also that entire military veteran community. You can see how much he means to them, too. So why? The powers [of the royal institution] are unfortunately greater than me."[14]

Never mind that since meeting Markle, Harry abandoned much risky behavior, including a penchant for cigarettes. Animal rights advocate Jane Goodall predicted that he would even give up hunting, a blood sport that most royals engage in but Markle dislikes. That Harry could possibly find happiness with his delightful wife and child is not even considered by their detractors. This is part of the misogynistic narrative that aggressively follows the couple. White-male-public apprehension over the apparent social death of the fun-loving Harry, and his boisterous partying, is masculinist and misogynistic.[15]

That Markle appears to have cultivated in her husband a newfound understanding of racism and sexism, and even inspired him to embrace the title *feminist*, is likely a big part of the British establishment's problem with her. During a conversation with feminist icon Gloria Steinem in 2020, Markle said: "I love that when [Harry] just came in he said, 'You know that I'm a feminist too, right Gloria?! It's really important to me that you know that.' ... And I look at our son and what a beautiful example that he gets to grow up with a father who is so comfortable owning that as part of his own self-identification."[16]

Dogged media accounts of his purportedly doom-and-gloom wife speak volumes about how white racism and male sexism still intersect. According to these accounts, Harry's new life is a cautionary tale of the extinguishing of elite-white-male entitlement by an uppity foreign-born feminist of color, who tore him away from his beloved family and country. First, he was lamented for no longer being free to party with his white male friends or to hang out in pubs with white male paparazzi. Then, after the couple stepped down as senior royals, he was pitied for being forcefully displaced by the domineering Markle. He was assumed to be under the spell of a manipulative wife, who is racially framed as a dangerous woman of color. That his white maleness has traditionally been revered makes her influence all the more tragic for many white Britons.

Evidently, not much has changed since Harry's mother joined the royal family decades earlier. Lady Diana Spencer had just turned 20 when she married 32-year-old Charles. He was expected to have sewn his wild oats, while any woman in serious contention to be future queen consort was not to *bed before she wed*. Hence, the huge emphasis on the age difference and Diana's virginity. The cultural critic Margo Jefferson observes that when a woman joins the royal family, "her body becomes a site of proprietary fantasy. The female body as a nation's procreative destiny."[17] This included the necessity of Diana's uncle publicly confirming her virginity, as if her body was a dowry. Markle's procreative destiny is far less prized than that of Diana. Most significant is her black body and heritage. She will not be providing the royal family with *an heir and a spare*; that is the purpose, like Diana before her, of the white British-born Kate.

Nothing about Markle, including apparently authentic claims she is a direct descendant of royalty (see Chapter 3), could atone for her non-whiteness. If she were much younger when she married Harry, never previously married, a virgin bride like her late mother-in-law, and/ or British-born, she would still likely be considered unsuitable. She, a mixed-race woman, poses a threat to white racial purity. The children she and Harry have will taint the royal bloodline, according to this racially framed narrative. Jefferson explains that mixed-race (the racist epithet is "mulatto") women like Markle have long been a cause for "social and erotic intrigue" and in need of "strict narrative policing." Typically, such women are racially framed by many whites in two ways: the "scheming seduc-tress" or the "tragic ... beautiful, seemingly white woman ... doomed by the taint of black ancestry." Decisively, as Jefferson points out, a recurring refrain in both framings is that these women fear the arrival of children, who will betray what they want hidden—their blackness.[18]

Pervasive white conjecture as to why Markle and Harry purportedly shrouded Archie's true appearance in early photographs of their son suggests whites' deep racial fears, which were then projected onto the family. Consider the official photo released to mark the duchess's first Mother's Day. Only the baby's feet and toes were visible, which caused much white pande-monium. What was being concealed and why was a common refrain among the white press and public. A photo of father and son in honor of the prince's first Father's Day caused further uproar. Harry was accused of purposefully obscuring the bottom half of Archie's face with his hand. One white-run media outlet noted that the photographer had used "a sepia-toned filter, dis-guising baby Archie's hair and eye colour—which has raised questions with royal fans."[19] The family's first Christmas card provoked similar white ire. Unlike insinuations that airbrushing was intended to make the child appear white in earlier photos, numerous responses to the image of Archie on the Christmas card suggest he looks Asian due to poor photo-editing.

> That kid looks Asian ... and mixed race children have very curly tight hair when babies.[20]
> Am I the only one that thinks this baby on the card looks Asian? His eyes are Asian. The whole card has been photoshopped. ... The baby is odd looking.[21]

Such criticism is generally focused on Markle, leading the editor-in-chief of *Majesty* magazine, Ingrid Seward, to comment: "I think [the anonymity for Archie] is quite Harry-led and it is putting Meghan in a very difficult position. ... She's the one getting all the flak." Seward suggests the public simply do not want to see "an arty Instagram shot of Archie's foot."[22] The hostile white reception to the baby photos was likely *not* rooted just in their stylized nature, as Seward claims. A familiar racist tone accompanied numerous white reactions.

That an officially released photo of Elizabeth II, Prince Philip, Doria Ragland, and the Sussexes, lovingly hovering over newborn baby Archie, was not more widely celebrated for the colossal symbol it was says much about white resistance to racial inclusivity. Markle told a friend that this photo made her "proud."[23] She likely saw it as a symbol of a potentially more inclusive and racially diverse royal family. The huge importance of the photo—or any photo of the queen's first biracial great-grandchild—seemed at least somewhat lost on the queen and her advisers. As she gave her annual televised Christmas message the year Archie was born, noticeably absent among the prominently displayed photographs of senior royals were the Sussexes. The largest of four photos viewers could observe throughout her message was of William, Kate, and their three children. The queen only vaguely referenced Archie in her Christmas message, saying she and her husband were "delighted to welcome our eighth great grandchild into our family."[24] The official explanation was that the photos selected for display were meant to illustrate the line of succession. Clearly, then, the next three (white male) British and Commonwealth heads of state have automatic pride of place in the monarchy, as opposed to the new racial diversity that Markle and her son symbolize.

Public online comments in reaction to photos of the Sussex family evoke Joel Kovel's landmark study *White Racism: A Psychohistory*. Recall from Chapter 2 that Kovel noted the collective propensity among white racists to frame people who are not white as unclean, even to link them directly with dirt itself. He wrote that many generations of whites have framed black people as "half ape and half men," and that their "skin color itself, that all-important yet trivial biological accident, contributed to their being fixed in the minds of whites as an essentially dirty and smelly people."[25] Many whites psychologically project onto black bodies conscious or half-conscious beliefs that blackness equals all things hazardous and strange. In highly racist societies like Britain, Markle and her son—living psychological inkblots—are constantly targeted by such emotional white-racist framing, often to the point of white dogmatism. Add to this misogyny and other male-sexist framing. In societies grounded in systemic sexism, such as Britain, one finds all kinds of female subjugation, including social exclusion, discrimination, androcentrism, disenfranchisement, violence, and sexual objectification. Fear and revulsion of independent women, particularly women of color, are implanted in the conscious and unconscious minds of many people from an early age.[26]

We pause here to accent how we conceptualize the gendered oppression we have noted thus far. As we see it, *systemic sexism* involves well-institutionalized patterns of subordinate and dominant social positions and roles for women and men, in a male-dominated hierarchical society like Britain. These patterns include the discriminatory practices of men directed against women, societal privileges and power unjustly provided to men, maintenance of gender inequalities by institutionalized reproduction mechanisms, and the dominant male-sexist frame rationalizing the everyday oppression of women. This omnipresent and powerful frame is a male-imposed worldview from which most men routinely operate. Over time this male-sexist frame has come to include a deep-seated and central pro-male subframe (a strongly positive placement of men and male virtue) and an anti-female frame (a negative placement of women, often viewed as unvirtuous). This dominant frame emphasizes male supremacy (patriarchy) and hegemonic masculinity, the latter usually being viewed in society as also white-racialized and heteronormative.[27]

The Color and Gender of Contemporary British Power

Royals and the Nobility: Male-Preference Primogeniture

Upon Markle's engagement to Harry, commentators justifiably remarked on the royal family's whiteness. Arguably, less attention was paid to the instutution's patriarchal character. The *Daily Mail* ran a headline asserting that Markle had a "proud feminist" manifesto and pronounced "in triumphant style how the new duchess's biography on the official royal website underscored her 'social justice and women's empowerment.'" Such headlines were commonplace, including claims that the royal wedding was "a coup for feminists" and involved Markle's "smashing the royal glass ceiling."[28] Of course, like assertions that her marriage to Harry was a coup for anti-racism, these claims were overstated at best.

The royal family has historically been a patriarchal system in which the eldest male is head of the family, while succession is traced through the male line. The fact that patriarchy and British royalty are one and the same should have captured much more attention from mainstream commentators, especially given that Markle does consider herself a feminist. When it was announced that the couple was expecting their first child, one apt article suggested an array of sexist headlines that "we can expect now that Meghan Markle is pregnant." The journalist sarcastically describes expectant royal women as "brood mares," while offering a rundown of other common sexist themes, including the "Bump watch" and the "Looking better than other pregnant women watch."[29]

By virtue of being the longest-reigning British sovereign in history and given her presence throughout the Commonwealth of Nations, Elizabeth II seems to contradict the notion that sexism is still entrenched in the monarchy. Many people seem unaware of the ongoing systemic sexism, or believe it to be a thing of the past. Prince William, for example, recently praised his grandmother, saying, "becoming Queen very young *and back in the day when it was a man's world* [made it] very difficult for her to carve her own career, carve what she was going to do, make a difference."[30] Note that William relegates patriarchy to the dustbin of history even as he acknowledges the extensive sexism his grandmother was up against. Indeed, the sole reason she became queen is because her father George VI had no sons.

Acknowledgement of systemic sexism by royals, other than by Markle, is so infrequent that when the queen gave her annual Christmas message in 2019, her fleeting mention of womankind seemed radical. Acknowledging the fiftieth anniversary of the Apollo 11 moon landing, she said: "[W]e watched Neil Armstrong taking a small step for man and a giant leap for mankind," adding, "*And indeed for womankind.*"[31]

Conversations about the patriarchal system, at the time of Markle's engagement to Harry, were undoubtedly restrained by the decision six years earlier to overturn the centuries-old tradition of male primogeniture. Starting with the offspring of William and Kate, the oldest male child no longer has the right to succeed to the British throne to the exclusion of an older female sibling.[32] Yet, this amendment was far less momentous than it may appear at first glance. Headlines such as *The New York Times*'s "British Monarchy Scraps Rule of Male Succession in New Step to Modernization" inadvertently suggest sweeping change where there was none. "The 16 countries that recognize the British monarch as head of state struck a historic blow for women's rights ... abolishing male precedence in the order of succession to the throne," read *The Times*'s article. "In the order of succession to the throne" was the operative phrase here. Other major inheritance rights still mostly favor the sons of royals and other nobles.[33]

In 2017, for example, when the 10th Baron Braybrooke passed away, none of his eight daughters could legally inherit his title or lay claim to his 6,000-acre Audley Estate. In 2019, there were 450 first-born daughters of peers and baronets excluded from inheritance rights. This led the women's rights group Daughters' Rights to campaign against the practice of male-preference primogeniture. In large part due to their work, the Hereditary Titles (Female Succession) Bill passed its initial 2019 reading with backing across party lines in the House of Commons.[34]

The abolition of male primogeniture was first proposed in the UK's House of Lords in 2004, but the then-ruling Labour government blocked it.[35] In 2011, a Conservative government ushered in the change. This decision to overturn the centuries-old male primogeniture tradition is also less significant than it appears given that other European monarchies already adopted equal or absolute primogeniture in the 1980s and 1990s. Nevertheless, the idea that it was a swift or revolutionary British change is widespread.[36]

Many other examples expose royal males' venerable gender privilege within the monarchy. A king holds a superior standing to a queen, for instance. For this reason, the consort of a queen is not referred to as king (e.g., Prince Philip) but a king's wife is queen consort. Clearly, a truly democratic society would altogether rid itself of such antiquated institutions like these traditional European monarchies.

Upper-Level Leadership: Realities and Recommendations

Notwithstanding decades of anti-discrimination laws, white-male privilege and entitlement still manifests across British society, not just among the nobility. White men very disproportionately dominate the British Parliament. Recall from Chapter 1 that even though the 2019 election was hailed as turning out the most diverse group of British Members of Parliament in the history of the country, women and racial-ethnic minority Members of Parliament still trail far behind white men in terms of proportionate representation.[37]

Almost all of those occupying the next level of the UK's political, cultural, financial, judicial, and security elite are white, according to a recent *The Guardian* study of 1,000 leaders. Only 36 of the 1,000 leaders are people of color and most of them are men. (Eleven are of African or Caribbean ancestry.) Gendered-racial disadvantage is obvious too, with a mere 0.7 percent of these leadership positions held by women of color. Clearly, women of color face the greatest of obstacles on the British social mobility ladder.[38]

In certain areas, including the police, military, Supreme Court, security services, top consultancies, and law firms, *The Guardian* found that there are no men or women of color in positions of leadership, including no police constables, trade union leaders, or local government CEOs.[39] An analysis of UK football managers, union leaders, and local authority CEOs also revealed how excluded people of color are from these leadership positions. For example, while 30 to 40 percent of Premier League footballers are people of color, there are no black managers in the League.[40] Diversity is also lacking among the country's leading charities. White men dominate there. Such a finding is problematic given that these important charities help the whole of an increasingly diverse UK nation.[41]

The Guardian's study also found that the upper echelons of leadership in England's local authorities, which deliver local government services, bear little resemblance to the increasing diversity of England. Among 50 authorities, not a single chief executive officer is a person of color, and a mere 4 percent of other leadership positions are held by "ethnic minorities." Few women hold leadership positions.[42] Similarly, among the leading 20 accountancy firms, only one is led by a CEO from a black, Asian, or minority ethnic background, while female leadership across these firms stands at a mere 15 percent. The highest stratum of leadership in the important accounting sector bears little resemblance to the diversity of UK society.[43]

The results of *The Guardian*'s survey call into question the effectiveness of UK racial equality legislation, including the 2000 Race Relations Amendment Act and the 2010 Equality Act. The 2010 Act was envisioned to legally protect people from workplace discrimination and inequity in the broader society. By supplanting earlier anti-discrimination laws with a single Act, the government aimed to create a user-friendly law, one intended to improve legal safeguards against discrimination in many situations.[44] Alas, such laws have failed to help advance people of color significantly into leadership positions.

The Guardian's survey generated important policy recommendations in regard to the private and public sectors. The people behind the survey advised schools, for example, to acknowledge distinctive challenges students from the inner city face; political parties to systematically "recruit, retain, and promote" from the diverse populace; and the public and private sectors to make "diversity pathways to leadership" explicit.[45]

Despite *The Guardian*'s much-publicized data, social media reaction to its findings and recommendations was predictable, with many Britons questioning why the results were considered bleak. Britain is mainly a white nation and "so what's the problem" was a common response to the survey. In part, the problem is that a lack of diversity in leadership and elsewhere ignores much-needed talent and knowledge to build a truly democratic society. This is especially worrying in post-Brexit Britain. Researchers have found that the more "ethnically diverse companies" are 35 percent more likely to surpass the industry's average annual earnings. Diversity generally gives rise to more comprehensive planning and advancements.[46] And so, promotion of diversity is not just a legal and ethical issue, but also a pragmatic issue.[47]

In Markle's country of birth, corporations have taken note of the benefits of diversifying. In 2016, for the sake of the bottom line and with almost $18 billion (£13.4 billion) in annual sales, the famous US manufacturer of food products General Mills required that its creative departments be staffed by a minimum of half women and a fifth people of color. Centering on 366 public companies, one major report concluded that firms in the top quartile for racial-ethnic diversity in management were significantly more likely to have financial returns beyond their industry's median level. Those in the top quartile for gender diversity were also more likely to have greater financial returns.[48]

Lack of diversity is not only a problem at the upper echelons of power. Government research in the UK has found that if an applicant has a seemingly foreign-sounding name (e.g., Asian or African), they will have to submit three times as many résumés to land a job interview as someone with a non-foreign-sounding British name (that is, white). Researchers sent out nearly 3,000 job applications using different-sounding names. Fabricated dossiers were generated with all candidates having analogous credentials, including British work experience and schooling. While applicants who appeared to be white sent out nine applications before receiving a positive response, applicants with Asian- or African-sounding names—with the same qualifications and experiences—sent out 16 applications before receiving similarly positive responses. Another UK study found that Bangladeshi and African college graduates are twice as likely to be over-qualified for a job. Indeed, black Britons have both higher educational qualifications and higher rates of unemployment.[49]

What's more, to have any genuine prospects of climbing the social ladder, customarily people of color must significantly embrace *white culture*—i.e., white speech, behavior, framing, and cultural norms and values. Markle's net worth and apparent ability to *pass as white* do not exempt her from the white expectation that she must wholeheartedly embrace white cultural norms and values (see Chapter 5). A common complaint among her detractors, even before she stepped down as a senior royal, was that she failed to embrace British (that is, white) norms and values. This commentary persists despite the fact that she once hired a London-born etiquette expert to teach her how to properly sip tea.[50] Consider, too, that she converted to the Church of England's Protestant Christianity—the UK's official religion. But this seems to matter little to her critics. As British-born Indian-descended Aatish Taseer suggests, white Britons are "perfectly happy to deal with people of color who know their place; it is the 'uppity wog,' or 'Paki,' who arouses in them an animal hatred."[51]

In a 2019 *Tatler* magazine survey, respondents were asked to respond to the statement, "Meghan Markle clearly understands British culture and our traditions." Only 16 percent of respondents agreed.[52] *Tatler*'s readers come mostly from the white upper-middle class and upper class, those readers concerned with high-society occasions. In that same year, *Tatler* observed that "Even though Britain has ten times more interracial relationships than the rest of Europe ... some of the antipathy [toward Markle] must be racist, as it was of the biracial President Obama."[53] Given that so much white media reporting denies that racial framing plays even a minor role in the treatment of Markle, *Tatler*'s brief words here were relatively radical.

As recently as the 1990s, non-elite Britons, including many whites, felt estranged from a "privileged, inward-looking, inbred royal family that was obviously dysfunctional."[54] They thus seemed to favor democratic modernization. In response, the queen introduced innovative policies to streamline the monarchy. She volunteered to pay income and capital gains taxes, and her personal income became taxable.[55] She permitted the decommissioning of the official royal yacht. In contrast, suggestions that a mixed-raced duchess is a modernizing force for Britain are troubling for many white Britons, including some in the royal family. When Markle and Harry announced they would step down as senior royals and become financially independent, while continuing to support the queen, they also said they wanted "to carve out a progressive new role within [the royal family]." This was widely seen as sanctimonious and an affront to the queen.[56] Again, Markle bore the brunt of the blame.

Recall, too, that the white racial frame is so pervasive and dominant that it is regularly internalized, to some degree, by many people of color. The South Asian-descended British CEO Perminder Mann—who is listed as one of the UK's 1,000 most powerful people and is known for introducing inclusive workplace policies—cites gender, social class, ethnicity, and her short stature as impediments to her climb up the corporate ladder. Still, she explains: "I've always thought... I've had to work that much harder to prove myself. But it's not been a problem, because with hard work and determination I've got where I have today."[57] According to Mann, then, if one works hard enough, one can climb the corporate ladder to the top, irrespective of socio-economic or racial locations. When the black British stand-up comedian Judy Love appeared on the chat show *Loose Women* to explain why Markle will never be truly accepted by the white public due to their racist framing, the panelist Saira Khan, a Briton of South Asian parentage, interrupted her to say, "Isn't that just what women in the media face? It's not because ... she's mixed-race?"[58] In another example a few years before Markle and Harry got engaged, Clarissa Tan—who describes herself as "ethnically Chinese"—wrote an article titled, "Britain Has Many Major Problems—Racism Isn't One of Them." In it, she inaccurately claims that racist incidents in the UK are rare.[59] As these examples show, one does not have to be white to operate out of the age-old and dominant white racial frame.

Despite commonplace downplaying of systemic racial and gender oppression, some business leaders and politicians recognize that a future diverse Britain needs to be much more representative in senior leadership positions. In 2017, the British book industry took decisive steps toward workplace equity. The Publishers Association announced its intent to boost the proportion of women in executive-level and other high-ranking leadership roles in its industry to at least 50 percent, and to boost the employees of color in its industry to at least 15 percent, over the next five years.[60] Compared to the current lack of diversity in many areas, such goals better reflect the actual composition of the UK population.

About the same time, the UK's Penguin Random House company launched an online questionnaire on demographic and identity issues, which new authors and employees were asked to voluntarily complete. The company publishes results annually, and its stated goal is to generate a composition of authors and staff more in line with national demographics by 2025, across racial-ethnic, gender, social mobility, sexuality, and disability lines. The company's CEO explains that he is determined to publish materials that more adequately reflect the diversity of UK society.[61] Other publishers have shown some intent to confront the glaring underrepresentation of authors of color. One example is Little, Brown Book Group's program of "Dialogue Books." These are envisioned to "source, nurture and publish writing talent—and reach audiences—from areas currently under-represented or not covered by the mainstream publishing industry."[62] Additionally, Channel 4, a British public-service television network, has been praised for introducing a significant diversity initiative. If executives at that network fail to meet goals for putting people of color, the disabled, and members of the LGBTQ community in leading network roles, their monetary bonuses will reportedly be cut.[63]

Too often such attempts fail because they do not address long-established systemic barriers. The prominent actor Sir Lenny Henry, among others, has long advocated for greater representation of people of color on British television through systemic changes. The failure of the BBC to significantly diversify its operations is especially problematic because the broadcaster serves as the UK's major public television network. When the BBC announced a plan to increase the number of people of color on air by 40 percent in three years, Henry pleaded with Members of Parliament to focus on long-term institutional changes rather than individual changes. He recognized that the oppressive treatment of people of color and other marginalized groups coexists with the professed national ideals of freedom, justice, and equality.[64]

A 2020 online survey found that 67 percent of black respondents, compared to just 27 percent of white respondents, believe there is too little representation of black people in the mass media. Only 17 percent of black Britons said there is essentially the right amount of representation of blacks on television and in film. The survey also found that considerably more black people than white people consider the removal of old blackface shows from television streaming services a good thing, and think that black celebrities endure worse treatment in the mainstream media than white celebrities.[65]

White-Male Arrogance

In a media piece aptly titled, "I've Had Enough of White People Who Try to Deny My Experience," the Afro-British journalist Afua Hirsch writes about the expectations that white colleagues have of her. They expect her to school them on racism issues, while simultaneously they lecture her on gendered racism. On one mostly white media panel on which she appeared, topics included US President Donald Trump's "shithole countries" depiction of several black nations and Jo Marney's racist remarks about Markle (see Chapter 2). Still, the insultingly naïve question "does racism exist any more?" was raised by the white panelists. One panelist remarked "Life's moved on from race," while another argued, "If it's well intentioned, it's not racism." Despondently, Hirsch wrote: "But I do know what I see.'"[66]

Hirsch further recounts the many ways that the white media panelists ought to have known that colorblindness is a myth and white racism is real. There are the British Attitudes Survey that found one quarter of Britons openly agree they are racist; a *YouGov* poll that determined that most Britons are proud of the British Empire, whose rationalizing dogmas were based on the purported superiority of the white race; a survey of more than 24,000 people that found that 30 percent of UK employees had personally seen or experienced racial harassment in the workplace during the preceding year; and a major 2017 racial disparity audit that established that the unemployment rate among people of color was almost twice that of white Britons. Hirsch notes that racial discrimination "intersects with class disadvantage and deprivation. ... While some white people are enjoying their colour-blindness, people of colour are getting on with having no choice but to live in a racialised reality." Matthew Ryder, a former deputy mayor of London, shares this exasperation. Speaking about an inquiry into the racially motivated murder of a black teenager, Ryder said he wishes "there was a rule that anyone publicly discussing racism, without at least a basic understanding ... could be politely asked to go away and read ... before continuing."[67]

Alas, too often whites take it upon themselves to give unsolicited advice on racial issues to people of color or make other offensive or credulous comments. For example, *white-male arrogance* is central in much contemporary white racial framing. Consider the actor Laurence Fox, who hails from a well-known thespian family. He gleefully told a talk show host that he walked around London donning a "Make America Great Again" hat, which has become a potent symbol of racism for many people in the Donald Trump era, especially people of color. He referred to his walk as a joke and described the white-nationalist slogan as benign. Fox is also known for his sexist reproach of actresses who wore black gowns to the 2018 Golden Globes to support the Time's Up campaign protesting sex discrimination in the film industry.[68] During a heated debate about Markle and white racism on a British television program, he remarked "it's so easy to throw the card of racism at everybody and it's really starting to get boring now."[69] Recall from Chapter 1 that the phrase *played the racism card* is a relatively recent white-created term added to the dominant white-racist framing, in this case a phrase attempting to denigrate anyone who questions the systemic racism of a country.

Piers Morgan personifies white-male arrogance. Referring to Markle's view of the extreme media criticism she faces as nonsense, he said: "I get it 10 times worse than she does. ... The problem is she wants to be a woke princess."[70] Fox has also used the word *woke* to deflect from discussions of systemic racism. These prominent white men are uninformed and speaking out of a conventional white framing of British society, which privileged white men often do. Woke, an expression first used by African Americans fighting for racial justice, is meant to signify authentic racial awareness and conscious blackness. Morgan and Fox would do well to stop brandishing that word ignorantly and without considering its painful historical context of racial injustice.[71]

The scholar André Brock describes how "expressions of black identity are subject to 'intense monitoring' by white people—a kind of accelerator for cultural appropriation." Whites' misuse of the word woke is the kind of racial misappropriation of which Brock writes.[72] The US sociologist Zuleyka Zevallos could have been reacting to Morgan and Fox when she wrote: "'Woke' is another Black term that White people have adopted in a cringe-worthy attempt to capitalize on Black culture, as well as a clumsy deflection of any criticism."[73]

When 72 British female Members of Parliament spoke out against the offensive and misrepresentative newspaper stories about Markle, Morgan tweeted: "Female MPs accuse press of being racist towards Meghan Markle. I hope they can justify that extraordinary claim, and that they urgently clarify which stories they think are unfairly intrusive?"[74] Morgan here and elsewhere denies the centrality of systemic racism and systemic sexism in modern Britain.

Undeniably, white-male arrogance is central to the white racial frame. Morgan and Fox seem to illustrate the maxim that those who profit most from white racial privilege are most in denial of, or oblivious to, its durable existence. They appear to be ignorant of the fact that their comfortable life experiences are not ubiquitous. Drawing on the book titled *White-Washing Race*, we might conceptualize such men as the proverbial fish who do not see the water they swim in: "Fish take the water they swim in for granted, just as [whites] take their race as a given, as normal. ... They cannot see how ... society produces advantages for them because these benefits seem so natural that they are taken for granted, experienced as wholly legitimate."[75] As enthralling as this narrative is, it is imprecise because those who possess white or white-male privilege usually do *see* it as their societal legacy. This mostly conscious understanding is especially true for those at the apex of the ruling elite.

Prince Andrew: Elite-White-Male Entitlement

Rich white men in the private sector such as Morgan and Fox clearly possess a heady dose of unchallenged entitlement and perpetual victimhood. The same is true of white men in other sectors of the British elite. Consider Prince Andrew, Elizabeth II's favorite son. He too sits at the apex of white-male power. Even as businesses and organizations around Britain and the Commonwealth disentangled themselves from him after his revealing BBC interview about his relationship with the late US pedophile Jeffery Epstein, many prominent whites continued to come to his defense. That it took such a revealing interview to finally catapult Andrew into damaging media headlines in Britain and elsewhere, says much about the lives of elite men who sit at the summit of the British racial, gender, and class hierarchies.

Andrew's relationship with Epstein had been public knowledge for years. In 2008, Epstein pleaded guilty to charges of soliciting prostitution and served a term in jail under a lenient plea bargain. After his release, Andrew again stayed in Epstein's Manhattan mansion. And while Andrew was forced to resign as Britain's representative for trade and investment due to his association with the convicted sex offender, he avoided having to publicly answer for his relationship with him until late 2019, at which time he gave the revealing interview to the BBC, in which he communicated a sense of innocence.[76]

Surely, whatever deviance Markle is accused of is inconsequential compared to what Epstein, and by association Andrew, are suspected of doing. But if you followed British press coverage of the two royals, you might not think so. As *Vanity Fair* put it: "Flying in a private jet in the era of climate change [what Markle did] is a morally dubious choice; so is remaining friends with a pedophile [what Andrew did]. And from the way the tabloids have covered them, you might think both choices carry equal weight."[77] Contrast, too, white British media reactions to Andrew's BBC interview with their reactions to the ITV documentary *Harry & Meghan: An African Journey*, filmed the same year. While Andrew was broadly condemned for, among other things, neglecting to denounce the convicted criminal Epstein and failing to voice empathy for his young female victims, Markle was extensively criticized for simply describing what she deems unfair treatment of her by British tabloids. One condemnation was late-coming and much deserved; the other was rife with gendered racism.

A media pundit warned it is a mistake "to say the whole world felt for Meghan Markle after watching her and Harry's ITV documentary."[78] In it, an emotional Markle thanks journalist Tom Bradby for asking if she is doing OK, "because not many people have asked if I'm O.K. But it's a very real thing to be going through behind the scenes." For this comment, the duchess was widely panned by many white media pundits.[79] They framed the "not many people have asked" remark as a swipe at her royal in-laws. It was later reported that palace aides interpreted her words as a snub to the royal establishment, and as an insinuation that the royal family did not act sufficiently to support the couple or protect Markle.[80]

Criticism by white royal watchers and public relations experts was rife after the ITV documentary aired, carelessly propagating dangerous messages about mental health. People who deal with mental health issues, as Markle and Harry so courageously disclosed they do, often have to face public stigma on top of their mental anguish. As researchers have found, such stigma is in turn a major barrier to people seeking essential profes-sional assistance.[81] In reaction to the documentary, famed royal biographer Penny Junor suggested that "it is best not to tell the entire world about your emotional state." A public relations expert referred to it as a "complete and utter disaster" and categorized it as "heart-on-sleeve" programing that violated the royal family's mantra "never complain, never explain."[82] In a tweet deriding the couple, Piers Morgan asked people to imagine "being two staggeringly privileged royal multi-millionaires going to Africa to make a documentary that supposedly 'shines a light' on poverty, violence against women/girls & racial inequality—then in fact making it all about their own terrible struggle."[83] Clearly, the Duchess of Sussex does not have a continuing gateway to victimhood like Prince Andrew.

Contrary to Morgan's claim, the ITV documentary is not "all about their own terrible struggle." According to our calculations, a fifth of the documentary focuses on the couple's personal struggles. Roughly 11 per-cent of the film is dedicated to Markle's frank comments about the British tabloids' unfair coverage of her. Harry speaks about his mother, his personal mental health struggles, his concerns for his wife's well-being, and his rela-tionship with his brother in approximately 9 percent of the documentary. The nearly 48-minute documentary mostly focuses on the couple's royal duties and the work of Harry's anti-land-mine-crusading mother—a cause the prince continues as a memorial to her. The couple's roles in the Queen's

Commonwealth Trust are chronicled. The film also accents their visit to Cape Town on Heritage Day and their efforts to help celebrate South Africa's diverse cultures. One can probably assume, given comments in the press and online, that not all Markle's detractors watched the documentary in full. Most seem to have seen excerpts widely shown on television or online. If Morgan had, for example, watched the entire documentary, he would have known that the royal couple did shine a light on poverty, violence against women and girls, and racial inequality, as well as other important social issues. He would have known the documentary was far from being just about the couple's (very real) personal struggles.[84]

After the documentary aired, another outspoken Markle critic, YouTuber "Murky Meg," slammed the duchess for using an alleged "sympathy and victim card."[85] Murky Meg's numerous followers repeated racist themes promoted by the YouTuber. Arguably, most disturbing were comments responding to the documentary's focus on lingering effects of South African apartheid and white racism. Such remarks often referenced a fictional "white genocide" against white South African farmers.[86] These comments drew in part on a racist myth perpetrated by white British commentators, as well as by US President Donald Trump and the neo-Nazi right in North America.[87]

No matter how nonthreatening Markle acts, many white Britons see her as a threat. She seemed to do her best to calm their likely racist reactions to the ITV documentary. When asked by the documentarian if she as a woman of color can "bring something new and interesting to the way the Royal Family" operates, she cautiously replied that she takes her role very seriously, recognizing her "incredible responsibility" to represent the royal family well across the Commonwealth.[88] When asked about her "experience of race in Britain and in America and being a mixed-race couple," she politely replies, "I would hope that … the world will get to a point where you just see us as a couple who's in-love, right? Because I don't wake up everyday and identify as being anything other than who I've always been."[89]

Just as in the essay she penned for *Elle* magazine in 2015, and her comments to *Pride* magazine that same year (see Chapter 3), in the 2019 documentary Markle appears unwilling or unable to speak about systemic racial oppression. However, as noted in Chapters 1 and 2, a year later, in a six-minute commencement speech to her former Los Angeles high school, following the police killing of George Floyd, an unarmed black man, she was more willing to begin that discussion, at least for the USA. When naming African Americans who have died at the hands of US police officers, she said their lives "mattered," lamenting that so little had changed in the decades since the exoneration of white Los Angeles police officers in the 1991 severe beating of the black man Rodney King, and the Los Angeles "riots" the following year. "I know you know that black lives matter," she told the graduating class, "so I am already excited for what you are going to do in the world, you are equipped, you are ready, we need you and you are prepared."[90] A spokesperson said the duchess "felt compelled to directly address and speak … about what's happening in [the USA] right now" and "what's been happening over many, many years and many, many generations to countless other black Americans."[91] Markle's expressed fear of raising these issues in her commencement speech may explain why, despite the importance of her black counter-framed words, she avoided underling systemic racism issues then and previously. Recall that, early on, commentators applauded her for her philanthropy but warned she likely would not use her royal status to bring awareness to British racial issues or their root causes in systemic racism (see Chapter 3).

One can understand Markle's fear. To speak up requires much risk and boldness, such as was on display in Glasgow, Scotland in the wake of George Floyd's death. There, anti-racism activists renamed streets in honor of black British victims of racism. For a brief moment, Cochrane Street, named after eighteenth-century slaveowner Andrew Cochrane, was renamed Sheku Bayoh Street. Bayoh was born in Sierra Leone and died in 2015 in police custody in Scotland. This and another makeshift street sign were soon removed but not before brave activists proved that white-racist oppression of Britons of color is hundreds of years old, systemic, and often opposed.[92]

Though Markle's class position, compared to ordinary Britons, protects her somewhat from the white elite's wrath, the contrasting media treatment of her and Prince Andrew, who refused to respond to sexual exploitation issues during his interview with the BBC (and apparently refuses to cooperate with law enforcement officials), speaks to the power that elite white men have, including over high-status people of color. It helps us to understand, too, Markle's genuine nervousness in simply saying *black lives matter*.

When asked by the BBC interviewer, "is there anything more you'd like to say?", Andrew could not at that time conjure up a single word of sympathy for his friend Epstein's many young victims. Yet, major publications like *Town & Country*, whose audience mainly consists of socialites and middle-class professionals, seemed to defend him. That publication noted that Andrew had elsewhere offered Epstein's victims sympathy.[93] A friend of the queen told *The Sunday Times*: "You've got a serious crime linked to the kind of behaviour towards women that people feel particularly strongly about at the moment."[94] "Feel particularly strongly about at the moment" is a strangely weak thing to say about felonious criminal actions that should be unconditionally condemned at all times.

Over eight months after Andrew stepped down as a working royal in the wake of the Epstein scandal, and roughly four months after Markle and Harry officially stepped down as senior royals in the wake of an endless volley of gendered-racist abuse directed at the duchess, their respective social media accounts were removed from the royal family's website. That it took half the time for this action to be taken in regard to the couple's account is telling. What's more, the removal of Andrew's account occurred amid renewed attention over the Epstein investigations after Ghislaine

Maxwell—a former friend of Epstein and Andrew—was charged with the crimes of enticement of minors and sex trafficking of underage girls. The removal of the Sussexes' social media account came just prior to the release of *Finding Freedom*, a book that the couple is widely believed to have influenced, and in which the royal family is criticized.[95] Here, again, we see the indulgence the royal establishment is willing to grant Andrew, who is suspected of having sex with trafficked underage girls and young women, which he denies. In contrast, we observe the lack of understanding the same establishment has for a mixed-race duchess (and, by association, her husband) who have done nothing of the kind. Markle's alleged blunders are quite minor compared to the felony accusations against Andrew.

The deferential treatment and support that Andrew receives from the royal establishment, the press, and other notables contrasts significantly to how the duchess has been treated by them. As we previously note, early reporting on Markle was so vicious that Harry took the unusual step to publicly condemn it. Then and later, the other royals remained publicly silent, leaving the couple concerned and perplexed as to why palace officials did nothing to counter misleading negative stories about Markle. The typically protective reactions for Andrew among the elite, including palace officials, leads one to question how they can defend the prince while singling out Markle so negatively or failing to support her publicly and otherwise. Clearly, the deference and support Andrew receives is an upshot of his racial and gender groups. He represents a white ruling class exerting its great exculpating power.[96]

A case study for future textbooks could be a comparison of the treatment of Andrew and Markle by ordinary white Britons, the white-run media, the UK establishment, and the royal family during her brief stint as a senior royal. Andrew benefits from the white-male privilege that his nation's institutions bequeath on certain of its citizens—a privilege that suggests many legal and informal norms that govern Britain are for non-elites only, and particularly non-elite people of color. Andrew's protectors and enablers are directly invested in upholding elite-white-male privilege, which is central to the country's systemic racism and sexism. Elite white men not only get away with what people of color and women never would, but, when they are exposed, they can count on the help of powerful protectors to bail them out.[97]

Scholars like Stuart Hall, the preeminent black sociologist discussed in Chapter 2, critically assessed such racial and gender injustices in 1970s Britain. In *Policing the Crisis: Mugging, the State and Law and Order*, Hall and his co-authors examine police brutality targeting Britons of color. This is an old problem in Western countries that persists today, and one to which the Black Lives Matter movement and other anti-racist efforts have brought attention. Hall and his colleagues underscore the racial reality they found: the "whole of the black proletariat is best conceived of as a *sub-proletariat*: the stratum of the working-class that is the object of two specific mechanisms: *super-exploitation* and *racial oppression*."[98] Other twentieth-century black

activists who focused on policing include Olive Morris, a young community leader in the 1970s Black Nationalist, women's, and squatters' rights
movements. Then, as now, a disparate number of black families in the
UK lived in poverty and were subject to much police brutality.[99] Morris
sits alongside other important black women activists, including Kathleen
Wrasama, Connie Mark, and Dawn Butler, who have long tried to force the
UK toward genuine democracy and liberty.

In dramatic contrast, elite white men are super-privileged actors in the
contemporary reality of systemic racism and systemic sexism. They thus stand
in the way of genuine democracy and liberty. Prince Andrew is not alone
in unchecked entitlement and perpetual victimhood. British Prime Minister
Boris Johnson (see Chapter 6) is fairly untouched politically or economically by his numerous marital affairs, allegations of plagiarism, and recurring
racist remarks. Like Andrew, he is "a pure product of the British elite."[100]
US President Donald Trump, who notoriously said he could shoot anyone
on Fifth Avenue in New York City and not lose any votes, has had numerous
extramarital affairs and business bankruptcies, and has made many white-
nationalist, anti-immigrant, and anti-black remarks. Trump has also been
accused of many crimes, including obstruction of justice, money laundering,
multiple counts of sexual assault, and inciting insurrection on the U.S. Capitol.
The corruption and venality of Johnson and Trump led one reporter to ask,
"Is there no limit to what rich white guys can get away with? ... Could you
imagine a woman or man of color getting away with any of that?"[101]

Another way that Andrew lives the customary life of an elite white
man is via his many ties to other elite men, including likely corrupt ones.
For example, he is socially linked to Sir Leonard Blavatnik (worth £14.4
billion), who landed in fourth place on a recent list of the 1,000 wealthiest
people in the UK, and who helped Trump with legal costs associated with
the investigation into the corrupting role of Russian operatives in the 2016
US presidential campaign. Blavatnik is a business partner and old friend
of a leading Russian oligarch who is close to the Russian dictator Vladimir
Putin. Business magnate Alisher Usmanov (worth £11.3 billion), in eighth
position on the list of the wealthiest people in the UK, also has close links
to Putin. The oligarch Roman Abramovich, ninth on the list, had close ties
to Russian President Boris Yeltsin in the 1990s, and his current relationship with dictator Putin has been described as like father and son. Andrew
has alleged ties to these and other disreputable elite men.[102] His extensive
socio-political networking underscores a very important aspect of contemporary class, gender, and racial hierarchies—just how interconnected they
are in the elite-white-male dominance system.

More Wizards of Oligarchy: Elite White Men Behind the Curtain

A few global oligarchs like those just mentioned are central to the maintenance of the UK's white-male dominance system. Even prominent
politicians tend to be less powerful than these elite figures. We have written

in previous books about this largely covert global network of mostly white and male oligarchs, including the US brothers Charles Koch and the late David Koch, who created Koch Industries, a gargantuan private conglomerate. This corporation encompasses oil pipelines and refineries; chemical, timber, and paper companies; commodity trading firms; and cattle ranches. The Koch holdings are worth a combined $120 billion, having put the brothers in the top group of richest men on the planet. The brothers have been among the principal funders of libertarian conservative causes globally, such as climate change denial.[103] For example, the powerful Koch network helped finance *Spiked*, a British internet magazine "dedicated to belligerent, populist, anti-environmental, Islamophobic 'analysis.'" In 2016, the year of the Brexit referendum and election of Donald Trump as US president, the Koch brothers made large donations to this magazine.[104]

David Koch once told a reporter: "If we're going to give a lot of money, we'll make darn sure they spend it in a way that goes along with our intent. And if they make a wrong turn and start doing things we don't agree with, we withdraw funding."[105] *Spiked* magazine must have pleased the brothers because in 2016–2018 they donated $170,000 for its general operating support.[106] A quick search of "Markle" on the *Spiked* website unearths a predictable trove of unenthusiastic articles, including denials of the white racism she faces.[107] *Spiked's* editor Brendan O'Neill gives us a glimpse into the influential classist, sexist, and racist framing by white oligarchs like the Koch brothers. O'Neill has called anti-racist movements "poisonous," denounced the welfare state and anti-capitalism, and panned movements like Black Lives Matter. He has disparaged "anti-Trump and anti-Brexit cultural elites," "feministic elites," "green elites," and "cosmopolitan politicians," such as the British Labour Party leader Jeremy Corbyn, and defended far-right figures like Katie Hopkins, who regularly vilifies Markle (see Chapter 1), and far-right Brexit Party leader Nigel Farage.[108]

In the period immediately preceding the critical 2016 Brexit referendum, and in the years since, prominent British politicians and Brexit campaigners, including Boris Johnson and Farage, traveled to the USA to meet with members of ideologically driven conservative research institutes (e.g., the Heritage Foundation), who helped make the UK's exit from the European Union essentially inevitable.[109] The progressive group DeSmog has further explained the extensive intercontinental connections among the elite, including widespread lobbying over Brexit with its conspicuous US influences: "A close look at the transatlantic connections of the London-based groups pushing for the most deregulated form of Brexit reveals strong ties to major US libertarian influencers. These include fossil fuel magnates the Koch brothers ... and ... Robert Mercer. At the heart of this network lies ... Matthew and Sarah Elliott ... [who] connect senior members of the [Leave.EU campaign] and groups pushing a libertarian free-market ideology ... to major US libertarian lobbyists and funders."[110] Mercer, once a co-owner of the American far-right news organization Breitbart, had his company Cambridge Analytica provide free expert advice to the Leave.EU campaign. Several other groups connected to such powerful US oligarchs have also financed British right-wing groups, including the Institute of Economic Affairs and the John Templeton Foundations. British right-wing organizations are also part of a worldwide coalition of 450+ conservative think tanks and campaign groups referred to as the Atlas Network.[111]

Conclusion

Grounded in many social science studies, our conceptual framework suggests that the non-elite—women and men of most racial backgrounds and most class positions—have long been subordinated to elite white men. In major British institutions, as we argued previously, the overwhelming majority of white women and virtually all women and men of color are subordinate in power and status to elite white men. In many ways, they lack substantial command over important areas of their lives. Locked within an elite-white-male dominance system, even privileged women of color like Meghan Markle often find themselves relatively powerless; they have, at best, modest impacts on that prevailing and oppressive system.

When she joined the royal family, Markle entered a systemically racist, gendered, classist, and otherwise elitist institution, one which has traditionally harmed, subjugated, and exploited many people racially and in other ways throughout its history. Her treatment by the British press and other white detractors did little or nothing to open her philanthropy-celebrating in-laws' eyes to systemic racism. But long before she married Harry the royal family ought to have known better. As we detail throughout this book, there is no shortage of data to show that colorblindness is a myth and white racism is real.[112]

When the current generation of British royals is long gone from this world, the elite-white-male dominance system of which that royal family is part will likely remain substantially in place. This is because of the kind of institutionalized power that elite white men have held and wielded for centuries. The latter long ago created a well-institutionalized dominance system, which remains central to UK society. Oligarchs rule over the UK aggressively and undemocratically, while often remaining concealed to and/or accepted by the many millions of Britons they have long routinely dominated.

As we consider the relative inconsequentiality of Markle in regard to changing systemic racism in Britain, we might consider what US historian Howard Zinn said about US President Barack Obama in 2010. Explaining why he was not disappointed in Obama for his failure to push forward aggressively on labor, feminist, and civil rights, Zinn remarked: "If there is going to be change, real change, it will have to work its way from the bottom up, from the people themselves. That's how change happens."[113] This is an important piece of wisdom for people waiting for Markle or any particular individual to effect real change in systemic oppressions. Unmistakably, a major international movement involving millions of ordinary people of all racial and national backgrounds is needed to effect the kind of racial change that many whites unrealistically fear Markle symbolizes and others unrealistically hope she will usher in.

At the time of writing, we see glimpses of the potential power of such an international undertaking, in this case a movement against systemic racism in Western policing systems, which has pressed successfully for significant policing reforms. Still, we regularly glimpse as well the hurdles the white male elite create against genuine democracy in the UK. Consider, for example, the viral debate Lloyd Russell-Moyle, a Labour Member of Parliament, ignited when he told a chat show host that he did not think anyone in the UK should be a billionaire. That host retorted, "Why on earth [not]?" She, like countless other Britons, non-elite and elite alike, seemed affronted by this radical notion. Russell-Moyle later wrote in *The Guardian*, "No one—however smart or hardworking—is worth a billion pounds or more. People only become billionaires because successive governments have organised our economic system, from taxes to property law to rights at work, to benefit the rich—often at the expense of the poor. In other words, their creation is a policy choice ... not to make policies that distribute wealth more fairly."[114] Add to this the reality that the political and policymaking system itself is organized to especially benefit wealthy white men.

We can only hope that yet more prominent voices, including perhaps Markle, will increase their emphasis on an array of systemic issues like Russell-Moyle raised, including, "How is it acceptable that a country that can afford to have billionaires can also afford to have 8 million people living in poverty ... 4 million of them children?"[115] Such queries must always begin from the premise of the intersectionality of societal power. Only by interrogating the overarching elite-white-male dominance system and its major subsystems—systemic sexism (including *heteronormativity*), systemic classism (including *predatory capitalism*), and systemic racism (including *gendered racism*)—does the UK have a real chance at genuine democracy in its future.

Notes

1 Rana Foroohar, "Facebook and the Creation of a US Oligarch," *Financial Times*, June 7, 2020, www.ft.com/content/0f2c8952-a719–11ea-92e2-cbd9b7e28ee6. Accessed June 9, 2020.
2 Joe R. Feagin and Kimberley Ducey, *Elite White Men Ruling: Who, What, When, Where, and How* (New York: Routledge, 2017).
3 Sandi Rankaduwa, "The British Royal Family Has More to Lose than Harry and Meghan Do," *BuzzFeed*, January 16, 2020, www.buzzfeednews.com/article/sandirankaduwa/meghan-markle-prince-harry-megxit-leaving-royal-family. Accessed August 22, 2020.
4 Erin Vanderhoof, "Donald Trump Returns to an Old Pastime: Insulting Meghan Markle," *Vanity Fair*, September 24, 2020, www.vanityfair.com/style/2020/09/donald-trump-meghan-markle-insults. Accessed October 13, 2020.

5 Marissa Laliberte, "13 Ways Meghan Markle Changed Prince Harry Since She Became a Royal," *Reader's Digest*, n.d., www.rd.com/culture/how-meghan-markle-changed-prince-harry/. Accessed December 13, 2019.

6 Deepansh Duggal, "#Megxit Misogyny: How Piers Morgan and British Tabloids Made Meghan Markle a Scapegoat," *The Economic Times*, January 14, 2020, https://economictimes.indiatimes.com/blogs/the-opinionated-lad/megxit-misogyny-how-piers-morgan-and-british-tabloids-made-meghan-markle-into-a-scapegoat/. Accessed May 21, 2020.

7 Public comments, "Harry & Meghan's Documentary—Murky Megs Opinions," YouTube user "Murky Meg," October 21, 2019, www.youtube.com/watch?v=9cgLU217tJY. Accessed December 14, 2019.

8 Public comments, "Why People Believe Harry and Meghan are Lying about Baby Archie," YouTube user "TheTalko", www.youtube.com/watch?v=s4CvboSiL2k. Accessed December 15, 2019.

9 Duggal, "#Megxit Misogyny."

10 Ulrika Jonsson and Jo Hemmings, "MAKING HER MARK Meghan Markle Walking Away from the Royal Family is Insulting and Will End in Tears, Says Ulrika Jonsson," *The Sun*, January 26, 2020, www.thesun.co.uk/news/10820762/why-meghan-markle-walked-away/. Accessed May 22, 2020.

11 Laura Clancy and Hannah Yelin, "'Meghan's Manifesto': Meghan Markle and the Cooption of Feminism," *Celebrity Studies*, 11 (3), pp. 372–377.

12 Omid Scobie and Carolyn Durand, *Finding Freedom: Harry and Meghan and the Making of a Modern Royal Family* (New York: HarperCollins), pp. 92–93, 328–329.

13 Terina Allen, "5 Things Prince Harry Might Regret After Leaving His Career and Royal Life," *Forbes*, January 31, 2020, www.forbes.com/sites/terinaallen/2020/01/31/5-things-prince-harry-might-regret-after-leaving-his-career-and-royal-life/#579a6c037c57. Accessed May 21, 2020.

14 Scobie and Durand, *Finding Freedom*, p. 337.

15 Chloe Wilt, "14 Things Prince Harry Gave Up to be with Meghan Markle," *Café Mom*, April 30, 2020, https://thestir.cafemom.com/celebrities/225042/prince-harry-gave-up-for-meghan-markle. Accessed May 21, 2020; George Driver, "Prince Harry Just Told the Public He's a Feminist and Yes to Modern Royalty," *Elle*, January 15, 2019, www.elle.com/uk/life-and-culture/a25899865/prince-harry-feminist/. Accessed December 15, 2019; Martin Robinson and Emma Reynolds, "Well, They Do Call it Close Protection: Prince Harry Pictured in Las Vegas Pool Party Jacuzzi with a VERY Relaxed Bodyguard (Who Failed to Stop Girl Taking Naked Snaps)," *Daily Mail*, August 27, 2012, www.dailymail.co.uk/news/article-2194207/Intimate-pictures-Prince-Harrys-wild-weekend-Vegas.html. Accessed December 14, 2019.

16 Caroline Hallemann, "Meghan Markle Opens Up about Prince Harry's Feminism with Gloria Steinem," *Town & Country*, August 26, 2020, www.townandcountrymag.com/society/tradition/a33807343/meghan-markle-prince-harry-feminism-gloria-steinem-quote/. Accessed August 30, 2020.

17 Margo Jefferson, "No Cinderella: Margo Jefferson on the Real Meghan Markle," *The Guardian*, May 5, 2018, www.theguardian.com/books/2018/may/05/meghan-markle-royal-wedding-margo-jefferson. Accessed December 14, 2019.

18 *Ibid.*

19 Delicia Smith, "Real Reason Harry and Meghan Hid Archie's Face," *Who*, n.d., www.who.com.au/why-harry-and-meghan-hid-archie-face. Accessed December 14, 2019.

20 Public comments, "Meghan Harry & Archie's Christmas Card is Photoshopped! How Many More Lies Do We Have To Take?", YouTube user "Yankee Wally," December 24, 2019, www.youtube.com/watch?v=KxSBu6cT8WE. Accessed December 26, 2019.

21 *Ibid.*

22 As cited in "Royal Shock: Why Baby Archie is REALLY Being Hidden," *New Idea*, n.d., www.newidea.com.au/why-prince-harry-and-meghan-markle-are-keeping-baby-archie-hidden. Accessed December 14, 2019.

23 Scobie and Durand, *Finding Freedom*, p. 288.

24 Amy Mackelden, "The Queen Mentioned Baby Archie in her Annual Christmas Day Speech," *Harper's BAZAAR*, December 27, 2019, www.harpersbazaar.com/celebrity/latest/a30345581/queen-christmas-broadcast-speech-transcript-2019-baby-archie/. Accessed August 22, 2020.

25 Joel Kovel, *White Racism: A Psychohistory* (New York: Columbia University Press, 1984), p. 83.

26 Lorraine Code, *Encyclopedia of Feminist Theories*, 1st edn (London: Routledge, 2000), p. 346; Cheris Kramarae, *Routledge International Encyclopedia of Women* (New York: Routledge, 2000), pp. 1374–1377.

27 For further discussion of systemic sexism, see Feagin and Ducey, *Elite White Men Ruling*.

28 Clancy and Yelin, "'Meghan's Manifesto,'" p. 3.

29 Glosswitch, "All the Sexist Headlines We Can Expect Now that Meghan Markle is Pregnant," *New Statesman* (America), October 15, 2018, www.newstatesman.com/politics/feminism/2018/10/all-sexist-headlines-we-can-expect-now-meghan-markle-pregnant. Accessed December 19, 2019.

30 "A Berry Royal Christmas—Kate Middleton and Prince William Christmas Special with Mary Berry," YouTube user "The House of Windsor," December 16, 2019, www.youtube.com/watch?v=1AkZ73KnfoM. Accessed December 26, 2019.

31 CBC/Radio Canada, "Queen's Christmas Message Reflects on 'Bumpy' 2019," YouTube user "*CBC News*," December 25, 2019, www.youtube.com/watch?v=yDZ6F-ncUtE. Accessed December 26, 2019.

32 For an important overview on succession laws throughout Europe, see Christine Alice Corcos, "From Agnatic Succession to Absolute Primogeniture: The Shift to Equal Rights of Succession to Thrones and Titles in the Modern European Constitutional Monarchy," 2012 *Michigan State Law Review* 1587 (2014), https://digitalcommons.law.msu.edu/lr/vol2012/iss5/9. Accessed December 26, 2019.

33 John F. Burns, "British Monarchy Scraps Rule of Male Succession in New Step to Modernization," *The New York Times*, October 28, 2011, www.nytimes.com/2011/10/29/world/europe/rule-of-male-succession-to-british-monarchy-is-abolished.html. Accessed December 19, 2019.

34 Stephen Moyes, "MEG-A AWKS This is Why the New Royal Baby WON'T Be Called Prince or Princess," *The Sun*, October 15, 2018, www.thesun.co.uk/news/6442840/prince-harry-and-meghan-markles-children-wont-inherit-title/. Accessed December 11, 2019; *Daughter's Rights* Staff, "Bill to Allow First-Born Daughters to Inherit Titles Passes First Stage," *Daughter's Rights*, March 8, 2019, http://daughtersrights.co.uk/bill-to-allow-first-born-daughters-to-inherit-titles-passes-first-stage. Accessed December 11, 2019.

Italics in original; "HEREDITARY TITLES (FEMALE SUCCESSION) BILL," *Daughter's Rights*, March 4, 2019, http://daughtersrights.co.uk/hereditary-titles-female-succession-bill/. Accessed December 11, 2019.

35 Rens Steenhard, "Equality in the Line of Succession," *Peace Palace Library*, February 26, 2010, www.peacepalacelibrary.nl/2010/02/equality-in-the-line-of-succession/. Accessed December 19, 2019.

36 As cited in Laura Barnett, "Is Royal Succession Gender Equality a Good Thing for Feminism?," *The Guardian*, June 4, 2012, www.theguardian.com/uk/the-womens-blog-with-jane-martinson/2012/jun/04/royal-succession-gender-equality-feminism. Accessed December 19, 2019.

37 Data Journalism Team, "Election 2019: Britain's Most Diverse Parliament," *BBC News*, December 17, 2019, www.bbc.com/news/election-2019–50808536. Accessed December 19, 2019.

38 *The Guardian* Staff, "Revealed: Britain's Most Powerful Elite is 97% White," *The Guardian*, September 24, 2017, www.theguardian.com/inequality/2017/sep/24/revealed-britains-most-powerful-elite-is-97-white. Accessed December 11, 2019; Colour of Power, "Main Findings," www.thecolourofpower.com/main-findings/. Accessed December 11, 2019.

39 *The Guardian* Staff, "Revealed"; Colour of Power, "Main Findings."

40 Colour of Power, "Main Findings."

41 *Third Force News* Staff, "Pale, Male and Stale? White Men Run UK's Charities," *Third Force News*, October 6, 2017, https://tfn.scot/news/britains-top-charities-lack-diversity. Accessed December 11, 2019.

42 Laura Sharman, "Unitary Councils Have 'Manifestly Failed' on Diversity," *The MJ.co.uk*, October 5, 2017, www.themj.co.uk/Unitary-councils-have-manifestly-failed-on-diversity/209042. Accessed December 11, 2019.

43 *The Institute of Leadership & Management* Staff, "Why the Accountancy Sector Must Address its Poor Diversity," *The Institute of Leadership & Management*, www.institutelm.com/resourceLibrary/why-the-accountancy-sector-must-address-its-poor-diversity.html. Accessed December 11, 2019.

44 Patrick Butler, "Key Points of the Race Relations Amendment Act Implementation Report," *The Guardian*, February 22, 2001, www.theguardian.com/society/2001/feb/22/policy.raceequality. Accessed December 15, 2019; *The Guardian* Staff, "Summary: The Race Relations (Amendment) Act 2000," *The Guardian*, February 22, 2001, www.theguardian.com/society/2001/feb/22/equality.raceequality. Accessed December 15, 2019; Government of the United Kingdom, "Equality Act 2010: Guidance," *GOV.UK*, February 27, 2013 (last updated June 16, 2015), www.gov.uk/guidance/equality-act-2010-guidance. Accessed December 15, 2019.

45 Colour of Power, "Main Findings."

46 Lester Holloway, "White Power is Holding Back Britain," *Huffington Post*, September 26, 2017, www.huffingtonpost.co.uk/lester-holloway/white-power-is-holding-ba_b_18099836.html. Accessed December 11, 2019.

47 Simon Woolley, "Britain's Elite is Bright White—But Doesn't Brilliance Come in All Colours?," *The Guardian*, September 25, 2017, www.theguardian.com/commentisfree/2017/sep/25/britain-elite-white-men-colour-of-power-national-self-interest. Accessed December 11, 2019.

48 Edward Helmore, "The Colour of the Boardroom—And Why it Might Affect the Bottom Line," *The Guardian*, September 30, 2019, www.theguardian.com/inequality/2017/sep/30/the-colour-of-the-boardroom-and-why-it-might-affect-the-bottom-line. Accessed December 11, 2019.

49 Rajeev Syal, "Undercover Job Hunters Reveal Huge Race Bias in Britain's Workplaces," *The Guardian*, October 18, 2009, www.theguardian.com/money/2009/oct/18/racism-discrimination-employment-undercover. Accessed December 11, 2019; Lucinda Platt, *Poverty and Ethnicity in the UK* (New York: Joseph Rowntree Foundation, April 2007), p. 1; Jermaine Haughton, "Government's Racial Inequality Audit Highlights BAME Injustices at Work," *Chartered Management Institute*, October 10, 2017, www.managers.org.uk/insights/news/2017/october/governments-racial-inequality-audit-highlights-bame-injustices-at-work. Accessed December 11, 2019.

50 *The Guardian* readers and Aidan Mac Guill, "'I heard the N-Word in a Board Meeting': Readers on Race and Power in the UK," *The Guardian*, September 29, 2017, www.theguardian.com/inequality/2017/sep/29/i-heard-the-n-word-in-a-board-meeting-readers-on-race-and-power-in-the-uk. Accessed December 11, 2019; Laura O'Callaghan, "US-Born Meghan Markle Doesn't 'Understand British Culture and Traditions' Says Shock Poll," *Daily Express*, October 26, 2019, www.express.co.uk/news/royal/1196048/meghan-markle-royal-news-prince-harry-poll-british-culture-queen. Accessed December 15, 2019.

51 Aatish Taseer, "Race and the Royals: An Outsider's View Inside Kensington Palace," *Vanity Fair*, May 2018, www.vanityfair.com/style/2018/04/race-and-the-royals-inside-kensington-palace. Accessed December 27, 2019.

52 O'Callaghan, "US-Born Meghan Markle."

53 *Tatler* Staff, "One Year of Meghanomania," *Tatler*, March 25, 2019, www.tatler.com/article/meghan-markle-mania. Accessed December 15, 2019.

54 Ellen Barry, "'I'm American. I Hug.' Meghan Markle's Looming Impact on the British Monarchy," *The New York Times*, May 18, 2018, www.nytimes.com/2018/05/18/world/europe/meghan-markle-monarchy-uk.html. Accessed December 15, 2019.

55 In 2021, it was revealed that five decades earlier, the queen's private lawyer had successfully pressured the government to alter a law to hide the true scale of her private wealth. For more, see David Pegg and Rob Evans, "Revealed: Queen Lobbied for Change in Law to Hide her Private Wealth," *The Guardian*, February 7, 2021, https://www.theguardian.com/uk-news/2021/feb/07/revealed-queen-lobbied-for-change-in-law-to-hide-her-private-wealth. Accessed March 1, 2021.

56 Allison Pearson, "Harry and Meghan's Bombshell Announcement is a Discourtesy to the Queen—And Smacks of Millennial Self-Absorption," *The Telegraph*, January 9, 2020, www.telegraph.co.uk/royal-family/2020/01/09/harry-meghans-bombshell-announcement-discourtesy-queen-smacks/. Accessed May 21, 2020.

57 Katherine Cowdrey, "Perminder Mann: 'Quotas Not the Right Solution' to Tackle Diversity," *The Bookseller*, October 2, 2017, www.thebookseller.com/news/perminder-mann-quotas-not-right-solution-tackle-diversity-645166. Accessed December 11, 2019.

58 "Will Meghan Ever Be Truly Accepted by Britain?," ITV's *Loose Women*, December 6, 2019, www.youtube.com/watch?v=aSVYZvZD1Dw, Accessed December 13, 2019.

59 Clarissa Tan, "Britain Has Many Major Problems—Racism Isn't One of Them," *The Spectator*, February 15, 2014, www.spectator.co.uk/2014/02/how-racist-is-britain/. Accessed December 19, 2019.

60 Benedicte Page, "The PA Introduces Diversity Targets and 10-Point Plan," *The Bookseller*, September 15, 2017, www.thebookseller.com/news/pa-introduces-diversity-targets-and-10-point-plan-638896. Accessed December 11, 2019.

61 *The Institute of Leadership and Management* staff, "Why the Accountancy Sector Must Address its Poor Diversity," *The Institute of Leadership and Management*, www.institutelm.com/resourceLibrary/why-the-accountancy-sector-must-address-its-poor-diversity.html. Accessed December 11, 2019.

62 *Ibid.*

63 Soraya Nadia McDonald, "Why are Black Brits Missing from PBS's 'Masterpiece'? Because They're Missing from British Television," *The Undefeated*, September 15, 2016, https://theundefeated.com/features/why-are-black-brits-missing-from-pbss-masterpiece-because-theyre-missing-from-british-television/. Accessed December 11, 2019.

64 Dawn Foster, "Lenny Henry Renews Call for BBC to Ringfence Funds to Boost Diversity," *The Guardian*, March 23, 2016, www.theguardian.com/media/2016/mar/23/lenny-henry-bbc-diversity. Accessed December 11, 2019. McDonald, "Why Are Black Brits Missing."

65 Richard Allen Greene, "Britain's Big Race Divide," *CNN*, June 22, 2020, https://edition.cnn.com/interactive/2020/06/europe/britain-racism-cnn-poll-gbr-intl/. Accessed August 12, 2020.

66 Afua Hirsch, "I've Had Enough of White People Who Try to Deny My Experience," *The Guardian*, January 24, 2018, www.theguardian.com/commentisfree/2018/jan/24/white-people-tv-racism-afua-hirsch. Accessed December 11, 2019.

67 *Ibid.*

68 Julia Llewellyn Smith, "Laurence Fox Interview: Let the Hipsters Hate Me—I Won't Dance to Their Politically Correct Tune," *The Times*, November 17, 2019, www.thetimes.co.uk/article/laurence-fox-interview-let-the-hipsters-hate-me-i-wont-dance-to-their-politically-correct-tune-5d7tdgwz7. Accessed December 11, 2019; Sarah Finley, "Actor Laurence Fox Slams Stars Who Wore 'Revealing' Black Dresses to Support Time's Up Campaign at the Golden Globes—and Rages that Harry and Meghan are 'Ultra-Woke Hypocrites,'" *Daily Mail*, November 17, 2019, www.dailymail.co.uk/femail/article-7694537/Actor-Laurence-Fox-slams-stars-wore-revealing-black-dresses-support-Times-campaign.html. Accessed December 11, 2019.

69 Celebretainment, "Laurence Fox 'Frightened' about Losing Career," *The McDuffie Progress*, April 26, 2020, www.mcduffieprogress.com/lifestyles/entertainment/laurence-fox-frightened-about-losing-career/article_7dbc99a5–340c-5fe1-a6fb-2e1f11f84f6b.html. Accessed April 29, 2020.

70 Francesca Specter, "Piers Morgan Criticises 'Woke Princess' Meghan Markle, Calls Racist Abuse Claims 'Nonsense,'" *Yahoo Style*, September 4, 2019, https://ca.style.yahoo.com/meghan-markle-piers-morgan-racist-abuse-claims-nonsense-095630330.html. Accessed December 11, 2019.

71 Michael Harriot, "The Definitive List of Get-Out-of-Racism-Free Cards," *The Root*, February 28, 2019, www.theroot.com/the-definitive-list-of-get-out-of-racism-free-cards-1832973113. Accessed December 29, 2019.

72 Amanda Hess, "Earning the 'Woke' Badge," *The New York Times Magazine*, April 19, 2016, www.nytimes.com/2016/04/24/magazine/earning-the-woke-badge.html. Accessed December 18, 2019.

73 Zuleyka Zevallos, "Whitewashing Race Studies," *Other Sociologist*, July 29, 2019, https://othersociologist.com/2019/07/29/whitewashing-race-studies/. Accessed December 18, 2019.

74 @piersmorgan, Twitter, October 29, 2019, https://twitter.com/piersmorgan/status/1189222313419513857?lang=en. Accessed December 11, 2019.

75 Michael K. Brown, Martin Carnoy, and Elliott Currie, *White-Washing Race: The Myth of a Color-Blind Society* (Berkeley, CA: University of California Press, 2005), p. 34.

76 Ben Quinn and Kevin Rawlinson, "Prince Andrew to Step Back from Public Duties 'For Foreseeable Future,'" *The Guardian*, November 20, 2019, www.theguardian.com/uk-news/2019/nov/20/prince-andrew-to-step-back-from-public-duties-for-foreseeable-future. Accessed December 14, 2019.

77 Erin Vanderhoof, "Why Can't Prince Andrew Get the Same Tabloid Scrutiny Meghan Markle Does?," *Vanity Fair*, August 22, 2019, www.vanityfair.com/style/2019/08/why-cant-prince-andrew-get-the-same-tabloid-scrutiny-meghan-markle-does. Accessed December 13, 2019.

78 Olivia Hayes, "The Reactions to Meghan Markle's ITV Interview were Very Intense Last Night," *her*, n.d., www.her.ie/celeb/intense-reactions-meghan-markles-itv-interview-last-night-485841. Accessed December 14, 2019.

79 Katie Nicholl, "Meghan Markle Gets Emotional in a Clip from an Upcoming Documentary," *Vanity Fair*, October 18, 2019, www.vanityfair.com/style/2019/10/meghan-markle-gets-emotional-in-a-clip-from-an-upcoming-documentary. Accessed December 14, 2019.

80 Scobie and Durand, *Finding Freedom*, p. 11, 312, 280–281.

81 Diana Rose, Graham Thornicroft, Vanessa Pinfold, and Aliya Kassam, "250 Labels Used to Stigmatise People with Mental Illness," *BMC Health Services Research*, 7 (97) (June 2007). DOI: 10.1186/1472–6963–7–97.

82 Caroline Davies, "Royal Experts Question Wisdom of Harry and Meghan Documentary," *The Guardian*, October 22, 2019, www.theguardian.com/uk-news/2019/oct/22/harry-and-meghan-documentary-an-utter-disaster-for-royals. Accessed December 14, 2019.

83 Joe Middleton, "Piers Morgan Says TV Rival Dan Walker is 'The Dullest, Most Excruciatingly Virtue-Signalling, Tediously Opinion-Devoid, Toe-Curlingly Snivelling Sycophant in TV' in Twitter Row over Meghan Markle," *Daily Mail*, October 22, 2019, www.dailymail.co.uk/news/article-7600379/Piers-Morgan-blasts-BBC-Breakfasts-Dan-Walker.html. Accessed December 14, 2019.

84 Tom Bradby, "Harry & Meghan: An African Journey," full documentary, FFTV, ITV, October 22, 2019, www.youtube.com/watch?v=j_c7ZhK0AKA. Accessed December 16, 2019.

85 Public comments, "Harry & Meghan's Documentary."

86 Public comments, "Harry & Meghan's Documentary."

87 Geoffrey York, "How the Fate of South Africa's White Farmers Became a Myth Used by Trump and the Far Right," *The Globe and Mail*, November 16, 2018, www.theglobeandmail.com/world/article-how-the-fate-of-south-africas-white-farmers-became-a-myth-used-by/. Accessed December 14, 2019.

88 Laura O'Callaghan, "US-Born Meghan Markle."

89 Tom Bradby, "Harry and Meghan."

90 Toyin Owoseje, Max Foster, and Jonny Hallam, "Meghan, Duchess of Sussex, Speaks Out on George Floyd's Death in Graduation Address," *CNN*, June 4, 2020, www.cnn.com/2020/06/04/uk/meghan-duchess-george-floyd-intl-scli-gbr/index.html. Accessed June 4, 2020.

91 Katie Nicholl, "'Like Hearing the Old Meghan': How Meghan Markle Decided to Finally Speak Out about George Floyd," *Vanity Fair*, June 4, 2020, www.vanityfair.com/style/2020/06/meghan-markle-george-floyd-black-lives-matter-speech. Accessed June 4, 2020.

92 *BBC* Staff, "Campaigners Rename Glasgow Streets Linked to Slave Owners," *BBC*, June 6, 2020, www.bbc.com/news/uk-scotland-glasgow-west-52950006. Accessed June 8, 2020.

93 Victoria Murphy, "Prince Andrew's Interview about Jeffrey Epstein was a Disaster," *Town & Country*, November 20, 2019, www.townandcountrymag. com/society/a29835327/prince-andrew-bbc-interview-jeffrey-epstein-disaster/. Accessed December 14, 2019.

94 As cited in Dominic Utton, "Prince Andrew. Victim or Villain?", *The Royals Monthly*, December 2019, p. 29.

95 Annabel Sampson, "Why the Royal Family has Made Some Pivotal Changes to its Website," *Tatler*, August 10, 2020, www.tatler.com/article/prince-harry-meghan-markle-and-prince-andrew-social-media-accounts-removed-from-royal-family-website. Accessed August 16, 2020; Hope Coke, "Prince Andrew's Website Taken Down amid Mounting Pressure over Epstein Investigations," *Tatler*, July 16, 2020, www.tatler.com/article/prince-andrews-website-taken-down-statement-on-royal-family-website. Accessed August 16, 2020; Scobie and Durand, *Finding Freedom*, et passim.

96 Kitching, "Prince Harry Hoax"; *The Guardian* Staff, "Key Quotes: Prince Andrew on the Epstein Scandal," *The Guardian*, November 16, 2019, www. theguardian.com/uk-news/2019/nov/16/transcript-prince-andrew-on-the-epstein-scandal. Accessed December 2019; Scobie and Durand, *Finding Freedom*, pp. 244, 297, 310, 314–315.

97 Chauncey DeVega, "The Brett Kavanaugh Case: This is How White Male Privilege is Destroying America," *salon*, October 4, 2018, www.salon. com/2018/10/04/brett-kavanaugh-this-is-how-white-male-privilege-is-destroying-america/. Accessed December 13, 2019.

98 Stuart Hall, Chas Critcher, Tony Jefferson, John Clarke, and Brian Roberts, *Policing The Crisis: Mugging, The State And Law And Order*, 35th Anniversary Edition (Berlin: Springer, 2013), p. 367. Italics in original.

99 Amie Tsang, "Overlooked No More: Olive Morris, Activist for Black Women's Rights in Britain," *The New York Times*, October 30, 2019, www. nytimes.com/2019/10/30/obituaries/olive-morris-overlooked.html, Accessed June 20, 2020.

100 As cited in Don Murray, "A 'Pure Product of the British Elite': How Europe Sees Boris Johnson's Brexit Manoeuvres," *CBC*, September 5, 2019, www.cbc.ca/news/world/a-pure-product-of-the-british-elite-how-europe-sees-boris-johnson-s-brexit-manoeuvres-1.5271267. Accessed December 19, 2019.

101 Emily Peck, "Boris Johnson and Donald Trump are Peak White Male Privilege," *Huffington Post US*, July 26, 2019, www.huffingtonpost.ca/entry/donald-trump-boris-johnson-male-privilege_n_5d39ff8ee4b0419fd339f939?ri18n=true. Accessed December 19, 2019.

102 Robert Booth, "Prince Andrew Hosted Tunisian Dictator's Son-In-Law at Palace," *The Guardian*, March 4, 2011, www.theguardian.com/uk/2011/mar/04/prince-andrew-tunisian-sakher-el-materi. Accessed February 6, 2020.

103 George Monbiot, "How US Billionaires are Fuelling the Hard-Right Cause in Britain," *The Guardian*, December 7, 2018, www.theguardian.com/commentisfree/2018/dec/07/us-billionaires-hard-right-britain-spiked-magazine-charles-david-koch-foundation. Accessed June 8, 2020.

104 Mike Small, "Revealed: US Oil Billionaire Charles Koch Funds UK Anti-Environment *Spiked* Network," *DeSmogUK*, December 7, 2018, www.desmog.co.uk/2018/12/04/spiked-lm-dark-money-koch-brothers. Accessed June 8, 2020.
105 Monbiot, "How US Billionaires."
106 Small, "Revealed."
107 *Spiked*, "Search Results for Markle," www.spiked-online.com/?s=markle. Accessed June 9, 2020.
108 *Ibid*.
109 Felicity Lawrence, Rob Evans, David Pegg, Caelainn Barr, and Pamela Duncan, "How the Right's Radical Thinktanks Reshaped the Conservative Party," *The Guardian*, November 29, 2019, www.theguardian.com/politics/2019/nov/29/rightwing-thinktank-conservative-boris-johnson-brexit-atlas-network. Accessed June 10, 2020.
110 Chloe Farand and Mat Hope, "Matthew and Sarah Elliott: How A UK Power Couple Links US Libertarians and Fossil Fuel Lobbyists to Brexit," *DeSmogUK*, November 19, 2018, www.desmog.co.uk/2018/11/18/matthew-sarah-elliott-uk-power-couple-linking-us-libertarians-and-fossil-fuel-lobbyists-brexit. Accessed June 8, 2020.
111 Christopher Hope, "Nigel Farage Meets Donald Trump for a Third Time amid Speculation of New Role Advising on UK/US Trade Deal," *The Telegraph*, December 15, 2016, www.telegraph.co.uk/news/2016/12/15/nigel-farage-meets-donald-trump-third-time-amid-speculation/. Accessed June 9, 2020; Lawrence, Evans, Pegg, Barr, and Duncan, "How The Right's Radical Thinktanks"; Rob Evans, David Pegg, Felicity Lawrence, and Caelainn Barr, "The US Donors who Gave Generously to Rightwing UK Groups," *The Guardian*, November 29, 2020, www.theguardian.com/politics/2019/nov/29/the-us-donors-who-gave-generously-to-rightwing-uk-groups. Accessed June 10, 2020. Please note: Dollars are taken from US tax filings and other public declarations with final amounts varying somewhat due to exchange rate fluctuations.
112 Sandi Rankaduwa, "Meghan Markle is the Future of a Monarchy with Racist Baggage," *BuzzFeed*, November 30, 2017, www.buzzfeednews.com/article/sandirankaduwa/itsamodernmarkle. Accessed November 11, 2019; Stephen Colegrave, "12 Facts that Prove Black Lives Don't Matter in Britain," *Byline Times*, June 8, 2020. https://bylinetimes.com/2020/06/08/black-lives-dont-matter-in-britain/. Accessed June 9, 2020.
113 As cited in Bob Herbert, "A Radical Treasure," *The New York Times*, January 29, 2010, www.nytimes.com/2010/01/30/opinion/30herbert.html. Accessed December 15, 2019. See also Stephen Bird, Adam Silver, and Joshua C. Yesnowitz, *Agitation with a Smile: Howard Zinn's Legacies and the Future of Activism* (New York: Routledge, 2014), p. 115.
114 Lloyd Russell-Moyle, "I Never Expected to Go Viral Just for Saying Billionaires Shouldn't Exist," *The Guardian*, November 1, 2019, www.theguardian.com/commentisfree/2019/nov/01/viral-billionaires-super-rich-exist. Accessed June 9, 2020.
115 *Ibid*.

5 Feminist Counter-Framer and Anti-Racist Counter-Framer

Disrupter of Elite White Dominance

Introduction

In the summer of 2017, a year after she met Prince Harry on a blind date and in the aftermath of the election of Donald Trump, Meghan Markle urged her two million Instagram followers to read Noam Chomsky's *Who Rules the World?*, telling them that that critical book "exposes the hypocrisy at the heart of America's policies and actions." Upon learning that the future duchess was a fan, Chomsky commended her in return. "Naturally pleased to hear it," he told *The Guardian* newspaper, "Sounds as though she may, for many reasons, shake up the royal family."[1] Markle and Harry have certainly shaken up the royal family but perhaps not in the way Chomsky and others envisioned. In early 2020 they announced their intention to step down as senior royals, giving pundits pause to reconsider the extent that Markle bound "herself to an institution whose very existence sits uncomfortably alongside the conceptions of equality and social justice beloved of Chomsky and his adherents."[2] Throughout this book we note an interesting paradox. Why would Markle choose to be part of a group of white royals with a long racist past and whose wealth and power are built on the global exploitation of people of color? Apparently, she did not like that harsh racial reality and, thus, soon opted out. This is likely an important example of her distinctive black counter-framing of that reality, which we examine in this chapter.

A mere three years after she advised her Instagram followers to read Chomsky, the former Speaker of the British House of Commons John Bercow suggested that the racist, sexist, and misogynistic treatment of Markle by the British press and public was because of her pre-royal condemnation of Trump's reactionary views (see Chapter 3) and her championing of feminism. Becrow was reacting to Home Secretary Priti Patel's inaccurate colorblind claims that Markle had not faced racism in the UK: "I'm not in that category at all where I believe there's racism at all. I think we live in a great country … great society, full of opportunity."[3] Patel is ideologically situated on the British Conservative Party's right wing. Perhaps, then, her conservative colorblind ideology is to be expected, despite the fact she is a woman of color descended from Ugandan Asians who immigrated to the UK. Her view seems to be a strong internalization of the dominant white frame. Note too that there is a social science literature on the ways in which people of color aggressively buy into some or much of the prevailing white framing in various white-dominated societies.[4]

In this chapter we consider the ways that Britons who are subjugated by class, racial, and gender oppression push back against those oppressions and their legitimating frames. Specially, we assess the degree to which Markle is a feminist counter-framer and anti-racist counter-framer. While her overt fight for social equality and justice makes her a disrupter of elite-white dominance, her brand of feminism and anti-racism—at least at the time of writing—embody a predominant focus on the *individual* sexist and racist. As such, she has mostly failed to shed much light on the underlying social structures that regularly thwart the achievements of women and girls and of people of color.

In this chapter we also give attention to Markle's periodic black counter-framing, such as during her wedding to Harry. She has, so far, mostly limited this resistance counter-framing to the marriage ceremony itself. Drawing again on the concept of the white racial frame, we illustrate how the ceremony demonstrates at least four major elements of the black counter-frame. We also detail how white British royals reacted to the counter-framing during the rather unique ceremony. We begin by highlighting some examples from Markle's advocacy for women, and then what some scholars call *intersectionality*. We offer examples of the ways in which white racism plays out differently for women of color, including Markle, than for men of color.

Intersectionality: Meghan Markle's Enduring Reality

Meghan Markle's Recurring Advocacy for Women

Markle is to be applauded for protesting a sexist soap advertisement at 11 years old (1993), for demanding that writers on the television series *Suits* cease with the unrelenting over-sexualization of her character (2014), for her role as a UN Women's Advocate for Women's Political Participation and Leadership (2015), for her open support of the #MeToo and Time's Up movements (2018), for her public support of the Black Lives Matter movement (2020), for her support of the National Association for the Advancement of Colored People (NAACP) (2020), and for acts such as telephoning Althea Bernstein after the 18-year-old biracial American was set on fire in an alleged hate crime (2020). She is to be praised for some of her public writings, such as for *Time* magazine, wherein she describes the stigma surrounding menstruation in the developing world in an attempt to raise awareness of how an absence of menstrual products there adversely impacts girls' education (2017), for her inaugural royal tour speech on women's right to education (2018), for scribbling messages of support on bananas for female sex workers (2019), for speaking about her future "feminist royal baby" (Archie) on International Women's Day (2019), and for engaging in discussions on the rights of Indigenous women (2020).[5]

Her recurring work against sexism and racism has been far from insincere or superficial. In 2016, for example, she visited Rwanda on behalf of World Vision Canada. She met with women parliamentarians in the country's capital and visited a refugee camp located just five miles from the border of the Democratic Republic of the Congo (formerly Zaire), in which, nearly two decades earlier, ethnic Tutsi refugees were brutally murdered in the Mudende Massacre.[6]

Markle's biography on the royal family's official website refers to her life-long philanthropy, and specifically to a speech she delivered on International Women's Day in 2015, in which she states she is "proud to be a woman and feminist."[7] Her pre-royal public statements on feminism include comments during a 2015 interview with US talk show host Larry King, when he remarked on her physical appearance. "You're not the average American woman, Meghan, admit it," he states, to which she responds, "No matter what you look like, you should be taken seriously. And for me also, I think it's really great to be a feminist and be feminine." King asks her "is feminist still a good word?" and Markle replies, "Yes. It's not the 'f' word."[8] In another interview Markle similarly remarks: "You don't have to play dress up to be a feminist. You are a feminist exactly the way you are. You can be a woman who wants to look good and still stand up for the equality of women. There's no uniform for feminism."[9]

The way the British press frames Markle contrasts strikingly to that of her sister-in-law, Kate Middleton. As journalist Helen Lewis explains, these women are ambassadors of opposing politics: "modern womanhood, outspoken and socially progressive" versus royal "traditionalism." Of Kate, Lewis writes:

> Tabloid headlines about her have become noticeably kinder since Harry's relationship with Markle was announced. She was once deemed vulgar and hopelessly bourgeois, a schemer who chose to study at the University of St Andrews in Scotland precisely to ensnare William. ... This new valorization of Kate is *racially* inflected, because Britain's most durable template of respectable womanhood—the "English rose"—is much less accessible to anyone foreign or dark-skinned.[10]

Lewis also notes that William and Harry, "despite their own different temperaments and approaches, are not being turned into cultural avatars in the same way."[11] Note too that in early 2020, when Markle and Harry announced their decision to become financially independent and step down as senior royals, the event was dubbed "Megxit" (a hybrid of "Meghan" and "exit," and playing on the word "Brexit"). Notice the sexism here, as the term for their decision is not some portmanteau of the words "Harry" and "exit." Since then, that negative, essentially sexist term has been adopted internationally by the press and the public, producing numerous internet memes in spite of the fact that Harry has accented his central role in the decision.

The "Intersectional Everywoman"?

In the lead-up to her May 2018 nuptials, Markle was dubbed the "intersectional everywoman" by *Glamour* magazine. Even as the magazine acknowledged that British society traditionally favors whites and that Britons of color "reckon with" racism every day, it defined Markle's personal worth largely in terms of her being the first person of color to wed a member of the British royal family. Supposedly, she was single-handedly transforming the meaning of British royalty by imparting "new life into archaic beliefs and long-held standards of acceptable leadership."[12]

Never mind that 14 years earlier, an Indigenous Polynesian man from New Zealand was the first person of color to wed a member of the British royal family (the eldest daughter of Elizabeth II's first cousin).[13] Never mind, too, that missing from the story of her as the intersectional everywoman is the major privilege Markle enjoyed as an American immigrating to the UK when many people of color were barred or deported from the country during the same period. The latter immigrants of color are, as social historian Paul Gilroy observes, victims of that white-racist "mentality which cannot grasp the connectedness of the postcolonial migrant to the machinery of British citizenship. ... Things that we thought we had disposed of, politically, have come up from the ground like zombies to consume our lives."[14]

Six months into her marriage, during an official royal tour of New Zealand with her husband, Markle appeared to offer a nod to the intersectionality of which *Glamour* magazine wrote. She declared: "The basic and fundamental human right of all people—including members of society who have been marginalized—whether for reasons of race, gender, ethnicity or orientation—is to be able to participate in the choices for their future and their community."[15] Closing her speech with what seemed to be a further reference to intersectionality, she borrowed the words of New Zealand suffragette Katherine Wilson Sheppard (1848–1934): "All that separates, whether race, class, creed, or sex, is inhuman, and must be overcome."[16]

Recall from Chapter 3 that, later still, when she and Harry visited South Africa, she told a cheering crowd that though she was a member of the royal family she wanted them to know that she was also there as a "mother," "wife," "woman," "woman of color," and "as your sister."[17] For many, her words indicated a commitment to exposing the UK's "long history of race-based colonial exploitation."[18] For Markle, however, her words were more singular. As she told journalist Tom Bradby when he asked about her declaration of sisterhood, it was simply a last-minute addition to the speech that came to mind, and that Harry told her to "go for it."[19]

Like all women of color in Britain and the USA, Markle constantly faces the intertwined realities of systemic racism and systemic sexism—and the intersectional identity and experience created by these oppressive realities. Female scholars and activists of color in the two countries have long recognized the intersectional oppression of racism and sexism. In the much-celebrated 1982 book *Empire*, two women of color wrote analytical essays on institutional sexism in the era of the black Windrush generation's immigration to the UK (1940s–1970s) and thereafter, including early black feminist resistance to it. Feminist scholar Gargi Bhattacharyya recently wrote that these women of color had early positioned black feminism centrally to serious study.

> Importantly to me, this was an approach where analysis of the experiences of racism and sexism was essential to any understanding of workplace struggles, where feminism was central to the struggle but white feminism was critiqued for an ignorance and sometimes an antipathy to the concerns of black women, and where ideologies of idealised families and parallel imaginings of gender and sexuality were identified as part of the repertoire of racist logic that informed state racisms.[20]

In their 1992 book *Racialized Boundaries*, the sociologists Floya Anthias and Nira Yuval-Davis explored the interconnections between race, gender, and class in the UK.[21] More recently, Anthias recounted how they began to develop their insights into what came to be called intersectionality.

> [We] ... decided we would write an article on gender, race, and class, which we did, and published it in *Feminist Review* in 1983. ... We talked about intersections and we talked about connections but did not talk about intersectionality as such. ... [O]ne of [our] main arguments was that you couldn't have a mechanical-additive approach: you couldn't say, "there's gender inequality, and then there's racial inequality, which you add, and then there's class inequality, and that it adds up to more inequality." ... Instead, we should look at the specificities of experience that emerge out of the cross-cuttings of these "social divisions," as we called them.[22]

In 1989, the US scholar Kimberlé Crenshaw coined the term *intersectionality* as part of a critique of conventional feminist studies for ignoring the intersectional position of black women, who face systemic racism and systemic sexism. The sociologist Patricia Hill Collins also pioneered in intersectionality studies, exploring in detail how racial subjugation intersects with gender subjugation for black women. She showed how this reality forms a unique black-feminist epistemological perspective and brings a "paradigmatic shift in how we think about oppression."[23] The sociologists Philomena Essed and Yanick St Jean also early developed the related concept of *gendered racism* to accent this intersectional reality (see Chapter 2).[24]

To understand why Markle must endure a white mythology is to understand more fully the operation of the contemporary dominant white racial frame. Women of color have long been the focus of much hostile white racial framing. A great many white Britons accept and accent the fictitious narratives constructed around Markle and other women of color because they have long relied on a white framing of alleged black and brown deviance from white racial norms. In this process they strengthen their acceptance and impression of white virtue and privilege. An example of this framing is the fetishization and exotification of women of color.

Feminist theorists and activists have claimed that at the core of systemic sexism is the material reality of sexuality and human reproduction, the former including how a woman is regarded physically and sexually by men and how she sees herself. As a case in point, black women have long faced many cruel forms of gendered racism, such as crude *jungle bunny* stereotypes.

White notions of blackness are commonly laden with sexuality. Since at least the 1600s, European writings have portrayed black women and men as naked and with hyperbolic sexual organs. In direct contrast to the emergent ideology of purity and modesty usually associated with white women's bodies, a scandalously sexualized black woman's body came into white consciousness by means of imperialism. This image has endured throughout several centuries now. Greatly influenced by and propagating such racist imagery, white men—including Britons on early Caribbean slave plantations—often sexually molested and raped black women. Currently, many social scientists have documented how some white men still see and seek out black women, and other women of color, as exotic sex objects. In this way, gendered racism is repeatedly inscribed on black female bodies.[25] Such exotification and fetishization has frequently been imposed on Markle.

The Exotification of Meghan Markle

In 2016, journalist Rachel Johnson, sister of Boris Johnson (then-British foreign secretary), wrote that the Windsors "will thicken their watery, thin blue blood and ... pale skin and ginger hair with some rich and exotic DNA." While racializing Markle's mother as "a dreadlocked African-American lady from the wrong side of the tracks who lives in LA," Johnson ironically concluded that "nobody cares that Miss Markle is mixed race."[26] Of course, these words are unreflectively about the white racial framing of Markle and her mother. Unsurprisingly, the Sussexes found Johnson's remarks especially upsetting.[27] She did eventually apologize. "I mean, I for one celebrated the fact that she was mixed race," Johnson explained, "but I used an unfortunate word, which was 'exotic'. I meant that in marvelous contrast to the gingery white blood of his own blood family on his maternal side."[28]

Johnson was not alone in categorizing Markle as exotic. Some German commentators covering the 2018 wedding repetitively referred to the bride and the black guests as exotic, even remarking that the gospel choir performing *Stand by Me* sang "beautifully *black*." Prominent German television presenter Aurel Mertz, himself a person of color, tweeted in response: "'Meghan radiates Afro-American spirit'—Officially the whitest sentence ever said #RoyalWedding."[29]

Many whites and some people of color consider the exotic reference to be a compliment or benign. That many people hold this view is evidence of the dangerous smog that is the persisting white racial frame and its role in perpetuating systemic racism. Exotification, when applied to women of color, suggests they are not genuinely beautiful because they fail to meet accepted white standards of beauty (e.g., light skin and eyes, straight hair, thinner bodies).[30] These standards were again applied to Markle after the birth of Archie, when she and Harry posted photos of their new family on their Instagram account instead of posing with baby Sussex on the hospital steps shortly after his birth, as is royal tradition. "Understand mom not wanting to be photographed after birth!," read one online post. "She has African hair that she likes styled and that can't be done the last weeks of carrying a child! All she had to do was wrap her hair or let Harry show child!"[31] Markle's post-birth looks, especially darker skin color and hair texture, came under scrutiny. "Is it my imagination or does Meghan Markle all of a sudden look like [she's] trying to be blacker?" tweeted another online critic.[32]

Unequivocal in this emotion-laden imagery is the centuries-old interpretation that women of color, including mixed-race women like Markle, are not as beautiful as prototypical white women. In the eighteenth-century expansion of the West's white racial frame, a hierarchy of female beauty was created. Since that era, white women have been the dominant standard. In contemporary UK society, as in other white-dominated societies, black females still bear considerable negative white imaging and commentary on their physical appearance via the media and the advertising, film, and fashion industries. Such racist framing repeatedly suggests their bodies and faces are not as beautiful as white bodies and faces. This framing is commonplace in countries outside of Europe and North America, a reality signaling how the white racial frame is spread globally, especially by Western media.[33]

According to data from OKCupid, a popular UK dating site, white men receive more messages than black and Asian men from possible dates. Black women receive the fewest messages. OKCupid's founder explains that all racial groups using the app, including some men of color, give black women "the cold shoulder."[34] US researchers have found a similar negative pattern on dating apps and in interviews with white men about their framing of black women.[35]

Despite Markle and Harry being fêted as representatives for modern intimate relations across racial lines, according to recent census data a mere 4 percent of white Britons have settled down with a person of color. This census also reports that about one in ten couples in England and Wales include two people of distinct "ethnicities," a substantial increase since the previous census. Like many public analysts of UK racism, however, the census-takers use ethnicities in a misleading way. The census even distinguishes between "British whites," "Irish whites," and "other whites" (mainly Eastern Europeans) in assessing these relationships. Indeed, the most frequent interethnic relationships comprise two white people whose family origins lie in different European countries.[36]

In the UK and the USA, black girls learn early on from their loved ones that the white frame's image of beauty is racially stereotyped—but also that, in contrast, "black is beautiful." In black households and friendship circles substantial efforts are needed to affirm black beauty and the full humanity of black women and girls. This is an unfair burden for black parents. In counter-framing against the intensively positive framing of white beauty, older generations of black Britons have passed down to youth positive interpretations of black beauty—also of black history, traditions, and humanity—just as older African Americans do in the USA. Black parents teach daughters that to be darker-skinned and of African descent is also to be beautiful. Such instruction is essential because over the course of their lives black girls and women will encounter countless positive white beauty images and assorted negative images of and commentaries on black female and male bodies and faces.[37] Currently, in some liberal circles, a clichéd description of light-skinned, curly haired mixed-race people is presented as the ideal symbol of Britain's exciting multicultural future, at the expense of darker-skinned black people with Afro hair. For this reason and on other bases, Markle's occasional statements about being "ethnically ambiguous" are controversial (see Chapter 3).[38]

Additionally, white-framed exotification often links women of color to certain non-human animals (e.g., tigers). Feminist Rachel Kuo explains that by identifying women of color as exotic, they are often reimagined as beasts in need of taming. A recent study of white undergraduates at a US university reveals that relative to white women, black women are more commonly the targets of a distinctive white gaze. In one study, white research participants obsessed more about black women's hips, waists, and chests than they did the hips, waists, and chests of white women. In related studies the white participants indirectly associated black women with words for non-human animals, as contrasted with words about humankind.[39]

Comparing the gendered-racist framing of Markle as exotic to the following counter-framed narrative by *Vogue*'s Michelle Ruiz sheds significant light on how the dominant white racial frame marginalizes and trivializes women of color.

> [I]t's all the more convenient to adhere to the Cinderella story that Markle is nothing more than a pretty girl ... [rather] than a successful 36-year-old woman who starred for seven seasons on a popular and positively reviewed cable drama ... and a longtime feminist and formidable activist in her own right. ... Markle was a U.N. Women's advocate, an ambassador for World Vision (traveling to Rwanda for the

organization's clean water campaign), and a counselor at One Young World, speaking out about gender equality and modern slavery.[40]

White racial framing is part of a colonial legacy that has long rationalized white hostility and violence toward women of color. This framing needs to be contextualized, as it is connected to Western colonization of non-European peoples over centuries. Entire nations, even continents, have been reduced and trivialized by white racial framing, including by white exoticization. In his acclaimed book titled *Queen of the World*, Robert Hardman emphasizes the exotic places to which Elizabeth II has traveled during her long reign. The back cover of the book includes such a mention: "The iconic monarch ... visited over 130 countries. ... It is a story full of drama, intrigue, *exotic* and sometimes dangerous destinations."[41]

The Fetishization of Meghan Markle

That Markle was an accomplished actress, a successful progressive activist, and a strong feminist before meeting Harry is largely or completely expunged from much mainstream reporting. A self-described theater nerd, she graduated from a top US university (Northwestern University), double-majoring in theater and international relations, and even held an internship at the US Embassy in Buenos Aires as part of her studies. Impressively, too, by her junior year she had finished nearly all credits for her under-graduate degree. These outstanding achievements are mostly removed from white-controlled media narratives of her life before her relationship with Harry. As with white exoticization, white racial framing, in concert with gendered-racist framing, allows the mainstream media to erase the complex woman Markle is by rendering her a damsel in distress, saved from oblivion by a virtuous white prince. The hyper-sexualization of her biracial body is an important part of this deflecting narrative.

Markle's sexual past elicits much commentary. *The Sun* declared "Harry's Girl's on Pornhub" on its front page, referencing the former actress's steamier scenes from the television series *Suits*. The show, US-rated TV-14, was hardly porn. *The Sun* would later be forced to apologize because video clips had been published unlawfully on that website, taken from the show without consent.[42] Her oft-cited brief stint as a scantily clothed model on the US game show *Deal or No Deal* is often noted, yet the future duchess told *Esquire* magazine that these appearances were "in the category of things I was doing while I was auditioning to try to make ends meet."[43]

These crude sexualizations of Markle illustrate the dominance of what we have termed the *male gender frame*; they suggest how its associated *white male gaze* works. While the male in their heterosexual relationship (Harry) once famously partied in the nude in Las Vegas and with photo proof, the white-male-controlled media tries to sexually shame Markle for her more modest nudity.

Meghan Markle, the Feminist

The Monarchy's Feminist Antithesis

In an article on representations of Markle, scholars Laura Clancy and Hannah Yelin challenge public claims that the duchess is the monarchy's feminist antithesis, destined to undo the patriarchy on which the royal institution is firmly based.[44] While they argue against disparaging Markle, headlines such as "Academics Accuse Meghan of Dropping Feminism Like a Hot Potato" soon followed their analysis. In the aftermath of such scare headlines, "Pro-Trump, pro-Brexit and pro-empire sentiment was intertwined with anti-feminist, anti-intellectual attitudes in abuse levelled against both [the authors] and Markle."[45]

Markle's modest nods to feminism during her 2018 wedding also opened her up to much online misogyny. The marriage ceremony was described by media pundits and other commentators as noteworthy for its many breaks with royal tradition. A royal bride walking herself down the aisle of St George's Chapel was deemed extraordinary, although her soon-to-be father-in-law, Prince Charles, met her near the altar to walk with her during the final steps, as if to serve as a buffer to more reformist components of the ceremony.[46] Much was made of the fact that the vow of obedience was not included in the ceremony, but few modern royal brides have included it. Even Harry's mother, then barely 20 years old, omitted obedience from her vows. Much notice was also made of the fact that Markle and Harry were pronounced "husband and wife" as opposed to "man and wife." Again, this is now commonplace and hardly consequential. Reportedly, at the reception, the duchess gave a speech in which she thanked the royal family for welcoming her, which was notable given that royal brides rarely give speeches.[47] In view of the British monarchy's role in preserving and spreading patriarchal and chauvinist traditions, the bride's speech was arguably momentous only because it occurred at a *royal* wedding reception.

Markle was from the get-go unfairly expected by many to breathe "new life and relevance" into the royal family, while relegitimating the monarchical power. In assessing this impossible burden placed on her shoulders, authors Clancy and Yelin describe a post-feminist media culture that "celebrates 'defanged, non-oppositional invocations' shorn of emancipatory potential … pivoting instead on notions of choice."[48]

Soon after the publication of their work, Yelin noted that Markle had had a positive impact on the royal family, including in its newfound inclusivity discussions and Prince Charles's acknowledgment of the British role in slavery. Yet, as the couple's departure from royal life demonstrates, Yelin wisely remained skeptical of substantial change, given that British royalty frames itself "as modernising while also conservatising the women … they're essentially using as a PR machine."[49]

Transforming the Individual versus Transforming Society

Despite Markle's public embrace of the label "feminist" and commendable attempts to advance women's education and bring attention to violence against women, among other examples, she has diluted her feminist message by regularly ignoring *systemic* forces of gender and racial oppression. She has, at the time of writing, remained publicly silent on the monarchy's continuing role in perpetuating male privilege and female oppression both within and beyond the institution.

While her overall intention is undoubtedly to help motivate and enable girls and women, her typically individualistic messages can have the opposite effect, in that she often propagates the notion that individual independence is all they need. This message is apolitical and neglectful of systemic sexism issues. That is, to this point in time at least, Markle has not sufficiently focused on transforming *society*. Rather, she mostly asks women to focus on transforming *themselves*.[50]

One prominent journalist described her feminist activism as such: "It is easy to champion diversity and urge girls to aim higher, but awkward to bring up the lack of state investment in child care and, well, the small matter of the class system."[51] Significantly, at a public event for International Women's Day in 2019, a senior editor at *The Economist* asked Markle to respond to accusations that her brand of feminism is "trendy." She replied that the notion of *trendy feminism* is illogical given that feminism is here to stay.[52]

In a general description of commercialized feminism, the sociologist Sara Goodkind describes a brand of feminism reminiscent of Markle's: "what began as a problem with men, created by men, is transformed into a problem with women, who, it is implied, are not confident and independent enough to use the power now available to them to achieve what they want and need."[53] Additionally, we might add the adjective "white" before men here and replace "women" with "people of color," and these words would then fit into the vast majority of Markle's public statements on racial matters, especially before mid-2020.

As noted previously, Markle has engaged in much admirable work to support women before and since marrying into the royal family. The royal tour to South Africa in 2019 is replete with such examples. She met with women entrepreneurs, mothers living with HIV, and prominent female leaders, including politicians, businesswomen, professors, and academics. Of meeting with Sophia Williams-De Bruyn, who in 1956 led 20,000 black women to protest against South Africa's totalitarian (apartheid) racial laws, Markle observed:

> I was recently reminded that the first one up the mountain often gets knocked down the hardest, but makes way for everyone behind them. These brave women have been able to see how their struggle can pave

the way for so many. For all young women organizers, activists and campaigners today, you must keep at it and know that you are working for this generation and the next, and also continuing the legacy of the generations of great women before you.[54]

While in South Africa, Markle visited the post office where Uyinene Mrwetyana, a Cape Town University student and activist, was raped and bludgeoned to death. She fastened a yellow ribbon and note to the post office's railings in remembrance of the young martyr. On the initial day of the tour, she and Harry spoke about gender-based violence.[55] Also while in South Africa, in celebration of International Day of the Girl, Markle shared the interview she gave at just 11 years old where she complained about a Procter & Gamble sexist advertisement. A comment accompanying the video read: "The Duchess of Sussex has been a long time advocate for women's and girls' rights and at the age of eleven campaigned against a sexist advertisement, which was then changed."[56]

Also in 2019, Markle spoke at an International Women's Day event, arguing that the education of both girls and boys is imperative if feminism is to advance. Here, she clearly touches on systemic educational issues. She also memorably remarks on her "hope that men are part of the conversation," adding, "My husband certainly is!" Additionally, she explains what gender equality means to her.

> For men to understand they can be feminists as well. You understand that your strength includes knowing your vulnerabilities. And your sense of self and security, your confidence, comes in knowing that a woman by your side, not behind you, is actually something you shouldn't be threatened about, but as opposed to that you should feel really empowered in having that additional support.[57]

At the same event, in response to the question how that "baby bump" was treating her, the pregnant duchess replied, "It's funny, I've actually been joking the last few weeks, I had seen this documentary on Netflix about feminism, and one of the things they said during pregnancy was 'I feel the embryonic kicking of feminism.' I loved that, so boy or girl, whatever it is, we hope that that's the case with our little bump."[58]

The year prior, while visiting the University of the South Pacific's Fiji campus, Markle addressed the importance of educating women, again touching on systemic educational issues. She remarked:

> Everyone should be afforded the opportunity to receive the education they want, but more importantly the education they have the right to receive. And for women and girls in developing countries, this is vital. ... Because when girls are given the right tools to succeed, they can create incredible futures, not only for themselves but also for those around them.[59]

As Patron of the Association of Commonwealth Universities, Markle announced a new monetary grant to the university and a second to Fiji National University. She explained, "female faculty members are able to encourage others to follow in their footsteps and enter higher education, and that more women become part of the decision-making process in academic institutions."[60]

In some of her remarks we see suggestions of systemic educational issues. But similar to her comments on racial matters, Markle's statements on gender equality mostly have an accent on individuals. Note, too, her lack of sophisticated consideration of how racial subjugation intersects with gender subjugation in numerous such cases for women of color.

In 2020, Markle supported the US organization The 19th* Represents's inaugural online summit on women's issues. Prominent US female leaders such as Kamala Harris, Hillary Clinton, Melinda Gates, and a slew of congresswomen and other notables participated too. A non-profit, non-partisan newsroom focusing on gender and politics, the group is named in honor of the major 19th Amendment to the US Constitution, which granted women the right to vote. Notably, in that year, 1920, the numerous states with racial segregation did not allow black women (or men) to vote. The asterisk in the organization's name serves as a reminder of these facts. Markle had earlier said of the group: their "commitment to reporting and storytelling that lifts up those who are too often underrepresented in the media has never been more important."[61]

At the summit's conclusion, the group's CEO, Emily Ramshaw, asked Markle what it was like as a biracial woman to return to the USA in the midst of intense conversations around racial justice. Markle replied:

> It was so sad to see where our country was in that moment. ... If there's any silver lining in that, I would say that in the weeks ... after the *murder* of George Floyd, in the peaceful protests that you were seeing, in the voices that were coming out, in the way that people were actually owning their role and acknowledging the role that they played either actively or passively in the discrimination of other people, specifically of the black community, it shifted from sadness to a feeling of absolute inspiration because I can see that the tide is turning. ... From my standpoint, it's not new to see this undercurrent of racism and certainly *unconscious bias*, but I think to see the changes that are being made right now is really ... something I look forward to being a part of.[62]

Her attention to individuals' unconscious bias, as opposed to systemic racism issues, is apparent. Note too her emphasis on staying positive, arguably another example of her focusing on transforming the individual as opposed to transforming society. Additionally, the duchess refers to the police killing of George Floyd as a murder. She suggests, like other progressive protesters at the time, that the US officers should not escape criminal charges. As the US civil rights attorney Benjamin Crump and legal scholar Jasmine Rand explain, "The officers knew that Floyd needed oxygen to live, but they never attempted CPR, never took his pulse and never tried to save his life."[63] That Markle appropriately refers to this as murder is a powerful public act, which arguably sheds light on her true feelings about such issues. Compare her reaction to that of US President Donald Trump, who, shortly after Markle made these comments, likened police shootings of unarmed black men to golfers who "choke" and "miss a 3-foot putt." Here, we clearly see the significant implication of a formerly silenced British duchess, who is now residing in the USA, referring to a police killing of an unarmed black man as a murder.[64]

During the summit, Markle also talked to The 19th* Represents's CEO about the importance of voting, saying: "I think it's often challenging ... to remember just how hard it was to get the right to vote. ... I really do hope ... what we're able to see happen through The 19th* over the course of the next few months is that women understand that their voices are needed now more than ever—and the best way to exercise that is through voting."[65]

By the time Markle spoke these words, the 2020 Donald Trump presidential campaign and the Republican National Committee had filed a chain of lawsuits and taken numerous other actions to curb access to the ballot box in that year's presidential election. Her words were thus striking for what they did not include, especially given that the arch-conservative US Supreme Court majority (all Republicans) had repealed critical provisions of the major 1965 Voting Rights Act designed to protect voters of color, just a few years earlier. Such anti-democratic political actions serve to reinforce the elite-white-male dominance system by dispossessing the growing numbers of women and men of color of the right to vote.

Martha S. Jones, author of *Vanguard: How Black Women Broke Barriers, Won the Vote, and Insisted on Equality for All*, recently spoke of the kind of systemic issues Markle failed to address at the summit, but which she would later take up, albeit in limited fashion, in an informal conversation with US feminist icon Gloria Steinem (see Chapter 4). Jones wrote that a US woman's "access to the polls is determined by where she lives" and because of the historical racial segregation in housing that shapes US towns and cities, voting access "often correlates with her race." Noting the coronavirus pandemic at the time, Jones explained that official voting policies, some of which limit the number of polling places or voting by mail, "may mean that fewer American women will cast ballots in fall 2020." She advised that the "history of the 19th Amendment is more than myth; it is a cautionary tale for our own time."[66]

As we see it, without significant utilization of a strong black feminist perspective, which many black female scholars and activists have advocated and utilized, Markle's own thinking and actions on gendered-racial oppression are likely to remain limited and limiting.[67] Moreover, the notion that her presence in royal circles would stimulate meaningful discussions and promote systemic change within the royal institution itself was always doubtful. After all, that monarchy's classed, gendered, and racialized framing and structures are foundational to British society.[68] The couple's jump from the proverbial royal ship would suggest an utter failure to make any tangible impact on the racialized and gendered inner workings of the royal family and related social institutions.

Meghan Markle: The Black Counter-Framer

Black Counter-framing in the UK: A Brief History

In *Theories of Race and Racism*, leading British sociologists Les Back and John Solomos bring attention to a lack of consideration by social scientists of anti-racist and anti-colonialist movements. They write:

> while much has been written about the impact of colonial expansion and imperial domination on racial attitudes there has been surprisingly little comment on the role and impact of anti-colonial ideas and movements. Given the extent of its influence on political and social discourses during this period, it is indeed surprising that we have little knowledge of both the nature of the anti-colonialist movements and the influence that they had on the changing ideas about race in Britain and elsewhere.[69]

In his conceptual work over decades now, the second author of the current book has outlined key elements typical of the black *counter-frame* in the USA, a counter-frame that has for centuries pushed back against the dominant white racial frame and the oppression it rationalizes. These elements include a strong critique of whites' anti-black stereotyping and narratives, calling out all white discrimination, and recognition of gendered racism. Other key elements include asserting firmly black humanity and societal achievements, well-honed perspectives on how to fight discrimination, insistence on authentic black American-ness, and a strong commitment to genuine liberty, justice, and equality for all.[70]

These features are also characteristic of the counter-framing developed by people of color in several European countries. There is a long history of black counter-framing in the UK, one contradicting and countering British framing of whites as virtuous and as frequent benefactors of black people, including claims of freeing slaves (see Chapter 1). For example, consider the black African Olaudah Equiano (c. 1745–1797). In the middle of the eighteenth century he was taken from Africa in chains to a British Caribbean plantation. After being resold several times, he bought his way out of enslavement and as a free black man in Britain became a prominent activist in the abolitionist group Sons of Africa. In a 1789 autobiography, he articulates a critical black counter-framing of the extreme brutality of the Atlantic slave trade, of the British Caribbean plantations, and, later, of racial oppression in Britain. At several points in his memoir, he sets this extensive oppression in terms designed to appeal to the British sense of justice and humanity: "Is not the slave trade entirely a war with the heart of man? ... I have often seen slaves, particularly those who were [small], in different islands, put into scales and weighed and then sold from three pence to six pence or nine pence a pound. ... And at or after a sale it was not uncommon to see negroes taken from their wives, wives taken from their husbands, and children from their parents, and sent off to other islands."[71] Equiano urges the English elite, including the monarch, to consider favorably the British abolitionists' petitions to eliminate this brutal slavery, again heavily accenting counter-framed ideals of black liberty and justice: "I hope to have the satisfaction of seeing the renovation of liberty and justice resting on the British government, to vindicate the honour of our common nature."[72]

Historian Kris Manjapra has offered numerous examples of black individual and community actions out of a survival-and-resistance black counter-frame during the slave trade and plantations era. For example, both enslaved and "free" black people on and around the Caribbean plantations established black trade throughout the plantations and adjacent settlements, promoted distinctive African spiritual practices, and celebrated black music and oral history—all active or passive resistance to the barbarity.[73] Significantly, what changes have come in systemic racism in Britain and its colonies over several centuries, from the slavery era to the present, have usually been generated by an oppositional dialectic—that is, by individual and group resistance on the part of those oppressed to their racially subordinated conditions.

A Black Counter-Framed Royal Wedding

As we show throughout this book, the white view that whites are culturally superior, even biologically superior, to people of color is enduring. This sense of superiority includes the expectation that black Britons and others of color must conform to white racial framing. People of color are viewed as more acceptable in the white-controlled society, and as more tolerable to whites, if they deport themselves according to established white racial norms and accept the negative white framing of them and the positive framing of whites.

Markle included elements in breach of these white norms and of the dominant racial framing in her wedding to Harry. She utilized some black counter-framing of the event, which connected her both with the black American and black British histories of resistance to white norms. Harry later called the ceremony "global" and said it was designed to be "inclusive."[74]

Of the aforementioned elements emblematic of the black counter-frame, we observe at least four in their wedding—an understanding and aggressive countering of negatively stereotyped framing of black people, a positive assertion of blacks' full humanity, an emphasis on the American-ness of African Americans, and a declaration of the positive aspects of black humanity and achievements.

At the time of the wedding, writer Afua Hirsch offered examples of this counter-framing, although not named as such. For example, she noted that the wedding featured black people, British and American, but as "more than adornment." It also featured a wedding sermon given by a leading black Episcopalian clergyman, Michael Curry, who prominently quoted Reverend Dr. Martin Luther King, Jr and foregrounded the wisdom of the spirituals (songs) of enslaved African Americans. He also accented Jesus as a revolutionary.[75] Hirsch notes other key counter-framing:

> The teenage cellist Sheku Kanneh-Mason was framed by flowers as he revealed the depth of talent that made him the first black person to win [the] BBC Young Musician of the Year award. The Kingdom gospel choir sang soul classic *Stand By Me*: a love song, yes, but one that first rose to fame in the midst of the civil rights movement. ... For people used to being part of the majority, these may be symbols they don't easily see. But for those who relate to Markle's situation—a person of colour entering perhaps the whitest and most exclusive of spaces in the world, the British royal family—they speak to an everyday sense of being the first, of bringing a heritage that changes the atmosphere.[76]

Britain actually has a long history of gifted black musicians. Some have been sent to the dustbin of history, while others have fortunately escaped being expunged by the white racial framers. Take, for example, the painting at the Royal Cornwall Museum titled, "A Musical Club, Truro," which includes Joseph Emidy, a black man, playing the violin alongside white musicians. Born in Africa, Emidy was enslaved by the Portuguese when a child. First brought to Brazilian slave plantations, he was later shipped to Portugal. In 1795, he was kidnapped and brought onboard a British ship to serve as fiddler to the crew. Eventually gaining his freedom, he became Britain's first African-origin composer and led the Truro Philharmonic Orchestra. His 1835 obituary states: "As an orchestral composer, his sinfonias [the Italian word for symphony] may be mentioned as evincing not only deep musical research, but also those flights of genius."[77] There was also the virtuoso Afro-British violinist George Augustus Polgreen Bridgetower (c. 1780–1860), to whom the German composer Ludwig van Beethoven originally dedicated his *Kreutzer Sonata*. The two performed it in Vienna. Bridgetower's musical genius is obvious in the fact that he had to sight-read the sonata, and did so successfully, with no time for rehearsal.[78]

Several other people remarked on black moments during the wedding ceremony. British Labour Party politician David Lammy tweeted: "A beautiful service and a beautiful couple. Making my beautiful mixed heritage family's shoulders stand a little taller."[79] Fashion editor Lindsay Peoples of *New York* magazine offered a list of what she deemed the "Best Black Joy Moments," adding that Markle did not come just to play, that "the melanin came all the way through." She noted Doria Ragland, Markle's black mother who showed "up in her locs in a twist out and her nose ring," and Rose Hudson-Wilkin, the first black female Anglican bishop and chaplain to a British queen. Lindsay Peoples also noted the flowers on Markle's veil, representing the nations of the British Commonwealth: "The duchess literally had black nations on her back, using one of the biggest days for the royal family to subtly note to their history of colonization and showing the world that all British people of color should be represented."[80]

These examples reveal an understanding and aggressive countering of negatively stereotyped framing of blacks (e.g., young black cellist Sheku Kanneh-Mason); a positive assertion of the full humanity of African Americans (e.g., Bishop Curry's sermon); a clear assertion of the American-ness of African Americans (e.g., a gospel choir singing *Stand By Me*); and an assertion of positive aspects of black humanity and achievements (most of the aforementioned examples). Interestingly, the participation of Bishop Curry and the gospel choir were suggested by Prince Charles.[81]

If we dig deeper into the song *Stand By Me*, which rose to fame during the US civil rights movement, we see even more clearly the black counter-framing. Published in the USA in the early 1900s by a man whose father had been enslaved and who grew up among others who had been enslaved, the song can likely be traced back even further in the black oral tradition. Then, decades later, the black R&B singer Ben E. King crooned, "No, I won't be afraid," and the tune became a song of dissent sung alongside the more famous "We Shall Overcome," which was based on an old African American hymn. Whether Charles and Markle were fully aware of this African American history or not, they had chosen a civil-rights anthem to be sung by an all-black choir during the wedding ceremony.[82]

As the newly married couple stood on the steps of St George's Chapel, the gospel choir sang "This Little Light of Mine," which was a US civil rights anthem in the 1950s and 1960s. Additionally, some 1960s black soul music, a cultural vehicle informed by and contributing to the US civil rights movement, provided the soundtrack for much of the post-wedding ceremony celebrations. The couple's first dance at the reception, for example, was to the 1968 megahit "I'm in Love" by Wilson Pickett, who was a prominent individual in the development of American soul music.[83]

Equally important, however, is Lammy's caveat about over-stressing the impact of this ceremony's black counter-framing. He told one British newspaper:

> Clearly one wedding isn't going to fundamentally alter the lives of Britain's ethnic minorities, many of whom are still subject to different forms of discrimination. ... These are paradoxical times, with a post-Brexit environment with rising hate crime, with the Windrush story [discriminatory treatment of Afro-Caribbean Britons] that brings us international shame. ... The ceremony was hopeful. It spoke both

of our Commonwealth past, our history, but also of a future. But we shouldn't read too much into it.[84]

Herman Ouseley, a former chair of the British Commission for Racial Equality, also noted that the wedding ceremony did not, of course, begin to rid Britain of racial and class oppression.[85] There is also Stafford Scott, who was even less enthusiastic about the significance of the wedding, remarking: "I heard there was a black choir and some people felt that was very symbolic. ... But, in terms of the black community's standing in this country, the difficulties we face are structural. White and black people have been mixing for generations and it hasn't, necessarily, led to any improvements, or deepening of understanding."[86]

Scott's assessment is supported by much social science data and by Markle's purported experiences within the royal family, such as when Princess Michael wore a racist brooch to a family lunch at Buckingham Palace: "... in the back of Meghan's mind, she wondered if there wasn't a message being sent."[87] In contrast, Lady Colin Campbell, a well-known critic of Markle, claimed the accessory "was not racist because it depicted a Moorish Venetian prince—and not a Sub-Saharan black slave." She maintained that it represents racial inclusivity and has been an element of "Venetian life for the last 700 years from the days when Venice and the Moors ended two of the great trading states."[88]

Markle's wedding choices, such as selecting a civil-rights anthem to be sung by an all-black choir, were assertive personal choices and a broader statement about the need for changes in who and what gets racially respected, especially in white British spaces. Still, as noted previously, when she married Harry, Markle had not yet moved to a higher level of black counter-framing that confronts *systemic* racism in Britain or the USA.

Backlash/Whitelash: White Royal Spaces, White Royal Racists

White resistance to even modest black counter-framing was obvious at the wedding. As black champion of civil rights Bishop Curry spoke, the queen's granddaughters, Zara Phillips (with mouth wide open) and Princesses Beatrice and Eugenie (donning matching smirks), were excruciatingly rude. Additionally, Harry's sister-in-law (Kate) side-rolled her eyes to Camilla (wife of Charles). Clearly, that eye-roll was not meant to convey appreciation for the bishop's eloquent address. Harry's brother William meanwhile had a fit of giggles as the bishop spoke.[89]

The white racial frame and its associated pro-white and anti-black subframes help explain why white adult royals—with every opportunity to learn proper social manners, and who are regularly exposed to the multiracial nation, Commonwealth, and world in which they live—would think it appropriate to giggle, eye-roll, smirk, and open mouths wide in disbelief during the bishop's savvy address. The white frame also helps to explain why so many whites (and others) were inclined to swiftly dismiss as harmless, find amusing, or not even notice such appalling racist behavior, clearly judging it as benign.

Imagine if the African American wedding guests had giggled or smirked when the white Archbishop of Canterbury Justin Welby spoke. Would their rude conduct be framed as a harmless response to a "quintessentially British address"? Would it go unnoticed or be deemed endearing? We doubt it because the difference is clear: Bishop Curry's "quintessentially *American* address" is code in the media for "quintessentially African American address," and according to the dominant white frame inferior to the traditional white way of addressing a British high-church service. This hyper-racist framing not only rationalizes Britain's still-systemic racism but also helps to prevent significant changes in that systemic racism.

As Hirsch put it, "For people used to being part of the majority, these may be symbols they don't easily see."[90] We put the matter less gently. Mocking the African American bishop is in keeping with the dominant racial frame; whereas, openly mocking a white Archbishop of Canterbury, who in many ways signifies white Britain, is in direct opposition to the white racial frame. Mocking one is acceptable; mocking the other is not. Incidentally, Archbishop Welby himself spoke quite positively about Bishop Curry's address (see Chapter 6).[91]

Significantly, at no time during the ceremony did the queen or her husband mock the black moments. In fact, another modest anti-establishment symbol on the wedding day came compliments of the monarch, who bestowed the titles Duke and Duchess of Sussex on the couple. In so doing, the newest member of the royal family became the first legal Duchess of Sussex. The much earlier Duke of Sussex, a son of George III, defied the white Anglo-Saxon royal tradition, refused to obey the 1772 Royal Marriages Act, and married who he wanted. A maverick royal, he advocated for the emancipation of Roman Catholics, fought to eliminate restrictions on Jews, supported parliamentary reform, and opposed slavery.[92] The queen possibly considered his anti-slavery advocacy when selecting this appropriate title for the newlyweds. It is a fitting designation because Markle has long been an advocate for numerous democratic causes.

More Backlash/Whitelash: Defending White Royal Spaces and Royal Racists

On the day of the wedding and subsequently, white pundits mostly described the rude behavior of the royals as inoffensive, and even as appropriate or understandable. They often drew on the myth of a post-racial and harmonious multicultural Britain to defend such ill-mannered racial behavior. One *CNN* commentator from the UK enthusiastically did so, explaining the royals' reactions to Bishop Curry thus:

> Look, there's nothing wrong [with the negative reactions]. He went on for 30 minutes. ... This is a high Church of England service in St.

George's Chapel. ... You did not necessarily, normally expect to have an American-style preacher. ... And I assure you, nobody was thinking oh, this is dreadful, this is awful. ... [D]on't forget, multi-cultural Britain, there are large populations, Asian, Indian, African populations right across the country.[93]

Note the overt white racial framing. By *American-style preacher* the arrogant *CNN* commentator means *African* American. And he is also wrong about the length of the bishop's sermon; he only spoke for 14 minutes, not 30. The anti-black subframe is unmistakable—the African American's style of preaching is not respectable or pious enough for a high Church of England service and certainly not in St George's Chapel in Windsor Castle. The country's systemic racism clearly encompasses its religious institutions. Of course, the Bishop's address, and Markle for that matter, are not typical because the dominant white racial frame has long *othered* people with physical complexions like theirs.

In contrast to the royals, Bishop Curry was the epitome of grace, respectability, and propriety. He honored Markle's African American heritage, which is no laughing matter. The address may not have been relatable to the mostly elite white guests at the wedding but it was to the majority of people living in the 54 member states of the Commonwealth (nearly all former territories of the British Empire). The ill-mannered royals could not *hear* him, but they would have greatly benefitted from his eloquent message. In contrast, Reverend Dr. Martin Luther King, Jr's daughter publicly approved of Curry's sermon. She understood what some of the royals could not, tweeting that her father's "life, teachings, and words still matter so much. ... Congrats Harry and Meghan."[94]

That May 2018 event was not the first time that bemused royals captured the media's attention for their racist giggling and other racialized behavior, and were excused by many whites. Visiting the Canadian Arctic in 2017, Charles and Camilla were caught on camera in a fit of laughter when Inuit (Indigenous people of Northern Canada) were throat-singing (katajjaq). One reporter remarked that the "royal couple did everything but stuff handkerchiefs in their mouths" to try to stop from snickering. The same journalist admitted to finding royals who get "the giggles quite endearing."[95] The couple should have prepared themselves for what to expect, educated themselves on this celebrated Inuit tradition, and honored Inuit culture. Given the historically oppressive, often *genocidal*, relationship between the Crown and Indigenous peoples in white-colonized Commonwealth countries across the globe, the couple ought to have known better.[96]

This history includes methodical and forced displacement of Indigenous peoples for the purpose of land theft and their use as forced laborers in colonial projects of resource extraction. It comprises both *physical* genocide—an attempt to extinguish the group by slaughtering its members—and *cultural* genocide, which expresses itself in involuntary assimilation policies directed toward a group.[97] According to the historian Dirk Moses, Britain's colonization of the so-called "new world" (e.g., Canada and Australia) was marked by genocide. The Beothuk was a group of Indigenous people living on the island of what is now Newfoundland. They were completely wiped off the face of the earth when white Europeans came to their shores. While the Canadian and Australian governments have apologized to Indigenous peoples, the British dominant narrative is that what transpired there "is a 'local' problem that has no implications for the settlers' country of origin or that country's state policy."[98] The truth is that these genocidal moments were motivated by the British elite's quest for *group dominance*, its *racialized arrogance*, and its *racialized anxiety* over real or imagined resistance from the oppressed peoples *there*.

Unmistakably, a central difficulty for Markle is that she is a woman of African American heritage, inhabiting a space presumed by many white Britons and others to legitimately belong to a white British-born woman. Aatish Taseer, a South Asian-descended, British-born man who once dated the daughter of Prince and Princess Michael of Kent (Lady Gabriella Windsor), explains.

> "The British don't like foreigners coming over and stealing their princes," a friend of Princess Michael's once said to me. It was an odd thing to say, because the royal family was not just chock-full of foreigners; it was basically *foreign itself*. It was why someone like [Gabriella] did not have a single English relation between her and Queen Victoria, who was herself of German descent and married to a German. But when Queen Victoria made the system of marital alliances that linked her family to every major royal family in Europe, Britain had been outward-looking.[99]

Conclusion

In Meghan Markle's now-defunct lifestyle blog The Tig, she shared favorite quotes, reminiscent of commercialized individualistic feminism, such as "Being yourself is the prettiest thing a person can be," "Of this be sure, you do not find the happy life … you make it," and "Travel often, getting lost will help you find yourself."[100] In advocating for a good and better life, Markle's words are notable for a failure to mention the many barriers, exclusions, and inequalities associated with class, gender, race, and sexuality. For example, not everyone can afford to travel—let alone often. That she is an avid reader of self-help books may partially explain her perspective on female empowerment. One of her favorite self-help authors is Brené Brown, who has said: "I believe that you have to walk through vulnerability to get to courage, therefore … embrace the suck. … and my motto right now is 'Courage over comfort.' "[101] Commercialized feminism especially manifests in this self-help industry.[102] Women and girls are guaranteed success and "happiness if only they can get the (self-) improvement script right."[103]

Like all such commercialized movements this type of individualistic feminism is, as Isabelle Kohn puts it, "less concerned with improving inequality" and more focused "on the canned, profitable image of self empowerment." It is also "inherently classist, with so-called feminist products selling at prices way outside the average person's budget."[104] Markle's brand of feminism reads, at least at times, similarly and thus as non-systemic.

Nonetheless, in no way do we wish to diminish Markle's significant contributions to female empowerment. For example, her continuing impact can be seen in the fact that some women and girls of color throughout the Commonwealth and the UK see her as a visible representation of themselves. Reflecting on this wide-reaching impression, the royal reporters Omid Scobie and Carolyn Durand summoned memories of the Sussexes' 2018 royal tour of Australia. "Teenage girls and boys, many of them Indigenous Australians," they recall, "spoke about how they saw Meghan as a symbol of female empowerment or a face that represented them in a way other members of the royal family hadn't before."[105]

But systemic sexism, like systemic racism, is a foundational, highly developed, well-institutionalized, and historically deep oppression that meaningfully shapes virtually every facet of British society today. This must be more widely recognized by all concerned. Much more than a royal wedding or a biracial duchess is needed to change a systematically racist and systemically sexist society like Britain. Among other things these changes are required: eradicating exploitative and other discriminatory practices that target Britons of color and women; eliminating the dominant British white racial (often male) hierarchy and its defense of white privilege and white power (and male privilege); and eliminating the British white racial frame that rationalizes and implements racial oppression, including its many racist prejudices, images, ideologies, emotions, interpretations, and narratives. Such action is required to end racial and gender inequalities long ago established in Britain by deep societal reproduction apparatuses and processes. As in the USA, serious dedication to genuine democracy and social justice in Britain will require a focus on *systemic* oppression as opposed to just *individual* bigotry and *individual* discrimination.

Notes

1 Katherine Hignett, "The British Royals Don't Do Politics, But Here's What Meghan Markle Said about Donald Trump Before She Joined the Family," *Newsweek*, June 2, 2019, www.newsweek.com/meghan-markle-donald-trump-royal-family-politics-prince-harry-1440580. Accessed June 22, 2019.
2 Maya Oppenheim, "Meghan Markle: How the Chomsky-Reading Trump Critic Will Have to Bite her Tongue When she Enters the Palace," *The Independent*, May 17, 2018, www.independent.co.uk/news/uk/home-news/meghan-markle-trump-royal-wedding-politics-feminism-prince-harry-a8356001.html. Accessed June 22, 2019.

3 Olivia Petter, "Meghan Markle is a Victim of Racism, Sexism and Misogyny, Says John Bercow," *The Independent*, February 2, 2020, www.independent.co.uk/life-style/royal-family/meghan-markle-john-bercow-racism-sexism-misogyny-sunday-times-magazine-a9313356.html. Accessed February 11, 2020.

4 See Joe R. Feagin and Kimberley Ducey, *Racist America: Roots, Current Realities, and Future Reparations*, 4th edn (New York, Routledge, 2019), et passim.

5 Mikhaila Friel, "7 Times Meghan Markle Was a Feminist Icon, From Calling Out Sexism in 'Suits' to Sending Notes to Sex Workers," *Insider*, March 8, 2019, www.insider.com/international-womens-day-meghan-markle-feminist-icon-2019–3. Accessed December 27, 2019; Eden Faithfull, "Canadian Organisation Opens Up about Working with Meghan," *Honey*, February 10, 2020, https://honey.nine.com.au/royals/meghan-markle-outing-justice-for-girls/af9124ca-c589–46e7-b00f-a19fef60c04c. Accessed February 11, 2020.

6 Aramide Tinubu, "Is Meghan Markle Really a Feminist?," *Showbiz Cheatsheet*, January 18, 2019, www.cheatsheet.com/entertainment/meghan-markle-feminist.html/. Accessed December 27, 2019.

7 *The Royal Household*, "The Duchess of Sussex," www.royal.uk/duchess-sussex. Accessed December 27, 2019.

8 Oppenheim, "Meghan Markle Outlines Fight for Feminism."

9 Tinubu, "Is Meghan Markle Really a Feminist?"

10 Helen Lewis, "Meghan, Kate, and the Architecture of Misogyny," *The Atlantic*, January 16, 2020, www.theatlantic.com/international/archive/2020/01/meghan-markle-kate-middleton-royals-culture-war/604981/. Accessed February 11, 2020. Italics added.

11 *Ibid.*

12 Samantha Willis, "Why Do We See So Much of Ourselves in Meghan Markle?" *Glamour*, May 18, 2018, www.glamour.com/story/royal-wedding-meghan-markle-representation-identity. Accessed December 20, 2019.

13 *Stuff* Staff, "Kiwi 'Royal' Gary Lewis Splits from Lady Davina Windsor After 14-Year Marriage," *Stuff*, March 26, 2019, www.stuff.co.nz/life-style/world/111544770/kiwi-royal-gary-lewis-splits-from-lady-davina-windsor-after-14year-marriage. Accessed December 26, 2019; Fiona Ward, "Buckingham Palace Confirm Divorce of Lady Davina Windsor and Gary Lewis After 14 Years Of Marriage," *HELLO!*, March 16, 2019, https://ca.hellomagazine.com/royalty/2019031670945/lady-davina-windsor-gary-lewis-royal-split-palace-confirms/. Accessed December 26, 2019.

14 Paul Gilroy, Sindre Bangstad, and Gard Ringen Høibjerg, "A Diagnosis of Contemporary Forms of Racism, Race and Nationalism: A Conversation With Professor Paul Gilroy," *Cultural Studies*, 33(2) (December 2019), pp. 173–197.

15 *Access* Staff, "Meghan Markle Delivers Passionate Speech About Women's Right to Vote: 'Feminism is About Fairness'," *Access*, October 28, 2018, www.accessonline.com/articles/meghan-markle-delivers-passionate-speech-about-womens-right-vote-feminism-about-fairness. Accessed December 11, 2019.

16 *Ibid.*

17 Anne-Marie O'Connor, "Opinion: Meghan Markle vs. the Tabloid Mob," *Los Angeles Times*, October 4, 2019, www.latimes.com/opinion/story/2019–10–04/meghan-markle-prince-harry-royals-tabloid-racism. Accessed November 11, 2019.

18 *Ibid.*

19 Tom Bradby, "Harry and Meghan an African Journey," *ITV, FFTV*, October 22, 2019, www.youtube.com/watch?v=j_c7ZhK0AKA. Accessed December 26, 2019.

20 Gargi Bhattacharyya, "Rereading The Empire Strikes Back," *Ethnic and Racial Studies*, 37 (10) (August 2014), pp. 1805.

21 Floya Anthias and Nira Yuval-Davis, *Racialized Boundaries* (London: Routlegde, 1992).

22 Matt Bryant Cheney, Lucía M. Montás, and James William Lincoln, "Translocational Social Theory After "Community": An Interview with Floya Anthias," *disClosure: A Journal of Social Theory*, 25 (19). DOI: https://doi.org/10.13023/disclosure.25.18.

23 Kimberlé Crenshaw, "Demarginalizing the Intersection of Race and Sex: A Black Feminist Critique of Antidiscrimination Doctrine, Feminist Theory and Antiracist Politics," *University of Chicago Legal Forum*, 140 (1989), pp. 139–167; Patricia Hill Collins, *Black Feminist Thought: Knowledge, Consciousness, and the Politics of Empowerment*, 2nd edn (New York: Routledge, 2000), pp. 221–228.

24 Philomena Essed, *Understanding Everyday Racism* (Newbury Park, CA: Sage, 1991); Yanick St Jean and Joe R. Feagin, *Double Burden: Black Women and Everyday Racism* (Armonk, NY: M.E. Sharpe, 1998).

25 Diane Roberts, *The Myth of Aunt Jemima: Representations of Race and Region* (New York: Routledge, 1994), p. 5; Brittany Slatton, *Mythologizing Black Women: Unveiling White Men's Racist Deep Frame on Race and Gender* (New York: Routledge, 2013); Marci Bounds Littlefield, "The Media as a System of Racialization: Exploring Images of African American Women and the New Racism," *American Behavioral Scientist*, 51 (January 2008), pp. 675–685; Patricia Hill Collins, *Black Sexual Politics: African Americans, Gender, and the New Racism* (New York: Routledge, 2005); Joe R. Feagin and Melvin P. Sikes, *Living with Racism: The Black Middle-Class Experience* (Boston, MA: Beacon Press, 1994).

26 Rachel Johnson, "RACHEL JOHNSON: Sorry Harry, but your Beautiful Bolter has Failed My Mum Test," *Daily Mail*, November 5, 2016, www.dailymail.co.uk/debate/article-3909362/RACHEL-JOHNSON-Sorry-Harry-beautiful-bolter-failed-Mum-Test.html. Accessed April 29, 2019.

27 Lulu Garcia-Navarro and Max Foster, "Inside the Racist Online Attacks on Meghan Markle," *NPR*, March 10, 2019, www.npr.org/2019/03/10/701987112/inside-the-racist-online-attacks-on-meghan-markle. Accessed April 29, 2019.

28 Rory O'Connor, "Royal Wedding 2018: Prince Harry and Meghan Markle Issued 'Race' Apology by Rachel Johnson," *Daily Express*, May 1, 2018, www.express.co.uk/showbiz/tv-radio/953390/Royal-Wedding-2018-Prince-Harry-Meghan-Markle-Race-Apology-Rachel-Johnson-Royal-Wives-ITV. Accessed April 30, 2019.

29 Amanda Erickson, "A German Broadcaster Called Meghan Markle Exotic," *The Washington Post*, May 21, 2018, www.washingtonpost.com/news/worldviews/wp/2018/05/21/a-german-broadcaster-called-meghan-markle-exotic-viewers-said-it-was-racist/?noredirect=on&utm_term=.89ae4d19d515. April 29, 2019.

30 Rachel Kuo, "4 Reasons Why Calling a Woman of Color 'Exotic' is Racist," *Everyday Feminism*, January 26, 2016, https://everydayfeminism.com/2016/01/calling-woc-exotic-is-racist/. Accessed April 29, 2019.

31 Richard Hartley-Parkinson, "Haters Target Royal Baby Archie as they Attack Harry and Meghan's Instagram," *Metro*, May 9, 2019, https://metro.co.uk/2019/05/09/racists-target-royal-baby-archie-harry-meghans-instagram-account-9459521/. Accessed June 9, 2019.

32 Kayla Hounsell, "'There's No Shortage of Negative Things': Pregnant Meghan Faces Online Bullying," *CBC News*, March 1, 2019, www.cbc.ca/news/world/meghan-markle-duchess-of-sussex-faces-online-bullying-1.5037143. Accessed June 17, 2019.

33 Yanick St Jean and Joe R. Feagin, *Double Burden: Black Women and Everyday Racism* (New York: M.E. Sharpe, 1998), pp. 90–91.

34 Amelia Murray, "The UK's Most Popular Dating Sites: What They Cost and What They Claim," *The Telegraph*, January 9, 2018, www.telegraph.co.uk/money/consumer-affairs/uks-popular-dating-sites-cost-claim/. Accessed November 9, 2019.

35 Slatton, *Mythologizing Black Women.*

36 Carlos Ballesteros, "Prince Harry's Engagement: It's Still Rare for a White Man to Marry a Nonwhite Woman in the U.K.," *Newsweek*, November 27, 2017, www.newsweek.com/harry-meghan-engaged-uk-interracial-marriage-low-723540. Accessed November 9, 2019.

37 Joe R. Feagin, *The White Racial Frame: Centuries of Racial Framing and Counter-Framing*, 2nd edn (New York: Routledge, 2013), p. 184; Adia Harvey Wingfield, *Doing Business with Beauty: Black Women, Hair Salons, and the Racial Enclave Economy* (Lanham, MD: Rowman & Littlefield, 2008); Debra Van Ausdale and Joe R. Feagin, *The First R: How Children Learn Race and Racism* (Lanham, MD: Rowman & Littlefield), pp. 190–196; Joe R. Feagin and Melvin P. Sikes, *Living with Racism: The Black Middle-Class Experience* (Boston, MA: Beacon Press, 1995), pp. 311–314; St Jean and Feagin, *Double Burden*, et passim. We are indebted here to scholarly comments by Brittany Slatton, Louwanda Evans, and Adia Harvey Wingfield.

38 Meghan Markle, "Meghan Markle: I'm More than an 'Other,'" *Elle*, December 22, 2016, www.elle.com/uk/life-and-culture/news/a26855/more-than-an-other/. Accessed June 20, 2019.

39 Kuo, "4 Reasons Why"; Joel R. Anderson, Elise Holland, and Courtney Heldreth, and Scott P. Johnson, "Revisiting the Jezebel Stereotype: The Impact of Target Race on Sexual Objectification," *Psychology of Women Quarterly*, 42 (4) (August 2018), pp. 461–476.

40 Michelle Ruiz, "Let The Misogynistic Public Shaming of Meghan Markle Now Commence," *Vogue*, December 4, 2017, www.vogue.com/article/meghan-markle-misogynistic-public-shaming. Accessed November 17, 2019.

41 Robert Hardman, *Queen of the World* (London: Century, 2018), back cover. Italics added.

42 *The Sun* Staff, "Miss Meghan Markle—An Apology," *The Sun*, February 11, 2017, www.thesun.co.uk/clarifications/2838630/clarification-miss-meghan-markle-an-apology/. Accessed November 12, 2019. Bold and italics in original.

43 Matt Goulet, "Meghan Markle Grew Up around TV Decades Before she Starred on *Suits*," *Esquire*, February 14, 2018. www.esquire.com/entertainment/tv/a23925/meghan-markle-interview/. Accessed November 17, 2019.

44 Laura Clancy and Hannah Yelin, "'Meghan's Manifesto': Meghan Markle and the Cooption of Feminism," *Celebrity Studies* (December 2018). DOI: 10.1080/19392397.2018.1541541, p. 3.

45 *Ibid.*, pp. 1, 3, 8.
46 Laura Clancy and Hannah Yelin, 2018, "'Meghan's Manifesto': Meghan Markle and the Cooption of Feminism," *Celebrity Studies*. DOI: 10.1080/19392397.2018.1541541, p. 2.
47 Maya Oppenheim, "Meghan Markle Outlines Fight for Feminism and Gender Equality on Royal Website," *The Independent*, May 21, 2018, www.independent.co.uk/news/uk/home-news/meghan-markle-feminism-royal-website-gender-wedding-prince-harry-a8361131.html. Accessed December 11, 2019.
48 Clancy and Yelin, "'Meghan's Manifesto,'", p. 3.
49 Sophie Wilkinson, "No, Meghan Markle Hasn't 'Dropped Feminism Like a Hot Potato,' Academic Tells Grazia," *Grazia*, December 18, 2018, https://graziadaily.co.uk/celebrity/news/meghan-markle-duchess-of-sussex-is-a-feminist-academics-critical-of-royals-say/. Accessed December 26, 2019.
50 Eve Livingston, "We Need to Abolish the Monarchy—Because it's Not Fair on Anyone, Including the Royals," *The Independent*, May 19, 2018, www.independent.co.uk/voices/royal-family-abolish-wedding-queen-monarchy-sexist-institution-why-meghan-markle-a8357266.html. Accessed December 12, 2019; Beverly Skeggs, *Formations of Class and Gender: Becoming Respectable* (London: Sage, 1997), p. 114.
51 Helen Lewis, "The Issue with Meghan Markle's *Vogue* Issue," *The Atlantic*, August 2, 2019, www.theatlantic.com/international/archive/2019/08/meghan-markle-vogue-radical-royalty/595288/. Accessed November 11, 2019.
52 Omid Scobie and Carolyn Durand, *Finding Freedom: Harry and Meghan and the Making of a Modern Royal Family* (New York: HarperCollins), p. 268.
53 Goodkind, "'You Can Be Anything You Want."
54 Katie Nicholl, "Meghan Markle Has a Feminist Focus in South Africa," *Vanity Fair*, September 29, 2019, www.vanityfair.com/style/2019/09/meghan-markle-south-africa-female-leaders-feminism. Accessed December 27, 2019.
55 *Ibid.*
56 Chloe Foussianes, "Meghan Markle Shares Her Feminist Childhood Interview to Celebrate International Day of the Girl," *Town & Country*, October 11, 2019, www.townandcountrymag.com/society/tradition/a29437425/meghan-markle-young-day-of-the-girl-instagram-video/. Accessed December 27, 2019.
57 Amy Mackelden, "Meghan Markle Discusses Prince Harry's Feminism & Describes How they Work in Tandem," *Harper's BAZAAR*, March 9, 2019, www.harpersbazaar.com/celebrity/latest/a26771213/meghan-markle-prince-harry-feminism-international-womens-day/. Accessed December 27, 2019.
58 Ashley Hoffman, "Meghan Markle Says She Can Feel the 'Embryonic Kicking of Feminism' at Women's Day Event," *Time*, March 8, 2019, https://time.com/5547951/meghan-markle-baby-bump/. Accessed December 27, 2019; See also, *NBC News* Staff, "Meghan Markle Discusses Feminism on International Women's Day Panel in London," *NBC News*, March 8, 2019, www.nbcnews.com/video/meghan-markle-discusses-feminism-on-international-women-s-day-panel-in-london-1454607939683. Accessed December 27, 2019.
59 Foussianes, "Meghan Markle's First Speech on the Royal Tour."
60 *Ibid.*
61 Robyn Morris, "Duchess Meghan's Next Public Appearance Revealed," *Woman & Home*, August 7, 2020, www.womanandhome.com/life/royal-news/duchess-meghan-public-appearance-virtual-summit-370874/. Accessed August 26, 2020.

62 The 19th, "The 19th Represents: On Race & Gender," YouTube user "The 19th," www.youtube.com/watch?v=qzjg3dl9cGM&feature=youtu.be, Accessed August 14, 2020.

63 Benjamin Crump and Jasmine Rand, "The Death of George Floyd Was an Act of Murder, Plain and Simple," *The Guardian*, May 29, 2020, www. theguardian.com/commentisfree/2020/may/29/george-floyd-death-benjamin-crump-jasmine-rand. Accessed August 28, 2020.

64 Quint Forgey, "Trump Compares Police Brutality to Golfers Who 'Miss A 3-Foot Putt,'" *Politico*, September 2, 2020, www.politico.com/news/2020/09/01/trump-police-brutality-golfers-406802. Accessed September 2, 2020.

65 The 19th, "The 19th Represents."

66 Martha S. Jones, "For Black Women, The 19th Amendment Didn't End their Fight to Vote," *National Geographic*, August 7, 2020, www.nationalgeographic.com/history/2020/08/black-women-continued-fighting-for-vote-after-19th-amendment/#close. Accessed August 25, 2020.

67 See, for example, Patricia Hill Collins, *Black Feminist Thought: Knowledge, Consciousness, and the Politics of Empowerment* (Boston, MA: Unwin Hyman, 1990).

68 See Clancy and Yelin, "'Meghan's Manifesto,'", p. 3.

69 Les Back and John Solomos (eds), *Theories of Race and Racism: A Reader*, 1st edn (New York: Routledge, 2000), p. 15.

70 Feagin, *White Racial Frame*, pp. 170–184.

71 Olaudah Equiano, *The Interesting Narrative of the Life of Olaudah Equiano, Or Gustavus Vassa, The African* (London, 1789), n. p., www.gutenberg.org/files/15399/15399-h/15399-h.htm. Accessed February 16, 2020.

72 *Ibid.*

73 Kris Manjapra, "When Will Britain Face Up to its Crimes Against Humanity?," *The Guardian*, March 28, 2018, www.theguardian.com/news/2018/mar/29/slavery-abolition-compensation-when-will-britain-face-up-to-its-crimes-against-humanity. Accessed December 26, 2019.

74 Scobie and Durand, *Finding Freedom*, p. 210.

75 Afua Hirsch, "Meghan Markle's Wedding Was a Rousing Celebration of Blackness," *The Guardian*, May 20, 2018, www.theguardian.com/uk-news/2018/may/19/meghan-markles-wedding-was-a-celebration-of-blackness. Accessed April 30, 2019.

76 *Ibid.*

77 Miles Davis, "Joseph Emidy: From Slave Fiddler to Classical Violinist," *BBC News*, June 21, 2015, www.bbc.com/news/uk-england-cornwall-33211440. Accessed December 28, 2019; Richard McGrady, "Joseph Emidy: An African in Cornwall," *The Musical Times*, 127 (1726) (1986), pp. 619–623.

78 British Library Staff, "Beethoven's Tuning Fork," British Library, www.bl.uk/collection-items/beethovens-tuning-fork. Accessed December 28, 2019.

79 @DavidLammy, Twitter, May 19, 2018, https://twitter.com/davidlammy/status/997809218655805440?lang=en. Accessed December 27, 2019.

80 Lindsay Peoples, "The 7 Best Black Joy Moments at the Royal Wedding," *The Cut*, May 20, 2018, www.thecut.com/2018/05/royal-wedding-best-black-joy-moments.html. Accessed April 30, 2019.

81 Scobie and Durand, *Finding Freedom*, p. 211.

82 Alan Connor, "Royal Wedding 2018: The Story Behind *Stand By Me*," *BBC News*, May 21, 2018, www.bbc.com/news/entertainment-arts-44200577. Accessed December 27, 2019.

83   Kim Ruehl, "10 Essential Civil Rights Songs," *Thought.Co*, June 24, 2020, www.thoughtco.com/essential-civil-rights-songs-1322740. Accessed August 19, 2020; Erin Hill, "Meghan Markle and Prince Harry's Soulful First Dance Song Revealed," *People*, August 11, 2020, www.msn.com/en-us/music/celebrity/meghan-markle-and-prince-harrys-soulful-first-dance-song-revealed/ar-BB17PxWN. Accessed August 19, 2020.
84   Kimberley Ducey, "Royal Wedding of Meghan Markle and Prince Harry: Black Counter-Framing," *Racism Review*, May 22, 2018, www.racismreview.com/blog/2018/05/22/royal-wedding-of-meghan-markle-and-prince-harry-black-counter-framing/. Accessed April 29, 2019.
85   Caroline Davies, " 'It Really Was a Black Service': World Reaction to Royal Wedding," *The Guardian*, May 20, 2018, www.theguardian.com/uk-news/2018/may/20/it-really-was-a-black-service-world-reaction-to-royal-wedding. Accessed April 30, 2019.
86   *Ibid.*
87   Maria Puente, " 'Finding Freedom' Tells Harry and Meghan's Reasons for Flight: 'Blindsided' by Racism, Tabloid Coverage," *USA TODAY*, August 11, 2020, www.usatoday.com/story/entertainment/books/2020/08/11/finding-freedom-harry-meghan-tell-their-side-new-book/3340413001/.   Accessed August 12, 2020.
88   Julie Miller, "Lady Colin Campbell, Author of the Other Harry and Meghan Book, Swears it's Not a Takedown," *Vanity Fair*, July 30, 2002, www.vanityfair.com/style/2020/07/lady-colin-campbell-swears-its-not-a-takedown?itm_content=footer-recirc. Accessed August 14, 2020.
89   Char Adams, "Kate Middleton's Side-Eye and Zara Phillips' Jaw Drop During Bishop's Sermon Rule Twitter," *People*, May 19, 2018, https://people.com/royals/royal-wedding-prince-harry-meghan-markle-preacher/. Accessed April 29, 2019; Bronte Coy, "Royal Wedding: Harry and Meghan Stifle Giggles as US Bishop Steals the Show," *news.com.au*, May 20, 2018, www.news.com.au/entertainment/celebrity-life/royals/royal-weddings/royal-wedding-harry-and-meghan-stifle-giggles-as-us-bishop-steals-the-show/news-story/d95d9ea0d483ada2d66dbbe75f07a07c. Accessed April 30, 2019.
90   Hirsch, "Meghan Markle's Wedding."
91   Megan Friedman, "The Archbishop of Canterbury Gushed over Bishop Michael Curry's Royal Wedding Sermon," *Harper's BAZAAR*, May 20, 2018, www.harpersbazaar.com/celebrity/latest/a20763941/bishop-michael-curry-royal-wedding-sermon-archbishop-canterbury/.   Accessed   April 30, 2019.
92   Lyndsey Matthews, "The Last Duke of Sussex was an Anti-Slavery Advocate," *Town & Country*, May 19, 2018, www.townandcountrymag.com/society/tradition/a20751869/duke-of-sussex-anti-slavery-abolitionist-royal-wedding/. Accessed April 30, 2019; Royal Collection Trust Staff, "Augustus Frederick, Duke of Sussex (1773–1843) c.1791," Royal Collection Trust, www.rct.uk/collection/420973/augustus-frederick-duke-of-sussex-1773–1843. Accessed April 30, 2019.
93   *CNN* Staff, "CNN LIVE EVENT/SPECIAL," The Royal Wedding, Aired 11–12p ET, www.cnn.com/TRANSCRIPTS/1805/19/se.11.html. Accessed April 30, 2019.
94   *Ibid.*

95 Peter Bradshaw, "OK, I Admit It: I Find Royals Who Get the Giggles Quite Endearing," *The Guardian*, July 5, 2017, www.theguardian.com/commentisfree/2017/jul/05/royals-giggles-endearing-inuit-throat-singing-charles-camilla. Accessed April 30, 3019.

96 "Billy Connolly—Journey to the Edge of the World—Waterstone's," YouTube user "Waterstones," www.youtube.com/watch?v=Vb-Nh3J2Fg4. Accessed June 21, 2019.

97 Leora Bilsky and Rachel Klagsbrun, "The Return of Cultural Genocide?," *European Journal of International Law*, 29 (2) (May 2018), p. 379.

98 Martin Shaw, "Britain and Genocide," *Open Democracy*, January 29, 2010, www.opendemocracy.net/en/britain-and-genocide/. Accessed August 21, 2020.

99 Aatish Taseer, "Race and the Royals: An Outsider's View Inside Kensington Palace," *Vanity Fair*, May 2018, www.vanityfair.com/style/2018/04/race-and-the-royals-inside-kensington-palace. Accessed December 27, 2019. Italics added.

100 Craig Brown, "*Finding Freedom* is Full of Fluff, Guff, Gobbldegook and Gush that has Meghan Markle's Fingerprints All Over It," *Daily Mail*, August 15, 2020, www.dailymail.co.uk/news/article-8631205/CRAIG-BROWN-Finding-Freedom-fluff-Meghan-Markles-fingerprints-it.html. Accessed August 26, 2020.

101 Brené Brown, "Researcher. Storyteller. Texan," About Brené, https://brenebrown.com/about/, Accessed August 26, 2020. See also Scobie and Durand, *Finding Freedom*, p. 123.

102 Goodkind, "'You Can Be Anything You Want," p. 400.

103 Andrea L. Press, "'Feminism? That's So Seventies': Girls and Young Women Discuss Femininity and Feminism in *America's Next Top Model*," in *New Femininities: Postfeminism, Neoliberalism and Subjectivity*, eds Rosalind Gill and Christina Scharff (New York: Palgrave Macmillan, 2011), p. 118.

104 Isabelle Kohn, "The Commercialization of Feminism Has Made it More Visible, But at a Steep Price," *Rooster*, June 9, 2017, https://therooster.com/blog/commercialization-feminism-has-made-it-more-visible-steep-price. Accessed December 27, 2019.

105 Scobie and Durand, *Finding Freedom*, pp. 238, 262.

6 "Where Is This Racism You Keep Talking About?"

Sincere Fictions of the Virtuous White Self

Introduction

In 2020, after Meghan Markle and Prince Harry announced they were stepping down as senior royals, a collective of black female professionals from the British media, law, health, education, and publishing sectors penned an open letter to the broadcast media. The trigger for their action was white commentator Piers Morgan's badgering of black columnist Afua Hirsch when she appeared on the *Good Morning Britain* television show to discuss her *New York Times* article titled, "Black Britons Know Why Meghan Markle Wants Out. It's the Racism." The women noted how Morgan's treatment of Hirsch amounted to bullying and described how the latter had been denied sufficient media time to respond to the former's volley of racialized allegations.[1]

Hirsch, author of a major book on race and identity in Britain, has much knowledge to offer on the subject as a scholar and through her lived experience. Her being silenced by a badgering Morgan was a great loss to *Good Morning Britain*'s viewership. As she told *CNN*, the "white person in this debate always centers it on themselves. ... It would make more sense if somebody said: I haven't got a lived experience of racism. I would like to understand your perspective."[2]

In this chapter, we focus more centrally on illustrating collective myths—or *sincere white fictions*—wherein white Britons, like other white Westerners, see themselves as "not racist" and as "good people" even while they think and act in anti-black and other racist ways. We show how such powerful collective myths are on full display and are enduring. Members of the British commentariat and polity, most especially white men, commonly view allegations of British racism as exaggerated or false, and allege that *reverse-racism* is the real problem of which they as whites are the victims. They ignore much evidence to the contrary. Here, we also assess the significant role of black Britons from Roman times onward and the oppression they have long endured. And we provide much detail on the many examples of senior royals' links to decades of racism and fascism, with much lack of social virtue demonstrated there.

Sincere White Fictions and Other White-Racist and Gendered-Racist Framings

Sincere white fictions are central to the deep-rooted white racial frame. While Markle and Harry did not explicitly cite systemic racism as a motivating factor in their decision to step down as senior royals, they did voice a belief "in a free, strong and open media industry, which upholds accuracy and fosters inclusivity, diversity, and tolerance."[3] Later, with the publication of the book *Finding Freedom*, what was long obvious to many people of color was confirmed therein: racist and *gendered-racist* framing by the British establishment, media, and monarchy played significant roles in the couple's exit from royal life.[4]

In the UK, young people and liberals, of whom a majority voted to remain in the European Union, lean toward support for the couple; whereas, older and more conservative folks, of whom a majority voted to leave the European Union, tend to be more disparaging of them and protective of the monarchy.[5] In the USA, too, older conservative whites tend to talk about Markle in white-racist terms while clinging to their sincere white fictions. In the aftermath of the couple's announcement that they were stepping down as senior royals, Lynda McLaughlin, a producer for a conservative US talk show, framed Markle as "uppity," a term long applied by whites to black Americans, one with very racist undertones. McLaughlin added: "She is one of those liberal elitists, you know?"[6] Nearly a decade earlier, arch-conservatives the late Rush Limbaugh and Glenn Beck claimed that the then-First Lady of the USA, Michelle Obama, demonstrated "uppity-ism." Notably, one US media commentator remarked that white "Brits treated Meghan worse than people here treated … Michelle Obama. And that's saying a lot."[7] When called out for this anti-black framing today, prominent whites often assert ignorance of its historical links to past black oppression. In the USA's Jim Crow South, such terms were widely used by whites to describe black people who did not accept their subordinate place in the racial hierarchy.[8]

Whites and people of color in Britain, as in the USA, live in different societal worlds. In Britain, white women media pundits act much like their white male counterparts on racial matters. Add to this the fact that royal correspondents and commentators are primarily white. Penny Junor, the prominent white biographer of the British royal family, told Gayle King on *CBS This Morning* that she did not "believe race is a factor" in the press coverage of Markle.[9] "Harry was a very cheerful, happy, happy man. Always laughing, always joking, always taking the mickey out of someone. That cheerful, charming man seems to have disappeared. And in his place we have an angry, disgruntled, really seriously disgruntled man," she told King, who is African American. King retorted wisely, noting that "[h]e admits though, Penny, that he's angry and frustrated by the treatment of his wife, who he loves and adores, and his son. He's very concerned about her safety and her wellbeing."[10] As a further example of this white denial,

Nigel Farage, leader of the arch-conservative Brexit Party, was asked if racism had anything to do with the couple's decision to step down as senior royals. "Any suggestion that there was even an inch of racism in what's happened is simply wrong and deeply insulting to a country that is very relaxed about these things," he said, adding that the couple had "chosen exile."[11]

Junor's yearning for the pre-Markle prince, which includes him once dressing in a German Nazi uniform for a costume party, brings to mind African American sociologist Jennifer Sims's words on the significance of the couple's pairing. Sims explains that notwithstanding the fact that in earlier US history white men often had intimate relations with black and mixed-race women, including a great many rapes and other non-consensual relations, when such men love, marry, and protect the women and their offspring, there is often an extreme white backlash. Such white men are frequently framed as "traitors to their race."[12] In 2018, an image of Harry was circulated on social media, calling for him to be shot because he was such a "race traitor." A *BBC* investigation found a British-based neo-Nazi group was responsible for the post, one closely linked to a similar US-based group.[13]

Junor's nostalgia for the good old days brings to mind efforts by some in the British media to frame Markle as deliberately isolating Harry from his family and friends. The forensic psychologist Mikhaila Friel said she is routinely asked leading questions, such as, "Can you confirm that isolating someone from their family is a tactic used by controlling partners?" in a misogynistic bid for an anti-Markle spin. Friel believes the duchess has endured much mass media bullying. "I've been asked by various media to write/contribute to articles accusing Meghan ... of manipulation, coercive control, exploiting Harry's mental health struggles etc., I say no to this."[14]

The Megxit storyline offered the white press a chance to draw on allegations previously espoused—for example, Markle is ungracious, self-centered, demanding, and selfish. As one media source summarized this storyline, the Duchess of Sussex has been blamed for damaging her husband's well-being and portrayed as a palace-wrecker who has put the future of the monarchy in jeopardy. Markle has even been likened to Yoko Ono (who was married to John Lennon, one of the members of the famous British rock band the Beatles) for "trampling on tradition, causing chaos, ruining everything and then runs and hides." As the same source put it, "[T]here are some notable parallels between Meghan and Ono, as two women who stand accused of breaking up historic and beloved British institutions. ... [T]he distrust and demonization they face is, at least in part, rooted in their race."[15]

Media Mistreatment and Black Counter-Framing

In stark contrast to the views of these privileged whites, in a NBC News report noted in Chapter 1, a group of young black Britons laugh at the notion that Markle has been treated fairly in Britain. A teenager in the group, displaying that lived experience gives one insights beyond one's years, tells NBC: "Of course, no one is going to call [Markle the] ... N-word in a headline. ... Instead, you can see it in their mannerisms. ... Even if you're rich and of a certain status, you're still black. ... You're black first and foremost before you're rich." Another teenager tells NBC that the Duchess of Sussex's treatment by the mainstream media "really just emphasizes the notion that Britain is racist." Another in the group adds that the British media is "blinded by their white privilege. It's the older, white men."[16]

Unmistakably, prominent white analysts like Piers Morgan and Penny Junor are biased by their white power and privilege. In response to Afua Hirsch critiquing a reference to Markle's "exotic" DNA, Morgan retorts: "Is her DNA not exotic by royal standards? She's the first mixed-race person to enter the royal family. Why do you take exception to the word exotic?" Hirsch explains what the above-mentioned group of black teen girls likely would also have told Morgan: "Because it *others* [Markle] and associates her with a history that has posited people of African heritage as other."[17] (See Chapter 5 for more on this exotification issue.)

While Morgan's white female co-host pleads with him to allow Hirsch a fair chance to reply to his arrogant-white barrage of questions, he quips: "You can't just say these things are racist when they're not." Hirsch firmly retorts: "I'm telling you that as someone who's lived the experience of being a person of African heritage in this country that there are narratives that are regularly ..." but then, Piers interrupts her to ask if she is accusing him of being racist. "I'm saying that the narratives that you're perpetuating are racist," she replies, referencing a key part of still-commonplace white racial framing. Morgan then forcefully scolds Hirsch, declaring, "You say we're demonising a woman of colour. You're the one bringing race into this." When Hirsch cites as an example of racism the *BBC* broadcaster Danny Baker's racist tweet that included a picture of a baby chimp as a stand-in for baby Archie (see Chapter 2), Morgan ardently defends that racist action of Baker: "Baker's not remotely racist as anyone who knows him knows. [He] was unceremoniously beaten up on Twitter and within seven minutes he apologised. He got fired and vilified." With a grace under fire that no mere mortal could conjure under such racial bombardment, Hirsch replies: "My definition of racism is that we've inherited a very racialised history. Either you're committed to trying to dismantle and change that history of racism, or you're part of it."[18] Clearly, Morgan is an influential part of it.

Noting that the conduct of Morgan is symptomatic of a broader white pattern, in the open letter mentioned in the introduction to this chapter, black professional women criticize the constant racialized questioning by media hosts and other whites, who insist there is no systemic racism in Britain. The letter includes examples such as when:

> white male historian Robert Lacey ... confidently declared "when you look at the newspapers, they're sensationalist, they're vulgar, I don't

see racism there," in the presence of black woman broadcaster and musician Jamelia. He went on further to add that "there are dreadful racist societies, we [white Brits] are not so bad as the others."[19]

Even after Jamelia recounts how she has been a victim of covert racism, and that "it pales in comparison to what I've seen happen to Meghan. … It's not just social media; it's not. It's mainstream media; it's tabloid media," Lacey remains incredulous. "I'd like to see the evidence of that," he retorts.[20] Jamelia's response is poignant and to the point: "Most of the people who are getting to speak about this are old, white men. Where are all the women of colour who are able to speak from experience?"[21]

The open letter continues with what should be obvious, including to white men: "Having to engage, articulate, and explain racism again and again to predominantly white hosts, white men, and white guests is draining and exhausting." The authors of the open letter connect this reality to what they term the UK's *culture of racism*, which often includes the racialization of much mainstream journalism.[22]

More Media Mistreatment and Counter-Framing

The day after Morgan's dismissive treatment of Hirsch, and in the aftermath of the queen belatedly releasing an official statement in support of the Sussexes (see Chapter 1), the legal scholar and activist Shola Mos-Shogbamimu appeared on *Good Morning Britain*. Morgan's attacks on Mos-Shogbamimu—as with Hirsch—were notable for his claims that systemic white racism does not exist, even as he spoke and acted in anti-black ways. Mos-Shogbamimu responded to him as follows.

> You are a man privileged to have power and influence, and you're using your platform so irresponsibly to spout out this personal vendetta with nasty and vile comments knowing fully well that your words are containing bigotry, misogyny, sexism and racism, and you're not taking responsibility for how you have contributed to the so-called royal crisis. … It's the fact you can't see it because of your privilege. It is not my job to educate you Mr. Morgan but you refuse to get educated. … It makes me question where have you been the last two years. White privilege whitewashes racist and inflammatory language as unconscious bias. It perpetuates the bigotry of intolerant white people as ignorant.[23]

Following her appearance on *Good Morning Britain*, Mos-Shogbamimu tweeted: "It's reprehensible that we not only have to defend ourselves from racism; but then [are] expected to explain it & also bear the brunt of denials of our lived experience."[24] In solidarity, Ayesha Hazarika of the *Evening Standard* tabloid tweeted, "Shout out to all my sisters of colour who have been summoned on national broadcast to be told there's no racism and it's all in our heads and then have to deal with the fallout here."[25]

As Olive Pometsey, an editor for British *GQ*, explains, suddenly "booking agents at every news station are frantically calling up prominent women of colour in the industry to coax them onto TV debates during which they're expected to play the snowflake against a panel of predominantly white men explaining why Meghan Markle and Prince Harry's decision to step back as senior royals has nothing to do with race." Pometsey interviewed the broadcaster Amna Saleem, who like countless other black women has gone head-to-head with white male broadcasters suffering from white denial and male hyper-sensitivity. During an appearance on *BBC* Scotland, Saleem left in tears as a result of badgering she endured from a white male reporter. She tells Pometsey:

> What I don't understand is that people keep saying that race has nothing to do with this, but when you look at the headlines of papers and the way that [Markle has been] contrasted and compared to Kate, it's undeniable. ... Kate [is] often described as introverted and sweet and you have Meghan ... a mixed-race black woman described as sexual or dominating, which is just a classic hyper-sexualisation of black women.[26]

When asked why white men like Piers Morgan accuse people of color of "playing the race card," Saleem adds an in-depth explanation of how racism is systemic: "I think that white people can't see it, because it doesn't affect them, so they think that it's not happening. ... When we talk about racism, we're mostly talking about it systematically and institutionally and they refuse to hear it because it's not overt."[27] Anti-racism campaigner Nova Reid similarly explains: "We are coming from completely different starting points—we, as in Black people."[28]

The scholar Maya Goodfellow argues that the incessant attempts at a refutation of racism by white journalists illustrates how deeply engrained white-racist framing is, including its racial biases, narratives, and emotions. Paradoxically, she writes, the debate over whether the British media coverage is racist has reproduced white racism while negating its pervasiveness.[29] Moreover, early media coverage was inundated with unconvincing "platitudes of progression," including the suggestion that the pairing of Markle and Harry was a mark of modern times and that a mixed-race woman joining the royal family was a momentous progressive event in British history.[30]

As we show throughout this book, between the time it was announced that the couple was dating (2016) and when Markle publicly acknowledged the difficulty of dealing with tabloid journalists (2019), a lot happened. Consider the media's double-standards as applied to Markle and Kate Middleton (see Chapter 1), as well as the deafening silence of Buckingham Palace regarding the gendered racism Markle endured from the media, even as Palace officials defended Prince Andrew in the midst of the Jeffery Epstein scandal. Yet, when confronted with evidence that media coverage of Markle has not been generally heartfelt or hospitable, many whites ask: "Is it really racism, though?"[31] Yes, as we have shown empirically, it really is *white* racism that is basic and systemic in Britain.

Like most other black Britons, the rapper Stormzy has said that the unfettered animosity hurled toward Markle is because she is black. The acclaimed rapper considers the UK a racist country, a belief for which he has received significant condemnation. He has also said that UK racism has grown direr under the leadership of openly racist Prime Minister Boris Johnson.[32]

While racial diversity in the British Parliament has expanded in recent years, in 2019 a little more than 8 percent of Members of Parliament were non-white. An Amnesty International study found that a third of offensive tweets alluding to women Members of Parliament in the lead-up to the 2017 general election targeted a single black Member of Parliament, Diane Abbott. She was the Labour Party's shadow home secretary, whose job was to scrutinize Conservative Party government policy on domestic affairs, including on national security, criminal justice, and citizenship.[33]

Equally disconcerting is the fact that Andrew Sabisky, an important adviser to Prime Minister Johnson, resigned in 2020 in the wake of outrage over his overtly racist assertions that blacks have lesser intelligence than whites. In one racially framed post he suggests that (white) politicians should consider the racial differences in intelligence when devising immigration policies. Adopting an old racist eugenics perspective, he recommends that the government might "legally enforce universal uptake of long-term contraception at the onset of puberty" of certain people to inhibit a "permanent underclass." In a book review, he contends that applicants of social welfare "tend to be less conscientious and agreeable," and should be urged to have fewer children than people with more "pro-social personalities."[34] A member of the opposition Labour Party suggests that Sabisky was "hired because of these views, not despite them." In the aftermath of his resignation, a government spokesperson repeatedly declined to comment on whether Prime Minister Johnson shared Sabisky's highly racist opinions.[35]

Conservative politicians from communities of color also objected to Sabisky's appointment, noting it was detrimental to the party's dealings with those communities. "I'm not necessarily against hiring intellectually interesting people with sometimes controversial views, but this guy just doesn't seem very smart, and if you are not very smart and at the very least appear bigoted that cannot be a good look for the party," explained one such Conservative Member of Parliament. "By all means we should be against ultra-woke nonsense, but we should also stand against alt-right nonsense too." Another said the prime minister's failure to take a stand against Sabisky's racist rantings was severely damaging to the party's position with constituents of color. Meanwhile, a prominent geneticist referred to Sabisky as being "bewitched by science, without having made the effort to understand the areas he is invoking, nor its history." "The history here is important," he said, "because this process is exactly what happened at the birth of scientific racism and the birth of eugenics."[36]

In such a racialized climate, the *CNN* headline that stated plainly, "The Backlash against Meghan and Stormzy Shows that Britain is in Denial about Racism," is accurate and uncanny. And as the same *CNN* article demonstrates the *white speaker effect* is alive and well too. The same week that Stormzy was met with disdain for calling out white racism in the UK, praise was showered on white English football coach Gary Neville when he spoke publicly about racism in the country's football sector.[37]

A Note on Persisting Systemic Racism

Recall that *systemic* signifies and calls out the dominant white-racist practices, which were long ago institutionalized and manifested in all significant societal stations, geographical areas, and institutions (e.g., popular culture, politics, education, employment). This began with the brutal British slave system and the conquest, colonization, and expropriation of foreign lands, including the genocide of Indigenous peoples in pursuit of predatory capitalism and British Empire-building. Recall, too, from Chapter 1, that if you break a well-crafted, three-dimensional hologram into smaller parts and shine a laser through one part, you can project the whole holographic image again from that one part. Like such a hologram, each apparently separate British institution reflects in many ways the reality of centuries-old systemic racism. Expectedly, each major institutional component of systemic racism is connected, directly and indirectly, to the other key institutional components.[38]

As we see it, an understanding of such racial truths should necessitate a genuine commitment to dismantling this systemic white racism. This will require that the many sincere fictions of the white British self be faced and deframed. Alas, however, many whites continue to resist and deny the deadly racial framing and discrimination. A 2020 online survey of 1,535 British adults found that black respondents "are at least twice as likely as [white respondents] to say there is discrimination in British policing and media; three times as likely to think the country has done far too little to address historic racial injustice; and significantly more likely to believe that the country's governing Conservative Party is institutionally racist."[39]

When black British Member of Parliament Dawn Butler's car was pulled over by London police in 2020, she accused them of racially profiling her. She told the media, "There is an institutional racism in the police. ... It is cancerous and it needs to be cut out." Prime Minister Boris Johnson responded to the incident, saying the police should treat people with fairness and equality but his representatives said he "did not share Ms Butler's view that the [police force] was 'institutionally racist.'"[40] An abundance of evidence, including that which we share in this book, clearly shows Butler is quite correct and Johnson is quite wrong. Following a fact-finding trip to the UK, for example, a UN Special Rapporteur on racism commented in 2018 on the recurring criminalization of youth from racial-ethnic minorities, especially black male youth. "They are over-represented in police stops and searches, more likely to face prosecution under the country's joint enterprise provisions, and are over-represented in the prison system," she plainly stated.[41]

White Amnesia and Revisionist History

As we previously showed, and illustrate further here, much historic and contemporary evidence confirms that Britain and its major institutions, including the royal family, continue to be white-racist in their recurring framing and everyday actions. Next, we examine how dominant white framers have routinely diminished or expunged people of color from the annals of British history. Britain was never a racial monoculture. Analysts asserting white privilege and implementing white power unashamedly fight for a past that never was. That Britons of color share a heritage with whites is still unthinkable to many whites (and others) who believe Britishness is historically synonymous with whiteness.[42]

Recall the definition of white racism that black journalist Afua Hirsch offered the white host Piers Morgan as she responded to hostile questions: "we've inherited a very racialised history. Either you're committed to trying to dismantle and change that history of racism, or you're part of it."[43] Ironically, Hirsch and lawyer-activist Shola Mos-Shogbamimu were forced to listen to Morgan as he accused them of "trying to turn the Meghan debate into a race divide." Yet, it is the white elite that has long promoted racial division, while deliberately oppressing and deriding people of color in the interest of their white social, political, and economic betterment.[44]

Blacks in Roman Britain

The racialized history of which Hirsch speaks is evident in the fact that in spite of consensus among scholars that there were people in Roman Britain who fit the contemporary description of black, much opposition to that idea persists among whites. This became clear after a cartoon incited heated debate on social media. Not long after Markle and Harry announced their engagement, the *BBC* released an animated short featuring an affluent black family, with English accents, including a father who works for the Roman Empire.[45] The short caught the wrath of *Infowars*, a far-right conspiracy and fake news website: "Thank God the BBC is portraying Roman Britain as ethnically diverse. I mean, who cares about historical accuracy, right?" Obviously, *Infowars* did not. When Mary Beard, the renowned scholar on the Roman Empire, weighed in and said it was "indeed pretty accurate, there's plenty of firm evidence for ethnic diversity in Roman Britain," all hell broke loose. Her attackers included the conservative US economist and philosopher Nassim Nicholas Taleb, who brought genetics into the debate and accused Beard of "talking bullshit."[46] The historian A.R. Kushner sheds light on white denial of such historical facts, arguing that entrenched British racism restricts studies of the pluralism of British history, making it hard to move beyond time-worn accounts that have erased people of color as historical actors.[47]

Public comments in response to the animated short are troublingly reminiscent of Piers Morgan's and other white pundits' white hyper-sensitivity and amnesia. The pejorative use of the term *SJW* (social justice warrior) for people on the left of the political spectrum is found in numerous online comments. Additional hostile themes comprise attacks on the political left, including at least one extremist commentator who links the short film to a feminist and anti-white agenda: "[T]here [are] so many leftist codes in this cartoon like anti-whiteness and feminism, but worst of all is the fact that this is projected at kids, so demonic." Still other online responses include accusations that the broadcaster is engaging in blackwashing and appropriating white culture. Perhaps most disturbing are the many angry replies that include contemptuous remarks like this: "Ah yes I remember learning about the great [African] [R]oman aristocrat Bigus Niggus." Many livid online responders strongly challenge the historical accuracy of the animated short: "WTF? Made up history? Yeah, let's just make it up and claim it's real for today's standards."[48]

As Beard noted, archaeological evidence strongly confirms that people of African-origin long ago called the British Isles home. In the third century, North African troops served with Roman forces guarding Hadrian's Wall, a defensive fortification in the Roman province of Britannia. In 2016, historian and broadcaster David Olusoga erected the first 20 plaques memorializing Britain's earliest-known African community.[49]

The "Ivory Bangle Lady"—a skeleton found in York, a northeastern English city established by ancient Romans, which was more multicultural under the Romans than today—also confirms that people of African origin long ago called the British Isles home. Forensic techniques determined that the "Ivory Bangle Lady," who died in the fourth century, was of North African descent and spent her childhood in the west of Britain or in coastal areas of Western Europe. Once the forensic results were made public, she became a lightning rod for white-racist commentary online and elsewhere. A second ancient skeleton found in East Sussex is said to be of sub-Saharan African descent. Isotope analysis indicates this second woman grew up in southeast England and lived during the Roman period, which is interesting given that sub-Saharan Africa was not then part of the Roman Empire. Her discovery, too, proved unpopular with right-wing social media commentators.[50]

Blacks in Eighteenth-Century England

In the second half of the eighteenth-century, approximately 15,000 black people lived in England, mostly in the larger cities of London, Liverpool, and Bristol. A majority worked in paid and unpaid (enslaved) domestic service. Evidence of their lives has survived. If one visits Boughton House, one of Britain's best-preserved stately homes, one can catch a glimpse of Charles Ignatius Sancho, servant to the Duchess of Montagu. He survives in a 1720s portrait. Dressed in a servant's uniform, he stands to the side of the duchess as she towers over him from her elevated chair. The African Caesar Shaw was enslaved by Prince Harry's maternal ancestors in the eighteenth century. Evidence of his life is found in portraits on display at Althorp House, the Spencer family estate, which is also where Harry's mom (née Lady Diana Spencer) is interred.[51] A painting hanging in the famous intellectual Samuel Johnson's house is of his servant, Francis Barber, who was born enslaved in Jamaica. The friendship between the men, even as Britain exported millions into slavery, was apparently so cherished that when Johnson died he left Barber the majority of his fortune. Recently, Barber's (seemingly white) great-great-great-grandson unveiled a plaque commemorating his black ancestor, saying of the estimated millions of Britons with a black ancestor: "We are going around in disguise … in camouflage."[52]

Doctor Who: Upsetting the White Frame on Contemporary Television

Recall that the concept of the white racial frame incorporates not only the stereotyping, bigotry, and racist ideology emphasized in traditional race relations theories, but also the visual images, assortment of emotions, sounds of accented language, interspersed interpretations and narratives, and proclivities to discriminate—all essential to that white frame's routine operations. We see these elements at work in opposition to the aforementioned *BBC* animated short. As a further example of these elements at work, there is the nearly identical hullabaloo that arose when the iconic British time-traveling television series *Doctor Who* included a few black actors in episodes in which the titular character and his companions travel to Britain's past.

In one 2004 episode, when Doctor Who and his black companion visit Shakespeare's London, a small black population appears on the screen. The companion worries for her own personal safety given this was the era before emancipation. Doctor Who remains indifferent to her legitimate concerns. The show's producers were accused of misrepresenting the past in the name of multicultural sensitivities. Fewer viewers critiqued them for representing Britain's past as "happy" and "benign"—that is, as trivializing white racial oppression in that era.[53]

In a 2017 episode, when Doctor Who and another black companion time-travel to Regency London (approximately 1795–1837), the presence of black faces again ignited wrath among white fans claiming "political correctness" run amok. Walking around 1814 London, the Doctor's black female companion notes that the city was "a bit more black than they show in the movies." "So was Jesus," jokes Doctor Who, adding that "History's a whitewash." Doctor Who is quite correct! Nevertheless, charges of historical inaccuracy, reminiscent of those directed at the *BBC*'s animated short, were again falsely leveled at the provocative episode. Here, we witness an especially alarming hostility toward anyone (scholar, animator, or media producer) who endeavors to include non-whites in an honest presentation of Britain's complex racialized past.[54]

Racial Framing by Meghan Markle's In-Laws

For those who confuse aristocrats, royals, and ordinary folks, perhaps historian Philip Ziegler put it best: "There are *the people*, there is *the aristocracy* which is slightly more important than the people, and there are *the royals*, who are different."[55] What white folks among the three groups have in common is that they have long been part of the creation and maintenance of systemic racism, including the intergenerational transmission of its rationalizing white racial frame. This includes Markle's white in-laws.

As we demonstrate throughout this book, the royal family has long had strong ties to, and propagated, the dominant white frame and its subframes, especially via their allegiance to the British Empire, colonialism, and white racial purity. They are arguably the principal emblem of whiteness in the UK and throughout the Commonwealth. Their presence, symbolic and material, is felt far beyond these realms through their extended family ties. For example, Elizabeth II's paternal great-great-grandmother, Queen Victoria, had 42 grandchildren. During her lifetime, she was known as the "Grandmother of Europe" because her children had married into so many European royal dynasties. Her many grandchildren eventually followed suit. Among them were Queen Maud of Norway (1869–1938); Queen Sophie of Greece (1870–1932); Tsarina Alexandra, Empress of Russia and wife of Tsar Nicholas II of the House of Romanov (1872–1917); Queen Marie of Romania (1875–1938); Queen Victoria Eugenie of Spain (1887–1969); and a disconcerting number of actual Nazis, including Charles Edward, Duke of Saxe-Coburg and Gotha (1884–1954), whose grandson is King Carl XVI Gustaf (1946–), currently the longest-reigning monarch in Swedish history.[56] Victoria's most notable grandsons include Kaiser Wilhelm II, the famous German Emperor and King of Prussia (1888–1918) and King George V of the UK and the British Dominions and Emperor of India (1910–1936). The Kaiser, George V, and the Russian Tsarina's husband, Tsar Nicholas II (1894–1917), were first cousins. Before World War I, these three white men ruled half the globe.[57]

In addition to Queen Elizabeth II and King Carl XVI Gustaf, current reigning monarchs descended from Victoria include Queen Margrethe II of Denmark (1972–), King Harald V of Norway (1991–), and Felipe VI of Spain (2014–). And while King Phillippe of Belgium (2013–) is not a descendant, he has hereditary links to Victoria and her husband, Prince Albert, via their mutual uncle. The last monarch of Romania, King Michael I (1927–1930; 1940–1947), was also related to Victoria. The routine intertwining of European royalty is perhaps best illustrated by Felipe VI and his mother Queen Sofia (1975–2014), who, like Carl XVI Gustaf of Sweden, is descended from Queen Victoria in multiple ways.[58]

British Royalty's Links to European Nazism

Recall from Chapter 5 that Queen Elizabeth II's cousin, Lady Gabriella Windsor, does not have a single English relation between her and Queen Victoria, and that Victoria herself was of German descent and married to a German. There is a strong connection between the British royal family and Germany, including via an embarrassing number of Nazis.

Charles Edward, who from 1900 to 1918 was head of the House of Saxe-Coburg and Gotha, a German royal dynasty, was born in England. In his early teens, at his grandmother Victoria's insistence, he was carted off to assume the ducal throne of Saxe-Coburg and Gotha. His war-mongering first cousin, the German Kaiser Wilhelm II, held much sway over the young duke. World War I (1914–1918) brought Germany into conflict with Britain and Charles Edward found himself an enemy of his native land. Upon the defeat of Germany and its allies, he was declared a "traitor peer" by the British government and stripped of his British royal titles.[59]

If one were to watch the 2007 British documentary titled *Hitler's Favourite Royal*, one might be conned into feeling sympathy for Charles Edward, in spite of the fact that during World War II (1939–1945) he was one of Hitler's staunchest supporters. As one film critic notes, "What cannot be interpreted as tragic (or in any way forgivable) was Charles Edward's ... enthusiastic embracing of Nazism. As one of the first of the old elite to endorse Hitler he may well have been 'instrumental' in his rise to power ... In 1943 [Charles Edward's] home town of Coburg was officially declared 'Jew-free.'" As the film critic further notes, irrespective of the documentary's inclusion of such particulars, the filmmakers largely frame Charles Edward as a victim of circumstance. In the final minutes of the film, viewers are encouraged to picture him in 1954, not as a war criminal but as a doting and harmless old man alone in a theater watching the coronation of his cousin Queen Elizabeth II. We are meant to feel bad that he could not partake in the festivities. Such is the *perpetual victimhood* that elite whites like Charles Edward often evoke. In the aftermath of the "Crowngate" controversy—that is, when the *BBC* edited a trailer falsely depicting Elizabeth II indignantly leaving a photoshoot—the film critic surmises that the filmmakers whitewashed the monarch's aggressively Nazi cousin so as not to further offend her.[60]

Concerns with upsetting royalty bring to mind reactions to a British tabloid's 2015 publication of a 1930s video of the future Queen Elizabeth II giving the infamous Nazi salute alongside her mother. Although Princess Elizabeth was no more than seven years old at the time, her mother was in her thirties. Hostile reactions focused on the decision to release the video and not on its disturbing content. Defenses ranged from assertions that the young princess and her mother were merely waving to claims that "everyone was doing it" back then. Of the latter point, a pundit provocatively wrote, "arguing that the salute was normal ... because the entire British ruling class was a gang of fascists isn't exactly comforting."[61]

Official and unofficial responses from Buckingham Palace were telling. A spokesperson told the press that the tabloid that published the video had exploited it. Sources inside the palace accused the press of copyright infringement and criminality. Powerful insiders threatened a police investigation and inquiry by the Independent Press Standards Organisation, the regulator of most UK newspapers. The German historian Karina Urbach disapproved of such tactics, arguing that the material should have been in the public domain decades earlier. And the prominent expert on British royalty Ingrid Seward likewise argued that archived images of the queen add to historical knowledge and should be in the public domain.[62]

To be sure, the British royal family has a complicated history with German and other European Nazism. Prince William's recent pilgrimage to the tomb of his great-grandmother, Princess Alice, located in East Jerusalem is a reminder of that complexity. Alice, mother of Prince Philip, saved the Cohens, a Greek-Jewish family, from an almost certain monstrous death during the Holocaust. In 1983, she was named "Righteous Among the Nations," the highest distinction Israel bestows on non-Jews who endangered themselves to protect Jews during World War II. In contrast, three of Alice's daughters (Philip's sisters) were married to prominent Nazis. In tribute to Hitler, Philip's sister Sophie even named her son Karl Adolf. Her husband was director of the Third Reich's Ministry of Air Forces, which was in charge of the bombing of Britain. In her memoir, written toward the end of her life, she remarks thus on Hitler: "I have to say here, that, although [my husband] and I changed our political view fundamentally some years later, we were impressed by this charming and seemingly modest man, and by his plans to change and improve the situation in Germany." Because of their associations with Nazism, Philip's sisters were not invited to his 1947 wedding to the future Queen Elizabeth II. Photos of 16-year-old Philip, taken in 1937, as he followed the swastika-draped coffins of another sister, Cecilie—a member of the Nazi Party—and her fascist husband, can be found online today. Notably, in 2015, Philip and Elizabeth II made an official visit to Frankfurt, Germany to visit his relatives, including descendants of his Nazi sisters.[63]

In her book *Go-Betweens for Hitler*, Karina Urbach documents how the old German aristocracy facilitated Hitler's rise to power and eventually aided his foreign ambitions. They drew on their influential European networks in an attempt to advance the German Nazi Führer's connections to that larger elite. For German princes, including the brothers-in-law of Prince Philip, networking directly with Hitler served as a safety net for their own continuing power and privilege.[64]

During World War II, the aging Kaiser Wilhelm II was in exile in the Netherlands and safe from the clutches of the Allies due to that country's reigning monarch, Queen Wilhelmina, who refused to extradite him. He actually hoped that his eldest grandson might become the new kaiser of Germany under Hitler. He, too, made an attempt to woo Hitler, including in a letter of praise following the 1939 German-Soviet invasion of Poland. Hitler was no fan of Wilhelm, and thus his attempts to win favor proved futile.[65]

Perhaps no chronicle of the royal family's links to European Nazism would be complete without the inclusion of King Edward VIII, the famous uncle of Elizabeth II, who abdicated the British throne to marry an American divorcée (Wallis Simpson). In 1937, Edward and Wallis visited Hitler and other high-ranking Nazis in Germany. Thirty-three years later, the former king apparently told a friend he never considered Hitler "such a bad chap."[66] As for his shameful Nazi salute during the 1937 visit, which his defenders have argued was merely a wave, Edward admitted that he "did salute Hitler ... but it was a soldier's salute."[67] The former king also appears in the 1930s video of the young Princess Elizabeth making the same gesture.[68]

People's Uprisings and Elite Reactions: More Fascist Collaboration

We would be remiss not to describe the people's uprisings in Europe, which punctuated the World War II era, and some elite reactions to them. According to Donny Gluckstein, "[i]n many European countries sections of the upper class eagerly *collaborated* with the Nazis (the classic example being Vichy France), because they feared the radicalism of their own working-class people *more than* German occupation." In addition, the elite-white-male leaders of the Allied powers openly viewed Western wartime actions as necessarily aimed at extending their existing capitalistic empires. One was the ever-conservative and imperialistic Winston Churchill, who "was always very clear that his mission in the war was to defend the British empire, not promote the interests of ordinary citizens. He was *not* ideologically committed to destroy fascism."[69]

Fascism, including Nazism, was and is central to the elite-white-male-dominance system, and not some cancerous add-on. During the early to mid-1930s, sympathy for Hitler and other fascists was rife among that elite. Frank McDonough, author of *The Gestapo: The Myth and Reality of Hitler's Secret Police*, explains that many in the British establishment, including key aristocrats and newspaper owners, "were keen supporters of Hitler up until the invasion of Czechoslovakia." They saw him as the "best means of preventing the spread of communism. They tended to turn a blind eye to anti-Semitism and the attacks Hitler made on communists, socialists, and other internal opponents." They took encouragement from the astonishing economic and emotional revitalization of Germany in the 1930s, which in their view would stem the tide of communism. What's more, until the outbreak of war in 1939, white British debutantes were still doing "the coming-out season" in Germany, appearing at balls in search of aristocratic or upper-class husbands. Intermarriage between upper-class Britons and Germans was even viewed by the British elite as a way to safeguard peace.[70]

Clearly, the European Nazis had powerful friends among the British elite. This includes Harold Harmsworth, the prominent newspaper proprietor who developed the *Daily Mail* and the *Daily Mirror*. He notoriously penned an editorial titled, "Hurrah for the Blackshirts," in which he commends Oswald Mosley, leader of the British Union of Fascists, for his "sound, commonsense, Conservative doctrine." Harmsworth also applauds the German occupation of Czechoslovakia (1938–1945). In secret papers recently declassified, he extols Hitler for "great and superhuman work in regenerating your country," and encourages him to attack Romania.[71]

This British complicity is also seen in how the elite reacted to the 2003 death of one of their own fascists, Lady Diana Mosley. The historian Francis Beckett explains that the response to her passing was a vestige of the snooty country that Britain is: "this rich, stupid, superficial, selfish woman, who sneered at Jews and blacks in an upper-class accent, was fawned on by the establishment right up to her death."[72] In her autobiography, Mosley scoffs at black immigrants to Britain and at racial relations laws.[73] Yet when she died, the historian Andrew Roberts referred to her as "funny, charming, intelligent, glamorous," and considered the question of how to treat an unrepentant Nazi a peculiar issue for "British upper-class etiquette."[74] Alas, this is a question suitable for the USA as well. Upon her death, the liberal *New York Times* proclaimed, "Lady Diana Mosley, Fascist Who Dazzled, is Dead at 93."[75] They left out of this headline that she was a Nazi, a fanatical supporter of Hitler, and thus a one-time enemy of the UK and the USA.

Unsurprisingly, British elite investment in and attraction to fascism is not limited to the German Nazi period. In *Franco's Friends: How British Intelligence Helped Bring Franco to Power in Spain*, author Peter Day exposes the British Military Intelligence Section 16's (MI16) involvement in the rise of Spanish fascism. A plane chartered by an MI16 agent took Francisco Franco—the Spanish general who would rule over Spain from 1939 to 1975 as a murderous dictator—from the Canary Islands to Morocco at the start of his military coup. MI16 continued working in Spain up until the start of World War II in order to ensure that the financial interests of British capitalists were maintained. Its agents bribed Franco and other Spanish generals to retain the country's neutrality, securing continuing profits for Britain's capitalists from 1939 to 1945. Once the bloody Spanish civil war (1936–1939) was under way, many pro-Franco lobbyists were welcomed at the British Foreign Office, including British businessmen set to benefit financially from the defeat of the Spanish Republic. Meanwhile, hundreds of non-elite young Britons traveled surreptitiously to Spain to fight for that democratic Spanish Republic, while some elite young Britons went to fight for fascist dictator Franco.[76] Clearly, the British establishment has long benefitted from a globalizing and capitalistic/fascist framework.

Prince Philip, Duke of Edinburgh

We can broaden this discussion to contemporary royals who have continued to operate out of an aggressive version of the dominant white racial frame. Consider that Prince Philip, Elizabeth II's husband, has an extensive record of racist framing, including telling a group of British students during a royal tour of China that if they remained "much longer you'll all be slitty-eyed"; commenting that an antiquated fuse box looked "as if it was put in by an Indian"; inquiring into how a British student who had been trekking in Papua New Guinea had "managed not to get eaten"; asking an Indigenous man during a royal tour of Australia if he still threw "spears"; and remarking, after reading the name tag of entrepreneur Atul Patel at a Palace reception for British Indians, "There's a lot of your family in tonight." He is also famous for saying of a 14-year-old boy while visiting a Bangladeshi youth club, "So who's on drugs here? … He looks as if he's on drugs"; for asking a black islander in the Cayman Islands if "most of you [are] descended from pirates"; and for telling the president of Nigeria, who was dressed in traditional robes, that he looked like he was "ready for bed."[77] The prince's so-called gaffes—often a euphemism for elite racism and ethnocentrism—reemphasize the point documented before that there is "fun" to be had when engaging in white-framed and anti-other racist performances.

Yet, when called out for their racist actions, most whites fervently maintain that such performances are not racist. A case in point is the respected filmmaker Robert Hardman, who is known for his work on the royal family. In describing some of the same gaffes we include here, he defends Philip, writing: "the local reaction to a gaffe would bear little comparison to the banner headlines in Britain. A joke … was big news back home, but passed virtually unnoticed [abroad]. The Governor of the Cayman Islands … was irked that the only international media coverage from an otherwise dizzying royal visit in 1994 was [Philip's] joke." As for Philip's feelings about such racist gaffes, Hardman explains that the prince once told a biographer that there are times when "he might be skating on very thin ice."[78] That is, he is quite aware of his white-racist framing.

Prince Harry, Duke of Sussex

Prince Harry's racist words and actions are also part of the public record. When attending a racist "Colonials and Natives" costume party in 2005, he wore a Nazi uniform, similar to those worn by the Afrika Korps during the North African Campaign (1940–1943). Among other acts, this German expeditionary force is known for plundering Jewish property along the Libyan coast and working Jewish forced laborers to death.[79]

In 2008, video footage emerged of Harry making racist comments while training at the Sandhurst Military Academy. Filming his fellow trainees, he zooms in on a British cadet of Asian descent and remarks: "And here is our Paki friend." In a second incident, the prince is heard telling another cadet: "Fuck me, you look like a rag-head," which is a racist expression for Muslims, Arabs, or all Middle-Easterners.[80]

Such incidents are regularly excused in the mainstream media and by Palace officials, which underscores how the white racial frame operates to rationalize whites' racist behavior—that is, whites with power get to define what is racist and what is not. The views of people of color, as here, are not even considered.

The Afro-British historian Paul Gilroy refers to the incident where Harry wore the Nazi uniform as trivializing the history of the British Empire "so that it becomes congruent with the playful mood of the fancy-dress party that imperial rule always was."[81] Inadequate media interpretations of Harry's conduct emphasize the failure of his elite education, his immaturity, and dysfunctional family. Gilroy argues:

> To leave interpretation of his conduct on that level would be to miss an opportunity to understand something fundamental about the cultural life of a post-colonial country that has never dealt with the consequences of its loss of empire. Harry's behavior ... raises mainstream themes. ... That nihilistic outlook dictates that conflicts against Hitler and Hitlerism remain imaginatively close while Britain's many wars of decolonization—particularly in Africa, Malaya, Cyprus and Aden—are to be actively forgotten. Standing firm against Nazis comforts Brits by making them feel righteous and perennially innocent. Being forced to reckon with the ongoing consequences of imperial crimes makes them uncomfortable in equal measure.[82]

The ever-savvy Gilroy adds that there is a psychological dimension to the white British memory of victory over German Nazis, even as whites engage in celebration of a distant British Empire that involved colonial oppression. In this white behavior we clearly see an application of the dominant white racial frame, including racialized "fun" and the doggedly airbrushed image of colonial history that is used to morally uplift whites' view of themselves as virtuous. Psychological repression of the racialized reality of these bloody historical realities helps to explain why contemporary white Britons have flocked to the racist far-right or neo-fascist political parties (e.g., the British National Party).

Harry's relationship with Markle has clearly changed him. Unlearning racism is a life-long journey nonetheless. When a visibly pregnant Markle was congratulated on the impending birth of their son during a 2019 tour of Morocco, Harry joked, "What, you're pregnant?" followed by, "Is it mine?" As one pundit explains, "[w]hile it's apparent that the Duke and Duchess of Sussex were engaging in a playful exchange, it's problematic for a Black woman to have the assertion that her baby daddy may not be the daddy in a world that already thinks Black women are loose."[83] This is a view most people of color would instantly understand, yet again revealing how elite whites engage in racist joking with little consequence.

Significantly, even before Markle and Harry announced their engagement, British colonialism scholars Nalini Mohabir and Jermain Ostiana asked the prince to "co-conspire in our decolonising vision and engage in an act of royal rebellion by thinking about what liberation might mean for his girlfriend's family, and others who walk in slavery's shadow." They added, "show us how woke you are, and atone for the royals' institutional role in slavery."[84] And three years later, Omid Scobie, co-author of the book *Finding Freedom*, remarked that Harry's "experience of witnessing Meghan face racist remarks and commentary would have been the first time he'd seen someone in his life or someone he was particularly close to affected by it in a certain way. Harry's really had to become more attuned to and learn to see when it happens in front of him."[85]

Prince Andrew, Duke of York

Prince Andrew has routinely used racist humor to entertain the British elite at social gatherings and in conversations with key politicians. Apparently, this behavior has been common knowledge for some time, but in the aftermath of his infamous 2019 *BBC* interview (see Chapter 4) more people are coming forward with such stories. At a dinner in honor of Saudis at Buckingham Palace, Andrew supposedly made racist comments about Arab people. In response, a Buckingham Palace spokesperson stated that the prince "has many friends from the region. He does not tolerate racism in any form."[86]

Offering on Andrew's behalf the standard white "some of my best friends are" defense serves to propagate the myth that proximity to people of color inoculates whites from white racism. It is a time-honored custom used by whites when they face such allegations. As *The New York Times* notes, this white defense shows "a reluctance to have blunt conversations about race" and "a failure to acknowledge racial difference altogether."[87] To this, we would add that the white racial frame and its numerous subframes create space for whites to cultivate intimate connections to people of color, while simultaneously retaining sincere racial fictions of the white self. Buckingham Palace officials, mouthpieces of the royal family, once again missed a chance to genuinely address rampant white racism in the UK and within the family.

The moral licensing behind the "some of my best friends" defense is a prevalent research topic in behavioral psychology. Daniel Effron, for example, demonstrates that white participants overemphasize how modestly good past conduct should persuade others that their current or future conduct is not racist. He concludes that "when people anticipate needing evidence of their morality, they expect their [current] behavior to be judged against lower moral standards [in the past] and thus to earn them better moral credentials [in the present]." Effron uses Radovan Karadžić, President of Republika Srpska during the Bosnian War, as a major example. Karadžić claimed he felt no ill-will toward Muslims because his ex-barber was

Muslim. Yet in 2016 he was found guilty of genocide and crimes against humanity, including the mass murder of 8,000 Muslim males. Similarly, US scholar Tyler Parry has found that the use of blacks as political props was common in nineteenth-century debates on US slavery. In that antebellum era, some ex-slaveowners commonly defined their association with those they had brutally enslaved as "friendships."[88]

Among other allegations of racism that Andrew has faced is his use of the N-word in an official meeting with Rohan Silva, former adviser to British Prime Minister David Cameron (2010–2016). Silva, the son of Sri Lankan immigrants to the UK, recalls that in response to the question of whether the Department for International Trade "could be doing a better job," Andrew replied: "Well, if you'll pardon the expression, that really is the nigger in the woodpile."[89] At an earlier meeting with Andrew, when discussing the European Union, Silva alleges that the prince told him to remember "that you'll never get anywhere by playing the white man." Silva was dismayed to find that Andrew had used an adage, common in the British colonial era, that implies that only whites "can be trusted to follow the rules, unlike dark-skinned natives." Silva later wrote, Andrew "clearly wasn't taken to task very often by the people around him, which meant offensive language could go unchallenged."[90] As we note in Chapter 4, elite white men like Andrew sit at the apex of white male power and seldom have to answer for any racist remarks or actions, or much else, at least not on a timely basis.

Charles, Prince of Wales

Exactly one month before Markle married his son, Prince Charles told Anita Sethi, a British writer of South American Guyanese descent, that she did not look like she was from Manchester, England. That this incident occurred during a Commonwealth People's Forum, in which civil society representatives from around the world meet to deliberate on the major issues that British Commonwealth peoples face, is all the more distressing. Sethi wrote a scathing piece about the incident for a newspaper. "If this is how he thinks, he shouldn't be the next head of the Commonwealth," she reasons. She had a message for the prince: "Your Royal Highness, you asked me: 'Where are you from?' To adapt a phrase from the late Ambalavaner Sivanandan: I am here because you were there." She also courageously excoriates Charles for his framing.

> That the ... next leader of an organisation that represents one-third of the people on the planet commented that I, a brown woman, did not look as if I was from a city in the UK is shocking. This is exactly why some people, including the prince, urgently need a history lesson about immigration, the British empire, the Commonwealth and colonialism. Because I do look like I'm from Manchester, actually—a city in which many people of colour have been born and bred.[91]

Also, recall from Chapter 5 the incident when Charles and his second wife Camilla were caught on camera laughing throughout a throat-singing performance by Inuit in Northern Canada. This was yet another time when he, operating out of the white racial frame, proved to possess an utter lack of understanding and respect for Commonwealth diversity.[92]

Charles's coldness to the plight of marginalized peoples seems deep-rooted. He, knowingly or involuntarily, appears to act regularly out of an unsophisticated version of the white racial frame and its corresponding subframes, often accenting white virtuousness. In 2001, he wrote the highest-ranking state officer, the Lord Chancellor, about the European Convention on Human Rights, referring to it as "compensation culture." Sounding more like Boris Johnson than future daughter-in-law Markle, he grumbled that "our lives are becoming ruled by a truly absurd degree of politically correct interference."[93] In anger, on a memo he received in defense of the broad-reaching Act on human rights, he wrote: "[T]his is rubbish—we're a society based on rights alone."[94] A year later, Charles wrote about "ever-more prescriptive laws—for example, health and safety at work legislation, the blame culture … and the bureaucratic red tape which accompanies new rules."[95]

Recently, his black personal secretary, who he had employed for a decade, quit because of years of racist and sexist mistreatment. Elizabeth Burgess notes that there were "always black jokes and names going round because it is the Royal Family and it is still very protected." She asserts that Charles's valet referred to her as "a fucking nigger typist." She consistently experienced derision from members of the prince's household who were "very much the old school and had not really accepted black people." "They wanted a white face," she explains. She adds that the royal family "has its own rules and regulations. … They haven't got on with race or being politically correct with race or disability issues."[96]

The white racial frame, as shown previously, is not simply a matter of individual bias and bigotry. Like most other whites, the royals learn and perpetuate that framing in systemic ways, such as in their aristocratic educations, including via a firm embrace of their imperial legacy. Thus, when Charles and Camilla toured the Caribbean in 2019, they continued the tradition of royals ignoring and whitewashing the wrongs of the British Empire. In 2016, Harry did the same, leading to the headline, "Welcome to the Caribbean, Prince Harry. Will You Dare Speak Out about Slavery?"[97]

The motivation and rituals of royal tours foreground the false perception of an enlightened relationship between the Caribbean and the former imperial epicenter. Plainly, Harry was sent to the Caribbean to promote the empire's continuing centrality. A photo of him with Olympic gold-medalist sprinter Usain Bolt did just this, going viral. This spectacle intended to show that the racist past is in the past.

In the present, royals are attentive to British triumphs throughout their realm, and the monarch maintains her standing as Commonwealth leader. As colonialism scholar Nalini Mohabir suggests, this grand spectacle also reflects the fact that the royal family, despite its wealth, expects former colonies around the Caribbean to subsidize expensive royal tours. Commenting on Charles's and Camilla's 2019 tour, Mohabir notes that the Barbadian government subsidized a wreath-laying ceremony by Charles at the Tomb of the Unknown Soldier to commemorate those who had died in the world wars. Not mentioned was the fact that many black soldiers had signed up to prove they were worthy of the obscure civil rights the elite white leaders of the British Empire had vaguely promised them in return for their service.[98]

Why members of the British royal family—the personification of Anglo-imperialism—are asked to be part of their former colonies' Independence Day events remains an important question.[99] The answer lies in the still-dominant white racial frame. As we have seen, a substantial literature demonstrates the many ways in which some people of color, especially those in the elite, aggressively conform and buy into the dominant white racial framing of society, often to the harm of their own communities of color. Of them, Mohabir writes:

> Islands of [non-white] elites connected through their own privileges seem willing to show hospitality and welcome to the royals in exchange for a sprinkle of royal prestige. ... [They are] eager to wash away a history of empire through a facile notion of friendship and cooperation across the Commonwealth. ... What if, instead, Caribbean countries said *no* to all royal tours until the Caricom reparations commission demands [for British compensation for continuing suffering from the Atlantic slave trade] are met?[100]

Queen Elizabeth II's Mother: The Queen Mother

Royal diarist Sir Roy Colin Strong framed the late Queen Mother with the timid "colour prejudiced," while claiming he concealed her many harsh racist slurs because they were "too awful" to publish during her lifetime. Operating out of a white racial framing, he did not include them in diaries he published regarding dealings with the royal family. On one occasion she allegedly said to him, "Beware the blackamoors," a pejorative white-framed term in Europe for a black servant or dark-skinned individual. A lady-in-waiting to the Queen Mother corroborates Strong's account, stating that she had a patronizing colonial view of the African continent, remarking at one point, "poor darlings; the Africans just don't know how to govern themselves—it's just not their form. What a pity we're not still looking after them."[101]

Since her death in 2002, the image of the "doddery grandmother-of-the-nation" has been tarnished. Included in her white framing, which she often "spun as patriotism," were her "reservations about Jews," opposition to democratic elections in India, and endorsement of white-supremacist rule in the African colony of Rhodesia.[102] Alongside her husband, George VI, she supported Prime Minister Neville Chamberlain's appeasement of Adolf Hitler, which allowed unbridled German expansion. The royal couple's actions included welcoming Chamberlain on Buckingham Palace's balcony after he signed the infamous 1938 Munich Agreement, which allowed the Germans to annex part of Czechoslovakia.[103] In *Elizabeth, The Queen Mother*, the author Hugo Vickers notes that in her later years she made far less effort to hide her racist views. For example, "When Crown Prince Naruhito of Japan, son of Emperor Akihito, was staying for [the Royal Ascot horseraces], she insisted that the Japanese sword of surrender be put on display ... for his special interest."[104]

Shortly before Markle's and Harry's first wedding anniversary, the *Royal Foibles* chronicler wrote the following about generations of royal racism:

> One can only imagine how many times [the Queen Mother] turned over in her tomb at St. George's Chapel, Windsor ... when her great-grandson, Prince Henry of Wales, plighted his troth with the divorced, American, half blackamoor actress, Meghan Markle. ... From Queen Elizabeth I granting the royal warrant that initiated England's entry into the Atlantic Slave Trade, to the late Diana, Princess of Wales privately joking in the '80s that Father's Day was an example of social confusion in Brixton, a majority black part of London; the annals of British royal history are littered with bigoted personages one can surmise had scarce regard for Africa's contributions to world civilization beyond its once bountiful supply of slave labor.[105]

Rebelling against Anachronistic Framing and Morality: Justin Welby, the White Archbishop of Canterbury

Markle's in-laws and other elite whites would do well to emulate Justin Welby, the current Archbishop of Canterbury, head of the Anglican Church. Consider, for example, his actions at the memorial to the victims of the Jallianwala Bagh massacre on its one-hundredth anniversary in 2019. About 500–600 unarmed Indian civilians were massacred there by British colonial troops in 1919. At the memorial site, the archbishop lay on the ground, as if imitating Indians who were given a "crawling order" by Brigadier General Reginald Dyer, with many of them killed at the soldiers' bayonet points. In contrast, when Elizabeth II visited the site of the massacre in 1997, like Prime Ministers David Cameron and Theresa May later on, she avoided apologizing for that horrific massacre. Reluctance on the part of white officials to criticize their country's violent history, including brutal actions under the oppressive banner of imperialism, makes any real movement toward genuine equality and democracy in Britain impossible. That the 1919 massacre has usually been framed as a rare event for which a single officer (Dyer) was responsible is part of an ongoing pattern of white denial.[106]

Elizabeth II also refused to apologize for or acknowledge other brutal oppression perpetrated by the British. On a visit to South Africa, she rebuffed calls that Britain apologize to the Afrikaner people there for its actions during the Anglo-Boer War (1899–1902). Instead, she said: "It is fitting that we should remember that tragic chapter in the history of both our countries. We should remember with sadness the loss of life and suffering not only of British or Boer soldiers [Afrikaners, white descendants of Dutch colonists] but of all those caught up in the war—black and white, men, women and children."[107]

The queen has been consistent in this white-rescuing approach. When she traveled to Barbados in 1966, the history of slavery, sugar, and British royalty were unpleasantly entangled in the visit. For one, she stayed on a former sugar slave plantation. As the astute colonialism analysts Mohabir and Ostiana poignantly put it: "This visit is not ancient history; it's living memory for our parents and grandparents, and Prince Harry's grandmother too."[108]

Over four decades later, during the two-hundredth anniversary of the abolition of the transatlantic slave trade, black British activists demanded an official apology for this brutal history of slavery. The queen refused. When Jamaican activists earlier asked for a public apology, the basis of her absurd refusal was the view that slavery was not a crime against humanity at the time it was established by the British there. Significantly, and in direct contrast to the actions of Elizabeth II, the Duchess of Sussex refers to slavery as a "shatteringly recent" occurrence. Following the British Emancipation Proclamation of 1862, her three-times great-grandfather— who had been enslaved—renamed himself Wisdom.[109] Recall too that Markle's four-times great-grandmother was born into US slavery in 1820s Georgia (see Chapter 1).

In direct opposition to the views of Archbishop Welby, others in the elite continue to revel in the bloody colonial past. In 2005, when white conservative Gordon Brown (later prime minister) was head of Her Majesty's Treasury, he proclaimed that expressions of regret for the country's colonial past must cease. He emphasized that Britons had fashioned the noblest ideas in world history, as he called for a return to the great British values of "freedom, tolerance, and civic duty." He aggressively accented restoring British patriotism, even while on an official tour of Dar es Salaam, Tanzania. One of Britain's former African colonies, and famous as a site of armed resistance to white imperialism, Dar es Salaam served as a sanctuary for African activists fighting the white colonialists. It was here that the African National Congress (ANC) had made its base during its war against official racial segregation in South Africa. In one of the most egregious examples of white colonial and racial framing, Brown spoke about the so-called British values of "fair play, of openness, of internationalism," in Dar es Salaam, of all places.[110] Conveniently, he left out many pivotal facts, such as the British government being active in strengthening racial segregation there and privileging white colonists over Indigenous black residents.[111]

Also in direct contrast to the example set by Archbishop Welby, in 2017 then-Foreign Secretary Boris Johnson was caught on camera publicly repeating a passage from the white-nationalist poet Rudyard Kipling's poem titled "Mandalay." While inside the most sacred Buddhist site in the Southeast Asian nation of Myanmar, he uttered, "The temple bells they say/ Come you back you English soldier." Johnson's actions were all the more outrageous if one considers that the British government brutally colonized Myanmar from 1824 to 1948, fighting wars to quash Indigenous opposition there to British imperialistic rule. The British ambassador to Myanmar even had to convince Johnson to stop quoting, just before he could recite a viciously disrespectful verse about the Buddha. That the white-supremacist Kipling barely knew anything about this Southeast Asian nation, having traveled there for a mere three days when in his twenties, seems to matter little to elite white Britons like Johnson, who gleefully accept such white-racially framed misrepresentations. The Labour Member of Parliament and chair of the All-Party Parliamentary Group on Democracy in Myanmar, Rushanara Ali, said at the time: "I can think of a long list of reasons why Boris Johnson isn't fit to be prime minister. This can be added to that list."[112]

And even though in 2019 Johnson, then a nationalistic candidate for British prime minister, publicly balked when President Donald Trump told four US Democratic congresswomen of color to "go back and help fix" their "broken and crime-infested" countries, he too has a long history of similar racist comments. "You simply cannot use that kind of language," he said of Trump's statements during a British debate. "It went out decades and decades ago and thank heavens for that. It's totally unacceptable." These sentiments were politically motivated for the purpose of securing British votes. After all, Johnson had previously penned newspaper columns about "piccaninnies with watermelon smiles" and publicly described niqab-wearing Muslim women as "letterboxes."[113]

Similarly, his insincere anti-racism was evident in the aftermath of the 2020 UK Black Lives Matter protests. After calling anti-racism protesters "thugs," Johnson blithely remarked, "Let us work peacefully and lawfully to defeat racism and discrimination wherever we find it, and let us continue to work together as we put Britain back on its feet." One Scottish journalist retorted: "Man who spoke of black people as 'piccaninnies' now instructs us about his achievements in race relations."[114]

Archbishop Welby's commentaries and actions against white racism illustrate that change is possible among whites, including those with significant societal power. He fearlessly argues that the incendiary language used by white-nationalist politicians, including Prime Minister Johnson, must end. "I think we have become addicted to an abusive and binary approach to political decisions," he explains, "'it's either this or you're my total enemy.'"[115] Of course, he was widely panned for such talk by Brexiters, those in favor of withdrawing from the European Union. In defense of Welby, a prominent white Anglican bishop explains in terms that seem to underplay the many centuries of British racism: "It is essential

... for the leaders of both sides and throughout our society to challenge the attacks, the xenophobia and the racism that seem to have been felt to be acceptable *at least for a while.*"[116]

The long Brexit effort was principally led by white men, who said little about the racial- and gender-equality ramifications of leaving the European Union, which makes dissenting voices like Welby's all the more crucial.[117] The approximate four-year sequence of leaving the union generated a rebirth of strong white-British nationalism, which persists to the present day.

In 2019, the archbishop publicly called on fellow Christians to use online social media with truth and kindness, lamenting the reality of false "alternative facts."[118] It would be a mistake to confuse such an influential call with religious sentimentality. His words and actions are bold attempts to direct white and other Britons on a path toward genuine equality, social justice, and democracy. "Within an environment where we've seen the biggest rise in hate crime, and particularly antisemitic crime and Islamophobic crime," he explains, "the amplification given by social media makes it extraordinarily dangerous to use careless comments."[119] While his language here is a bit understated, his point about ending hate crime is clear.

Another example of the Archbishop's courageous quest for a more democratic Britain occurred during the 2019 general election. He called on political candidates "to reject the language of prejudice and not to stoke stigma or hatred towards people on the grounds of their religion, their culture, their origin, their identity or their belief." He mentioned numerous groups—expressly Jews and Muslims—who are vulnerable to ongoing xenophobic and religious attacks. Political parties "must make it an absolute priority to offer positive reassurance and avoid anything that increases the perception of fear," he said. Welby has made clear his vision of a just society, including a fair economic system, justice for the oppressed, and "a commitment to combat climate change and adapt to its effects." He has also emphasized that contemporary Christians must atone for past antisemitism.[120]

In 2020, amid the Black Lives Matter protests and the ensuing public discussions over racist and colonial symbols, the Archbishop's commitment to anti-racism was on display yet again. He said the Church of England would carefully review religious statues for links to slavery: "the statue needs to be put in context. Some will have to come down. Some names will have to change." When asked by the *BBC* if it was incumbent on the Western church to reconsider how it portrays Christ—with the interviewer mentioning US activists' calls to remove murals and statues representing Jesus as European—Welby replied: "Yes of course." He explained that across the world Anglican churches depict "black Jesus or a Chinese Jesus or a Middle Eastern Jesus—which is of course the most accurate. You see Jesus portrayed in as many ways as there are languages, cultures and understandings. ... I do think saying 'that's not the Jesus who exists, that's not who we worship,' it is a reminder of the universality of the God that became fully human."[121]

Conclusion

"Thank God they are free. Nobody should tolerate bullying and abusive behavior because of the color of their skin," said one Londoner of Caribbean descent in the aftermath of the Sussexes' decision to step down as senior royals. "All of this is about [Markle's] race. I know it because as a Caribbean woman who did not grow up here, I have experienced it myself."[122] Similar sentiments are regularly expressed by people of color in Britain and throughout the world. They know well what most whites everywhere refuse to concede, that the racist and gendered-racist press coverage of the Duchess of Sussex is ever-present, and has frequently fueled similar attacks on an array of social networking websites.

Amna Saleem, a Scottish Pakistani writer, notes that "much of Britain desperately wants to be absolved of its racist history without doing any work to combat racism—treating marginalisation and discrimination like imagined annoyances not worth confronting."[123] We agree with Saleem, but would clarify and emphasize that the "much of Britain" to which she refers is mostly *white* Britain. Whites generally do not seek a mere pardon; rather, they furiously try to refute the existence or impact of past and contemporary racism. As we show in this chapter, elite whites like Justin Welby, Archbishop of Canterbury, are certainly exceptional in not perpetrating such racial falsehoods.

Notes

1 *InfluencHer*, "Black British Group Pens an Open Letter to the British Broadcast Media on Racism and Meghan Markle," *InfluencHer*, January 15, 2020, http://influencher.org/index.php/2020/01/15/an-open-letter-to-the-british-broadcast-media-on-racism-and-meghan-markle/. Accessed February 15, 2020.
2 Monica Sarkar, "The Backlash against Meghan and Stormzy Shows that Britain is in Denial about Racism," *CNN*, January 27, 2020, www.cnn.com/2020/01/26/uk/uk-meghan-stormzy-racism-denial-intl-gbr/index.html. Accessed February 16, 2020.
3 The Duke and Duchess of Sussex, "Media," *The Royal Household*, https://sussexroyal.com/media/. Accessed February 16, 2020.
4 Omid Scobie and Carolyn Durand, *Finding Freedom: Harry and Meghan and the Making of a Modern Royal Family* (New York: HarperCollins), pp. 349, 126–127.
5 Mark Landler, "'Megxit' is the New Brexit in a Britain Split by Age and Politics," *The New York Times*, January 15, 2020, www.nytimes.com/2020/01/15/world/europe/harry-meghan-megxit-brexit.html. Accessed February 16, 2020.
6 Martha Ross, "Sean Hannity's Producer: Meghan Markle was 'Very Uppity,'" *The Mercury News*, January 17, 2020, www.mercurynews.com/2020/01/17/sean-hannitys-producer-meghan-markle-was-very-uppity/. Accessed February 16, 2020.
7 Elizabeth Wellington, "Meghan Markle Proved Being a Princess Isn't What It's Cracked Up to Be—Especially If You're Black," *The Philadelphia Inquirer*, January 15, 2020, www.inquirer.com/columnists/meghan-markle-prince-harry-megxit-queen-elizabeth-kali-nicole-gross-rutgers--20200115.html. Accessed February 16, 2020.

8 Elspeth Reeve, "Yep, 'Uppity' is Racist," *The Atlantic*, November 22, 2011, www.theatlantic.com/politics/archive/2011/11/yep-uppity-racist/335160/. Accessed February 16, 2020.

9 @CBSThisMorning, Twitter, https://twitter.com/CBSThisMorning/status/1216710409819914242. Accessed February 16, 2020.

10 Blue Telusma, "Gayle King Checks Royal Family Biographer over Megan Markle Racial Remark on 'CBS This Morning,'" *The Grio*, January 13, 2020, https://thegrio.com/2020/01/13/gayle-king-checks-royal-family-biographer-over-megan-markle-racial-remark-on-cbs-this-morning/. Accessed February 16, 2020.

11 Erin B. Logan, "A Month After Meghan Markle's Exit, Britons Continue to Debate the Role of Race," *Los Angeles Times*, February 11, 2020, www.latimes.com/world-nation/story/2020-02-11/meghan-markle-racism-england-black-britons. Accessed February 16, 2020.

12 Rachel Hatzipanagos, "Royalty, Social Class Could Not Shield Meghan from Racism in Britain," *The Washington Post*, January 16, 2020, www.washingtonpost.com/nation/2020/01/16/meghan-obama-class-race/. Accessed February 16, 2020. On the hundreds of thousands of white male rapes of black women in US history, see Rachel Feinstein, *When Rape was Legal: The Untold History of Sexual Violence during Slavery* (New York: Routledge, 2019), et passim.

13 *NPR* Staff, "Inside the Racist Online Attacks on Meghan Markle," *NPR*, March 10, 2019, www.npr.org/2019/03/10/701987112/inside-the-racist-online-attacks-on-meghan-markle. Accessed November 11, 2019.

14 Mikhaila Friel, "Racism in the British Media May Have Been a Driving Force behind Meghan Markle's 'Step Back' from the Royal Family," *Insider*, January 20, 2020, www.insider.com/racism-british-media-meghan-markle-prince-harry-royal-step-back-2020-1. Accessed February 16, 2020.

15 Sandi Rankaduwa, "The British Royal Family Has More to Lose than Harry and Meghan Do," *BuzzFeed*, January 16, 2020, www.buzzfeednews.com/article/sandirankaduwa/meghan-markle-prince-harry-megxit-leaving-royal-family. Accessed February 16, 2020.

16 Alexander Smith, "Meghan Markle and British Racism: What Her Saga Says to Black Britons," *NBC*, February 10, 2020, www.nbcnews.com/news/world/meghan-markle-british-racism-what-her-saga-says-black-britons-n1132181. Accessed February 16, 2020.

17 Cydney Yeates, "Piers Morgan Clashes with Afua Hirsch in Explosive Meghan Markle 'Racism' Debate," *Metro*, January 13, 2020, https://metro.co.uk/2020/01/13/piers-morgan-clashes-good-morning-britain-guest-explosive-meghan-markle-racist-media-coverage-debate-12048124/. Accessed February 16, 2020. Italics added.

18 *Ibid*.

19 InfluencHer, "Black British Group Pens an Open Letter."

20 Rankaduwa, "The British Royal Family Has More to Lose."

21 Olive Pometsey, "Meghan and Harry have Blown Britain's Racism Debate Wide Open," *GQ*, January 10, 2020, www.gq-magazine.co.uk/politics/article/meghan-and-harry-racism. Accessed February 16, 2020.

22 InfluencHer, "Black British Group Pens an Open Letter."

23 Charlie Nash, "Piers Morgan Erupts during Debate on Meghan Markle Press Treatment: 'Where is the Racism?,'" *MediaITE*, January 14, 2020,

www.mediaite.com/tv/piers-morgan-erupts-during-debate-on-meghan-markle-press-treatment-where-is-the-racism/. Accessed February 15, 2020.

24 @SholaMos1, Twitter, https://twitter.com/sholamos1/status/1217049937227 190274?lang=en. Accessed February 15, 2020.

25 Olive Pometsey, "Amna Saleem on Meghan Markle: 'Why Should We Expect Racism?,'" *British GQ*, www.gq-magazine.co.uk/politics/article/amna-saleem-meghan-markle-prince-harry. Accessed February 15, 2020.

26 *Ibid.*

27 *Ibid.*

28 Richard Allen Greene, "Britain's Big Race Divide," *CNN*, June 22, 2020, https://edition.cnn.com/interactive/2020/06/europe/britain-racism-cnn-poll-gbr-intl/. Accessed August 12, 2020.

29 Maya Goodfellow, "Yes, the UK Media's Coverage of Meghan Markle Really is Racist," *Vox*, January 17, 2020, www.vox.com/first-person/2020/1/17/21070351/meghan-markle-prince-harry-leaving-royal-family-uk-racism. Accessed February 16, 2020.

30 Amna Saleem, "Harry and Meghan Were Meant to Embody Post-Racial Britain. So Much for That," *The Guardian*, January 11, 2020, www.theguardian.com/commentisfree/2020/jan/11/post-racial-britain-harry-meghan-tabloids. Accessed February 16, 2020.

31 Goodfellow, "Yes."

32 *BBC* Staff, "'Stormzy: No 'Credible' Reason to Hate Meghan Markle," *BBC*, January 14, 2020, www.bbc.com/news/newsbeat-51102826. Accessed February 16, 2020; Antonello Guerrera, "Stormzy E Ghali Gemelli Di Versi," *Rep*, December 18, 2019, https://rep.repubblica.it/pwa/anteprima/2019/12/18/news/stormzy_ghali_intervista_doppia_trap_rap_brexit_salvini_boris_johnson-243704497/?refresh_ce. Accessed February 16, 2020.

33 Sarkar, "The Backlash against Meghan and Stormzy."

34 Rowena Mason, "Boris Johnson Adviser Quits over Race and Eugenics Controversy," *The Guardian*, February 17, 2020, www.theguardian.com/politics/2020/feb/17/boris-johnson-adviser-quits-over-race-and-eugenics-writings. Accessed February 18, 2020.

35 Luke McGee, "Boris Johnson's Adviser Who Voiced Support for Eugenics has Resigned," *CNN*, February 17, 2020, www.cnn.com/2020/02/17/uk/boris-johnson-advisor-andrew-sabisky-intl-gbr-scli/index.html. Accessed February 18, 2020.

36 Mason, "Boris Johnson Adviser Quits."

37 Sarkar, "The Backlash against Meghan and Stormzy."

38 For more details on social reproduction of racism, see Joe R. Feagin, *Systemic Racism: A Theory of Oppression* (New York: Routledge, 2006), et passim.

39 Greene, "Britain's Big Race Divide."

40 Lamiat Sabin, "Labour's Butler Calls for Action to 'Cut Out Cancerous' Institutional Racism in Policing after Officers' Car Stop," *Morning Star*, August 10, 2020, https://morningstaronline.co.uk/article/b/dawn-butler-calls-action-cut-out-cancerous-institutional-racism-policing-after. Accessed August 12, 2020.

41 Office of the High Commissioner for Human Rights (UN Human Rights), "UN Rights Expert Hails UK for Anti-Racism Action but Raises Serious Concerns over Immigration Policy, Prevent Programme and Brexit," May 11, 2018, www.ohchr.org/EN/NewsEvents/Pages/DisplayNews.aspx?NewsID=23074&LangID=E. Accessed February 16, 2020.

42 Chitra Ramaswamy, "Black and British: A Forgotten History Review—This is What it Means to Share a Heritage," *The Guardian*, November 10, 2016, www.theguardian.com/tv-and-radio/2016/nov/10/black-and-british-a-forgotten-history-review-this-is-what-it-means-to-share-a-heritageAccessed   December 28, 2019.

43 Yeates, "Piers Morgan Clashes with Afua Hirsch."

44 Stephanie Soteriou, "POOR SHO Piers Morgan Comes to Blows with Shola Mos-Shogbamimu after Mispronouncing her Name in Fiery Meghan Markle Debate," *The Sun*, January 14, 2020, www.thesun.co.uk/tvandshowbiz/10733046/piers-morgan-shola-mos-shogbamimu-meghan-markle/. Accessed February 16, 2020.

45 *BBC*, "Life in Roman Britain History The Story of Britain," YouTube user "Fritzman," www.youtube.com/watch?v=WjuYhBPwaQs. Accessed December 28, 2019.

46 Sarah Zhang, "A Kerfuffle about Diversity in the Roman Empire," *The Atlantic*, August 2, 2017, www.theatlantic.com/science/archive/2017/08/dna-romans/535701/. Accessed December 28, 2019.

47 A.R. Kushner, "Selling Racism: History, Heritage, Gender and the (Re)production of Prejudice," *Patterns of Prejudice*, 33 (4) (December 2010), pp. 67–86.

48 *BBC*, "Life in Roman Britain."

49 Ramaswamy, "Black and British."

50 Stephany Leach, Hella Eckardt, Carolyn Chenery, and Gundula Müldner, "A Lady of York: Migration, Ethnicity and Identity in Roman Britain," *Antiquity*, 84 (323) (March 2010), pp. 131–145; Emily Hanscam, "Postnationalism and the Past: The Politics of Theory in Roman Archaeology," *Theoretical Roman Archaeology Journal*, 2 (1) (2019), p. 3; Jo Seaman, "The Mystery of Beachy Head Lady: A Roman African from Eastbourne," *Museum Crush*, May 4, 2018, https://museumcrush.org/the-mystery-of-beachy-head-lady-a-roman-african-from-eastbourne/. Accessed December 29, 2019.

51 Historic England Staff, "Black Lives in England," Historic England, https://historicengland.org.uk/research/inclusive-heritage/the-slave-trade-and-abolition/sites-of-memory/black-lives-in-england/. Accessed December 28, 2019; Boughton House Staff, "Experience 'The English Versailles,' " Boughton House, www.boughtonhouse.co.uk/. Accessed December 28, 2019; Historic England Staff, "Servants," Historic England, https://historicengland.org.uk/research/inclusive-heritage/the-slave-trade-and-abolition/sites-of-memory/black-lives-in-england/servants/. Accessed December 28, 2019.

52 Ramaswamy, "Black and British."

53 For an exception, see Lindy A. Orthia, " 'Sociopathetic Abscess' or 'Yawning Chasm?' The Absent Postcolonial Transition in Doctor Who," *Journal of Commonwealth Literature*, 45(2) (June 2010), pp. 207–225.

54 David Olusoga, "Black People Have Had a Presence in Our History for Centuries. Get Over It," *The Guardian*, August 13, 2017, www.theguardian.com/commentisfree/2017/aug/12/black-people-presence-in-british-history-for-centuries. Accessed December 28, 2019.

55 Channel 4 Documentary, *Three Kings At War*, December 14, 2006 (original air date), www.channel4.com/programmes/three-kings-at-war. Accessed December 28, 2019.

56 See Julia P. Gelardi, *Born To Rule: Five Reigning Consorts, Granddaughters of Queen Victoria* (New York: St Martin's Griffin Press, 2006) and Jonathan Petropoulos,

Royals and the Reich: The Princes Von Hessen in Nazi Germany (Oxford: Oxford University Press, 2008).

57 Nosheen Iqbal, "Has Meghan Markle Changed Britain's Attitude to Race and Royalty?" *The Observer*, May 13, 2018, www.theguardian.com/uk-news/2018/may/13/has-meghan-markle-changed-britains-attitude-race-and-royalty. Accessed June 12, 2019; Will Dahlgreen, "The British Empire is 'Something to be Proud Of,'" *YouGov*, July 26, 2014, https://yougov.co.uk/topics/politics/articles-reports/2014/07/26/britain-proud-its-empire. Accessed November 10, 2019; Jone Johnson Lewis, "Queen Victoria's Children and Grandchildren," *ThoughtCo.*, September 17, 2019, www.thoughtco.com/queen-victorias-children-and-grandchildren-3530653. Accessed December 28, 2019; Channel 4 Documentary, *Three Kings At War*.

58 Lauren Hubbard, "Queen Victoria's Descendants Still Reign over Europe," *Town & Country*, February 17, 2019, www.townandcountrymag.com/society/tradition/a26193545/queen-victoria-descendants-on-the-throne/. Accessed May 3, 2020.

59 *Hitler's Favourite Royal*, DOCS, https://documentaries.io/hitlers-favourite-royal-world-war-2-documentary-timeline/. Accessed December 29, 2019.

60 Gerard O'Donovan, "Last Night on Television: *Hitler's Favourite Royal* (Channel 4) – Spoil (Channel 4)," *The Telegraph*, December 7, 2007, www.telegraph.co.uk/culture/tvandradio/3669780/Last-night-on-television-Hitlers-Favourite-Royal-Channel-4-Spoil-Channel-4.html. Accessed December 28, 2019.

61 Sam Kriss, "No One Should be Surprised by the Royal Family's Nazi Salute," *Vice*, July 24, 2015, www.vice.com/en_ca/article/kwx7ge/royal-family-nazi-salute-british-empire-history-fascism-832. Accessed December 29, 2019.

62 Josh Halliday and Louise Osborne, "Queen's Nazi Salute Footage Raises Pressure on Royals to Open Archives," *The Guardian*, July 20, 2015, www.theguardian.com/uk-news/2015/jul/19/queens-nazi-salute-video-pressure-mounts-on-royals-to-open-up-archives. Accessed December 29, 2019.

63 Elena Nicolaou, "How were Prince Philip's Sisters Connected to Nazi Germany?," *Refinery29*, December 14, 2017, www.refinery29.com/en-us/2017/12/185268/prince-philip-sister-cecile-nazi-the-crown-season-2. Accessed December 28, 2019.

64 Karina Urbach, *Go-Betweens For Hitler* (Oxford: Oxford University Press, 2015).

65 Tobias Buck, "Descendants of Last German Kaiser Fight to Reclaim Royal Property," *Financial Times*, July 26, 2019, www.ft.com/content/c2699d52-af85-11e9-8030-530adfa879c2. Accessed December 28, 2019.

66 Rory Tingle, "When Edward VIII Went to See Hitler: Never-Before-Seen Photos Emerge for Sale of Duke of Windsor's Infamous Trip to Nazi Germany in 1937," *Daily Mail*, September 10, 2016, www.msn.com/en-gb/news/royals/when-edward-viii-went-to-see-hitler-never-before-seen-photos-emerge-for-sale-of-duke-of-windsors-infamous-trip-to-nazi-germany-in-1937/ar-BBO86rd. Accessed August 26, 2020. See also Andrew Morton, *Wallis in Love: The Untold Life of the Duchess of Windsor, the Woman Who Changed the Monarchy* (New York: Grand Central Publishing, 2018).

67 Andrew Morton, *17 Carnations: The Royals, the Nazis, and the Biggest Cover-Up in History* (New York: Grand Central Publishing, 2018), p. 133.

68 Halliday and Osborne, "Queen's Nazi Salute."

69 Interview with Donny Gluckstein, *New Left Project*, https://plutopress.wordpress.com. Accessed December 25, 2015. Italics added.

70 Tom Sykes, "How British High Society Fell in Love with the Nazis," *Daily Beast*, April 14, 2017, www.thedailybeast.com/how-british-high-society-fell-in-love-with-the-nazis. Accessed April 29, 2020; Frank McDonough, *The Gestapo: The Myth and Reality of Hitler's Secret Police* (New York: Skyhorse, 2017), et passim.

71 Sykes, "How British High Society Fell in Love with the Nazis."

72 As quoted in Francis Beckett, "A Better Class of Fascist," *The Guardian*, August 16, 2003, www.theguardian.com/politics/2003/aug/16/race.thefarright. Accessed April 29, 2020.

73 Diana Mitford, *A Life of Contrasts: The Autobiography* (London: Gibson Square, 2012).

74 Beckett, "A Better Class of Fascist."

75 Sarah Lyall, "Lady Diana Mosley, Fascist Who Dazzled, is Dead at 93," *The New York Times*, August 14, 2003, www.nytimes.com/2003/08/14/world/lady-diana-mosley-fascist-who-dazzled-is-dead-at-93.html. Accessed April 29, 2020.

76 Peter Day, *Franco's Friends: How British Intelligence Helped Bring Franco to Power in Spain* (London: Biteback Publishing, 2011); Francis Beckett, "Franco's Friends by Peter Day—Review," *The Guardian*, September 30, 2011, www.theguardian.com/books/2011/sep/30/francos-friends-peter-day-review, Accessed April 29, 2020.

77 Hamid Dabashi, "The Priceless Racism of the Duke of Edinburgh," *Al Jazeera*, August 13, 2017, www.aljazeera.com/indepth/opinion/2017/08/priceless-racism-duke-edinburgh-170810082226234.html. Accessed November 10, 2019; Johnny Lieu, "25 Things Prince Philip Said that will Make You Full-Body Cringe," *Mashable*, May 4, 2017, https://mashable.com/2017/05/04/prince-philip-gaffes-list/. Accessed November 10, 2019.

78 Robert Hardman, *Queen of the World* (London: Century, 2018), p. 59.

79 Valerie Wade, "What Meghan Markle's Engagement to Prince Harry Says About How We Think of Black Royalty," *Allure*, November 29, 2017, www.allure.com/story/meghan-markle-engagement-black-royalty. Accessed April 30, 2019. For more on the Afrika Korps, see Robert Satloff, *Among the Righteous: Lost Stories from the Holocaust's Long Reach into Arab Lands* (New York: PublicAffairs, 2006).

80 Mary Dejevsky, "Prince Harry Called a Fellow Soldier His 'Little Paki Friend,' " *The Independent*, January 11, 2009, www.independent.co.uk/news/uk/home-news/prince-harry-called-a-fellow-soldier-his-little-paki-friend-1299804.html. Accessed November 12, 2019.

81 Paul Gilroy, "Why Harry's Disoriented about Empire," *The Guardian*, January 18, 2005, www.theguardian.com/uk/2005/jan/18/britishidentity.monarchy. Accessed May 16, 2020.

82 *Ibid.*

83 Stephanie Petit, " 'Is It Mine?' Watch Prince Harry Act Shocked While Being Congratulated on Meghan Markle's Pregnancy," *People*, February 26, 2019, https://people.com/royals/prince-harry-jokes-meghan-markle-pregnancy-is-it-mine/. Accessed June 12, 2019; Kia Morgan-Smith, "Prince Harry's Crass Joke 'Is it Mine' about Meghan Markle's Pregnancy Leaves Black Women Feeling Some Type of Way," *The Grio*, February 27, 2019, https://thegrio.com/2019/02/27/prince-harrys-crass-joke-is-it-mine-about-meghan-markles-pregnancy-leaves-black-women-feeling-some-type-of-way/. Accessed June 12, 2019,

84 Nalini Mohabir and Jermain Ostiana, "Welcome to the Caribbean, Prince Harry. Will You Dare Speak Out about Slavery?", *The Guardian*, November 21, 2016, www.theguardian.com/commentisfree/2016/nov/21/carribean-prince-harry-slavery-slave-trade-meghan-markle-royalty. Accessed May 17, 2020.

85 Brittany Vonow, "SET FREE Meghan Markle Guided Prince Harry on his 'Journey to Wokeness' after he 'Witnessed her Facing Racism', Author Claims," *The Sun*, August 10, 2020, www.thesun.co.uk/news/12359216/meghan-markle-guided-prince-harry-wokeness/. Accessed August 10, 2020.

86 Chris Baynes, "Prince Andrew Made Racist Comments about Arabs at Buckingham Palace Dinner, Claims Former Home Secretary," *The Independent*, November 19, 2019, www.independent.co.uk/news/uk/home-news/prince-andrew-racist-arabs-saudi-royal-family-dinner-jacqui-smith-epstein-a9209391.html. Accessed December 29, 2019.

87 John Eligon, "The 'Some of My Best Friends are Black' Defense," *The New York Times*, February 16, 2019, www.nytimes.com/2019/02/16/sunday-review/ralph-northam-blackface-friends.html. Accessed December 29, 2019.

88 Daniel A. Effron, "Making Mountains of Morality from Molehills of Virtue: Threat Causes People to Overestimate their Moral Credentials," *Personality and Social Psychology Bulletin*, 40 (8), p. 983; Terry Tang and Deepti Hajela, "Many View 'Black Friend Defense' as a Tired, Hollow Argument," *Associated Press*, March 1, 2019, https://apnews.com/c7e6681046e3463aa9967a8302e5a102. Accessed December 29, 2019.

89 Baynes, "Prince Andrew Made Racist Comments."

90 Rohan Silva, "Rohan Silva: Prince Andrew's Use of Language Left Me Reeling—and I Still Regret Not Challenging his Choice of Words," *Evening Standard*, November 18, 2019, www.standard.co.uk/comment/comment/prince-andrew-rohan-silva-language-a4289571.html?utm_medium=Social&utm_source=Twitter#Echobox=1574076679. Accessed December 29, 2019.

91 Anita Sethi, "Dear Prince Charles, Do You Think My Brown Skin Makes Me UnBritish?" *The Guardian*, April 19, 2018, www.theguardian.com/world/commentisfree/2018/apr/19/prince-charles-brown-skin-british-people-head-of-commonwealth. Accessed December 29, 2019.

92 Peter Bradshaw, "OK, I Admit It: I Find Royals Who Get the Giggles Quite Endearing," *The Guardian*, July 5, 2017, www.theguardian.com/commentisfree/2017/jul/05/royals-giggles-endearing-inuit-throat-singing-charles-camilla. Accessed April 30, 3019.

93 Rob Evans and Robert Booth, "Prince Charles Faces Fresh Meddling Claim over Letters to Ministers," *The Guardian*, December 16, 2009, www.theguardian.com/uk/2009/dec/16/prince-charles-letters-to-ministers. Accessed May 21, 2020.

94 Michael McDonough, "Charles 'Rubbished Human Rights Act Defence," *The Guardian*, March 2, 2006, www.theguardian.com/uk/2006/mar/02/monarchy.pressandpublishing. Accessed May 21, 2020.

95 Christopher Hope, "Neutrality of Prince of Wales Might be Questioned if 'Black Spider' Memos Made Public, Former Aide Warns," *The Telegraph*, September 18, 2012, www.telegraph.co.uk/news/politics/9551222/Neutrality-of-Prince-of-Wales-might-be-questioned-if-black-spider-memos-made-public-former-aide-warns.html. Accessed May 21, 2020.

96 Clare Kitchen, "Royal Staff Accused of Racism," *Daily Mail*, November 10, 2019, www.dailymail.co.uk/news/article-88454/Royal-staff-accused-racism. html. Accessed November 10, 2019.

97 Mohabir and Ostiana, "Welcome to the Caribbean, Prince Harry"; "Prince Harry to Visit the Caribbean," *The Royal Household*, November 10, 2016, www.royal.uk/prince-harry-visit-caribbean. Accessed May 17, 2020.

98 Nalini Mohabir, "What if the Caribbean Refused Royal Visits until Reparations were Paid?," *The Guardian*, March 20, 2019, www.theguardian. com/commentisfree/2019/mar/20/caribbean-reparations-charls-camilla-slavery-empire. Accessed May 17, 2020.

99 Mohabir and Ostiana, "Welcome to the Caribbean, Prince Harry."

100 Mohabir, "What if the Caribbean Refused."

101 Bella Brennan, "Shocking New Claims: Was the Queen Mother a Racist?," *now TO LOVE*, June 6, 2017, www.nowtolove.com.au/royals/british-royal-family/was-the-queen-mother-racist-38064. Accessed December 30, 2019.

102 Tanya Gold, "The Queen of Unkindness," *The Guardian*, September 15, 2009, www.theguardian.com/commentisfree/2009/sep/15/tanya-gold-queen-mother. Accessed December 30, 2019.

103 London Staff, "Chamberlain's Return from Munich," *The Guardian*, October 1, 1938. www.theguardian.com/news/1938/oct/01/leadersandreply. mainsection. Accessed June 15, 2020.

104 Hugo Vickers, *Elizabeth, The Queen Mother* (London: Arrow, 2006), p. 372.

105 *Royal Foibles* Blogger, "Prince Harry's Rebuke of his Ancestors' Racism," *Royal Foibles*, March 21, 2019, www.royalfoibles.com/prince-harrys-rebuke-of-his-ancestors-racism/. Accessed December 30, 2019.

106 Kim Wagner, "Justin Welby has Apologised for Amritsar. But Britain Still won't Face the Reality of Empire," *The Guardian*, September 13, 2019, www.theguardian.com/commentisfree/2019/sep/13/archbishop-canterbury-apologises-amritsar-government. Accessed December 27, 2019.

107 *The Irish Times* Staff, "Queen Faces Demands for Apology over Treatment of Boers," *The Irish Times*, November 11, 1999, www.irishtimes.com/news/queen-faces-demands-for-apology-over-treatment-of-boers-1.248797. Accessed December 30, 2019.

108 Mohabir and Ostiana, "Welcome to the Caribbean, Prince Harry."

109 *Ibid.*

110 Benedict Brogan, "It's Time to Celebrate the Empire, Says Brown," *Daily Mail*, January 15, 2005, www.dailymail.co.uk/news/article-334208/Its-time-celebrate-Empire-says-Brown.html. Accessed November 10, 2019.

111 See, for example, Sarah L. Smiley, "The City of Three Colors: Segregation in Colonial Dar es Salaam, 1891–1961," *Historical Geography*, 37 (December 2008), pp. 178–196.

112 Robert Booth, "Boris Johnson Caught on Camera Reciting Kipling in Myanmar Temple," *The Guardian*, September 30, 2017, www.theguardian. com/politics/2017/sep/30/boris-johnson-caught-on-camera-reciting-kipling-in-myanmar-temple. Accessed December 27, 2019.

113 Smith, "Meghan Markle and British Racism."

114 Gavin Esler, Twitter, https://twitter.com/gavinesler/status/12700823223233 78177, Accessed June 9, 2020.

115 Frances Perraudin, "MPs' Brexit Rhetoric Risks Igniting Divisions, Warns Justin Welby," *The Guardian*, October 27, 2019, www.theguardian.com/politics/2019/oct/27/brexit-rhetoric-petrol-volatile-issue-justin-welby-archbishop. Accessed December 30, 2019.

116 Aamna Mohdin, "Brexiters Tell Archbishop of Canterbury Not to Interfere," *The Guardian*, August 27, 2019, www.theguardian.com/uk-news/2019/aug/27/dont-interfere-with-brexit-archbishop-of-canterbury-justin-welby-told. Accessed December 27, 2019. Italics added.

117 Sarah Donilon, "Brexit Is for Boys," *Foreign Policy*, June 19, 2019, https://foreignpolicy.com/2019/06/19/brexit-is-for-boys-boris-johnson-jeremy-hunt-michael-gove-tories/. Accessed December 30, 2019.

118 Alex Hern, "Archbishop of Canterbury Warns against 'Alternative Facts' Online," *The Guardian*, July 1, 2019, www.theguardian.com/world/2019/jul/01/church-of-england-publishes-social-media-guidelines. Accessed December 27, 2019.

119 Perraudin, "MPs' Brexit Rhetoric Risks Igniting Divisions."

120 Harriet Sherwood, "Church of England Urges UK Voters to 'Leave their Echo Chambers,'" *The Guardian*, November 20, 2019, www.theguardian.com/world/2019/nov/20/church-of-england-urges-uk-voters-to-leave-their-echo-chambers. Accessed December 30, 2019.

121 *Times of Israel* Staff, "Archbishop of Canterbury Calls to Reassess Depictions of Jesus as White," *The Times of Israel*, June 26, 2020, www.timesofisrael.com/archbishop-of-canterbury-calls-to-reassess-depictions-of-jesus-as-white/. Accessed August 12, 2020.

122 Yeginsu, "Black Britons Wonder."

123 Saleem, "Harry and Meghan."

7 Concluding Thoughts

The Royals, British Racism, and the Coronavirus Pandemic

Introduction

We conclude this book with an examination of our themes of systemic racism and its white racial frame, especially as they have been illustrated during the coronavirus pandemic era. In the early months of the international pandemic, the UK and USA registered the greatest number of coronavirus deaths globally. Prime Minister Boris Johnson and President Donald Trump had risen to political power on the promises to "Get Brexit Done" and "Make America Great Again." When faced with the globalizing pandemic, both responded slowly and squandered the advantages of months of time, ample scientific data, and the instructive negative cases of China and Italy. "Flippant and ill-prepared" is how *The Guardian* columnist Nesrine Malik described their response. "Two nations that prided themselves on their extraordinary economic, historical and political status have been brought to their knees. Their fall from grace is the outcome of a damaged political culture and distinct form of Anglo-American capitalism." She continued: "Without radically challenging Anglo-American capitalism, they have nothing else to offer their voters. And so they must separate economic suffering from politics, and attempt to blame it on immigrants and outsiders." Unsurprisingly, Britons and Americans of color continue to pay the heftiest price for this imprudent Anglo-American predatory capitalism, which is firmly rooted in weak government, predacious markets, privatization, and stamping out labor rights.[1]

Johnson and Trump blamed other countries and transnational institutions like the World Health Organization (WHO) for the deadly setbacks their countries faced during the pandemic. In societies where white racism is systemic, whites often blame people of color. In early 2020, when Trump was asked about his continuing use of the term "Chinese virus," especially given the increasing racist incidents targeting Chinese Americans for purportedly spreading the coronavirus, he claimed the term was "not racist at all. ... Because [the virus] comes from China." In response, the executive director of the WHO's emergencies program explained: "it's really important we be careful in the language we use lest it lead to the profiling of individuals associated with the virus." Around the same time that

Trump defended his use of the racial slur, the Chinese-born White House correspondent Weijia Jiang tweeted: "This morning a White House official referred to #Coronavirus as the 'Kung-Flu' to my face. ... Makes me wonder what they're calling it behind my back."[2] Trump also publicly called the coronavirus the "Kung flu."[3] Similarly, many ordinary whites and some people of color, who internalize the white racial frame, have used racial slurs and sought scapegoats for the coronavirus.

Johnson's and Trump's growing enemies lists led both men to aggressively cut ties with other countries and international institutions during the coronavirus. Prior to the pandemic, Trump tried to withdraw funding from key disease prevention organizations such as the WHO and the Centers for Disease Control and Prevention, while in the UK the pandemic served as an annoyance to Johnson and his conservative Cabinet, who were entangled in disputes over Brexit and with their own civil service.

Politicians like Johnson and Trump have long proved critical to the creation, preservation, and extension of the old elite-white-male-dominance system. Given this exceedingly skewed dominance arrangement, the male-oriented version of the white racial framing of Meghan Markle, which we detail throughout this book, is predictable. So, too, is the insensitivity and callousness shown by many in the white elite, including senior royals, toward those most vulnerable to the ravages of the deadly coronavirus pandemic.

The coronavirus pandemic is another critical juncture when the elite rework and hone the oppressive predatory system that has served them well over centuries. Elite white men, like Johnson and Trump, have jostled to provide major banks and other major corporations with extraordinary resources to save them from financial ruin, but will not scramble as much to save ordinary human lives. As Malik unforgettably put it, nurses will don garbage bin liners as personal protective equipment longer than a failing capitalistic bank will be without a government bailout.[4] After all, in the UK and the USA, pro-business, anti-regulation, white old-boy networks connect government officials, heads of capitalistic corporations, and other elite economic players in this aggressively market-centered (neoliberal) era of oligopoly capitalism.

As the social scientist Anthony Weems explains, equally important are the broader connections between ordinary whites, the elite-white-male-dominance system, and the current pandemic in the USA—and, we would add, in the UK.

> In light of the murders of black people, and countless other uses of brutal force by white police officers and other white men in recent months, I want to emphasize the central role of the "white army"—that is, that ordinary whites will continue to increasingly deploy violent methods as an integral component of maintaining white supremacy in the United States. This also connects directly to ... the geopolitical ramifications of the COVID-19 pandemic. As a process that was

already accelerating before the virus, that persisting white army will continue to polarize the U.S. political landscape while physically and metaphysically erasing other people. In the wake of the coronavirus, ordinary whites—who again are armed with major weapons and a substantial white "American" framing of society—will often choose whiteness over human lives. It is indeed a "death cult," to the tune of liberty and justice for some. Elite whites are or will be happy to ride the wave of white nationalism while sponsoring and controlling the ways in which it is resisted.[5]

Weems's perceptive view also helps us to understand the large-scale white (mostly male) attack on the US Capitol building on January 6, 2021, near the peak of the coronavirus pandemic. Thousands of largely unmasked white supremacists and other extremists, many armed with various weapons and assuming they were following the command of outgoing President Donald Trump, attempted to stop a constitutional congressional assembly there to certify the authentic election of Joe Biden, the new President of the USA.

In this chapter we discuss the failure, at the time of writing, of senior white royals to acknowledge that some Britons are much more at-risk from the coronavirus than others, and to own their multiple racial, class, and gender privileges underscored by the pandemic. We discuss how World War II is germane to the pandemic given that for European monarchs the crisis resembles wartime, and in times of war royals are expected to perform admirably. We also detail how Markle and Harry have been pilloried for purportedly being self-absorbed during the pandemic, while other royals have been inundated with praise for their public performances. To begin, however, we examine how the coronavirus pandemic highlights in dramatic ways the UK's anti-Asian racism—one major type of the country's anti-others racism.

Perpetual Foreigners, Racialized Maskaphobia, and Hate Crimes

The *perpetual foreigner* stereotype is one racialized form of xenophobia in which naturalized and native-born citizens, including those who have lived in a country for generations, are marked as alien because they belong to a racial or ethnic minority.[6] Examples include the genocidal oppression and mass murder of Jews in Nazi-occupied Europe in the 1930s–1940s and the 1940s internment of Japanese Americans and Japanese Canadians in the name of illusory national security during World War II. These were the racialized scapegoats that dominant racial-ethnic groups sought to blame for dire economic conditions or wartime calamities.

As we show throughout this book, nativist xenophobia has long been a part of British history. In the midst of the coronavirus crisis in 2020, it took new and old forms. In the first three months of 2020, about 260 hate crimes against people of Chinese ancestry were recorded in the UK, compared to a total of 375 hate crimes in the entire previous year. The sociologist Yinxuan Huang found that virtually all instances of these racist crimes were prompted by *racialized maskaphobia*—a particular fear of people of Chinese descent who wear protective face masks. When it was possible, thus, Chinese international students fled numerous UK universities for China amid this surge in racist attacks instigated by white maskaphobia. In those months, numerous similar hate crimes against other people of Asian descent were likewise recorded, also many more than for the previous year. Because numerous police forces do not report, or do not report accurately, hate crimes, the actual number is likely to be much higher. This racialized maskaphobia also appeared in a rash of anti-Asian hate crimes in the USA during this same period.[7]

The psychologist Binna Kandola notes that this level of overt racist action, which ranges from spontaneous "jokes" to violent assaults, had already forced Britons of Asian ancestry to retreat from public areas before the pandemic lockdown. He completed 29 in-depth interviews with people of East Asian descent in mid-2020. More than half reported having suffered increased racial discrimination during the pandemic. One respondent abandoned her morning exercise because of racist abuse. Another reported being so fearful that she wore a sign: "Please don't fear me—I don't have the virus." Kandola views such incidents as scapegoating, resulting from a need for (usually white) control of society in uncertain times. He explains: "As long as there is that anxiety about people's own personal welfare and this idea that somebody's responsible ... I think there will be an increase [in overt racist actions]."[8]

Similar to the black Britons who question whether they will ever be truly accepted as British in light of Markle's treatment by the press and public, and the many more who conclude they never will be, Kandola reports that Chinese-descended people who had lived their entire lives in the UK began to ask the same question in light of the coronavirus-instigated racist attacks. One respondent explains: "I was born in Wales and I've lived here all my life. I've experienced racism, unfortunately, and I've had to put up with it. I've never felt in danger though but now it's different." Another remarks: "Nearly every British-born Chinese person I've spoken to is genuinely very shocked about what has happened. They ... feel like outsiders now."[9] Still, even Kandola appears not to recognize that the white-racist framing and oppression of Britons of color are *not* at all new, but have been systemic since at least the seventeenth century to UK society.

British Royals during the Coronavirus Pandemic

A monarch's statements are usually at least as much about politics as morale-boosting. As the royal historian Carolyn Harris explains, the "presence of the sovereign in a constitutional monarchy demonstrates the continuity of the government, even in times of crisis."[10] How then did the queen and other senior royals respond to reports of this coronavirus-instigated racism, including anti-Asian maskaphobia? When it was widely reported that the coronavirus disease was killing black Britons at twice the rate of whites, how did they respond? How did they react when it was reported that South Asian Britons were dying disproportionately too?[11] Did they call on Britons to cease their racist acts? At the time of writing, we have found no such royal denunciations. Instead, when these data on racial discrimination and inequality were coming to light, Prince William claimed Britain was "at its best when ... in a crisis."[12] Here, we have an example of ahistorical white racial framing, in which long-term structural forces resulting in major racial inequalities that advantage white Britons over Britons of color are willfully ignored.

During her official address to the British people amid the first months of the pandemic, the queen characterized fellow Britons as possessing "self-discipline," "good-humoured resolve," "fellow-feeling," and an "instinctive compassion to heal." She also said: "The pride in who we are ... defines our present and our future." Perhaps more noteworthy were her remarks that the pandemic reminded her of the "very first broadcast I made, in 1940, helped by my sister. We, as children, spoke from here at Windsor [Castle] to children who had been evacuated from their homes and sent away for their own safety. Today, once again, many will feel a painful sense of separation from their loved ones. But now, as then, we know, deep down, that it is the right thing to do."[13] Here, the queen, like her grandson William, presents an ahistorical white racial framing that ignores the highly relevant racial discrimination and inequalities of this time. Significantly, some 67 percent of Britons watched her pandemic address, and 70 percent of them reported feeling positive afterwards.[14]

Throughout World War II, like during the coronavirus pandemic, the notion of "being all in it together" was a theme vigorously spouted by the white royals. Such wartime propaganda was central to positively and successfully marketing the royal family to the common (white) Briton. As a *BBC* writer recently noted, it "has played well in the royal family's favour ever since: the present Queen could hardly have been so prominently and sympathetically associated with the commemoration of wartime anniversaries had that not been the case."[15]

While the young Elizabeth was protected behind castle walls at Windsor (west of London), nearly one in six people killed during the German bombing of London (1940–1941) were children. Many were also seriously wounded. The government planned the evacuation of four million people, predominantly women and children, from the cities, including London, to avoid this. But nearly half the children returned because of homesickness and other reasons. Unlike Princess Elizabeth, many evacuated children did not have the familiarity of a much-loved home or close relations with whom to sequester.[16]

Recently, Alexander Chancellor wrote an important *The Guardian* article, aptly titled "It's Time to Explode the Myth that All Children Evacuated from the Blitz Were Well Treated." He observes that "it is clear from the first-hand accounts ... that for many children evacuation meant misery and desperate homesickness. And this was often because the British were not always suffused with the warm feelings of national solidarity and goodwill towards each other that are supposed to have characterised the Dunkirk spirit."[17]

Photos from the time show the future Elizabeth II and her family reading in Windsor Castle's drawing room and biking amid grand scenery.[18] Historical photos of ordinary children capture a different story. An image captioned, "Homeless and orphaned children settle down to sleep in the air raid shelter at John Keble Church Mill Hill London," tells us much about the class disparities evident during the war.[19] In her first radio broadcast in October 1940, nonetheless, the future queen told British children, "[w]e know from experience what it means to be away from those we love most of all."[20]

To counter ill-will toward the royal family, a wartime public relations campaign was launched. Prime Minister Winston Churchill said that by the war's end the king (George VI) was "more beloved by all classes and conditions than any of the princes of the past." That the royal family was regularly filmed for cinematic newsreels at a higher frequency than in the pre-war era certainly helped. Upon seeing images of the king touring Buckingham Palace after it was bombed, one national survey participant said: "Now the king is clapped not so much as a man but as a symbol of the country."[21] The scholar Darren Kelsey has studied the making and propagation of the myth of Britons greatly bonding in resistance during the German blitz. He assessed how the saga was reported in newspapers following the London bombings, how it was framed, and the ideological role it took once the attacks concluded. At the time, significant societal conflicts and complexities were habitually suppressed by these official messages, which were intended to arouse a spirit of Britishness as delineated by earlier white generations.[22]

During the coronavirus pandemic, official public relations messages seemed to remain the same. Even Prince Harry engaged in such dialogue. Months into the crisis, when publicly thanking the UK's National Health Service and all volunteers, he remarked: "It's such a wonderfully British thing that we all come to help when we need it. ... but I really, really hope that this keeps going after ... this whole pandemic has come to a close."[23]

Collective Forgetting: Whitewashing the Past and the Present

As we show throughout this book, Britishness and whiteness have long been synonymous. As another example, even after seven decades, British soldiers of color are still not officially recognized in Britain for their wartime contributions and heroics. Happily, in 2020, a play performed by school children at the Imperial War Museum in London paid homage to one such person, Nigerian-born Ita Ekpenyon. He embodied valor during the blitz. Actually, there were 15,000 Afro-Britons in London at the time, yet their human stories have been drowned out by tales of white wartime gallantry.[24]

Ekpenyon, like 200,000 other Londoners, served as an air-raid protection warden. Too old for combat duty, he extinguished countless bomb fires, performed first aid, and helped with census-taking. His records reveal that the notion of "being all in it together" was false. Whites often operated out of a racial framing during the German blitz. Ekpenyon had to stop an irate group of them from ejecting black people from a bomb shelter, as the whites grumbled that "such people" should not be in the same shelter. Ekpenyon also wrote for a *BBC* propaganda program titled, "Calling West Africa." That program intended to show the German Nazi leadership that the entire British Empire was united against fascism. The truth, however, was different. Colonial subjects of color, and other people of color, served the Allied cause even while they were considered and targeted as "subhuman."[25]

Ekpenyon's daughter, a prominent historian, reflects extensively on her father's wartime efforts.

> [P]eople like my father, the contributions they made to the war effort and their willingness to serve, are all too often overlooked and forgotten. Their commitment both during the years of conflict and those immediately after the war were vital to Britain. The reconstruction during the post war years was in no small measure due in part to those people of colour who supplied the labour force that was important to Britain's recovery. There is a whole generation of young Britons who do not understand how people of colour helped to shape the nation.[26]

Black Londoners displayed bravery in countless ways. A black housewife living in meager housing wrote Prime Minister Churchill, pleading with him to end discrimination faced by black citizens. They were refused "decent and reasonably priced" lodgings, she explained. Churchill arranged for her to speak to the welfare officer in the Colonial Office. She explained to him that black people were treated poorly by white air wardens and even ejected from bomb shelters. That officer encouraged her to urge black Britons to report discriminatory incidents to him.[27]

Black Britons still face gross injustices, as their higher death rates during the coronavirus pandemic help to confirm. This World War II history is germane to the pandemic, given that the coronavirus's impacts have resembled wartime, and in times of war royals are expected to perform supportively and publicly. During the early months of the pandemic in 2020, one media commentator explained that Europe's monarchs

> have been thrust onto primetime broadcasts in recent weeks to calm and instruct their people in a way rarely seen since World War II. The stakes for these messengers—hauled back into national emergency mode much like retired doctors are being called back to hospitals—are

higher than usual. Get it right, and the crisis could become a defining moment, an opportunity to turn an oft-maligned and increasingly antiquated institution into a source of national strength.[28]

Speeches like the one delivered by George VI at the dawn of World War II, cautioning Britons against dark days ahead, are mostly seen today as inspired morale boosts.[29] Unsurprisingly, thus, Elizabeth II calling out white Britons for obvious and extensive racism during the pandemic does not fit well into this old public relations rulebook, which like much else in the UK is defined by the dominant white racial frame. Until she or her successors, together with other key members of the British elite, denounce and reframe their white racial framing, and take action to remove racialized structural forces that greatly advantage white Britons over Britons of color, nothing substantial about systemic racism will change. In our view, if elite and non-elite whites believe in genuine democracy, they must regularly speak out and take much concrete action against systemic white racism in all its major forms.

Lessons of the Coronavirus Crisis: Some Humans are More Human than Others

In the past, stately homes and estates were opened to those in need. During both world wars, for example, the Earl of Harewood and the 4th Marquess of Salisbury allowed their homes to serve as auxiliary military hospitals. During the early days of World War II, at the bequest of its then-owner, an Anglo-American heiress, Leeds Castle was home to many Commonwealth airmen recovering from serious burn injuries. Similarly, Lady Carnarvon converted Highclere Castle into a military hospital at the start of World War I.[30] More recently, a nineteenth-century Vatican palace became home to the poor and the homeless, who Pope Francis said "society treats as rejects, victims of today's throwaway culture." Imagine all the "nobles of the streets"—to use the Pope's terminology—who would find comfort in some of the 1,000 rooms at Windsor Castle.[31] Or imagine how Buckingham Palace—with its 52 royal and guest bedrooms and 188 staff bedrooms—could be transformed into a shelter for the poor and the homeless, including during the coronavirus pandemic.[32]

Likely, such suggestions would be labeled as absurd by many people despite the historical and contemporary precedent set by others. After all, there is the elite's resounding silence about racial hate crimes during the pandemic, at least at the time of writing. In spring 2020, one prominent British politician called on Members of Parliament and of the aristocratic House of Lords to unreservedly condemn hate crimes against people of Chinese ancestry.[33] Few responded to the call, while the British monarch said nothing. The queen's comments could have been simple, such as "all forms of racism are unacceptable." As noted in previous chapters, Elizabeth II has long side-stepped such critical racial issues.

Only when Prince Charles was diagnosed with a mild case of the coronavirus did William and Kate say the crisis "hit home." Discussing his father, William explained: "I have to admit, at first, I was quite concerned. He fits the profile of somebody at the age he's at, which is fairly risky, and so I was a little bit worried. ... I think very carefully about my grandparents who are at the age they're at, and we're doing everything we can to make sure that they're isolated away and protected from this, but it does worry me."[34] We, of course, do not fault William for worrying about his father and grandparents, but as second-in-line to the throne we expect him to have a broader view. In his comments, there is no mention of other vulnerable Britons—including those who are elderly or people of color, both groups being especially susceptible to the coronavirus, if for different reasons. There is also no acknowledgment of the huge privileges that allow his aging loved ones to remain especially safe and secure.

Notably, William also tested positive for coronavirus around this time. With two direct heirs infected, he chose to conceal his diagnosis for fear of provoking panic among Britons. At least one tabloid journalist has since claimed that "William's experience ... helped him understand the severity of the virus and the need for measures to stop the spread." The prince, of course, had the benefit of "palace doctors," among other advantages, which makes his "experience" quite different to that of most Britons battling the virus, and living in fear of it.[35]

In the early months of the pandemic, William and Kate called on their fellow Britons to prioritize mental health—an essential issue to be sure, but they publicly discussed it without referencing its causes, including widespread racial discrimination and inequality. Speaking on a video call, and again without mention of the most vulnerable Britons, William described what is most important to the couple when it comes to the pandemic and their fellow Britons' well-being:

> We felt very strongly that, now more than ever, [the mental health initiative Every Mind Matters] was a vital tool and a vital service that people could easily access at home [online] to guide them and give them just some very basic tips to mind their mental health [and] well-being through this process. ... [S]taying connected, staying positive and being able to talk to friends and family is so crucial.[36]

These apparently simple solutions, not to mention false expectations that all Britons easily access online sources, are problematic at best. William did remark that some might think they are "not worthy of support" given the burdens on mental health services during the pandemic: "It's important that other people aren't forgotten and those who do need help, and do need support, and haven't necessarily ever had to think about their mental well-being, start to do that in this weird climate we're in."[37] Still, he failed to address obvious systemic racism or classism issues.

Mainstream media commentary told the whitewashed story of how William's "family is in coronavirus lockdown with most everyone else in Britain ... on {*their*} *sprawling royal estate*," with apparent obliviousness to the fates of many Britons who have little or no such space.[38] In slight contrast, *The Guardian* reporter wrote an article titled, "Super-Rich Jet Off to Disaster Bunkers amid Coronavirus Outbreak." We write *slight* contrast given that there is no mention in the article of white British royals darting off to royal estates and castles, some near their customary homes. *The Guardian* reporter offers details about how the world's richest people are protecting themselves and their families: from chartering jets so they can isolate themselves in holiday homes or disaster bunkers, to taking personal doctors or nurses with them lest they become infected, to demanding private coronavirus tests.[39] In our view, such stories need to explain not just this classism but also associated white racism and male sexism, and how these oppressions overlap and intersect. The royal family's realities should be at the center of such critical analyses.

A second noteworthy *The Guardian* story from the period is titled, "We're About to Learn a Terrible Lesson from Coronavirus: Inequality Kills."[40] Again, this is a commendable attempt on the part of the writer to expose racial and class inequality but it misses a crucial point. Britons of color and the poor already know that inequality kills. Whether one considers health, education, housing, employment, or criminal justice, Britons of color are more likely to die as a result of intentional discrimination and associated inequalities than whites, including before, during, and after serious health crises.

In the early months of the coronavirus pandemic, racial, class, and gender insensitivities of elite white men were on full display when the British government selected Prince Charles as the face of its "Pick for Britain" campaign, which was launched by fruit farm owner and Environment Secretary George Eustice. "So far removed are the Conservatives from the sentiments of the UK population that they never stopped to consider the impact of a bone-idle multi-millionaire landowner [Charles] urging workers furloughed during the COVID-19 pandemic, students and the unemployed to sign up as seasonal fruit pickers and farm labourers" and work for subsistence wages, writes the socialist Robert Stevens. "Speaking against the backdrop of the vegetable garden on his 53,000-acre Scottish estate," continues Stevens, Charles "felt obliged to educate his 'subjects' on the hitherto unknown fact that 'Food does not happen by magic; it all begins with our remarkable farmers and growers.'" That harvest could have potentially rotted in the fields because the tens of thousands of poor Eastern European migrants, who gathered the produce in previous years, were unavailable to work owing to British anti-immigration policies associated with Brexit and the coronavirus pandemic.[41] Our proverbial hats are off to Stevens and others who point out this royal absurdity, but we repeat our earlier point that such assessments need to be broadened to explain not just this classism but also the associated white racism and male sexism that are involved—and explain how these class, racial, and gender oppressions overlap and intersect.

For too long, even well-intended white analysts have assumed to speak for all Britons, while ignoring the significant impact a consideration of racial identity would have on their conclusions. In his 1991 book *Talking of the Royal Family*, psychologist Michael Billig examines how non-elite Britons converse about the royal family. He writes: "A public fascination with a family possessing incalculable wealth should itself signify an interesting academic puzzle."[42] Data gleaned from 63 English families led Billig to determine that ordinary people see themselves as better off in certain ways than the royals, while the royal family is viewed as a symbol of continuity in national consciousness. This helps explain a lack of crusading against their avaricious riches, he concludes.[43] Then, in 2015, a year before Markle met Harry and a recession year when UK economic inequalities had become more publicly obvious, researchers replicated Billig's findings in a study of young people's impressions of celebrities. These young Englanders describe how celebrities, including Prince Harry, are unenviably subject to relentless media attention and seem pretty ordinary. These non-elite youth generally believe that celebrities deserve their riches and status.[44]

The racial make-up of the research participants in the 1991 and the 2015 studies seem unimportant to the analyses. We suggest that the whiteness of the British royal family would make Billig's academic puzzle less mystifying if one separately considers non-white Englanders' views, which would likely be more critical. The sociologist Claire Alexander has written about how young Britons of color often identify generally as black and have collectively struggled against discrimination. This "political blackness" is at the center of their collective sense of being unwelcomed by whites.[45] Results from a 2020 online survey of 1,535 British adults also suggest that black Britons would likely have a different understanding of white celebrities, including white royals, than do whites. Significantly, 50 percent of white respondents versus 21 percent of black respondents said they believe black celebrities are treated no better or worse by the media than white celebrities; whereas, 16 percent of white respondents versus 48 percent of black respondents said that black celebrities are treated worse than white celebrities.[46]

Pillorying of Meghan Markle amid the Coronavirus Crisis

Canada's *Globe and Mail* newspaper got it partially right when it declared: "As the COVID-19 outbreak spreads across Britain, the Queen and members of the Royal Family have won plaudits for their morale-boosting efforts and messages of support. The same can't be said for Harry and Meghan. ... The Royal Family—except for Harry and Meghan—has been everywhere during the crisis." The Sussexes, the *Globe and Mail* continues, "have been pilloried for appearing self-absorbed during the pandemic. They've been mocked for relocating to Los Angeles when the outbreak took hold and roundly criticized for announcing a new 'media relations policy' for tabloid journalists just as the number of deaths from the virus topped 18,000 in the United Kingdom."[47]

First, there is the question here of how many plaudits the queen and the royal family are entitled. After all, they have time, many servants, and live in castles or royal estates that keep them well-isolated and protected. Meanwhile, Britons of color are much more likely than even non-elite whites to live on low incomes and in overcrowded housing. Such socio-economic realities certainly help explain why people of color are over-represented in groups at risk of serious illness, including during the coronavirus pandemic. And yet, senior royals appear mostly oblivious to these critical facts of class and race, usually even self-absorbed. That they may not be entitled to special plaudits seems lost on mainstream journalists and perhaps on them.

Second is the question of why the mainstream media praises senior royals while they are quick to condemn Markle and Harry and frame them as self-absorbed. Contrary to the *Globe and Mail*'s claim, the Sussexes were very active during the coronavirus pandemic. Once excerpts from the book *Finding Freedom* began appearing in the British press, the onslaught against them increased, however. Writing for MailOnline, the website of the conservative *Daily Mail* newspaper, Piers Morgan viciously remarked:

> as the rest of the world struggles with the very real hell of the worst pandemic for 100 years ... [Markle and Harry] expose themselves as a pair of appallingly bitter, staggeringly self-obsessed, utterly deluded, and woefully tone-deaf laughing stocks. The title of [*Finding Freedom*] alone has made me shake my head ever since it was announced. It is obviously derived from Nelson Mandela's autobiography *Long Walk To Freedom*... *In their eyes, they had become Nelson Mandela*, the victims of a terrible miscarriage of justice now trapped in a world of unending misery. So, they broke "free". ... Unlike Mandela, who emerged from his very real prison with extraordinary positivity, an astonishing lack of bitterness, and an intense desire to unify not divide, the Sussexes seem even more unhappy now than they were before and intent on causing as much division as possible.[48]

The irony that the elite white male Morgan, who has long denied the foundational and systemic nature of British racism, would lecture Markle (or any person of color) about Mandela serves to highlight the depth and arrogance of the white racial frame. Also important is the fact that the book's title is not inspired by Mandela's autobiography. What's more, Morgan offers no empirical evidence to suggest that the Sussexes believe "they had become Nelson Mandela."

Despite dire warnings not to travel during the global health crisis, some British tabloids falsely accused the duchess of preventing her husband from visiting Prince Charles after his father's coronavirus diagnosis.[49] "I don't know what's going [on] at all with [Markle and Harry]," said the prominent royal biographer Penny Junor. "It seems while the country and the world are losing loved ones and desperately trying to keep safe, they're focusing on tabloid newspapers." Renowned historian Robert Lacey similarly remarked: "I'd say that Meghan and Harry have not done very well during the COVID-19 crisis, what with upstaging the Queen's brilliant [pandemic] broadcast with their own mistimed announcement [of a new media relations policy for tabloids]."[50]

The mostly white British commentariat and polity neglect to accent, as they often do, the truth about the couple's significant humanitarian activities. Not only have they delivered meals in Los Angeles for Project Angel Food, a non-profit organization that provides food for people with serious illnesses, but similar to William and Kate they hosted video chats to boost the morale of Britons. The couple had intended to remain tight-lipped concerning their work for the Project Angel charity but were pleased that the organization received attention.[51] Markle also chatted with women from a community kitchen in London, while Harry talked to families with special-needs children to learn how they were surviving the pandemic. To the families, Harry said: "Full respect to every single one of you. This is hard on everyone, but it is especially hard on you."[52] Via a podcast months into the devastating pandemic, Harry encouraged British veterans to volunteer to help during the crisis through a private organization bringing skilled military veterans and first responders together to serve disaster-affected communities. To mark International Day of the Girl, they met with the Pakistani activist for female education and the youngest Nobel Prize laureate, Malala Yousafzai, to discuss the difficulties girls face in accessing education amid the coronavirus pandemic. The couple also participated in fundraising efforts for Save the Children. On Archie's first birthday, Markle read to their son as Harry cheered the two on. Markle's video was shared widely by Save the Children UK.[53]

In response to the video, US author Emily Giffin—a self-professed royals watcher, who has a history of targeting Markle—insisted that the duchess is a controlling wife who stole Harry from his family, is "fake and forced," and is "unmaternal." She posted a screenshot of the video with the words "Happy birthday, Archie. Go away, Megan" written across it. Giffin has repeatedly reposted Gary Janetti's attacks on the duchess. A purported satirist, Janetti uses Prince George, eldest child of William and Kate, as the avatar for his gendered-racist rants against Markle. In Giffin's posts, we glimpse how a female acolyte of the white male elite perpetuates dominant racial, class, and patriarchal-sexist frames. Sadly, as we show throughout this book, such gendered-racist attacks against Markle are not unique. Indeed, Giffin's comments are reminiscent of remarks made by many white royal reporters and tabloid journalists.[54] Also, as documented throughout this book, many whites seek gratification, amusement, and pleasure from engaging in white-framed, anti-other racist performances. Clearly, Giffin took such satisfaction from targeting Markle. When she came under fire for her gendered-racist posts, she returned to the internet and Instagram to defend her actions: "I enjoy following celebrities and analyzing them with my readers. ... To be clear, I absolutely loved that a biracial, American woman was marrying into the Royal Family." Her self-defense continues with claims that she recently changed her opinion of the royal couple after they decided to step down as senior royals.[55]

The attention Markle and Harry bring to systemic racism and sexism issues, including during the pandemic—even if rather limited—is not deemed as valuable as the work of other royals by many in the British commentariat and polity. Some of the couple's critics even view their civic engagement as obnoxious, politically correct do-gooding, or as inappropriate partisanism, while applauding or excusing the royal family for remaining apolitical. Recall from Chapter 3, for example, that Piers Morgan said the Sussexes' royal titles should be removed because of Markle's public comments on the importance of voting in the 2020 US presidential election.[56]

The age-old argument that *good royals are apolitical* is rolled out as a justification for the royal family's characteristic silence on such issues and as a reason for criticizing the Sussexes. For those invested in the white racial frame, anti-racist activism is not to be applauded. Hence, when the couple met with a group of young leaders from the British Commonwealth in summer 2020 and spoke candidly about the enduring legacy of slavery and other ongoing racial injustices, the meeting did little or nothing to change the white British establishment's framing of them as overindulged good-for-nothings. One of the young leaders mentioned the transatlantic slave trade's continuing impacts today, which is tied to a whole slew of issues, including mental health. Harry responded as follows: "There's no way we can move forward unless we acknowledge the past, and I think so many people have done such an amazing, incredible job of acknowledging the past and trying to right those wrongs. ... But I think we all acknowledge there is so much more still to do." To which Markle added: "It's not just in the big moments, it's in the quiet moments where racism and unconscious bias lies and thrives. ... We're going to have to be a little uncomfortable right now because it's only in pushing through that discomfort that we get to the other side of this." Such remarks led a *Vanity Fair* writer to observe: "Meghan and Harry have the potential to address Britain's history of colonialism, and the damage it has done, more than any royal ever has." Furthermore, "[w]ith Prince Harry's departure from the [royal family], he has newfound freedom to speak about a previously taboo topic ... he can (and should) speak as someone who has directly benefited from the monarchy's colonial past."[57]

The counter-framing and assertive management of the racist mobbing endured by Markle and countless other people of color reveals their imagination, ingenuity, and vision. They are forced to participate in an unending struggle to survive white racial malice and subjugation. In the aftermath of

Markle and Harry stepping down as senior royals, an online commentator movingly noted:

> the narrative of the difficult, angry Black woman leaving a momentary smear on the monarchy has likely been perched on some editor's mantle for two years now, just waiting for a reason ... to be dusted off and disseminated on a world stage. And yet, it never happened. Meghan kept her cool, even when her voice cracked on camera and you could see the tears welling up in her eyes. The spirit of all the Black women who had come before her stood at her side as she put on a brave smile and waved to crowds of people who she knew considered her unworthy of her throne.[58]

Conclusion

Prior to his election as US president, Barack Obama unequivocally criticized elements of the centuries-old white racial framing of US society in his appropriately titled autobiography *The Audacity of Hope: Thoughts on Reclaiming the American Dream*. He categorically declared that his personal economic and political successes did not erase the fact that white-racist attitudes significantly restrict opportunities for Americans of color. Obama argued that the white-racist framing still limits access to the American Dream, including affordable housing, education, safety, health, and financial security for most people of color. Notwithstanding his black counter-framing and critique of the white-proclaimed American Dream, in the wake of his 2008 election numerous white pundits and politicians aggressively urged him to take the lead in exposing what they deemed the myth of white racism. They wanted him to publicly say that the (white) American Dream was open to all. Some, like the editors at the conservative *Wall Street Journal*, vigorously demanded he do so.[59]

At the time of writing, we have less evidence to suggest that Meghan Markle yet fathoms the depths of this enduring white racial framing as much as Obama has. After all, she commended *Suits*'s producers on what she termed race-neutral casting (see Chapter 3). What is certain is that white racial framing in UK history, and the openly and covertly racist treatment of Markle by much of the British press, conceal the great effort to which elite and non-elite whites are willing to go to prevent significant racial integration in the country's major institutions. To put it simply, most are afraid of the increased racial diversification of Britain and its historically white institutions. They fear they will have to truly democratize the nation.

The idea that Markle and Harry will find sanctuary from white racism in the USA, of course, is preposterous. Elite and non-elite whites in the USA, as in the UK, are willing to go to extreme lengths to prevent thorough racial integration of all major US institutions. What's more, the assertion on both sides of the Atlantic by whites that the mainstream media coverage of Markle has not been racist confirms just how poorly systemic white racism and its white racial frame are understood by most whites in both countries.[60]

In 2018, when a book tour took Michelle Obama to the UK, Markle was sitting in the audience in London when the former First Lady said: "What happens to black women is that we become a caricature. ... People will take the things from us that they like. Our style, our swag becomes co-opted, but then we're demonized. We are angry, we are too loud, we are too everything. *And I experienced that.* How dare I have a voice and use it."[61] Throughout this book we describe numerous incidents when Markle *experienced that.* In 2018, we could only speculate about what the duchess was thinking as Michelle Obama spoke these poignant words. When two years later Markle publicly said, "I know what it's like to have a voice, and also what it's like to feel voiceless" (see Chapter 3), we were given a glimpse into what she may have been thinking back then.[62]

Notes

1 Nesrine Malik, "It's No Accident Britain and America are the World's Biggest Coronavirus Losers," *The Guardian*, May 10, 2020, www.theguardian.com/commentisfree/2020/may/10/anglo-american-coronavirus-crisis. Accessed May 11, 2020.

2 Dan Mangan, "Trump Defends Calling Coronavirus 'Chinese Virus'—'It's Not Racist at All,'" *CNBC*, March 18, 2020, www.cnbc.com/2020/03/18/coronavirus-criticism-trump-defends-saying-chinese-virus.html. Accessed October 17, 2020.

3 Nicquel Terry Ellis, "'Stand Back and Stand By': Rhetoric Some Call Racist has Marked Trump's Entire Presidency," *USA TODAY*, October 13, 2020, www.usatoday.com/story/news/politics/elections/2020/10/13/hate-speech-common-theme-trumps-presidency/5873238002/. Accessed October 17, 2020.

4 Malik, "It's No Accident."

5 Anthony Weems, email correspondence to Joe R. Feagin, May 10, 2020. Used with permission.

6 George J. Sefa Dei and Shukri Hilowle (eds), *Cartographies of Race and Social Difference*, 1st edn (New York: Springer, 2018).

7 Sally Weale, "Chinese Students Flee UK after 'Maskaphobia' Triggered Racist Attacks," *The Guardian*, March 17, 2020, www.theguardian.com/education/2020/mar/17/chinese-students-flee-uk-after-maskaphobia-triggered-racist-attacks. Accessed May 10, 2020; David Mercer, "Coronavirus: Hate Crimes against Chinese People Soar in UK During COVID-19 Crisis," *Sky News*, May 5, 2020, https://news.sky.com/story/coronavirus-hate-crimes-against-chinese-people-soar-in-uk-during-covid-19-crisis-11979388. Accessed May 10, 2020. See also Jingqui Ren and Joe R. Feagin, "Face Mask Symbolism in Anti-Asian Hate Crimes," *Ethnic and Racial Studies*, 43 (2020). DOI: 10.1080/01419870.2020.1826553.

8 Staff, "Chinese People 'Too Scared to Venture Out Alone' amid Rising Coronavirus Abuse," *UK News*, May 7, 2020, www.expressandstar.com/news/uk-news/2020/05/07/chinese-people-too-scared-to-venture-out-alone-amid-rising-coronavirus-abuse/. Accessed May 10, 2020.

9 *Ibid.*
10 Janet Davison, "The Pandemic Puts the Royals Online—and 'At Their Best,'" *CBC*, April 19, 2020, www.cbc.ca/news/world/royal-fascinator-pandemic-royals-online-1.5536530. Accessed May 12, 2020.
11 Benjamin Mueller, "Coronavirus Killing Black Britons at Twice the Rate of Whites," *The New York Times*, May 7, 2020, www.nytimes.com/2020/05/07/world/europe/coronavirus-uk-black-britons.html. Accessed May 10, 2020.
12 Rhiannon Mills, "Prince William Says Britain is 'At Its Best When We're In A Crisis,'" *Sky News*, April 13, 2020. https://news.sky.com/story/coronavirus-prince-william-says-britain-is-at-its-best-when-were-in-a-crisis-11972447. Accessed May 10, 2020.
13 Peter Stubley, "Queen's Speech: Read Monarch's Coronavirus Address to Nation in Full," *The Independent*, April 5, 2020, www.independent.co.uk/news/uk/home-news/queens-speech-coronavirus-full-transcript-text-read-a9448531.html. Accessed May 10, 2020.
14 Jack Royston, "Exclusive Poll: Majority of British People Say Prince Harry and Meghan Markle Should Not Return to Royal Duties," *Newsweek*, April 17, 2020, www.newsweek.com/britons-oppose-prince-harry-meghan-markle-coronavirus-response-1498454. Accessed August 9, 2020.
15 *History Extra* Staff, "The Windsors at War: What Did the Royal Family Do During WW2?," *History Extra*, September 10, 2019, www.historyextra.com/period/second-world-war/windsors-war-ww2-royal-family-what-did-they-do-nazi-germany-george-vi-elizabeth/. Accessed May 12, 2020.
16 *IWM* Staff, "Growing Up in the Second World War," *Imperial War Museum*, February 1, 2028, www.iwm.org.uk/history/growing-up-in-the-second-world-war. Accessed May 10, 2020; *The History Press Staff*, "The 'Dead End Kids' of the London Blitz," *The History Press*, n.d., www.thehistorypress.co.uk/articles/the-dead-end-kids-of-the-london-blitz/. Accessed May 12, 2020.
17 Alexander Chancellor, "It's Time to Explode the Myth that All Children Evacuated from the Blitz were Well Treated," *The Guardian*, September 3, 2020, www.theguardian.com/commentisfree/2009/sep/03/alexander-chancellor-wartime-evacuees. Accessed May 12, 2020.
18 *History Extra* Staff, "The Windsors at War."
19 Jacob Miller, "20 Photographs Depicting British Children during the Blitz of World War II," *History Collection*, n.d., https://historycollection.co/20-photographs-depicting-british-children-blitz/. Accessed May 12, 2020.
20 *History Extra Staff*, "The Windsors at War."
21 *Ibid.*
22 Darren Kelsey, "Hero Mythology and Right-Wing Populism," *Journalism Studies*, 17 (8) (March 2015), pp. 971–988.
23 Raven Saunt, "'Proud' Prince Harry Praises British Public's Response to Coronavirus Pandemic and 'Selfless' Captain Tom—As He and Wife Meghan Markle are Seen on the Streets of LA for a Second Time Wearing Masks to Deliver Packages to the Needy," *Daily Mail*, April 19, 2020, www.dailymail.co.uk/news/article-8233343/Prince-Harry-praises-British-publics-response-coronavirus-pandemic-selfless-Captain-Tom.html. Accessed May 12, 2020.
24 "War Blitz: Forgotten Black British History Remembered," *Operation Black Vote*, September 9, 2020, www.obv.org.uk/news-blogs/war-blitz-forgotten-black-british-history-remembered-0. Accessed May 12, 2020.
25 *Ibid.*

26 *Ibid.*

27 Stephen Bourne, *Mother Country: Britain's Black Community on the Home Front, 1939–45* (Cheltenham: The History Press, 2020).

28 Charlie Duxbury, "The Crown vs. Corona," *Politico*, April 1, 2020, www.politico.eu/article/the-crown-vs-coronavirus-king-monarchy-europe/. Accessed May 12, 2020.

29 *Ibid.*

30 Alexandra Fraser, "Ten Stately Homes which Became Hospitals during the First World War," *Country Life*, November 19, 2019, www.countrylife.co.uk/architecture/ten-stately-homes-became-hospitals-first-world-war-185211. Accessed October 17, 2020; Rose Staveley-Wadham, "A Look at the Fascinating History of Highclere Castle—Setting of Downton Abbey," *The British Newspaper Archive*, September 20, 2019, https://blog.britishnewspaperarchive.co.uk/2019/09/10/a-look-at-the-fascinating-history-of-highclere-castle-setting-of-downton-abbey/. Accessed October 17, 2020.

31 Sylvia Poggioli, "Pope Francis Turned a Vatican Palazzo into 'Palace of the Poor' for Homeless People," *NPR*, February 7, 2020, www.npr.org/2020/02/07/803423754/pope-francis-turned-a-vatican-palazzo-into-palace-of-the-poor-for-homeless-peopl. Accessed May 12, 2020.

32 Leah Silverman, "These are All of Queen Elizabeth's Homes," *Town & Country*, December 12, 2017, www.townandcountrymag.com/leisure/real-estate/g14106752/queen-elizabeth-homes/. Accessed April 29, 2020.

33 David Mercer, "Coronavirus: Home Secretary Urged to Act on 'Unacceptable' Rise in Anti-Chinese Hate Crimes," Sky News, May 6, 2020, https://news.sky.com/story/coronavirus-home-secretary-urged-to-act-on-unacceptable-rise-in-anti-chinese-hate-crimes-11983731. Accessed May 10, 2020.

34 *CBC News* Staff, "Prince William and Kate Speak Out on Coronavirus, as Britain Extends Lockdown," *CBS This Morning*, April 17, 2020, www.cbsnews.com/news/prince-william-kate-coronavirus-britain-lockdown/. Accessed May 20, 2020.

35 Katie Nicholl and Erin Vanderhoof, "Prince William's Coronavirus Diagnosis was "No Secret" among the Royal Family," *Vanity Fair*, November 2, 2020, www.vanityfair.com/style/2020/11/prince-william-coronavirus-diagnosis-was-no-secret-royal-family. Accessed January 28, 2021.

36 Meaghan Wray, "Prince William, Kate Middleton Give Rare Interview about Mental Health during Coronavirus Pandemic," *Global News*, April 17, 2020, https://globalnews.ca/news/6831871/prince-william-kate-middleton-coronavirus-interview/. Accessed May 12, 2020.

37 *BBC* Staff, with analysis by Jonny Dymond, "Coronavirus: Royal Couple Say Lockdown 'Stressful' on Mental Health," *BBC*, April 17, 2020, www.bbc.com/news/uk-52308863. Accessed May 12, 2020.

38 Maria Puente, "Happy 5th Birthday, Princess Charlotte! Palace Releases New Photos of Will and Kate's Daughter," *USA Today*, May 1, 2020, www.usatoday.com/story/entertainment/celebrities/2020/05/01/princess-charlotte-turns-5-prince-william-duchess-kate-daughter-birthday/3032849001/. Accessed May 20, 2020. Italics added.

39 Rupert Neate. "Super-Rich Jet Off to Disaster Bunkers amid Coronavirus Outbreak," *The Guardian*, March 11, 2020, www.theguardian.com/world/2020/mar/11/disease-dodging-worried-wealthy-jet-off-to-disaster-bunkers. Accessed May 10, 2020.

40 Owen Jones, "We're About to Learn a Terrible Lesson from Coronavirus: Inequality Kills," *The Guardian*, March 14, 2020, www.theguardian.com/commentisfree/2020/mar/14/coronavirus-outbreak-inequality-austerity-pandemic. Accessed May 10, 2020.

41 Robert Stevens, "The Berries of Wrath: Prince Charles Demands "Hard Graft" from Furloughed Workers," *World Socialist Website*, May 21, 2020, www.wsws.org/en/articles/2020/05/21/frui-m21.html. Accessed May 21, 2020.

42 Michael Billig, *Talking of the Royal Family* (New York: Routledge, 1991), p. 14.

43 *Ibid.*

44 Laura Harvey, Kim Allen and Heather Mendick, "Extraordinary Acts and Ordinary Pleasures: Rhetorics of Inequality in Young People's Talk about Celebrity," *Discourse & Society*, 26 (4) (2015), pp. 436–437.

45 Claire Alexander, "Quartz: "Political Blackness": A Very British Concept with a Complex History," *The University of Manchester*, March 3, 2018, www.research.manchester.ac.uk/portal/en/media/quartz-political-blackness-a-very-british-concept-with-a-complex-history(c151eb83-4972-4b6a-968e-6640cf2f5945).html. Accessed May 16, 2020.

46 Richard Allen Greene, "Britain's Big Race Divide," *CNN*, June 22, 2020, https://edition.cnn.com/interactive/2020/06/europe/britain-racism-cnn-poll-gbr-intl/. Accessed August 12, 2020.

47 Paul Waldie, "Meghan and Harry Called 'Self-Absorbed' during Pandemic," *Globe and Mail*, April 24, 2020, www.theglobeandmail.com/world/article-meghan-and-harry-called-self-absorbed-during-pandemic/. Accessed May 10, 2020.

48 Piers Morgan, "Meghan and Harry's New Book Only Confirms They're the World's Most Tone-Deaf, Hypocritical, Narcissistic, Deluded, Whiny Brats—AND That Most of the Stories the 'Lying' Press Wrote about them Were 100 Percent True!," *Daily Mail*, July 27, 2020, www.dailymail.co.uk/news/article-8564033/PIERS-MORGAN-Meghan-Harrys-new-book-confirms-theyre-worlds-tone-deaf-whiny-brats.html. Accessed August 7, 2020. Italics added.

49 Amanda Woods, "Meghan Reportedly Forbids Harry from Visiting Charles after Coronavirus Diagnosis," *Page Six*, March 26, 2020, https://pagesix.com/2020/03/26/meghan-markle-reportedly-forbids-prince-harry-from-visiting-uk-prince-charles/. Accessed May 11, 2020.

50 Waldie, "Meghan and Harry Called 'Self-Absorbed.' "

51 Saunt, " 'Proud' Prince Harry."

52 Davison, "The Pandemic Puts the Royals Online."

53 *Associated Press* Staff, "Prince Harry, Meghan Markle Team with Malala Yousafzai to Discuss Pandemic's Impact on Young Women," *The Hollywood Reporter*, October 8, 2020, www.hollywoodreporter.com/news/prince-harry-meghan-markle-team-with-malala-yousafzai-to-discuss-pandemics-impact-on-young-women. Accessed October 17, 2020; Saunt, " 'Proud' Prince Harry."

54 Kayleigh Donaldson, "Emily Giffin's Hatred of Meghan Markle and the Racism of Royal Fandom," *Pajiba*, May 7, 2020, www.pajiba.com/celebrities_are_better_than_you/emily-giffins-hatred-of-meghan-markle-and-the-racism-of-royal-fandom.php. Accessed May 10, 2020.

55 Katherine Singh, "Why were People So Mad at Meghan Markle on Archie's Birthday?," *Flare*, May 7, 2020, www.flare.com/celebrity/emily-giffin-meghan-markle-archie-birthday/. Accessed May 10, 2020.

56 Maija Kappler, "People are Furious Because Meghan Markle Encouraged Americans to Vote," *Huffington Post*, August 23, 2020, www.huffingtonpost. ca/entry/meghan-markle-royals-voting_ca. Accessed August 26, 2020.

57 Erica Gerald Mason, "How Prince Harry and Meghan Markle could Actually Combat Colonialism's Destructive Legacy," *Vanity Fair*, August 14, 2020, www. vanityfair.com/style/2020/08/how-prince-harry-and-meghan-markle-could-actually-combat-colonialisms-destructive-legacy. Accessed August 14, 2002.

58 Blue Telusma, "How Meghan Markle Exposed Racism in the British Media (Then Bounced)," *The Grio*, January 14, 2020, https://thegrio.com/2020/01/14/how-meghan-markle-exposed-racism-in-the-british-media-then-bounced/. Accessed May 11, 2020.

59 Deborah F. Atwate, "Senator Barack Obama: The Rhetoric of Hope and the American Dream," *Journal of Black Studies*, 38 (2) (November 2007), pp. 124, 125; Barak Obama, *The Audacity of Hope: Thoughts on Reclaiming the American Dream* (New York: Crown, 2006), pp. 81, 233; Editor, "Text of Obama's Speech: A More Perfect Union," *The Wall Street Journal*, March 18, 2008, http://blogs.wsj.com/washwire/2008/03/18/text-of-obamas-speech-a-more-perfect-union/. Accessed May 11, 2020; "President-Elect Obama: The Voters Rebuke Republicans for Economic Failure," *The Wall Street Journal*, November 5, 2008, www.wsj.com/articles/SB122586244657800863. Accessed May 11, 2020.

60 Telusma, "How Meghan Markle Exposed Racism."

61 Omid Scobie and Carolyn Durand, *Finding Freedom: Harry and Meghan and the Making of a Modern Royal Family* (New York: HarperCollins), p. 250. Italics added.

62 Emily Dixon, "Meghan Markle Opens Up to *Marie Claire* about Why She's Voting in November," *Marie Claire*, August 11, 2020, www.marieclaire.com/celebrity/a33572727/meghan-markle-why-im-voting-marie-claire/. Accessed August 14, 2020.

Index

Abbott, Diane 189
Abramovich, Roman 141
Abrams, Stacey 102
Acuña, Rodolfo 59
Adegoke, Yomi 83
Adichie, Chimamanda Ngozi 84
African Americans 43, 99, 138, 160, 170, 173–4
Ali, Rushanara 207
Alice, Princess 196
Al-Kadhi, Amrou 39, 44
Al Manaar Muslim Cultural Heritage Centre 114–15
Althorp House 193
American Broadcasting Corporation (ABC) 103
Amnesty International 77, 189
Anderson, Claud 36–7
Andrew, Prince, Duke of York 8, 108, 124, 136–41, 188, 201–2; stepping down as a senior royal 139
animalistic imagery 73, 77, 79, 160
Anthias, Floya 157
anti-black feeling 73–85, 106, 183
anti-racism 128, 139, 142, 154, 208
anti-radicalization strategy 98
anti-semitism 208
apolitical nature of royalty 17, 19, 61, 84, 95, 110–11
apology, refusal of 205–6
appeasement 204–5
Archewell charity 96
Archie (son of Meghan Markle and Prince Harry) 77–8, 86, 99, 109, 125–7, 154, 184, 186; "Asian" look of 126
Ardern, Jacinda 84
aristocracy 24–5, 194
Armstrong, Neil 129
Atlas Network 142
Audley Estate 129

Back, Les 75, 167
Baker, Danny 77–8, 186
Barbados 65, 204, 206
Barber, Frances 193
Beard, Mary 191–2
Beatrice, Princess 171
beauty, female 159–60
Beck, Glenn 184
Beckett, Frances 198
Bell, Derrick 35, 59
Bercow, John 153
Bernstein, Althea 154
Bhattacharya, Gargi 68–9, 157
Bhopal, Kalwant 100
Biden, Joe 123
Biggar, Nigel 13
birther movement 101
Black, Jeremy 13
black Britons 140, 183, 191–4
Black Lives Matter movement 1–2, 15–19, 26, 31–2, 58, 85, 106, 138–42, 154, 207–8
black man's burden 71
black musicians 169
black women with light complexions 105
Blackburn, Robin 34
blackness 127
Blair, Charles 37
Blavatnik, Sir Leonard 141
Blyton, Enid 75–7
Boer War (1899–1902) 206
Bolt, Usain 203
Bonilla-Silva, Eduardo 100
book industry 133
Boughton House 193
Bowers, Nancy 29–30, 35, 41
Bradby, Tom 137, 156
Braybrooke, Baron 129
Brexit 22, 27, 44, 96, 98, 131, 142, 207–8

Bridgetower, G.A.P. 169
Bristol 31
British Attitudes Survey 134
British Broadcasting Corporation
   (BBC) 29, 58, 80, 134–9, 185, 188,
   191–5, 201, 208
British Council of Churches 63
British Empire 12–14, 25–6, 39,
   62–3, 68, 71, 82, 95, 134, 190,
   194, 197, 200, 203–4
British Fashion Council (BFC) 8
British National Party 200
British South Sea Company 33
Britishness 95, 191
Brixton 98, 205
Brock, André 135
Brown, Brené 174
Brown, Gordon 206
Browning, Elizabeth Barrett 37
Brunsma, David 113
Buckingham Palace 23; staff of 137,
   196, 201
Burgess, Elizabeth 203
Burke, Edmund 67
Burrow, Ava 79
Busnel, François 76
Butler, Dawn 1–2, 16, 141, 190

Cabot, John 25–6
Cameron, David 21, 37–8, 205
Camilla, Duchess of Cornwall 33, 108,
   171, 173, 203–4
Campbell, Lady Colin 9, 11–12, 171
Canada 29, 36, 74
capitalism 33–4, 42, 198
Caricom Commission 204
Carl XVI Gustaf, King of
   Sweden 194–5
Carlyle, Thomas 70
Carty-Williams, Candice 62, 95
Castile, Philando 16
casting for television 104–5
Cayman Islands 199
CBS This Morning 184
census-taking 159–60
Chamberlain, Joseph 71
Chamberlain, Neville 204–5
changes needed in Britain 175
Channel Four 133
Charles, Prince of Wales 17, 23–4, 38,
   83, 125, 162, 170, 173, 202–4
Charles Edward, Duke of Saxe-Coburg
   and Gotha 194–5
Charles II, King 33
Charlotte, Princess 77

chief executive officers 130
children's comics and magazines 69
Chomsky, Noam 153
Christie, Agatha 76
Christmas cards 126
Church of England 124, 132, 208
Churchill, Winston 26, 31, 44, 197
Clancy, Laura 124, 162
classism 144
Clinton, Hillary 101, 165
closed-mindedness 105
CNN 58, 82, 190
Cochrane, Andrew 139
collective forgetting 64
collective myths 183
Collins, Patricia Hill 60, 80–1, 157
colonialism 13, 25, 29–32, 35, 60, 71,
   75, 194, 200, 206
Color of Change (organization) 16, 107
"colorblind" attitudes 100, 134, 142
colorism 104–5
"coloured people", use of the term 2
Colston, Edward 31–2
Commission for Racial Equality 72
Common Sense Media 107
Commons, House of 20
Commonwealth, the 19, 73
Conservative Party 98–9, 189–90
constitutional monarchy 19–23
Consultative Committee on Overseas
   Coloured Workers 63
Cooper, Anna Julia 59–60
Corbyn, Jeremy 142
coronavirus pandemic (2020–21) 15,
   23–4, 102–3, 109–10
counter-framing 153–4, 160, 167–74
Country Life 83
Cox, Oliver C. 59
Crenshaw, Kimberlé 157
criminality and criminalization
   79, 190–1
critical race theory (CRT) 5
The Crown 62
"Crowngate" controversy 195
Crump, Benjamin 166
Cugoano, Ottobah 67
cultural differences 44, 63, 79–82, 132
Cummings, Dominic 2
Curry, Michael 169–73
Czechoslovakia 198, 205

Dadzie, Stella 81
"Daffodils" (poem) 71
Daily Mail 3, 7, 79, 83, 106, 123,
   128, 198

Daily Mirror 57, 198
Dampier, Phil 109
Dar es Salaam 206
Darkest Hour (film) 39, 44
Darwin, Charles 73–4
Darwin, John 14
Darwinism 74
Daughters' Rights group 129
Davis, Angela Y. 59–60, 80–1
Davis, Mike 17
Day, Peter 198
Deal or No Deal (game show) 161
debutantes 197–8
decolonization 68
Defoe, Daniel 33
Delgado, Richard 59
Department for International
   Trade 202
DeSmog group 142
Diana, Princess of Wales 61, 96,
   125–6, 137, 162, 193, 205
Dick, Cressida 16
Dickens, Charles 69, 72–3
Dilke, Charles 68, 70
discrimination 10, 19, 27–8, 45, 97,
   100, 114, 134, 190
diversity, promotion of 131, 133
Doctor Who (television series) 193
Dokoupil, Tony 2, 4
Douglass, Frederick 59
Downton Abbey 62
Du Bois, W.E.B. 59
Duchy of Cornwall 23
Duggal, Deepanish 124
Durand, Carolyn 175
Dyer, Reginald 205

East India Company 30, 40
Eddo-Lodge, Reni 81
education 131, 164–5
Edward, Prince of Wales 62
Edward VIII 197
Effron, Daniel 201
elite white men, dominance of 74,
   122–3, 130, 136, 140–4
Elizabeth, Princess 197; *see also*
   [the] queen
Elkins, Caroline 63–4
Ella Baker Center for Human
   Rights 106
Elle magazine 99, 104–5, 112–13, 138
Elliott, Matthew and Sarah 142
Emidy, Joseph 169
The Empire Strikes Back (book, 1982)
   5–6, 68–9, 157

Engels, Friedrich 7
Enninful, Edward 83–4
Epstein, Jeffery 136–40, 188
Equiano, Olaudah 167–8
Erase the Hate campaign 105–6
Esquire magazine 161
Essed, Philomena 60, 80–1, 157
ethnic minorities 27, 190–1
eugenics 74, 189–90
Eugenie, Princess 171
European Convention on Human
   Rights 17, 203
European Union 142, 183, 208
Evaristo, Bernardine 81

Farage, Nigel 142, 184–5
fascism 197–8
Feagin, Joe R. (co-author) 113–14, 167
Feeding Britain (charity) 110
Felipe VI, King 194–5
feminism 59, 80–1, 84, 125,
   128, 154–5, 158, 162–7, 175;
   commercialized 111
Ferguson, Sarah, Duchess of York 8
Le Figaro 76
films and the film industry 39, 44, 135
Finding Freedom (book, 2020) 4, 140,
   184, 201
First World War 195
Floyd, George 16, 19, 138–9, 165–6
Fox, Laurence 135–6
Franco, Francisco 198
Fraser, Malcolm 22
free trade 35
French Revolution 66
Friel, Mikhaila 17, 185
Frogmore Cottage 109
Froude, James Anthony 68
Fryer, Paul 65, 70

Galton, Francis 74
Gates, Melinda 165
gender equality 164
gendered racism 60–1, 79–81, 101,
   109, 112, 115, 122–3, 157–8, 188
genealogy 97
General Mills 131
genocide 138, 173, 202
George III 67
George V 62, 108, 184
George VI 7, 86, 129, 204–5
George, Prince 8, 77
Germany 76; revitalization of (in the
   1930s) 197
Ghana 62

Gillray, James 67
Gilroy, Paul 5, 44, 156, 200
Gladstone, John 37
Gladstone, William 37
Glamour magazine 156
Gluckstein, Danny 197
Goldsmith, Oliver 65–6
Good Morning Britain 183, 187
Goodall, Jane 85, 125
Goodfellow, Maya 18, 188
Goodkind, Sara 163
Gramsci, Antonio 60–1
Grant, Bernie 38
Greene, Graham 37
Grenfell Tower fire (2017) 18, 58, 114
The Guardian 3, 130–1, 144

Haggard, H. Rider 74
Haitian Revolution 66
Halbwachs, Maurice 9
Halifax, Earl of 33–4
Hall, Catherine 38
Hall, Stuart 59–60, 71–2, 81, 140
Hannan, Jason 17
Hardman, Robert 62, 161, 199
Harmsworth, Harold 57, 198
Harris, Kamala 102, 165
Harry, Prince 1, 4–12, 16–17, 57–8,
    73, 82–5, 184–5, 199–203; changes
    seen in 107–10, 122–5, 184, 200;
    see also Sussex, Duke and Duchess of
*Harry & Meghan: An African
    Journey* (television documentary)
    114, 137–8
hate crime 24, 98, 208
hate speech 59, 103, 107
Hawkins, Sir John 25
Hazarika, Ayesha 187
Henley, Jon 21
Henry, Sir Lenny 133–4
Henry VIII 25
Henty, George Alfred 75
The Heritage Foundation 142
Higginbotham, Elizabeth 80–1
Hirsch, Afua 95, 134, 169, 172, 183,
    186–7, 191
historical scholarship 13–14
Hitler, Adolf 17, 195–200, 204–5
Hocking, Jenny 22
Hong Kong 26
HOPE not hate group 82
Hopkins, Katie 10–11, 142
Horne, Lena 105
Howe, Stephen 64
Hudson-Wilkin, Rose 170

Huffington Post 83
Hutchinson, Leslie 62
hybrid role as royals 125

identity, racial 100, 113–14
immigrants 44, 96; hostility towards 5
imperialism 71
Independent Press Standards
    Organisation 196
India 39–40, 86, 204–5
individualism 100, 103–7
Industrial Revolution 39
inequality, social 23
Infowars (website) 181
ingroups and outgroups 7
Inside Out London program 29
Institute of Economic Affairs 142
institutional racism 10, 15–16, 18–19,
    31, 85, 98–9, 190
institutions, links between 190
intersectionality 81, 101, 123, 144,
    153, 156
Inuit culture 173
investment 34
"Ivory Bangle Lady" 192

Jalianwala Bagh massacre (1919) 205
Jamelia 187
Jefferson, Margo 126
Jephson, Patrick 11
Jesus Christ, portrayal of 208
Jewish communities 204
job applications 131
John Templeton Foundation 142
Johnson, Boris 2, 18–19, 22, 27,
    31–2, 98, 103, 141–2, 189–90,
    203, 207
Johnson, Jo 13–14
Johnson, Linton K. 81
Johnson, Rachel 158
Johnson, Samuel 193
Johnson, Stanley 8
joking, racist 77, 200–3
Jones, Claudia 81
Jones, Martha S. 166
Junor, Penny 2–4, 108, 137, 184–6

Kanneh-Mason, Sheku 169–70
Karadžić, Radovan 201–2
Karim, Abdul 39
Kate (Middleton), Duchess of
    Cambridge 2–3, 8–9, 12, 58, 72,
    80, 83, 110, 126–7, 155, 171, 188
Kay, Jackie 81
Kay-Task, Haunani 59

Kennedy, Jackie 62, 64
Kensington Palace staff 3, 7–10
Kenya 63–4
Kerr, Sir John 22
Khan, Sadiq 11
Khan, Saira 133
Kilby, James 22
King, Ben E. 44, 170
King, Gayle 2, 4, 184
King, Larry 155
King, Martin Luther 169; daughter of 173
King, Rodney 138
Kipling, Rudyard 70–2, 207
Koch, Charles and David 142
Koh-i-Noor diamond 14
Kohn, Isabelle 175
Kovel, Joel 85, 127
Kuo, Rachel 160
Kurten, David 102
Kushner, A.R. 191–2

Labour Party 22, 98–9, 142
Lacey, Robert 186–7
Lammy, David 169–71
Lancaster, Duchy of 24
Lawrence, Doreen 18–19
Lawrence, Stephen 18–19
leadership positions 130–3
legal proceedings 57, 61–4
legislation 12, 25, 130–1
Leishang (company) 76
Lennon, John 185
Levin, Angela 8–9
Levy, Andrea 81
Lewis, Helen 84, 155
Life magazine 62–3
Limbaugh, Rush 184
Little, Brown (book group) 133
Long, Edward 65
Lords, House of 20, 129
Louis, Prince 77
Love, Judy 133
Lytton, Sir Edward Bulwer 70

Macaulay, Thomas Babington 38
McDonough, Frank 197
MacKenzie, John 71
McLaughlin, Lynda 184
McQuade, Aidan 41
Maher, Bill 107–8
The Mail on Sunday 57
Majesty (magazine) 23, 127
Major, John 95
"male, pale and stale" thinkers 83

male supremacy 128; *see also* elite white men, dominance of
Manjapra, Kris 36, 168
Mann, Perminder 132–3
Mansfield, William M. 66
Margaret, Princess 62–3
Mark, Connie 141
Markle, Meghan 1–12, 16–17, 39, 44–5, 57–62, 72–3, 77–84; advocacy for women's rights 154, 175; changes initiated by 124–5; exotification of 158–61; as a feminist 162–7; fetishization of 161; influence of 124, 154–5, 162–3, 167; lifestyle blog of (The Tig) 174; opposition to 8–11, 61–2, 72–3, 77–84, 108, 123–8, 132–42, 184–5, 188–9; popularity of 107–10, 122; relations with in-laws 194–5; relationship with her father 4; staff of 58; support for 2–3, 58, 184; as a trophy of diversity 96–9, 15; *see also* Sussex, Duke and Duchess of
Markle, Thomas 97, 113, 124
Marney, Jo 78–9, 134
Martin, Trayvon 106
Marx, Karl 7
mass media 134
Matsuda, Mari 59
Maxwell, Ghislaine 139–40
May, Theresa 28, 205
media coverage 3–4, 7, 10–11, 57–8, 61, 66, 72, 106, 111–12, 137, 187
media security 114
Meghan Markle's Royal Sparkle 80
"Megxit" 82, 155
Meinzer, Kristen 38
Members of Parliament 27–8, 57, 130, 135–6, 189
menstruation 154
mental health 58, 137
Mercer, Robert 142
Mertz, Aurel 158–9
Metropolitan Police 19
Michael, Princess 171
military appointments 125
Milne, Seumas 95
minstrel shows 69
Mirza, Munira 31
MI16 198
misogyny 125
mixed-race parentage 63, 77–8, 82, 99, 104–6, 112–15, 126, 158–61, 186, 188

Mizra, Heidi 81
Mohabir, Naini 201–6
monarchy 25, 95–6, 203; arguments for and against 95; powers 20, 22
monkey chants 78
Morgan, Piers 102–3, 106–7, 124, 135–8, 183, 186–8, 191–2
Morris, Olive 141
Moses, Dirk 173–4
Mosley, Lady Diana 198
Mosley, Oswald 198
Mos-Shogbamimu, Shola 187, 191
Mountbatten, Lord Louis 62
Mrwetyana, Uyinene 164
Mullen, John 69
Munich Agreement (1938) 17, 205
Murdoch, Rupert 57, 102
"Murky Meg" 138
music 44, 69
Myanmar 207

Naruhito, Prince 205
National Association for the Advancement of Colored People (NAACP) 107, 154
National Portrait Gallery 40–1
National Trust 30
nationalism 5, 208
natural selection 73–4
Nazi regime: collaboration with 197–8; royalty's links to 195–7; uniform and salute of 195–6, 199–200
NBC 1, 185–6
Nehlen, Paul 78
the Netherlands 196–7
networks and networking 85, 141, 196
Neville, Gary 190
New York Times 1, 106, 129, 198, 201
The New Yorker 10
Newsweek magazine 109
Newton, Isaac 33
Nicholas II, Tsar 184
The 19th* Represents summit (2020) 165–6
Nolan, Christopher 44
norms and values 132, 140
nudity 161
N-word 76

Obama, Barack 31, 78, 83, 101, 106, 113–14, 132, 142
Obama, Michelle 78, 101, 184
Ocasio-Cortez, Alexandria 101
offensive language 202
Ogbuani, Peace 1

OkayAfrica 72–3
OKCupid 159
Olusoga, David 32, 37, 39, 44, 192
O'Neill, Brendan 142
Ono, Yoko 185
opinion polls 134
Order of St. Michael 18
Orwell, George 71
Ostiana, Jermain 201, 206
"othering" 8, 85, 95, 100, 186
Ouseley, Herman 171

Pampers 71
Parry, Tyler 202
"passing as white" 106
Patel, Atul 199
Patel, Priti 31, 153
patriarchy 128–9
Peaky Blinders 62
Pears' Soap 70
Penguin Random House 133
Peoples, Lindsay 169–70
Philip, Prince, Duke of Edinburgh 23, 127, 129, 172, 196, 199; gaffes of 199
Phillips, Zara 171
Pickett, Wilson 170
Piper, Adrian 59
"playing the race card" 11, 135, 188
policing 15–19, 31, 79, 111, 140–1, 144, 165, 190
"political correctness" 193, 203
politicization 16–17
Pometsey, Olive 188
popular culture 74
Porten, Lucy 30
post-racial Britain 86, 97–100
Powell, Ted 96
Pride magazine 104–5, 112, 138
primogeniture 129
Privy Council 20–1
Procter & Gamble (company) 70–1, 164
professors 82–3
protocol 110–11
public relations 137
purity 126
Putin, Vladimir 122, 141

Qiaobi cleaning liquid 76–7
the queen 17–25, 38, 40, 58, 62–4, 95–6, 108, 110, 125–9, 161, 172, 187, 195, 205–6; *see also* Elizabeth, Princess
Queen Mother 204–5
Queen's Commonwealth Trust 16

race disparity audit 28–9, 134
Race Relations Act (1965) 25
race transcension 112–13
racialization 19, 45, 59–63, 85, 98,
    100, 186, 190–1, 194
racism: denial of 1–2, 9, 12–14,
    107, 136, 183–92, 199, 205; in
    reverse 10, 27, 84, 183; *see also*
    systemic racism
"rag-heads" 200
Ragland, Doria 79, 99, 127, 170
Ramshaw, Emily 165
Rand, Jasmine 166
Rankaduwa, Sandi 96, 122–3
rationalization 134
Rees, Marvin 32
Rees-Mogg, Jacob 21
Reid, Nova 188
Remi, Georges 72
reproduction of oppression 15
Republic group 108
Rhodes, Cecil 70
Rhodesia 204
Rice, Tamir 16
Roberts, Andrew 198
Robinson, Art 75
Robinson, Rashad 16
Rockquemore, Kerry Ann 113
Rothermere, Viscount *see*
    Harmondsworth, Harold
"rough sleepers" 24
Royal Africa Company (RAC) 31, 33
royal family 95–6, 194, 203–4;
    functionality of 132; Markle's
    impact on 162, 167; official website
    of 155; popularity of 108–9; public
    funding of 109; rude behavior at
    Markle's wedding 171–3; survival of
    108, 123
royal titles 110
royal tours 204
royal yacht 132
Ruiz, Michelle 160–1
ruling class in Britain 7, 20–5, 115,
    136, 144
Rwanda 155, 160–1
Ryder, Matthew 134–5

Sabisky, Andrew 189
St. Jean, Yanick 80–1, 157
Saleem, Anna 97, 188, 209
Sambo, use of the name 75–7
Sancho, Charles Ignatius 193
scholars of colour 59
Schwarz, Bill 68–9

Scobie, Omid 175, 201
Scott, Sir George Gilbert 37
Scott, Stafford 171
Scottish independence 110
Second World War 63–4, 195–7
"The Secret Teacher" (blog) 26
Seeley, John Robert 68
Sethi, Anita 202
Seward, Ingrid 23, 127, 196
Sewell, Rob 22
sexism 69; *see also* systemic sexism
Shaw, Caesar 193
Shrubsole, Guy 24
Silva, Rohan 202
Simpson, Audra 59
Simpson, Wallis 97
Sims, Jennifer 63, 185
sincere fictions 183–4, 190
60 Minutes program 10–11
Slave Compensation
    Commission 35–42
slavery and the slave trade 12, 17,
    29–44, 65–7, 162, 202, 206;
    abolition of 34–42, 66–7; British
    experience compared with that of
    the US 42–4; legacies of 29–31;
    resistance to 41; Smith, Mary 96
Smith, Zadie 81
social Darwinism 74
social justice warriors (SJWs) 192
social media 8–9, 14, 16, 26, 58, 62,
    73, 77–8, 82, 103, 107–11, 114,
    124, 131, 139–40, 153, 159,
    185–6, 189, 208
socialization 85
Sofia, Queen 195
Solomos, John 75, 167
"some of my best friends" defense 201
Somerset, James 66
Spain 198
Spencer, Baldwin 35
Spencer, Herbert 74
Spiked magazine 142
Steinem, Gloria 102–3, 125, 166
Stephens, Britt 3
stereotyping 58, 72–3, 78–80, 100
Stewart, Charles 66
Steyer, Jim 107
Stop Hate for Profit campaign 107
Stormzy 189–90
Strong, Sir Roy Colin 204
subtle racism 1, 4
Suits (television series) 104–5,
    154, 160–1
Sumner, William Graham 74

The Sun 161
"survival of the fittest" 74
Sussex, Duke of (son of George III) 172
Sussex, Duke and Duchess of 58, 97–9, 103–12, 125–7, 139–40, 159; first child *see* Archie; stepping down as senior royals 58, 82–5, 99, 107–12, 124, 132, 153, 155, 184–5, 188, 209; wedding ceremony 97–8, 108, 128, 154, 162, 168–72; *see also* Harry, Prince; Markle, Meghan
Swift, Jonathan 33
systemic racism 1–16, 18–19, 25–6, 29–32, 38, 45, 58–9, 64–5, 73, 76, 79, 85, 95–107, 113, 115, 122–3, 136, 139–44, 156, 175, 184, 187–90, 194; and the white racial frame 4–9
systemic sexism 123, 127–9, 136, 140–1, 144, 158, 163, 175

"taking the knee" 16
Taleb, Nassim Nicholas 191
Tan, Clarissa 133
Taseer, Aatish 132, 174
Tatler magazine 8, 132, 110
Taylor, Breonna 16
The Telegraph 10, 84
There Ain't No Black in the Union Jack (film) 44
Thistlewood, Thomas 42
Thomas, Bumi 18
Thunberg, Greta 98
Time magazine 154
Tindley, Charles 44
The Today Programme 83
Tominey, Camilla 9–10, 84
Town & Country 16, 139
trade monopolies 35
Treasury Department 38–9
Trump, Donald 27, 98, 101–3, 106, 123, 134–5, 138, 141, 153, 168, 207
Ture, Kwame 59
Tuvalu 72

Umoja, Safiya 102
United Nations Children's Fund 70–1
United States (US) 1–2, 6, 17, 29, 63, 66, 74, 100, 113–15, 122, 124, 131, 138–9, 168; Constitution 43, 165; Supreme Court 166
"uppityism" 132, 184

uprisings in Europe 197–9
Urbach, Karina 196
Usmanov, Alisher 141

Vanity Fair 136
Vernon, Patrick 19
Vickers, Hugo 205
Victoria, Queen 14, 17, 20, 39–40, 86, 174; many grandchildren of 194–5; monarchs related to 194–5
View Park-Windsor Hills neighbourhood 79
Vogue 10, 83, 85
voter suppression 101–2
voting rights 101

Wade, Lisa 71
Wade, Valerie 98, 105
Wagner, Kim 12–13
Walker, David 59
wars of colonization 200
Welby, Justin 172, 205–9
Wells-Barnett, Ida B. 59–60
West, Cornel 59
The White Man's Burden 70–1
white racial framing 2–10, 14–15, 29–45, 59–70, 73–9, 83–6, 96, 103, 115, 127, 132–6, 153–4, 157–61, 168, 171, 173, 188, 191, 194, 199–207; in the 18th Century 64–7; in the 19th Century 67–70; and systemic racism 4–9
Whitelock, Anna 111
Whitlam, Gough 22
Wilberforce, William 40–1
Wilhelm II, Kaiser 194–7
Wilhelmina, Queen 197
William, Prince, Duke of Cambridge xi, 8, 12, 72, 78, 108, 110, 124, 127, 129, 137, 155, 171, 196
William IV, King 66–7
Williams, Eric 35
Williams-De Bruyn, Sophia 163–4
Wilson Sheppard, Katherine 156
Windrush Scandal 6, 18–19, 96
Windsor, Amelia 16
Windsor, Lady Gabriella 174, 195
Windsor Caste and Home Park 23–4, 173
Winfrey, Oprah 101
Wingfield, Adia Harvey 80–1, 100, 113–14
"woke", use of the expression 135
Wootton, Dan 102
Wordsworth, William 71

worldviews 5–6, 103, 128
Wrasama, Kathleen 141

xenophobia 75, 208

Yancy, George 29
Yasir, Rami 61–2
Yelin, Hannah 124, 162

Yeltsin, Boris 141
Yuval-Davis, Nina 157

Zane, Rachel 104
Zephaniah, Benjamin 81
Zevallos, Zuleyka 135
Ziegler, Philip 194
Zinn, Howard 142